MULTIPARTY AND LINKED CONTRACTS, TRANSPORT LOGISTICS AND THE UNIFORM TRANSPORT LAW

This book introduces legal aspects of business n[illegible] example of shippers' co-operation in cargo bundling, which is the practice of manufacturing and distributing companies (shippers) consolidating cargo before the engagement of a carrier. Shippers agree to co-operate and to detect cargo matching opportunities before shipment. As a result, shippers can organize joint transportation, yielding significant efficiency gains in both logistics and sustainability terms. However, the current legal framework is not adapted to co-operation in cargo bundling.

This book not only clarifies the operation of laws (with the special focus on international uniform transport laws) but also provides legal solutions facilitating legal certainty in co-operation. It is the first comprehensive book on the legal aspects of shippers' co-operation in logistics, particularly liability issues in multiparty contracts, network contracts, and long-term contracts in the international carriage of goods domain. It is also the first providing an interpretative framework for transport conventions considering new business models and new technologies. Proposals are made for solutions at regulatory levels but also for contracts, which are especially important because contractual solutions can facilitate shippers to enter co-operation and help Transport Orchestrators operating through online platforms to prepare standard terms and conditions. The comparative part of the text features mainly three jurisdictions (Poland, Germany, and England), which offer readers an insight into how multiparty context in the carriage of goods operates at the crossroads of national laws and international transport conventions.

This book is written for interested legal practitioners, policymakers, lobbying bodies, industry professionals (logistics, management of selling, and producing companies), and scholars. It will also broadly appeal to those dealing with sustainable logistics and concepts such as sharing economy in logistics.

Marta K. Kołacz is Assistant Professor in Private Law at Maastricht University in the Netherlands. Marta obtained her Doctor of Law degree at the Erasmus University Rotterdam, the Netherlands and University of Antwerp, Belgium (double degree). Her main areas of interest are the regulation of new technologies, regulation of sustainable logistics, and transport law.

CONTEMPORARY COMMERCIAL LAW

Maritime Law in China: Emerging Issues and Future Developments
Edited by Johanna Hjalmarsson and Jenny Jingbo Zhang

Illegality in Marine Insurance Law
Feng Wang

Insurance Law Implications of Delay in Maritime Transport
Ayşegül Buğra

Online Arbitration
Faye Fangfei Wang

Double Insurance and Contribution
Nisha Mohamed

The Law and Autonomous Vehicles
Matthew Channon, Lucy McCormick and Kyriaki Noussia

FIDIC Yellow Book: A Commentary
Ben Beaumont

The Contract of Carriage: Multimodal Transport and Unimodal Regulation
Paula Bäckdén

FIDIC Red Book: A Commentary
Ben Beaumont

Blockchain Technology and the Law: Opportunities and Risks
Muharem Kianieff

Third Party Protection in Shipping
Carlo Corcione

Multi-sided Music Platforms and the Law: Copyright, Law and Policy in Africa
Chijioke Ifeoma Okorie

Comparative Analysis of Interim Measures: Interim Remedies (England & Wales) v Preservation Measures (China)
Vivek Jain, Thomas Macey-Dare QC and Shengnan Jia

Knock-for-Knock Indemnities and the Law: Contractual Limitation and Delictual Liability
Edited by Kristoffer Svendsen, Endre Stavang & Greg Gordon

Managing International Trade Risk: Customs, Revenue and VAT Compliance
Mark Rowbotham

Company Directors' Liability and the Protection of Creditors
Andrew Kaey

Causation in Insurance Contract Law
Meixian Song

Multiparty and Linked Contracts, Transport Logistics and the Uniform Transport Law: Legal Solutions for Co-operation in Cargo Bundling
Marta K. Kołacz

For more information about this series, please visit: www.routledge.com/Contemporary-Commercial-Law/book-series/CCL

MULTIPARTY AND LINKED CONTRACTS, TRANSPORT LOGISTICS AND THE UNIFORM TRANSPORT LAW

LEGAL SOLUTIONS FOR CO-OPERATION IN CARGO BUNDLING

MARTA K. KOŁACZ

informa law
from Routledge

Designed cover image: shironosov/Getty Images

First published 2025
by Informa Law from Routledge
4 Park Square, Milton Park, Abingdon, Oxon OX14 4RN

and by Informa Law from Routledge
605 Third Avenue, New York, NY 10158

Informa Law from Routledge is an imprint of the Taylor & Francis Group, an informa business

British Library Cataloguing-in-Publication Data
A catalogue record for this book is available from the British Library

ISBN: 978-1-032-58608-3 (hbk)
ISBN: 978-1-032-58609-0 (pbk)
ISBN: 978-1-003-45080-1 (ebk)

DOI: 10.4324/9781003450801

Typeset in Times New Roman
by Apex CoVantage, LLC

CONTENTS

FIGURES

Chapter 1

Chapter 2

Chapter 3

Chapter 4

Chapter 5

Chapter 6

Chapter 7

Chapter 8

Chapter 9

TABLES

TABLE OF LEGISLATION AND OTHER DOCUMENTS

European Union

1 Commission Recommendation of 6 May 2003 concerning the definition of micro, small, and medium-sized enterprises [2003] OJ L 124/36

2 Commission, 'A competition policy fit for new challenges' (Communication) COM (2021) 713 final

3 Commission, 'A European agenda for the collaborative economy' (Communication) COM (2016) 356 final

4 Commission, 'Closing the loop – An EU action plan for the Circular Economy' (Communication) COM (2015) 614 final

5 Commission, 'Fact-finding studies in support of the development of an EU strategy for freight transport logistics Lot 1: Analysis of the EU logistics sector Final Report' (2015) <https://bit.ly/32uCiGh> accessed 1 April 2020

6 Commission, 'Freight transport logistics action plan' (Communication) COM (2007) 607 final

7 Commission, 'Roadmap to Single Transport Area – Towards a competitive and resource efficient transport system' (White Paper) COM (2011) 144 final

8 Commission, 'Sustainable and Smart Mobility Strategy – putting European transport on track for the future' (Communication) COM (2020) 789 final

9 Commission, 'Sustainable Products in a Circular Economy – Towards an EU Product Policy Framework contributing to the Circular Economy' (Staff Working Document) SWD (2019) 91 final

10 Commission, 'The EU's freight transport agenda: Boosting the efficiency, integration, and sustainability of freight transport in Europe' (Communication) COM (2007) 606 final

11 Commission, 'The European Green Deal' (Communication) COM (2019) 640 final

12 Commission, 'Guidelines on the application of Article 81 of the EC Treaty to maritime transport services' [2008] OJ C 245/2

13 Consolidated Version of the Treaty on European Union [2008] OJ C115/13

14 Consolidated Version of the Treaty on the Functioning of the European Union [2008] OJ C115/47

15 Council Directive 86/653/EEC of 18 December 1986 on the co-ordination of the laws of the Member States relating to self-employed commercial agents [1986] OJ L 382/17

16 Directive 2000/31/EC of the European Parliament and of the Council of 8 June 2000 on certain legal aspects of information society services, in particular

electronic commerce, in the Internal Market (Directive on electronic commerce) [2000] OJ L 178/1

17 Directive 2006/123/EC of the European Parliament and of the Council of 12 December 2006 on services in the internal market [2006] OJ L 376/36

18 Eurostat, 'Manufacturing statistics – NACE Rev. 2' (2020) <https://bit.ly/3kZAOtZ> accessed 16 March 2020

19 Eurostat, 'Eurostat Statistic Explained, Greenhouse gas emission statistics – emission inventories' (2019) <https://bit.ly/3DNjK1x> accessed 1 April 2020

20 Regulation (EU) 2019/1150 of the European Parliament and of the Council of 20 June 2019 on promoting fairness and transparency for business users of online intermediation services [2019] OJ L 186/57

21 Regulation (EU) 2022/2065 of the European Parliament and of the Council of 19 October 2022 on a Single Market For Digital Services and amending Directive 2000/31/EC (Digital Services Act) [2022] OJ L 277

Treaties and international law and travaux préparatoires

1 Agreement concerning the International Carriage of Dangerous Goods by Road (ADR) with the amendments in force since 1 January 2021 (ECE/TRANS/300, Vol. I and II and Corr.1 and Corr.2)

2 Budapest Convention on the Contract for the Carriage of Goods by Inland Waterway (CMNI) (adopted 3 October 2000, entered into force on 1 April 2005) CMNI/CONF(99)2/FINAL

3 Commission Economique pour L'Europe Comite des Transports Inerieurs, Sous-Comite des transports routiers, Groupe de travail charge des questions juridiques, 'Project de Convention Relative au Contract de Transport International de Merchandises par la Route' TRANS/WP.9/11 10 October 1949

4 Convention for the Unification of Certain Rules Relating to International Carriage by Air (adopted 12 October 1929, entered into force 13 February 1933) (Warsaw Convention)

5 Convention for the Unification of Certain Rules Relating to International Carriage by Air (adopted on 28 May 1999, entered into force 4 November 2003) International Civil Aviation Organization Doc 9740 (Montreal Convention)

6 Convention on the Contract for the International Carriage of Goods by Road (CMR) (adopted 19 May 1956, entered into force 2 July 1961) 399 UNTS 189

7 Economic Commission for Europe, Inland Transport Committee, Sub-Committee on Road Transport, Working Party on Legal Questions, 'Report of the Small Committee, Preliminary Draft Convention Concerning the Contract for the International Transport of Goods by Road' TRANS/WP9/22 21 December 1953

8 ILC, 'Report of the Study Group of the International Law Commission on the Fragmentation of International Law: Difficulties Arising from The Diversification and Expansion of International Law' (13 April 2006) UN Doc A/CN.4/L.682

9 International Maritime Dangerous Goods (IMDG) Code (adopted in 1965) International Maritime Organization, resolution A.716(17)

10 ILC, 'Draft Articles on The Law of Treaties with Commentaries' (1966) Yearbook of the International Law Commission vol. II 187

11 Note from the Netherlands Government on the liability of the carrier TRANS/WP9/16. 22.12.1950 (CMR travaux préparatoires)

12 Protocol to Amend the Convention for the Unification of Certain Rules Relating to International Carriage by Air Signed at Warsaw on 12 October 1929 (adopted 28 September 1955, entered into force 1 August 1963) (The Hague Protocol 1955)
13 Protocol to Amend the International Convention for the unification of certain rules of law relating to bills of lading, signed at Brussels on 25 August 1924. (adopted 23 February 1968, entered into force 23 June 1977) No. 23643
14 The Brussels Convention for the Unification of Certain Rules of Law relating to Bills of Lading (adopted 25 August 1924, entered into force 2 June 1931) Trb. 1953, 109, 004127 (Hague Rules)
15 *The Travaux Préparatoires of the Hague Rules and of the Hague-Visby Rules* (Comite Maritime International (CMI)
16 UNCITRAL, 'Consolidated Official Reports on the Preparation of the United Nations Convention on Contracts for the International Carriage of Goods Wholly or Partly by Sea ("The Rotterdam Rules"), 41st Session of UNCITRAL (A/63/17' <https://bit.ly/3nq1hRK> accessed 3 March 2020
17 Uniform Rules concerning the Contract of International Carriage of Goods by Rail (COTIF-CIM) adopted 9 June 1999, entered into force 1 July 2006) [International Carriage by Rail (COTIF) of 9 May 1980, as amended by the Vilnius Protocol of 3 June 1999] CR 24/NOT/Add.5 21.12.2009]
18 United Nations Convention on the Carriage of Goods by Sea (adopted 31 March 1978, entered into force 1 November 1992) 1695 UNTS 4 (Hamburg Rules)
19 Vienna Convention on the Law of Treaties (adopted 23 May 1969, entered into force 27 January 1980) 1155 UNTS 331 (Vienna Convention)

National law

1 Bürgerliches Gesetzbuch in der Fassung der Bekanntmachung vom 2. Januar 2002 (BGBl. I S. 42, 2909; 2003 I S. 738) (with further changes) (BGB)
2 Bürgerliches Gesetzbuch 18.8.1896 Bundesgesetzblatt I S. 42, 2909; 2003 I S. 738 ze zm.
3 Carriage of Goods by Sea Act 1936 46 USC 30701 (US COGSA)
4 Carriage of Goods by Sea Act 1992 c.50
5 Civil Liability (Contribution) Act 1978 c.47
6 Codice civile italiano, Regio Decreto 16 marzo 1942, n. 262 (GU Serie Generale n. 79 del 04-04-1942)
7 Contracts (Rights of Third Parties) Act 1999 c.31
8 Decreto legge 10 febbraio 2009, n. 5 convertito con modificazioni dalla L. 9 aprile 2009, n. 33 (in SO n. 49, relativo alla GU 11/04/2009, n. 85)
9 Handelsgesetzbuch vom 10. Mai 1897 (RGBl. S. 219) BGBl. III/FNA 4100–1 (with further changes)
10 Kodeks morski Dz.U. 2001 Nr 138, poz. 1545 (with further changes) 11. Partnership Act 1890
11 Prawo Przewozowe Dz. U. 1984 Nr 53 poz. 272
12 Unfair Contract Terms Act 1977 c 50
13 Ustawa z dnia 23 kwietnia 1964 r. – Kodeks cywilny Dz.U. 1964 nr 16 poz. 93 (with further changes) (Kodeks Cywilny, KC)
14 Ustawa z dnia 15 września 2000 r. Kodeks spółek handlowych Dz.U. 2000 nr 94 poz. 1037 (with further changes)

TABLE OF CASES (BY COUNTRY)

Poland *(extracted from: https://legalis.pl/, https://orzeczenia.ms.gov.pl/, www.sn.pl/orzecznictwo/)*

1 Sąd Najwyższy 29.06.1995 III CZP 66/95
2 Sąd Najwyższy 17.11.1998 III CKN 23/98
3 Sąd Najwyższy 19.03.1999 II CKN 231/98
4 Sąd Najwyższy 14.05.1999 I CKN 2/98
5 Sąd Najwyższy 03.09.2003 II CKN 415/01
6 Sąd Najwyższy 25.09.2003 V CK 204/02
7 Sąd Najwyższy 27.01.2004 II CK 389/02
8 Sąd Najwyższy 06.10.2004 I CK 199/04
9 Sąd Apelacyjny w Katowicach 18.04.2005 I ACa 2051/04
10 Sąd Najwyższy 26.01.2006 V CSK 111/05
11 Sąd Najwyższy 20.07.2006 V CSK 115/06
12 Sąd Apelacyjny w Katowicach 27.10.2007 I ACa 400/07
13 Sąd Najwyższy 22.11.2007 III CSK 150/07
14 Sąd Najwyższy 29.10.2008 IV CSK 237/08
15 Sąd Najwyższy 05.10.2011 IV CSK 65/11
16 Sąd Rejonowy w Gorzowie Wielkopolskim 12.09.2012 V GC 693/11
17 Sąd Okręgowy w Szczecinie 14.12.2012 VIII Ga 385/12
18 Sąd Okręgowy w Szczecinie 28.02.2013 VIII Ga 435/12
19 Sąd Apelacyjny w Gdańsku 16.07.2003 I ACa 1387/02
20 Sąd Najwyższy 11.10.2013 I CSK 769/12
21 Sąd Apelacyjny w Krakowie 27.11.2013 I ACa 1056/13
22 Sąd Najwyższy 19.12.2013 II CSK 70/13
23 Sąd Apelacyjny w Gdańsku 17.04.2014 V ACa 136/14
24 Sąd Apelacyjny w Krakowie 27.05.2014 I ACa 541/14
25 Sąd Okręgowy w Szczecinie 26.09.2014 VIII Ga 239/14
26 Sąd Okręgowy w Szczecinie 26.09.2014 VIII Ga 241/14
27 Sąd Rejonowy dla m. st. Warszawy w Warszawie 08.10.2014 XV GC 1377/14
28 Sąd Apelacyjny w Krakowie 05.11.2014 I ACa 1097/14
29 Sąd Apelacyjny w Szczecinie 05.11.2014 I ACa 19/14 I ACz 23/14
30 Sąd Apelacyjny w Łodzi, 06.11.2014 I ACa 623/14
31 Sąd Apelacyjny w Warszawie 12.11.2014 VI ACa 89/14
32 Sąd Apelacyjny w Szczecinie 23.12.2014 I ACa 461/14
33 Sąd Okręgowy we Wrocławiu 23.02.2015 I C 413/14

34 Sąd Apelacyjny w Krakowie 16.09.2015 I ACa 750/15
35 Sąd Apelacyjny w Krakowie 06.10.2015 I ACa 840/15
36 Sąd Apelacyjny w Gdańsku 28.10.2015 I ACa 410/15
37 Sąd Okręgowy w Szczecinie 27.11.2015 VIII Ga 354/15
38 Sąd Rejonowy w Przemyślu 02.12.2015 V GC 103/15
39 Sąd Apelacyjny w Warszawie 10.03.2016 VI ACa 238/15
40 Sąd Rejonowy Szczecin-Centrum w Szczecinie, 07.04.2016 XI GC 1338/15
41 Sąd Najwyższy 14.04.2016 II CSK 338/15
42 Sąd Apelacyjny w Gdańsku 14.07.2016 I ACa 1106/15
43 Sąd Okręgowy w Warszawie 05.08.2016 XXIII Ga 632/16
44 Sąd Apelacyjny w Warszawie 07.09.2016 I ACa 1421/15
45 Sąd Rejonowy w Kaliszu 14.09.2016 V GC 1206/15
46 Sąd Okręgowy w Poznaniu 16.12.2016 XII C 101/15
47 Sąd Apelacyjny w Gdańsku 04.01.2017 I ACa 466/16
48 Sąd Okręgowy w Szczecinie 03.02.2017 VIII Ga 32/16
49 Sąd Okręgowy w Łodzi 13.03.2017 XIII Ga 892/16
50 Sąd Okręgowy w Rzeszowie 16.03.2017 VI Gz 10/17
51 Sąd Okręgowy w Krakowie 23.03.2017 XII Ga 575/16
52 Sąd Apelacyjny w Białymstoku 07.04.2017 I ACa 894/16.
53 Sąd Okręgowy w Krakowie 10.04.2017, IX GC 1091/14
54 Sąd Rejonowy w Bydgoszczy 19.05.2017 VIII GC 2113/15.
55 Sąd Apelacyjny w Katowicach, 25.10.2017 I ACa 503/17
56 Sąd Okręgowego w Łodzi 24.11.2017 X GC 321/14
57 Sąd Apelacyjny w Katowicach 28.12.2017 V ACa 163/17
58 Sąd Najwyższy 20.02.2018 V CSK 205/17
59 Sąd Okręgowy w Szczecinie 20.04.2018 VIII Ga 133/18
60 Sąd Najwyższy 23.05.2018 IV CSK 425/17
61 Sąd Apelacyjny w Krakowie 26.07.2018 I AGa 176/18
62 Sąd Okręgowy w Katowicach 09.08.2018 XIX Ga 1025/17
63 Sąd Okręgowy w Białymstoku 15.10.2018 VII Ga 281/18
64 Sąd Okręgowy w Łodzi 30.10.2018 X GC 270/18
65 Sąd Najwyższy 28.03.2019 I CSK 387/18
66 Sąd Okręgowy w Poznaniu 12.04.2019 XII C 2611/14
67 Sąd Najwyższy 18.06.2019 II CSK 670/18
68 Sąd Najwyższy 27.08.2019 V CSK 191/18
69 Sąd Rejonowy w Gdyni 06.11.2019 VI GC 928/18
70 Sąd Rejonowy w Gdyni 06.11.2019 VI GC 532/19
71 Sąd Najwyższy 26.11.2019 IV CSK 415/18
72 Sąd Apelacyjny w Białymstoku 04.12.2019 I AGa 68/19
73 Sąd Apelacyjny w Białymstoku 21.05.2020 I AGa 149/19
74 Sąd Najwyższy 08.10.2020 II CSK 773/18
75 Sąd Okręgowy w Łodzi 04.12.2020 XIII Ga 1378/19

Germany *(extracted from: https://beck-online-beck-de.peacepalace.idm.oclc.org/)*

1 OLG München 12.04.1990 23 U 3161/88
2 BGH 02.12.1991 II ZR 274/90 (Hamm)
3 BGH 14.07.1993 I ZR 204/91

4 OLG München 31.03.1998 25 U 4876/97
5 OLG Düsseldorf 02.06.2004 18 U 37/0
6 BGH 01.12.2005 I ZR 108/04
7 OLG München 13.09.2006 7 U 3872/05
8 OLG Düsseldorf 27.09.2006 18 U 61/06
9 BGH 14.02.2008 I ZR 183/05
10 BGH 17.07.2008 IZR 181/05.
11 BGH 15.01.2009 I ZR 164/06
12 OLG Hamburg 16.07.2009 6 U 173/08
13 LG Hamburg 03.9.2010 308 O 27/09
14 LG Hamburg 30.08.2012 409 HKO 126/11
15 LG Düsseldorf 05.12.2013 31 O 101/12
16 BGH 22.05.2014 I ZR 109/13
17 OLG Nürnberg 14.04.2015 3 U 1573/14
18 LG Hamburg 17.7.2015 412 HKO 117/14
19 LG Aachen 21.03.2017 41 O 57/15
20 OLG Nürnberg 04.07.2017 12 U 2204/15
21 LG Stuttgart 02.10.2017 44 O 27/17 KfH
22 OLG München 26.10.2017 23 U 1699/17
23 BGH 23.11.2017 I ZR 51/16
24 LG Saarbrücken 27.06.2018 17 HK O 9/16
25 OLG Brandenburg 15.1.2020 7 U 119/18
26 OLG Hamburg 13.2.2020 6 U 182/17
27 *Immonet/Immowelt* [2014] B6–39/15 (Bundeskartellamt)
28 *Verivox/ProSiebenSat1* [2015] B8–76/15 (Bundeskartellamt)

UK *(extracted from: www.bailii.org/; https://uk-westlaw-com.eur.idm.oclc.org/)*
1 *'Giannis N.K' Effort Shipping v Linden Management S.A. and Others* [1998] 1 Lloyd's Rep 337
2 *A/S Dan Bunkering Ltd v FG Hawkes (Western) Ltd* [2009] EWHC 3141 (Comm)
3 *Aegean Sea Traders Corp v Repsol Petroleo SA & Anor ('The Aegean Sea')* [1998] C.L.C. 1090
4 *Albacora SRL v Westcott & Laurence Line* [1966] S.C. (H.L.) 19
5 *Alianca Navegacao e Logistica Lda v Ameropa SA (The Santa Isabella)* [2020] Bus. L.R. 360
6 *Alize 1954 and another v Allianz Elementar Versicherungs AG and others (The Libra)* [2019] EWHC 481 (Admlty)
7 *AP Moller-Maersk A/S (t/a Maersk Line) v Kyokuyo Ltd* [2018] Bus. L.R. 1481
8 *Aqualon (UK) Ltd. and Another v. Vallana Shipping Corporation and Others* [1994] 1 Lloyd's Rep 669
9 *Arnold v Britton* [2015] UKSC 36
10 *Bell v Ivy Technology Ltd* [2020] EWCA Civ 1563
11 *British American Tobacco Denmark A/S and others (Respondents) v Kazemier Transport BV (Appellant)* [2015] UKSC 65
12 *Bunga Seroja* [1999] 1 Lloyd's Rep 512
13 *Cho Yang Shipping Co. Ltd. V Coral (UK) Ltd.* [1997] 2 Lloyd's Rep 641
14 *D. Mildon QC* [1999] I.J.S.L. 99

15 *Datec Electronics Holdings Ltd and others v United Parcels Service Ltd* [2007] UKHL 23
16 *Exportadora Valle de Colina SA (t/a Exportadora Santa Elena) v AP Moller-Maersk A/S (t/a Maersk Line)* [2010] EWHC 3224 (Comm)
17 *Filatona Trading Ltd v Navigator Equities Ltd (Danilina v Chernukhin)* [2020] EWCA Civ 109
18 *Filikos Shipping Corporation of Monrovia v Shipmair BV "Filikos"* [1982] 10 WLUK 241
19 *Gefco UK Ltd. v Mason* [1998] 2 Lloyd's Rep 585
20 *Geofizika DD v MMB International Ltd* [2010] 2 Lloyd's Rep 1
21 *Glencore Energy UK Ltd and Glencore Ltd v Freeport Holdings Ltd (The "Lady M")* [2019] EWCA Civ 388
22 *Goodwin, Ferreira & Co. Ltd., and others v. Lamport & Holt, Ltd.* [1929] 34 Ll.L.Rep. 192
23 *Goodwin, Ferreira & Co. v. Lamport & Holt Line Ltd* [1929] 34 Lloyd's Rep. 19
24 *Investors Compensation Scheme Ltd. v West Bromwich Building Society* [1997] UKHL 28
25 *J. Y.A. Lamaignere v Selene Shipping Agencies Ltd* [1982] C.L.R. 227
26 *Jindal Iron & Steel Co Ltd v Islamic Solidarity Shipping Co Jordan Inc TCI Trans Commodities AG v Islamic Solidarity Shipping Co Jordan Inc (The Jordan II)* [2004] UKHL 49
27 *JJ Silber v Islander Trucking Patenta GmbH v Islander Trucking* [1985] 2 Lloyd's Rep 243
28 *Kala Ltd v. International Freight Services (UK) Ltd [1998] QBD and Inco Europe Ltd v. First Choice Distribution* [1999] 1 WLR 270
29 *Kyokuyo Co Ltd v AP Moller-Maersk A/S (t/a Maersk Line)* [2017] Bus. L.R. 1270
30 *Laemthong International Lines Co Ltd v Artis (The Laemthong Glory) (No.2)* [2005] 1 C.L.C. 739
31 *Magellan Spirit ApS v Vitol SA (The Magellan Spirit)* [2016] EWHC 454 (Comm)
32 *Midlothian Council v Bracewell Stirling Architects* [2018] CSIH 21
33 *Ministry of Food v Lamport & Holt Line Ltd* [1952] 2 Lloyd's Rep 371
34 *MVV Environment Devonport Ltd v NTO Shipping GmbH & Co. KG MS "Nortrader" MV "Nortrader"* [2020] EWHC 1371 (Comm)
35 *Nisshin Shipping Co Ltd v Cleaves & Co Ltd* [2004] 1 Lloyd's Rep 38
36 *Noble Chartering Inc v Priminds Shipping Hong Kong Co Ltd (Tai Prize)* [2021] EWCA Civ 87
37 *Pirie v Richardson* [1927] 1 K.B. 448
38 Pyrene v. Scindia Navigation [1954] 2 QB 402
39 *Quantum Corp v. Plane Trucking* [2002] 2 Lloyd's Rep 24
40 *Quantum Corporation Inc. and others v Plane Trucking Ltd. and Another* [2002] 2 Lloyd's Rep 25
41 *Sandeman v Tyzak* [1913] A.C. 680.
42 *Shell Chemicals UK Ltd v P&O Roadtanks Ltd* [1993] 1 Lloyd's Rep 114
43 *Silver and Layton v. Ocean Steam Ship Company* [1929] 35 Ll.L.Rep. 49
44 *Société de Distribution de Toutes Merchandises en Côte D'Ivoire (t/a SDTM-CI) v Continental Lines NV and Another* [2015] EWHC 1747 (Comm)

45 *Tetroc Ltd v Cross-Con (International)* [1981] 1 Lloyd's Rep 192
46 *The Athanasia Comninos and The Georges Chr Lemos* [1990] 1 Lloyd's Rep 277
47 *The Flowergate* [1967] 1 Lloyd's Rep 1
48 *Uber BV and others (Appellants) v Aslam and others (Respondents)* [2021] UKSC 5
49 *Ulster-Swift Ltd. and Another v Taunton Meat Haulage Ltd. v Fransen Transport NV (Third Party)* [1977] 1 WLR 625
50 *Vinnlustodin HF v Sea Tank Shipping AS (The Aqasia)* [2017] Bus. L.R. 730
51 *Volcafe Ltd and another v Compania Sud Americana de Vapores SA* [2018] UKSC 61

Other jurisdictions

1 CA Lyon 15.09.2016 n° 15/06269
2 Corte di Cassazione 19.3.2019–9133/2015
3 Hoge Raad, 01.02.2008, C06/082HR
4 Hoge Raad, 01.06.2012, 10/05322 S&S 2012/95
5 *Mississippi Shipping Co. v. Zander & Co. (S.S. Del Sud)*, 270 F.2d 345 (5th Cir. 1959)
6 Rechtbank Rotterdam, 28.10.1999, S&S 2000, 35

European Union

1 Case C-484/14 Tobias Mc Fadden v Sony Music Entertainment Germany GmbH [2016] ECLI:EU:C:2016:689
2 Case C-18/18 *Eva Glawischnig-Piesczek v Facebook Ireland Limited* [2019] ECLI:EU:C:2019:821
3 Case C-324/09 *L'Oréal SA and others v eBay International AG and others* [2011] ECR I-06011.
4 Case C-236/08 *Google France and Google* [2010] ECR I-02417;
5 Case C-291/16 *Schweppes SA v Red Paralela SL and Red Paralela BCN SL* [2017] ECLI:EU:C:2017:990
6 Case C-434/15 *Asociación Profesional Élite Taxi v Uber Systems Spain SL* [2017] ECLI:EU:C:2017:981
7 Case C-432/15 *Odvolací finanční ředitelství v Pavlína Baštová* [2016] ECLI:EU:C:2016:855;
8 Case C-71/18 *Skatteministeriet v KPC Herning* [2019] ECLI:EU:C:2019:660;
9 Case C-425/*06 Ministero dell'Economia e delle Finanze v Part Service Srl* [2008] ECR I-00897;
10 Case C-434/*15 Asociación Profesional Elite Taxi v Uber Systems Spain SL* [2017] ECLI:EU:C:2017:364, Opinion of AG Szpunar.
11 Case C-390/18 *Airbnb Ireland* [2019] ECLI:EU:C:2019:1112
12 Case C-434/15 *Asociación Profesional Élite Taxi v Uber Systems Spain SL* [2017] ECLI:EU:C:2017:981

FOREWORD

Dear Reader,
The book that is presented to you has several purposes:

Firstly, this book promotes legal solutions for sustainable transport. The book facilitates freight online platform makers, freight consolidation centres, manufacturing and distributing companies, and their legal support engaging in various models of multiparty co-operation for cargo bundling while knowing potential legal obstacles of such co-operation and how to prevent them. Furthermore, the book serves judges who might face cases concerning co-operation in cargo bundling for which they will often apply laws oriented to individual parties. Lastly, the book serves policymakers who might want to popularize effective logistics operations through improved legal systems. The latter has a special meaning at the time when this book is published. Improving efficiency across the whole transport system is crucial for many policies aiming at minimizing the environmental impact of transport including European Green Deal, Sustainable and Smart Mobility Strategy, and 'Fit for 55' package. Improved legal systems are also necessary to continue with the development of such ideas as logistics as a service or carbon-free last mile deliveries.

Secondly, the book offers another perspective on shipper's or sender's rights and liability under uniform international transport law, particularly under the Convention on the Contract for the International Carriage of Goods by Road of 1956 and the Hague-Visby Rules as amended by the 1968 Protocol. The specific attention is paid to joint rights and obligations that might be the result of, for example, packing goods together in one transport unit or implementing new business models such as horizontal co-operation in logistics that might involve multiparty contracts. As result, the discussion involves clarification of the methods of interpretation of the transport conventions, conventions' risk management frameworks and how to deal with various types of multiparty carriage contracts. In the end, the reader receives a picture on the legal role of shippers and senders in a wider transport network.

Thirdly, the book offers another perspective on transport intermediaries that are referred to in a book as Transport Orchestrators (TOs) who match cargo originating from different sources very often with the use of ICT solutions, and facilitate manufacturing and producing companies starting and running co-operation in logistics. The specific attention is given to the legal classification of these transport intermediaries and how the legal classification affects their liability. Although their online operations should not automatically exclude the possibility of classification as a common offline service, managing transport data instead of the cargo causes legal uncertainties in more legal frameworks compared to traditional offline logistics service providers.

Fourthly, the concepts and solutions in this book were not developed through purely academic glasses but explicitly take into account the issues and observations raised by stakeholders, here manufacturing and producing companies. The European manufacturing and producing companies were asked to express their preferences regarding legal solutions concerning co-operation in logistics and these preferences are discussed at various places in this book. Also, the cases used in the book are sufficiently general and representative to be able to keep a long life.

The book does not:

- Discuss the issues related to competition law. I fully acknowledge that issues related to competition law might hinder co-operation in logistics; however, the format of this book does not allow to discuss these. I did cover the topic elsewhere and I make references to this output.
- Offer a multidisciplinary approach to make it more accessible for the relevant audience. Related to the just mentioned, multidisciplinary approach affects complexity of the book and as a result might make it more difficult to receive. The book, although monodisciplinary, offers a comparative research focusing on different jurisdictions and takes into account the observations raised by manufacturing and producing companies that were collected through a survey.

I hope that this book will serve well the practice of co-operation in logistics. My thanks are due to Routledge for making it happen.

Marta K. Kołacz,
November 2023

CHAPTER 1

Co-operation in cargo bundling – business networks, multiparty, and linked contracts

Marta K. Kołacz

1 Introduction

Business networks are increasingly receiving attention because their organisational forms are legally constrained. In business networks, the factual interdependence between the enterprises might differ from their formal legal independence.[1] Business networks can be created for *ad hoc* or long-term co-operation, yet these purposes might not be reflected in written contracts or the creation of a company.[2] Instead, the co-operating partners may opt for informal contracting and relations based on trust.[3] Even if more formalised structures are used, business networks might not be supported by the law of contracts or that of corporations. The former is intended primarily for bilateral on the spot contracting, and the latter creates rigid structures which may make it difficult to respond to, among others, rapid changes in the composition of the network. Different aspects of various business networks have been discussed in works on labour law,[4]

1 Fabrizio Cafaggi, 'Introduction' in Fabrizio Cafaggi (ed), *Contractual Networks, Inter-Firm Cooperation and Economic Growth* (Edward Elgar 2011).

2 Stefan Grundmann et al., 'The Contractual Basis of Long-Term Organization – The Overall Architecture' in Stefan Grundmann et al. (eds), *The Organizational Contract. From Exchange to Long-Term Network Cooperation in European Contract Law* (Ashgate 2013) 20–37.

3 On building trust and reputation in co-operation (including in the online environment), see e.g.: Michael Luca, 'Designing Online Marketplaces: Trust and Reputation Mechanisms' (2017) 17 *Innovation Policy and the Economy* 77; Steven Tadelis, 'Reputation and Feedback Systems in Online Platform Markets' (2016) 8 *Annual Review of Economics* 321; Timm Teubner and David Dann, 'How Platforms Build Trust' (2018) <https://bit.ly/3rEJR7w> accessed 20 January 2019; Mário Franco and Heiko Haase, 'The Role of Reputation in the Business Cooperation Process: Multiple Case Studies in Small and Medium-Sized Enterprises' (2021) 14 *Journal of Strategy and Management* 82.

4 Chantal Mak, 'The Lion, The Fox, and the Workplace: Fundamental Rights and the Politics of Long-Term Contractual Relationships' in Stefan Grundmann et al. (eds), *The Organizational Contract. From Exchange to Long-Term Network Cooperation in European Contract Law* (Ashgate 2013).

DOI: 10.4324/9781003450801-1

the law of the sale of goods,[5] construction law,[6] competition law,[7] and the law of finance.[8]

This book focuses on co-operative logistics, which here takes the form of horizontal co-operation in cargo bundling (for brevity, co-operative logistics is also referred to as 'co-operation in cargo bundling', 'shipper co-operation', or 'horizontal co-operation'). Horizontal co-operation in cargo bundling is the practice of having shippers (manufacturing and distributing companies in this context) perform cargo consolidation before a carrier is engaged. The companies can agree on a form of long-term co-operation and identify matching opportunities prior to shipment. Consequently, they share their transport resources or services as well as the risks and benefits of co-operation. Shipper co-operation might be considered as a form of business network that could be found in supply chains alongside sales, purchasing, or franchising networks.[9] As with other supply chain business networks, co-operation in cargo bundling involves various organisational forms that could defy the traditional distinction between bilateral contracts and companies, especially because co-operation in cargo bundling might often involve multiparty contracts. In addition, co-operation in cargo bundling can be strongly influenced by context-dependent operations that are related to transportation. Lastly, shipper co-operation can involve economic agents that act in different capacities, which can add to the complexity of its organisational forms.

The present chapter links the aspects of co-operation in cargo bundling that are presented in the management and operations literature with the contractual structures that are discussed in the further chapters of this book. The focus is on the types of relations in the supply chain and their characteristics, the parallels and dissimilarities to groupage services, models of co-operation, and the role of new intermediaries and the specifics of their operations. At the same time, the cases used in the book and analysed problems are sufficiently general and representative to be able to keep a long life – as indicated earlier

5 Hugh Collins, 'The Weakest Link: Legal Implications of the Network Architecture of Supply Chains' in Marc Amstutz and Gunther Teubner (eds), *Networks Legal Issues of Multilateral Co-operation* (Hart Publishing 2009).

6 Cordula Heldt, 'Internal Relations and Semi Spontaneous Order: The Case of Franchising and Construction Contracts' in Marc Amstutz and Gunther Teubner (eds), *Networks Legal Issues of Multilateral Co-operation* (Hart Publishing 2009); Joasia A. Luzak, 'Linked Contracts and Construction Sector: A Builder's Contractual Obligation to Warn the Client About a Risk That Might Emerge from a Contract Between the Client and a Designer' in Ilse Samoy and Marco B.M. Loos (eds), *Linked Contracts* (Intersentia 2012).

7 E.g.: Marion Schultes, 'Company Networks and the Dichotomy and Statics of Competition Law – A Combined Dynamic Control of Conduct and Structure as a Solution Approach' in Stefanie Jung et al. (eds), *Business Networks Reloaded* (Nomos 2015).

8 Clayton P. Gillette, 'Contractual Networks, Contractual Design and Contract Interpretation: The Case of Credit Cards' in Stefan Grundmann et al. (eds), *The Organizational Contract. From Exchange to Long-Term Network Cooperation in European Contract Law* (Ashgate 2013).

9 Heldt (n 6; Reinhard Böhner, 'Asset-sharing in Franchise Networks: The Obligation to Pass on Network Benefits' in Marc Amstutz and Gunther Teubner (eds), *Networks Legal Issues of Multilateral Co-operation* (Hart Publishing 2009).

various business networks are present in day-to-day life, and they are challenged by the existing legal frameworks. Section 2 starts with an approach that is selected to present the content of this book. Section 3 presents types of co-operation in logistics. Section 4 concerns the characteristics of groupage services, shipper co-operation and orchestration, and their legal aspects, which are discussed further in the book. Section 5 presents models of co-operation in cargo bundling in which the network structures that are described in the operations literature are transposed to contractual structures. Section 6 concludes by listing the characteristics of shipper co-operation and connecting them to the problems that are posed by the choice of legal frameworks.

2 Approach

The reader should be firstly briefly introduced to the approach that is taken in this book. Linking the practical forms of co-operation in logistics that are presented in the management literature to the contractual structures that are discussed in the legal literature sets the scene for further legal analysis concerning legal problems that pertain to cargo bundling. The chosen theoretical framework touches upon different characteristics of contracts which are affected by different regulatory levels. Contractual solutions reflect the self-regulatory mechanisms through which the co-operating partners govern their behaviour.[10] The impact of different regulatory tools is such that the contracts in question are not instances of pure self-regulation.[11] The self-regulation of businesses results from freedom of contract. However, freedom of contract is limited by the existing legal frameworks, and contracts might be complementary or substitutive in relation to those frameworks.

The book focuses on the uniform transport law. Considerable importance is ascribed to the Hague Rules of 1924 as amended by the Visby Protocol of 1968 (HVR),[12] which are relevant to marine transport, and to the Convention on the Contract for the International Carriage of Goods by Road of 1956 (CMR),[13] which regulates transportation by road. The two conventions contain separate liability schemes. The carrier's liability under Article 17(1) CMR

10 John Braithwaite, 'Types of Responsiveness' in Peter Drahos (ed), *Regulatory Theory, Foundations and Applications* (Australian National University Press 2017) 140.

11 Joseph Ress, *Reforming The Workplace: A Study of Self-Regulation in Occupational Safety* (University of Pennsylvania Press 1988) 10–11.

12 The Brussels Convention for the Unification of Certain Rules of Law relating to Bills of Lading (adopted 25 August 1924, entered into force 2 June 1931) Trb. 1953, 109, 004127 and Protocol to Amend the International Convention for the unification of certain rules of law relating to bills of lading, signed at Brussels on 25 August 1924 (adopted 23 February 1968, entered into force 23 June 1977) No. 23643. Germany did not ratify the Hague-Visby Rules. The HVR operate at the level of national law with some modifications.

13 Convention on the Contract for the International Carriage of Goods by Road (CMR) (adopted 19 May 1956, entered into force 2 July 1961) 399 UNTS 189.

is very strict. It cannot be avoided by proving lack of fault but only by making out exoneration grounds.[14] In the HVR, the negligence of the shipper relieves the carrier from liability for damage to cargo.[15] The CMR model is followed by the Uniform Rules concerning the Contract of International Carriage of Goods by Rail (COTIF-CIM)[16] and the Convention on the Contract for the Carriage of Goods by Inland Waterway (CMNI).[17] The HVR model is followed by the United Nations Convention on Contracts for the International Carriage of Goods Wholly or Partly by Sea (Rotterdam Rules, RR)[18] and the Convention for the Unification of Certain Rules Relating to International Carriage by Air of 1999 (Montreal Convention, MC).[19] Since the framework for the interpretation of the conventions permits systemic interpretation, arguments are often supported with comparisons to other transport conventions (see further Chapter 2). The mandatory transport conventions leave certain issues that pertain to carriage contracts to domestic law. In the context of this book, the biggest uncertainty relates to the issue of shippers' individual or joint rights and liability (see especially Chapter 4, Chapter 5, and Chapter 6). Furthermore, since the transport conventions do not govern all aspects of the carriage of goods, the comparative analysis is essential to understanding, for example, national classifications of intermediaries, as in the case of TOs (Chapter 8) or the legal nature of co-operation agreements (Chapter 7). Mainly three jurisdictions are examined, and these are Poland, Germany, and England among the others because judges in these countries tend to interpret the international conventions differently.

As a result, the legal frameworks that influence contracts may be conceptualised within a regulatory pyramid (Figure 1.1). The pyramid refers to the idea that merchants should benefit the most from market regulation. Treating self-regulation as a fundamental element of the system is advantageous because shippers understand the operation of certain markets and the optimal means of improving their regulation.[20] A contract aids the design and planning of a deal.[21] The regulatory pyramid is used to achieve synergies between

14 Art. 17(2) and 17 (4) CMR.

15 Art. IV.2(q) HVR.

16 Uniform Rules concerning the Contract of International Carriage of Goods by Rail (COTIF-CIM) adopted 9 June 1999, entered into force 1 July 2006) [International Carriage by Rail (COTIF) of 9 May 1980, as amended by the Vilnius Protocol of 3 June 1999] CR 24/NOT/Add.5 21.12.2009]; Art. 23 COTIF-CIM.

17 Budapest Convention on the Contract for the Carriage of Goods by Inland Waterway (CMNI) (adopted 3 October 2000, entered into force on 1 April 2005) CMNI/CONF(99)2/FINAL. Art. 16 CMNI.

18 United Nations Convention on Contracts for the International Carriage of Goods Wholly or Partly by Sea (adopted 11 December 2008) Sea A/RES/63/122. Art. 17.1 and 17.2 RR.

19 Convention for the Unification of Certain Rules Relating to International Carriage by Air (adopted on 28 May 1999, entered into force 4 November 2003) International Civil Aviation Organization Doc 9740 (Montreal Convention). Art. 18.2 MC.

20 Hugh Collins, *Regulating Contracts* (Oxford University Press 1999) 254.

21 Collins (n 20) 148.

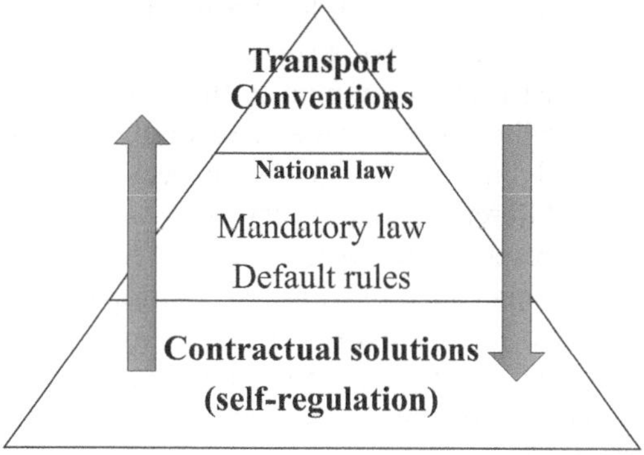

Figure 1.1 Summary of the interrelated regulatory levels

different regulations.[22] Furthermore, top-down and bottom-up approaches are combined.

The top-down approach reveals legal loopholes in the chosen legal framework and enables statutory regulation to facilitate and support the development of stronger and more effective systems of self-regulation.[23] Due to the breadth of the topic, several limitations were accepted. These related, in particular, to liability law, to company law, to competition law, and to some aspects of private international law. The competition law aspects of co-operation have been discussed elsewhere.[24] The references to extracontractual liability serve mainly to highlight the limitations of contracts in multiparty settings (e.g. Chapter 5). The observations concerning the area of company law focus on limited liability companies and unlimited liability companies that can be jointly created by the co-operating partners. In the context of these companies, the particular attention is given to the contribution of the partners to damage for which the jointly established company has to compensate the carrier (Chapter 8). Another important limitation of the study is that it is not a comprehensive text on private international law, and it does not cover matters, such as jurisdiction and the conflict of laws.

The bottom-up approach allows the identification of contractual solutions that align with statute and ensure certainty. Better understanding of interactions between various legal instruments contributes to the design of legal solutions that can be used to promote co-operation in cargo bundling (see

22 Neil Gunningham et al., *Smart Regulation: Designing Environmental Policy* (Clarendon Press 1998).

23 Roger Brownsword and Morgan Goodwin, *Law and the Technologies of the Twenty-First Century Text and Materials* (Cambridge 2012) 25.

24 Marta K. Kołacz, 'Co-Operation Between Manufacturers and Distributors for Sustainable Freight: Select Legal Obstacles Posed by Laws Oriented to Individual Parties' in Ellen J. Eftestøl et al. (eds), *Towards a Zero-Emissions and Digitalized Transport Sector: Law, Regulation, and Logistics* (Edward Elgar Publishing 2024).

Chapter 9). The bottom-up approach has been supported by a survey which had two aims. Firstly, the purpose of a survey was to illustrate what European manufacturing and distributing companies think about co-operative initiatives and how popular those initiatives are. Secondly, the survey enriches the legal analysis by supplying real-life data on expectations about shipper co-operation within the different regulatory levels.

The survey of 121 respondents were administered in 2017 and 2018. The survey was targeted at small, medium, and large European manufacturing and distributing companies. The companies that were approached were based in Poland, the UK,[25] Germany, Italy, and the Netherlands. This selection reflects considerations of access and capacity. Snowball sampling, direct distribution, and the Qualtrics[26] databases were used to reach respondents. All participants, howsoever approached, were assured of the privacy and confidentiality of their responses. This book reports only the survey questions that are relevant for the discussion of the selected legal frameworks.

There could be several reasons for the low response rate. First, the process of question design and data collection showed that, consistent with prior empirical studies, law plays a peripheral role in commercial activities.[27] As a result, potential respondents might have chosen not to participate in the study due to a lack of expertise or interest in the legal aspects of their work. Second, the respondents might have been deterred by the fact that the questions were not about a common practice, but rather one they were likely unfamiliar with. Lastly, businesses can be difficult to reach due to their network relationships, as they are often unwilling to reveal their methods of co-operation and their partners.[28] While the limited number of respondents does not permit definitive conclusions about market preferences, their responses do shed light on potential challenges in contract creation for cargo bundling co-operation.

3 Types of co-operation

Three types of co-operation between companies can be distinguished, namely the vertical, the horizontal, and the lateral (see Figure 1.2). Vertical co-operation aims to enable the partners to complement their attributes, horizontal co-operation targets improvements to their market positions, and the two purposes are combined in lateral co-operation.

25 The surveys were conducted before Brexit.

26 Qualtrics offers several products, including a subscription-software platform that can be used for the design and distribution of surveys as well as to gain access to different population databases. The licence of Erasmus University Rotterdam enabled me to use the software and to design and distribute the survey.

27 See e.g.: Stewart Macaulay, 'Non-Contractual Relations in Business: A Preliminary Study' (1963) 28(1) *American Sociological Review* 55.

28 Maryse Marpsat and Nicolas Razafindratsima, 'Survey Methods for Hard-to-Reach Populations: Introduction to the Special Issue' (2010) 5(2) *Methodological Innovations Online* 3, 4.

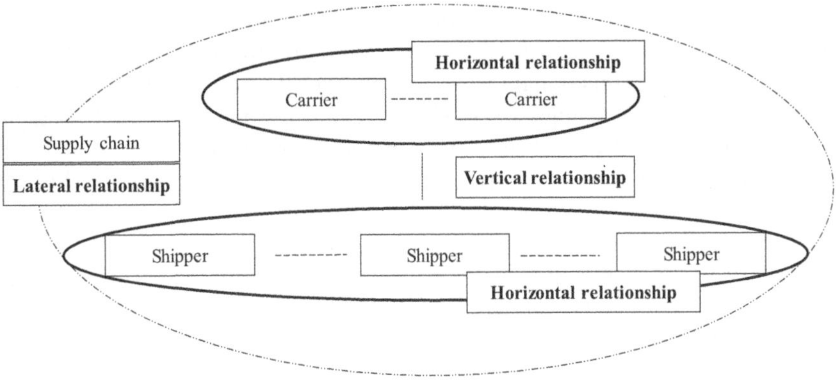

Figure 1.2 Types of co-operation

3.1 Vertical co-operation

Vertical co-operation creates mutual dependences.[29] It is a result of, among others, the introduction of products with shorter lifecycles and the increasing demands of customers, who value rapid delivery.[30] The partners to vertical co-operation operate at different levels of a supply chain. Their offerings complement those of the firms on the level below. The examples of vertical co-operation include groupage services (see Section 4.1) and urban logistic systems with cargo consolidation centres. The latter simplify the delivery of goods to customers who are located in different districts of a city.[31]

Vertical co-operation is a result of the outsourcing of some activities to logistics service providers (LSPs), including carriers, which often indicate that their management of the flow of goods extends beyond mere transport. Four types of interactions between the groups that participate in a supply chain for the management of the flow of goods can be distinguished. The first type, often referred to as 'first-party logistics', refers to shippers performing logistics services in-house because they possess assets such as trucks or warehouses.[32] The shippers therefore manage the production and transportation

29 Maria Bengtsson and Sören Kock, 'Coopetition in Business Networks – To Cooperate and Compete Simultaneously' (2000) 29(5) *Industrial Marketing Management* 411, 414.

30 E.g.: Frans Cruijssen et al., 'Horizontal Cooperation in Logistics: Opportunities and Impediments' (2007) 43(2) *Transportation Research Part E: Logistics and Transportation Review* 129, 129; Laetitia Dablanc et al., 'The Rise of On-Demand "Instant Deliveries" in European Cities' (2017) 18 *Supply Chain Forum: An International Journal* 203.

31 Marianna Jacyna, 'The Role of the Cargo Consolidation Center in Urban Logistics System' (2013) 8(1) *International Journal of Sustainable Development and Planning* 100.

32 Marcus Thiell and Sergio Hernandez, 'Logistics Services in the 21st Century: Supply Chain Integration and Service Architecture' in Zongwei Luo (ed), *Service Science and Logistics Informatics: Innovative Perspectives* (Information Science Reference 2010) 363–364.

of the goods, and they do not co-operate with service providers. First-party logistics is particularly considered in the chapter on the legal classification of co-operation contracts (Chapter 7). Second-party logistics (2PL) is the result of the outsourcing of logistics services.[33] The shippers concentrate on their core competencies, leaving transport, a minor aspect of their business activity, to carriers that own means of transportation. Some aspects of second-party logistics are examined in the discussion of the shipper's rights and liabilities vis-à-vis the carrier under the transport conventions (see Chapter 5 and Chapter 6). The term 'third-party logistics' (3PL) refers to specialised companies, such as freight forwarders, offering services that entail the complex management and co-ordination of logistics tasks, including warehousing, inventory management, packaging, cross-docking, and technology management.[34] Some aspects of third-party logistics are discussed in the analysis of the legal position of new transport intermediaries in Chapter 8. Fourth-party logistics focuses on supply chain integration and supply chain management. The overarching aim is to integrate all actors of a supply chain. Some of the aspects of fourth-party logistics, such as data management, are also covered in Chapter 8. Fourth-party logistics triggers lateral co-operation, which is presented later in Section 3.3.

3.2 Horizontal co-operation

Frans Cruijssen defined horizontal co-operation in transport and logistics as 'active cooperation between two or more firms that operate on the same level of the supply chain and perform a comparable logistics function'.[35] LSPs or shippers can co-operate horizontally in cargo consolidation. The key is, as Cruijssen underlines, is 'that the co-operating companies have direct control over the planning and execution of the logistics activities under consideration'.[36] Horizontal co-operation is different from one-off transactions that do not require co-ordination mechanisms and mergers that result in the creation of new entities at the expense of the independent existence of the partners.[37] Companies can co-operate horizontally for a long time without losing their independence.

33 Thiell and Hernandez (n 32); see also: Kristina Rimienė and Dainora Grundey, 'Logistics Centre Concept through Evolution and Definition' (2007) 4(54) *Engineering Economics* 87, who shows the evolution of the relations in the supply chain based on the concept of a logistics centre.

34 Thiell and Hernandez (n 37); Zach G. Zacharia et al., 'The Emerging Role of the Third-Party Logistics Provider (3PL) as an Orchestrator' (2011) 32(1) *Journal of Business Logistics* 40, 43.

35 Frans Cruijssen, *Horiozontal Cooperation in Transport and Logistics* (Center for Economic Research 2006) 12.

36 Cruijssen (n 35) 13.

37 On relations between businesses, see further e.g.: Andrzej Sznajder, *Alianse marketingowe. Partnerstwa przedsiębiorstw dla zwiększenia konkurencyjności* (Wolters Kluwer 2012).

3.2.1 Horizontal co-operation between carriers

Horizontal co-operation between carriers has been said to carry considerable benefits for companies that specialise in all transport modes.[38] Carriers co-operate to optimise vehicle routes and vehicle loading.[39]

Richard Clarke[40] analysed co-operation between container-ship companies, which are called 'conferences'. Shipping conferences were a response to the problem of overcapacity and falling rates in the shipping sector. Their use resulted in stable rates, improved customer service, and larger volumes of pooled and shipped goods. Terence Fan et al.[41] focused on horizontal co-operation in aviation and found that airlines began co-operating to strengthen their positions on the market, to provide better customer service, to develop joint marketing programmes, or to cross-sell on selected routes. Such co-operation has been found to be beneficial only if certain conditions are met. For example, Romero-Silva and Mujica Mota[42] found that with high dock capacity utilization, co-operative policies penalize collaborating actors. Hanif Sherali and Brian Lunday[43] examined co-operation in rail transport and suggested improved planning processes to enhance total fleet size on US railroads. The advantages of horizontal co-operation have also been investigated in the context of road transportation. Among the various initiatives that have been discussed, it is worth mentioning Frans Cruijssen et al.'s[44] work. They suggested that Flemish road transport companies begin co-operating horizontally to improve the efficiency of their operations. Horizontal co-operation has also been examined in the context of truck platoons, which are groups of vehicles that travel closely behind each another and are connected by Wi-Fi. For this

38 See further: Shenle Pan et al., 'Horizontal Collaborative Transport: Survey of Solutions and Practical Implementation Issues' (2019) 59(15–16) *International Journal of Production Research* 1.

39 E.g.: Margaretha Gansterer and Richard F. Hartl, 'Collaborative Vehicle Routing: A Survey' (2018) 268(1) *European Journal of Operational Research* 1; Margaretha Gansterer and Richard F. Hartl, 'Shared Resources in Collaborative Vehicle Routing' (2020) 28(1) *TOP* 1; Mouna Atik El Ftouh et al., 'Collaborative Transportation and Urban Routing Problems: State of Classification and Literature' (2020) 35(3) *International Journal of Logistics Systems and Management* 1.

40 Richard L. Clarke, 'An Analysis of the International Ocean Shipping Conference System' (1997) 36(4) *Transportation Journal* 17. See further: Elena A. Lezhnina and Yulia E. Balykina, 'Cooperation between Sea Ports and Carriers in the Logistics Chain' (2021) 9(7) *Journal of Marine Science and Engineering* 774 on how co-operation affects ports.

41 Terence Fan et al., 'Evolution of Global Airline Strategic Alliance and Consolidation in the Twenty-First Century' (2001) 7(6) *Journal of Air Transport Management* 349.

42 Rodrigo Romero-Silva and Miguel Mujica Mota, 'Trade-Offs in the Landside Operations of Air Cargo Hubs: Horizontal Cooperation and Shipment Consolidation Policies Considering Capacitated Nodes' (2022) 103 *Journal of Air Transport Management* 102253.

43 Hanif D. Sherali and Brian J. Lunday, 'Equitable Apportionment of Railcars Within a Pooling Agreement' (2011) 47(2) *Transportation Research Part E* 263.

44 Frans Cruijssen et al., 'Logistic Efficiency Through Horizontal Cooperation: The Case of Flemish Road Transportation Companies' (2006) (2006–14) CentER Discussion Paper <https://rb.gy/10d2jd> accessed 18 November 2023.

reason, the vehicles in the platoon can accelerate, brake, and cruise together.[45] Authors such as, among others, Danjue Chen et al.,[46] Wouter Verheyen,[47] S. Sivanandham, and M. S. Gajanand[48] have discussed various strategies for improving road safety and the uptake of platooning in order to conserve fuel.

Although horizontal co-operation between carriers is not the focus of this book, it can still benefit from certain parts of the legal analysis that is developed on these pages. Co-operation between carriers can result in uncertainties in respect of liabilities, a point to which especially Chapter 8 may be germane.

3.2.2 Horizontal co-operation between shippers and freight forwarders

Horizontal co-operation between shippers has been discussed from many perspectives, including those of logistics, distribution, and production. Manufacturing and distributing companies have incentives to co-operate, not only because of lower transportation costs but also (and often mainly) because of the availability of efficient supply chains.[49] Horizontal co-operation that aims only to ensure the efficient flow of goods by enabling demand-sensitive adjustments is discussed in relation to freight forwarders, to whom steering the flow of goods is a core activity.[50]

Efficiencies and product improvements have been said to be the main aims of co-operation.[51] Much attention has also been afforded to sustainability.

45 See further: Robbert Janssen et al., *Truck Platooning Driving the Future of Transportation* (TNO 2015).

46 Danjue Chen et al., 'Truck Platooning on Uphill Grades Under Cooperative Adaptive Cruise Control (CACC)' (2018) 94 *Transportation Research Part C: Emerging Technologies* 50.

47 Wouter Verheyen, 'Towards a Model for Sustainable Platooning Cooperation in Road Transport' in Ellen Eftestøl-Wilhelmsson et al. (eds), *Sustainable and Efficient Transport Incentives for Promoting a Green Transport Market* (Edward Elgar 2019).

48 S. Sivanandham and M.S. Gajanand, 'Platooning for Sustainable Freight Transportation: An Adoptable Practice in the Near Future?' (2020) 40(5) *Transport Reviews* 581.

49 E.g: William Ferrell et al., 'Horizontal Collaboration: Opportunities for Improved Logistics Planning' (2020) 58(14) *International Journal of Production Research* 4267; Belarmino Adenso-Díaz et al., 'Assessing Partnership Savings in Horizontal Cooperation by Planning Linked Deliveries' (2014) 66 *Transportation Research Part A* 268, who listed various European cases on horizontal co-operation between shippers; Fabrizio Cafaggi and Paola Iamiceli, 'Inter-Firm Networks in the European Wine Industry' (2010) AAWE Working Paper No. 77 – Business, 1 <https://bit.ly/3COHP72> accessed 18 November 2023, who focused on inter-firm networks in the European wine industry, particularly wine producers and distributors; Ozhan Yilmaz and Secil Savasaneril, 'Collaboration Among Small Shippers in a Transportation Market' (2012) 218(2) *European Journal of Operational Research* 408, who focused on small shippers that cannot ship truckloads regularly and thus make sporadic transportation requests.

50 E.g.: Minghui Lai et al., 'An Ascending Auction for Freight Forwarder Collaboration in Capacity Sharing' (2019) 54(3) *Transportation Science* 1175; Chalermpong Senarak, 'Shipping-Collaboration Model for the New Generation of Container Port in Innovation District: A Case of Eastern Economic Corridor' (2020) 36(2) *The Asian Journal of Shipping and Logistics* 65; Rene Leitner et al., 'Structural Concepts for Horizontal Cooperation to Increase Efficiency in Logistics' (2011) 4(3) *CIRP Journal of Manufacturing Science and Technology* 332, 334.

51 Ferrell et al. (n 49) 4276.

As far as efficiencies are concerned, horizontal co-operation can facilitate access to new markets and enable the use of services under favorable conditions.[52] Co-operation between small manufacturing and producing companies that cannot ship full truckloads regularly is triggered by the expense of pick-up and delivery services.[53] Horizontal co-operation also facilitates reducing the distribution costs of shippers.[54] Relatedly, a fall in CO_2 emissions has been observed. For this reason, some studies of horizontal co-operation focus primarily on the optimisation of routes by reference to environmental criteria.[55]

This book is relevant to co-operation between shippers, and freight forwarders because under contract law, both a producing company and a freight forwarding company can acquire the status of principal shipper or sender under a contract of carriage (see Chapter 5, Section 2). A freight forwarding company that is involved in a contractual chain can, in fact, end up as both a contractual carrier and a principal shipper (see further Chapter 5, Chapter 6, and Chapter 8).

3.3 Lateral co-operation

Lateral co-operation is defined as a combination of horizontal and vertical relations that ensures optimal supply chain performance.[56] Lateral co-operation circles on supply chain integration and supply chain management, with the overarching aim of integrating all actors in a supply chain.[57]

Integrators group shippers, freight forwarders, and carriers. They steer cargo flows and can administer co-operation on and between different levels.[58] Integrators function as single points of contact for shippers, carriers, and other LSPs. The attempts of Nestlé and PepsiCo to engage in the joint

52 Cafaggi and Iamiceli (n 49).

53 Yilmaz and Savasaneril (n 49).

54 Cruijssen (2006) (n 35) 29; Sebastián Lozano et al., 'Cooperative Game Theory Approach to Allocating Benefits of Horizontal Cooperation' (2013) 229(2) *European Journal of Operational Research* 444.

55 E.g.: S. Ubeda et al., 'Green Logistics at Eroski: A Case Study' (2011) 131(1) *International Journal of Production Economics* 44; Elena Pérez-Bernabeu et al., 'Horizontal Cooperation in Road Transportation: A Case Illustrating Savings in Distances and Greenhouse Gas Emissions' (2014) 22(3) *International Transactions in Operational Research* 585; Thomas Hacardiaux et al., 'Balancing Partner Preferences for Logistics Costs and Carbon Footprint in a Horizontal Cooperation' (2022) 44 *ORSpectrum* 121.

56 E.g.: Cruijssen (2006) (n 35) 21; Yi Tao et al., 'A Column Generation Approach for the Route Planning Problem in Fourth Party Logistics' (2017) 68 *Journal of the Operational Research Society* 165; Michael Dircksen and Gaelle Magnin, 'Evaluation of Synergy Potentials in Transportation Networks Managed by a Fourth Party Logistics Provider' (2017) 25 *Transport Research Procedia* 824.

57 François Fulconis et al., 'Exploring New Competences in the Logistics Industry: The Intermediation Role of 4PL' (2006) 7(2) *Supply Chain Forum: An International Journal* 68; François Fulconis and Gilles Paché, 'Supply Chain Monitoring: LLPs and 4PL Providers as Orchestrators' (2018) 238 *Procedia – Social and Behavioral Sciences* 9.

58 Fulconis and Paché (n 57).

packing and outbound distribution of fresh and chilled food products to retail customers in Belgium and Luxemburg, which was administered by a company called TRI-VIZOR, is an example of lateral co-operation.[59] Another example, also administered by TRI-VIZOR, was the co-operation between the retailer Spar and its suppliers.[60] The obligations that integrators undertake in the realization of its operations can influence legal classification of such service provider. For example, they can be legally classified as carriers (see Chapter 8). On the pages of this book integrators are also referred to as Transport Orchestrators (TOs).

4 Shipper co-operation, groupage, and orchestration

This book frequently refers to groupage services, shipper co-operation, and transport orchestration. While I was conducting the underlying research, I noticed that co-operation between shippers in cargo bundling is often associated with groupage. Since there are considerable differences between the two (see Figure 1.3 and further Chapter 4, Chapter 5, and Chapter 6), a comparison is provided. Likewise, new intermediaries, such as TOs or logistics platforms, have been said to provide novel services. However, those services can be subsumed under existing legal concepts. Thus, the characteristics of the new transport intermediaries are presented in light of the related legal problems.

4.1 Groupage

The consolidation of freight is not a new concept. It is 'a transportation option that combines different items, produced and used at different locations and different times, into single vehicle loads in order to minimize transportation costs and maximize vehicle utilization'.[61] In practice, Less-than-Container or Truck Loads (LCL) are transferred in Full-Container-or-Truck Loads (FCL), whereby small shipments are merged to reach volumes that are relatively close to capacity and are then transported via common routes.

Groupage services are organised reactively by service providers, which have networks of logistics assets at their disposal and organise the service according

59 Kurt Jacobs et al., 'Horizontal Collaboration in Fresh & Chilled Retail Distribution' (2014) CO^3 Test Project Report, Collaboration Concepts for Co-modality (CO^3 Project) <https://bit.ly/3G8Wf3Y> accessed 15 January 2019.

60 Sven Verstrepen and Lisa Van den Bossche, 'Retail Inbound Horizontal Collaboration' (2014) <https://bit.ly/3lnWakD> accessed 15 January 2019.

61 Adil Baykasoglu and Vahit Kaplangolu, 'A Multi-Agent Approach to Load Consolidation in Transportation' (2011) 42(7) *Advances in Engineering Software* 477, 477.

to the number of orders that they receive.[62] A contract is concluded every time an order is received, which indicates that a shipper wants to dispatch a consignment. Once the single consignments have been prepared by the shippers, they are declared to the LSP and collected, within a certain geographical area, according to its schedule.[63] The LSP, based on its knowledge of the cargoes that can be grouped, combines small freight shipments that do not require the entire capacity of the vehicle (LCL) if the shipment timings are identical and if there is a geographical match.[64] Relatedly, the LSP deals with the packing of containers. It is in the interests of the LSP to identify the most optimal solution that allows the best arrangement of rows, layers, stacks, and optimal stowage plans to be employed for each unit.[65]

From a legal perspective, it is important that the LSPs consolidate freight flows on the basis of a bilateral contract with each shipper. A bilateral contract is a basic and common type of arrangement that is used by business partners and regulated by different fields of law. Groupage contracts, which are bilateral, can often be classified as carriage contracts. The shipper is therefore legally responsible for securing the consignment, that is, for its proper packing. The LSP, which formally acts as a carrier under such contracts, in turn bears the risks of cargo matching, transport routes, factual consolidation, and transportation. In fact, consolidation is subsumed under transportation.[66] As a result, the LSP who has a legal status of a carrier is presumed to be liable unless it can establish that the damage was caused outside of the period for which it was responsible or, alternatively, if it makes out a valid exoneration ground (e.g. Article 17 CMR). In the analysis that is developed in different chapters of this book, the bilateral contract between a shipper and an LSP with a legal status of a carrier serves as a point of reference for the analysis of the liability issues that the different cargo bundling models engender (see further Chapter 5, Chapter 6, and Chapter 8).

62 Harald Gleissner and J. Christian Femerling, *Logistics Basics – Exercises – Case Studies* (Springer 2013) 89.

63 Gleissner and Femerling (n 62).

64 Gleissner and Femerling (n 62); Stefan Creemers et al., 'Tri-Vizor Uses an Efficient Algorithm to Identify Collaborative Shipping Opportunities' (2017) 47(3) *Interfaces* 244, 245.

65 See further e.g.: António G. Ramos et al., 'A New Load Balance Methodology for Container Loading Problem in Road Transportation' (2018) 266(3) *European Journal of Operational Research* 1140; Rodolfo Ranck Júnior et al., 'A Hybrid Approach for a Multi-Compartment Container Loading Problem' (2019) 137 *Expert Systems with Applications* 471; Çağatay Iris et al., 'Flexible Ship Loading Problem with Transfer Vehicle Assignment and Scheduling' (2018) 111 *Transportation Research Part B: Methodological* 113; Túlio A.M. Toffolo, 'A Two-Dimensional Heuristic Decomposition Approach to a Three-Dimensional Multiple Container Loading Problem' (2017) 257(2) *European Journal of Operational Research* 526.

66 See e.g.: Andrew Messent and David A Glass, *Hill & Messent CMR: Contracts for the International Carriage of Goods By Road* (LLP 2000) 283–294.

4.2 Shipper co-operation

Horizontal co-operation in cargo bundling is the practice of having shippers consolidate the cargo before a carrier is engaged. The shippers agree on a form of long-term co-operation and detect matching opportunities prior to shipment. Subsequently, they can share transport resources or services as well as the risks and benefits of co-operation.[67]

Horizontal co-operation in cargo bundling involves the proactive organisation of consolidation, in that matching possibilities are identified before the order is sent to an LSP.[68] The process of organising the actual consolidation is similar to that which is common in groupage service and involves three stages: Identification, preparation, and operation.[69] The difference is that these stages do not necessarily depend on the LSP (see Figure 1.3). In the identification phase, shippers collect information about possible matches between freight flows and attempt to forecast the amount of cargo that can be shipped together.[70] The consolidation does not always need to be based on spatiotemporal concordance.[71] Shippers can consolidate their cargo either with shippers in their vicinity or on common transport routes.[72] Due to this flexibility, shippers can adjust the planning of their shipments and create better, cheaper, and more sustainable distribution plans.[73] In the preparation phase, further data on freight flows must be collected, and LSPs must be selected. The shippers also decide on loading plans and transport routes.[74] The identification and preparation phases may overlap because additional partners can join or leave the co-operative arrangement. Accordingly, it might be necessary to adjust plans and preparations or seek out new shippers to join the scheme. Matching opportunities prior to shipment can strengthen the shipper's bargaining position vis-à-vis the carrier.[75] If the shipper demands more capacity than

67 Rahul Kale et al., 'Analyzing Private Communities on Internet-Based Collaborative Transportation Networks' (2007) 43 *Transportation Research Part E* 21, 28–30; Creemers et al. (n 64) 245; See also: Benoit Montreuil, 'Towards a Physical Internet: Meeting the Global Logistics Sustainability Grand Challenge' (2011) 3 *Logistics Research* 71, proposing a Physical Internet initiative that can boost advanced planning; and William Ferrell et al., 'Horizontal Collaboration: Opportunities for Improved Logistics Planning' (2019) 58(14) *International Journal of Production Research* 4267.

68 Yilmaz and Savasaneril (n 49).

69 Kurt Jacobs et al., 'CO^3 Test Project Report: Creation of an Orchestrated Intermodal Partnership Between Multiple Shippers' (2014) CO^3 Test Project Report, Collaboration Concepts for Co-modality (CO^3 Project) 21–32 <https://rb.gy/96uls0> accessed 15 November 2023.

70 Jacobs et al. (n 69).

71 Christine Vanovermeire and Kenneth Sörensen, 'Measuring and Rewarding Flexibility in Collaborative Distribution, Including Two-Partner Coalitions' (2014) 239(1) *European Journal of Operational Research* 157–158.

72 Creemers et al. (n 64) indicates that the opportunities include the bundling of shipments at origin and destination points in the same areas, at routes in opposite directions, and at different routes that tie in with each other.

73 Creemers et al. (n 64); See also: Jeroen Beliën et al., 'Collaborative Shipping: Logistics in the Sharing Economy' 44(2) *Informs* 20.

74 Jacobs et al. (n 69).

75 Kale et al. (n 72).

what the carrier actually possesses, the shipper may, firstly, be able to default on its contract with the carrier. Secondly, the shipper may be able to find better transport services on the market and adjust its own production.[76] The actual operation of co-operation involves the co-ordination and consolidation of goods and their subsequent transportation. Here, another difference from groupage services may be observed. In groupage, the LSP consolidates goods; in the case of shipper co-operation, the identity of the party that performs the consolidation depends on the type of operational solutions that are chosen (see further Section 5). Either shippers or the LSP may take charge of consolidation. If the shippers undertake it, they need to resolve partner- and transport-route selection issues as well as to manage the delivery and packaging of single loads and consolidated bundles.

Horizontal co-operation extends the current logistics market, but it is unlikely to fully replace traditional groupage services for two reasons. Firstly, it is rather improbable that all shippers will restructure their logistics operations simultaneously. Their human and financial resources are limited. For example, Gautam Ahuja[77] observed that the firms which have co-operated in the past are highly specialised and often exhibit advanced technological and commercial assets, which make them more attractive as potential partners. These findings are compatible with the conclusions of Fabrizio Cafaggi and Paola Iamiceli,[78] who observed that small and medium producers face obstacles in accessing distribution channels. Efficiency-management concerns in groups of co-operating businesses preclude the possibility of accepting members that are too small. Secondly, horizontal co-operation might be of little use for non-recurring or low-frequency transport operations.[79] Instead, it may be expected that shippers which are already organised in some way (for example, in industrial parks or as suppliers of a single distributor) will co-operate horizontally.[80]

Beyond the bilateral contracts that typify groupage, shippers can also organise their co-operation by using different contractual models, which range from multiparty contracts to linked contracts (see further Section 5). These different contractual arrangements and their varied operational contexts produce uncertainty. For example, if the LSP is considered a carrier, then, under the transport conventions, it is not clear whether shippers are jointly or individually liable under the multiparty contract of carriage. If a judge instead decides that national law applies to the LSP, different contractual structures may operate differently across jurisdictions (see particularly Chapter 5 and Chapter 6).

76 Kale et al. (n 67).

77 Gautam Ahuja, 'The Duality of Collaboration: Inducements and Opportunities in the Formation of Interfirm Linkages' (2000) 21(3) *Strategic Management Journal* 317.

78 Cafaggi and Iamiceli (n 49).

79 Michael Bogen and Sven Verstrepen, 'CO^3 Position Paper: Added Value of ICT in Logistics Horizontal Collaboration. Identifying the Need for an Integrated Approach' (2014) 9 <https://rb.gy/stsy06> accessed 15 November 2023.

80 Cruijssen (2006) (n 35) 138.

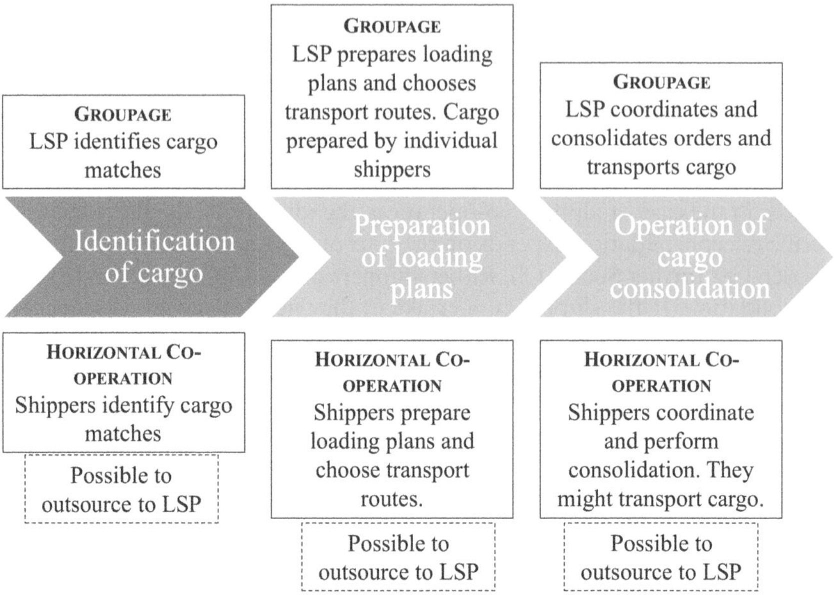

Figure 1.3 Horizontal co-operation v groupage

4.3 Orchestration

Although the phases of consolidation in horizontal co-operation can be performed by shippers, if those shippers are not specialised, they can outsource each stage to a LSP (see Figure 1.3). In consequence, the LSP might deal with the final product of the consolidation, perform it according to a plan devised by the shippers, or even transport goods if the shippers lack the requisite assets. The involvement of LSPs facilitates integrated supply chains, especially when efficiencies can be harnessed by combining horizontal and vertical co-operation (see Section 3.3.).[81]

The scope of orchestration services can differ depending on whether the LSP is involved in the creation of vertical, horizontal, or mixed forms of co-operation. Furthermore, whereas some orchestrators offer online services for the establishment of co-operative arrangements, others also maintain them. A review of the services that are offered by LSPs that match cargo flows reveals that the factual content of their operations, that is, the services that they advertise, might not match the corresponding contractual stipulations, that is, the terms and conditions that regulate the service and apportion or exclude liability (see Table 1.1).

81 Yilmaz and Savasaneril (n 49).

Table 1.1 Description of online services related to cargo matching and their self-categorization on the basis of Terms and Conditions (T&Cs). Information valid as of 15.11.2023

Provider	*Description of service*	*(Self-) Qualification in T&Cs*
Chronotruck *www.chronotruck.com/*	Chronotruck identifies a reliable carrier in real time on the request of a sender. Carriers receive freight offers near them.	1) Chronotruck is ***a freight forwarder*** and is providing expertise through this web portal and its mobile application(s). 2) As a freight forwarder, Chronotruck organizes the shipments of an ordering party (hereinafter the Sender), selecting a carrier (hereinafter the Carrier) and ensuring the smooth running of the service provision. Chronotruck invoices the ordering party on the fare basis applied to so-called services and enters into contract with the carrier who invoices it in turn
Eurosender *www.eurosender.com/*	Eurosender is a digital platform that facilitates efficient combinations of transport to meet the demand for *ad hoc* shipments as well as for shipping that is tailored to different logistics flows.	1) Eurosender ***acts as a commission agent and not as a freight forwarder*** 2) When placing the order through our website, the customer authorizes Eurosender to, in its own name (Eurosender's name) and on behalf of the client (commissioner), order transportation services with one of the carriers with which Eurosender has an agreement in place, provided that the carrier selected complies with the requirements for the execution of the commissioned service. 3) Eurosender is solely responsible for the selection of carriers and never for the execution of transportation. 4) The fulfilment of obligations inherent to the transportation service is the exclusive responsibility of the carrier, selected to execute transportation. It is them, and not Eurosender, who perform the pick-up, transportation and delivery of the shipments, who arrange the transportation and who are responsible for its/the execution.
Quicargo *https://quicargo.com*	Quicargo establishes connections between shippers and carriers by providing an (online/digital) platform.	1) Quicargo will ***act as an intermediary as described in*** **Article 8:60 of the Dutch Civil Code for the shipper**. 2) Quicargo is not responsible or liable for the contract including the conditions under which the carriage shall be carried out. Such an agreement is the responsibility of the carrier and shipper. 3) The shipper pays the carrier's costs through the invoice from Quicargo. Quicargo informs the shipper regarding its full financial commitment, including the fee to the carrier, the charge for Quicargo, VAT, and any other Quicargo known fees and charges.
TRI-VIZOR *www.trivizor.com/*	TRI-VIZOR proactively prepares, designs, and operates horizontal partnerships and collaborative communities for shippers.	***Impartial orchestrator*** for transport and logistics; creation (as 'architect') and managing (as 'trustee') horizontal collaboration partnerships and platforms.
uShip *www.uship.com/*	The marketplace helps shippers to connect with trusted feedback-rated service providers, such as large companies, small fleets, and single-truck owners that offer additional space for cargo at a discount.	1) uShip is a **neutral venue** and **digital clearinghouse**. 2) uShip is not a Transportation Service Provider or Shipper. Our website acts as a venue where Shippers and TSPs can interact and enter into agreements. uShip is not a party to any shipping agreement made between uShip users via the uShip software platform. As a result, we have no control over the quality, safety, or legal aspects of the transactions that take place on our website. 3) uShip does not set or control prices offered by Shippers or TSPs. 4) As a neutral venue, uShip does not set terms specific to Carrier cargo liability.
Saloodo! *www.saloodo.com/*	Saloodo! connects shippers and carriers on a digital freight platform. The platform offers the customer the technical means to request freight services provided by Saloodo! and its subcontractors.	'Unless mandatory provisions to the contrary (e.g. CMR) are applicable, Saloodo! shall be liable for all the services it provides in accordance with the **Allgemeine Deutsche Spediteurbedingungen 2017 – ADSp 2017 – (German Freight Forwarders' General Terms and Conditions 2017)** and if the ADSp 2017 do not apply for performing logistics services – with the Logistic-AGB (General Terms and Conditions of Logistics Services Providers), as of March 2006.'

These varied possibilities correspond to a plethora of contractual terms. Those terms regulate the relationships between the actors, the definition of the procurement criteria, and liability limitations. However, the advertised functionalities do not necessarily coincide with the legal obligations that the platform is prepared to assume. Notably, the LSPs often attempt to avoid legal classification as a provider of transport or transport-related services contractually. For example, Eurosender (see Table 1.1) matches cargo flows. Therefore, its offering resembles typical groupage services. In its terms and conditions, it excludes the possibility of being classified as a freight forwarder. Nevertheless, under German law, it could actually attract carrier liability (§ 460 HGB[82]). This tendency in the drafting of terms and conditions reveals an apparent mismatch between functionalities and self-descriptions, which invites questions about the weight of different factors in juridical classification. For LSPs that are active in both horizontal and vertical relationships, the mismatch can actually occur at both levels if a judge classifies each obligation separately (see further Chapter 8).

5 Shipper co-operation – models

This section presents the contractual models for co-operation in cargo bundling that are used in practice. The section also focuses on the practical aspects of co-operation, such as the performance of cargo bundling, because the operational context might be relevant to liability issues (see Chapter 4, Chapter 5, and Chapter 6), standard contract clauses, and other regulatory solutions (see Chapter 9).

5.1 Co-operation – operational governance

Operational governance concerns the daily organisation of activities within horizontal co-operation schemes.[83] It builds trust and rests on rules, policies, and procedures that allocate responsibilities between the partners.[84] In shipper co-operation, operational governance concerns, among others, strategies for consolidating and loading cargo.

82 Handelsgesetzbuch vom 10. Mai 1897 (RGBl. S. 219) BGBl. III/FNA 4100–1 (with further changes) (HGB).

83 Jan Simon Raue and Andreas Wieland, 'The Interplay of Different Types of Governance in Horizontal Cooperations: A View on Logistics Service Providers' (2015) 26(2) *The International Journal of Logistics Management* 401, 403; Melanie Schreiner et al., 'What Really Is Alliance Management Capability and How Does It Impact Alliance Outcomes and Success?' (2009) 30(13) *Strategic Management Journal* 1395, 1396.

84 Raue and Wieland (n 83).

Consolidation can be centralised or decentralised. Centralised consolidation occurs at consolidation centres, which can be operated jointly by all the shippers, owned by a single shipper, or in the purview of an LSP. Consolidation might occur at cross-docking points[85] where the goods are consolidated without being stored for long periods of time. Alternatively, goods can be consolidated at warehouses until a sufficient quantity is accumulated for an FCL load.[86] Decentralised consolidation can be the result of joint route planning.[87] Consolidation is possible because sharing information about shipments enables the identification of recurrent transport routes, and cargo is collected during milk runs or return trips.[88] The milk runs refer to situations when the goods are packed and loaded separately along the way. The identification of routes induces an increase in the circular movements of carriers between companies which ultimately results in respositories being avoided.[89]

Operational governance is important for the liability of partners to co-operation in cargo bundling. Firstly, legal uncertainty about operational governance[90] can hinder co-operation or at least worsen the situation of a carrier. For example, when the co-operating partners have separate contracts with a carrier yet pack goods together, and the carrier has no claim against its counterparty (e.g. due to insolvency), it may also be unable to sue any of the other partners (see Chapter 5). Secondly, operational governance influences risk management under the transport conventions. Despite the multiparty context, risk passes to the carrier when it receives the goods, and its passage can differ depending on whether it is receiving a bundle or separate goods (see Chapter 3).

85 E.g.: Feifeng Zheng et al., 'Heuristics for Cross-Docking Scheduling of Truck Arrivals, Truck Departures and Shop-Floor Operations' (2021) *Journal of Combinatorial Optimization* 1; Prashant Barsing et al., 'Cross-docking Centre Location in a Supply Chain Network: A Social Network Analysis Approach' (2018) 19(3) *Global Business Review* S218; Paul Buijs et al., 'Synchronization in Cross-Docking Networks: A Research Classification and Framework' (2014) 239(3) *European Journal of Operational Research* 593.

86 Jinxiang Gu et al., 'Research on Warehouse Operation: A Comprehensive Review' (2007) 177(1) *European Journal of Operational Research* 1.

87 E.g: Simon Emde et al., 'Scheduling Electric Vehicles Making Milk-runs for Just-in-Time Delivery' (2018) 50(11) *IISE Transactions* 1013; Huang Mei et al., 'The Modeling of Milk-run Vehicle Routing Problem Based on Improved C-W Algorithm that Joined Time Window' (2017) 25 *Transportation Research Procedia* 716; Özlem Ergun et al., 'Shipper Collaboration' (2007) 34 *Computers & Operations Research* 1551, 1552.

88 Leitner et al. (n 50) 334; Creemers et al. (n 64).

89 Özlem Ergun et al., 'Shipper Collaboration' (2007) 34 *Computers & Operations Research* 1551; Gansterer and Hartl (2018) (n 39).

90 On legal uncertainty in the operation of contracts, see: Ronald J. Gilson, 'Contract, Uncertainty, and Innovation' in Stefan Grundmann et al. (eds), *Contract Governance: Dimensions in Law and Interdisciplinary Research* (Oxford University Press 2015) 165.

5.2 Co-operation – structural governance models

Structural governance makes the behaviour of the co-operating partners predictable because legal structures set parameters, including legal safeguards, rights, and obligations, for both internal co-operation (see Section 5.2.1.) and the execution of contracts of carriage (see Section 5.2.2).

5.2.1 Internal co-operation

Shippers can use contractual structures and corporate forms to design horizontal co-operation schemes. These schemes may involve partners with different business profiles and varying levels of experience in co-operation. In addition, shippers might retain LSPs to establish, manage, or even execute the co-operation (see further Section 5.2.1.2.).

5.2.1.1 Shippers' profiles

The partners can be competitors or non-competitors with different levels of market power.[91] They may be from a single country[92] or from different ones.[93] The partners can share obligations.[94] Alternatively, one of the partners may lead the venture,[95] or leadership may be outsourced to an externat entity.[96] Shippers can be members of open groups, for example, on online marketplaces, or they can form closed groups. Since it might be difficult to share profits, to co-ordinate large numbers of partners and to compensate founding members for their initial investments,[97] it is common to retain an LSP or to settle on an exclusive form of co-operation.[98] Co-operation might involve partners who own transport assets, such as fleets or consolidation points. Those that own such assets can execute carriage contracts and consolidate goods.

From a managerial perspective, it is best to create synergies between compatible partners in order to realise efficiencies. From a legal perspective, the

91 Christoph Glock and Simon Hochrein, 'Purchasing Organization and Design: A Literature Review' (2011) 4(2) *Business Research* 149; Jacobs et al. (2014) (n 59).

92 E.g.: Jean-François Audy et al., 'An Empirical Study on Coalition Formation and Cost/Savings Allocation' (2012) 136(1) *International Journal Production Economics* 13.

93 E.g.: TRI-VIZOR, 'Horizontal Collaboration and Orchestration Among Shippers as a Solution to Create Multimodal Transport Opportunities, Case Study on the Trade Lane Belgium-Spain Focusing on the Zeebrugge-Bilbao Shortsea Service in Particular' (Short Sea, 11 July 2017) <https://bit.ly/3lwjIE5> accessed 15 November 2023.

94 Kale et al. (n 67); Audy et al. (n 92).

95 Audy et al. (n 92).

96 On the advantages of an external leader, see Verstrepen and Van den Bossche (n 65) 8.

97 Bas Groothedde et al., 'Towards Collaborative, Intermodal Hub Networks. A Case Study in the Fast Moving Consumer Goods Market' (2005) 41 *Transportattion Research Part E* 567, 580–581.

98 Groothedde et al. (n 97); see also: Vasco Sanchez Rodrigues, 'Horizontal Logistics Collaboration – An International Retail Supply Chain Case Study' in Peter Wells (ed), *Contemporary Operations and Logistics* (Springer 2019).

profile of a company might be relevant to competitive restrictions. Furthermore, obligations undertaken by a shipper and its role in the co-operation scheme can influence its legal classification. For example, the partner who owns transport assets and performs transport may acquire a legal status of a carrier. In this regard, the observations presented in Chapter 8 might be of relevance.

5.2.1.2 Models

Horizontal co-operation schemes can be of a short- or long-term character. For example, open electronic platforms may enable companies to establish non-recurrent co-operative arrangements without strong interdependences between the shippers. Alliances are conducive to long-term co-operation. Ard-Pieter de Man and Dave Luvison identified three types of alliance models: Sharing, specialisation, and allocation.[99] Under the sharing model, the capabilities of similar partners are combined to realise economies of scale and network effects. This model requires a high level of integration because the co-operation scheme must function as a single business.[100] Under the specialisation model, companies combine their complementary capabilities into innovative offerings. Such co-operation schemes can be managed at a low level of integration.[101] In the allocation model, the focus is on the overlapping capabilities of the partners. Value is created by allocating roles and responsibilities for risks efficiently.[102]

Short-term co-operation will likely result in contractual organization (Figure 1.4). Meanwhile, alliances necessitate the adoption of different structural governance models that vary with the requisite level of integration. A high degree of integration might require the establishment of a joint company that is owned by independent companies (Figure 1.5).[103] In such cases, the organization is supported by bilateral contracts between independent companies and a jointly created company that co-ordinates the network.[104] The jointly created company can take many legal forms, but the observations that are presented later, especially in Chapter 8, generally concern limited liability companies and unlimited liability companies. The relevant issues involve, among

99 Ard-Pieter de Man and Dave Luvison, 'Collaborative Business Models: Aligning and Operationalizing Alliances' (2019) 62 *Business Horizons* 473.

100 de Man and Luvison (n 99).

101 de Man and Luvison (n 99).

102 de Man and Luvison (n 99).

103 Cafaggi and Iamiceli (n 49).

104 Fabrizio Cafaggi, 'Contractual Networks and Contract Theory: A Research Agenda for European Contract Law' in Fabrizio Cafaggi (ed), *Contractual Networks, Inter-Firm Cooperation and Economic Growth* (Edward Elgar 2011) 74–84, 92; Gunther Teubner, *Networks as Connected Contracts* (Michelle Everson tr, Hart Publishing 2011) 8–9; Cafaggi and Iamiceli (n 49); Kale et al. (n 67).

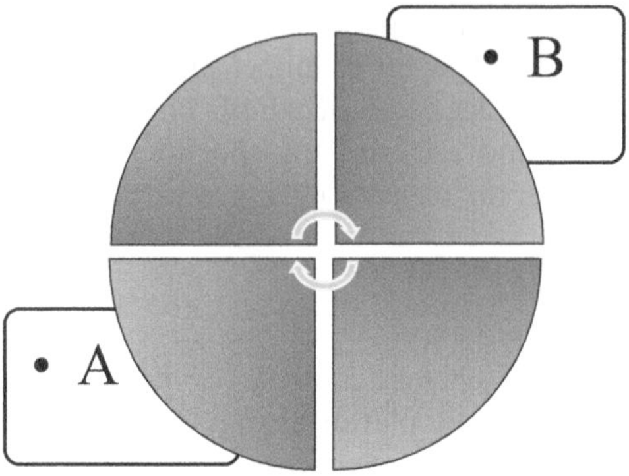

Figure 1.4 Multilateral contracts. Note: 'A' and 'B' denotes shippers

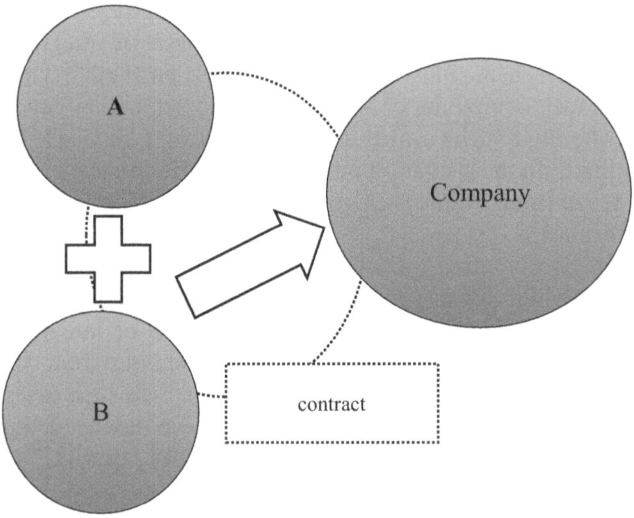

Figure 1.5 Institutional co-operation. Note 'A' and 'B' denote shippers

others, the contribution of the partners to damage for which the company has to compensate the carrier and for which the company may not claim against a shipper whose cargo has been defectively packed. Alliances that are based on agreements or jointly established companies are also common in co-operation arrangements between carriers.[105] For example, they are used to establish

105 Ahmed Karam et al., 'Horizontal Collaboration in the Freight Transport Sector: Barrier and Decision-Making Frameworks' (2021) 13(53) *European Transport Research Review* 1. However, in the case of joint route planning, the co-operation between the carriers is mostly

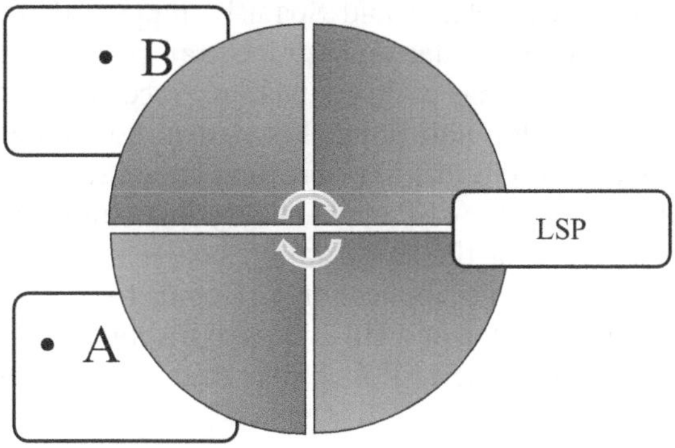

Figure 1.6 Co-operation that involves a Logistics Service Provider. Note 'A' and 'B' denote shippers

consolidation centres.[106] Low levels of integration can be managed through purely contractual means such as multiparty contracts between shippers.[107] Multiparty contracts could be seen, in this context, as framework (long-term) contracts.[108] Framework contracts are incomplete, in that their objectives are specified only imprecisely, and they are more flexible when it comes to the possibility of renegotiation. Framework contracts usually also contain more organisational elements, which pertain, for example, to the nature of membership in the scheme.[109] One of the problems with long-term co-operation agreements is that, being incomplete, they might not be classified as contracts of carriage, and they may even be deemed unenforceable (see further Chapter 7).

Multiparty contracts can be established exclusively between shippers or facilitated by an LSP (Figure 1.6). An LSP called TRI-VIZOR supported

contractual because the establishment of a central managing entity, being the result of combining the capital of the freight forwarders, has been considered inefficient. See: Herbert Kopfer and Giselher Pankratz, 'Das Groupage-Problem kooperierender Verkehrsträger' in Peter Kall and Hans-Jakob Lüthi (eds), *Operations Research Proceedings 1998. Operations Research Proceedings 1998 (Selected Papers of the International Conference on Operations Research Zurich, August 31–September 3, 1998)* (Springer 1999) 458. This might be the consequence of the more intensive form that competition in the freight forwarding sector takes.

106 Karam et al. (n 105); Guanghu Zhou et al., 'Strategic Alliance in Freight Consolidation' (2011) 47 *Transport Research Part E: Logistics and Transportation Review* 18, 18–19.

107 Tapon Kumar Das and Bing-Sheng Teng, 'A Resource-Based Theory of Strategic Alliances' (2000) 26(1) *Journal of Management* 31; Sascha Albers, *The Design of Alliance Governance Systems* (Kölner Wissenschaftsverlag 2005) 43–46; see also e.g: Gabriella Lojacono et al., 'Offshoring, Local Market Entry, and the Strategic Context of Cross-Border Alliances: The Impact on the Governance Mode' (2017) 26 *International Business Review* 435.

108 See further: Grundmann et al. (eds) (2015) (n 90); Grundmann et al. (eds) (n 2). For a practice-oriented view on the duration of contracts, see e.g.: Nina Gorovaiaa and Josef Windsperger, 'The Choice of Contract Duration in Franchising Networks: A Transaction Cost and Resource-Based View' (2018) 75 *Industrial Marketing Management* 125.

109 Ahuja (n 77).

a co-operation between Belgian and Spanish shippers that had appropriate freight flows.[110] An LSP that orchestrates transport but is also involved in a horizontal structure has a dual function. Specifically, it develops the inter-company relationship and thus takes part in horizontal co-operation, but it can also act as an intermediary, creating lateral structures (see further Chapter 8). Alternatively, the LSP might also perform transport services. This structure was employed in the co-operation between JSP (a company that produces lightweight plastic applications), Hammerwerk (a company that produces metal components), and HS-Line (a transport company).[111] In such instances, the position of the LSP is similar to that of a partner that owns transport assets.

5.2.2 Contracts of carriage

Shippers can take the lead in all stages of cargo consolidation. In consequence, they can also transport goods. Furthermore, shippers can rely on the complementary functions of the carrier that transports the consolidated goods (see Figure 1.3). Three structures can be distinguished, namely 1) a multilateral contract with a carrier, 2) a contract of carriage concluded by a TO or a company created by the partners to co-operations, and 3) a set of bilateral executory contracts with a carrier. These structures can create high interdependence between the parties and their common interests, especially when the parties want to benefit from a co-ordinated flows of goods that creates durable efficiencies. Fabrizio Cafaggi classifies such models as networks of contracts.[112] These features are absent from conventional groupage services. Operational governance (see Section 5.1) can be decisive not only for the qualification of concluded contracts but also for the passage of risk to the carrier. If the goods are consolidated at one point and handed to a carrier at once, risk passes immediately. However, if routes are planned jointly, the risk passes every time a single shipment is handed over for carriage.

The first model involves a set of independent bilateral contracts of carriage (see Figure 1.7). The shippers might enter into a co-operation agreement but continue concluding separate bilateral contracts with carriers. Nestlé and PepsiCo used such a structure in their co-operation for the retail distribution of fresh and chilled products.[113] Under these contracts, a carrier is obliged to deliver single cargoes to specific destinations. In this sense, the position of the carrier seems similar to that which results from the conclusion of groupage service contracts. However, the carrier may bear the consequences of operational governance decisions that are made by the shippers (see further Chapter 4 and Chapter 5).

110 TRI-VIZOR (n 93).
111 Jacobs et al. (n 69).
112 Cafaggi (n 104) 72–73.
113 Jacobs et al. (n 59) 3.

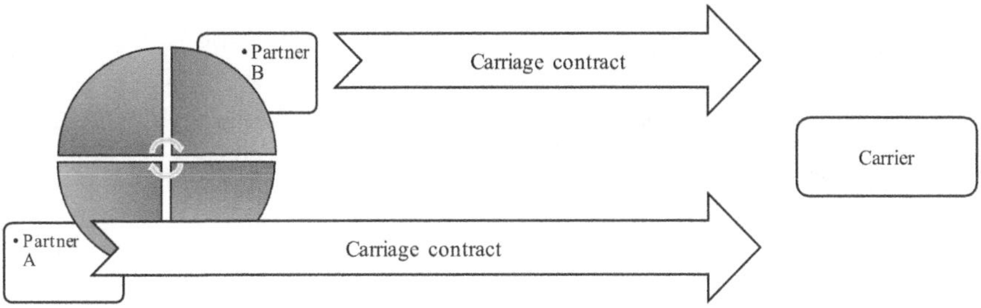

Figure 1.7 Execution model of cargo bundling co-operation in which the carrier enters into separate contracts of carriage with individual partners to co-operation in cargo bundling

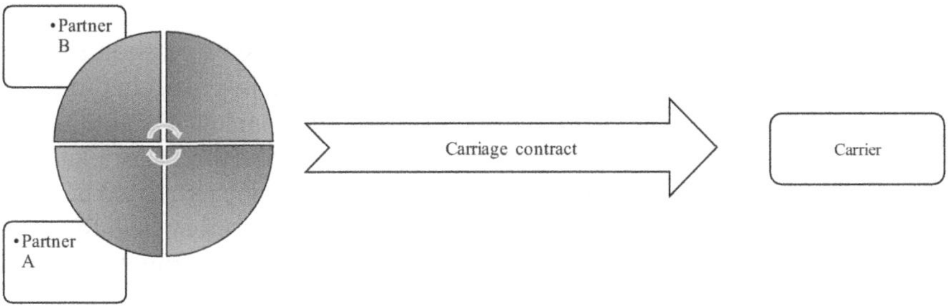

Figure 1.8 Execution model of cargo bundling co-operation in which the carrier enters one contract of carriage with several co-principals

In the second model, the shippers conclude a multiparty contract with a carrier (see Figure 1.8). Since a single contract is used, each party should understand its relationship to the other participants. For example, the obligation of each partner to provide cargo for transport might depend on the obligation of the other partners to deliver their parts of the load. The risks of non-performance and damage may also be shared. The legal analysis shows that this model is plagued by uncertainty, especially in connection to the position of the shipper or sender under the transport conventions (see Chapter 6).

In the third model, the shippers create a company, and the company contracts with a carrier (see Figure 1.9). This model resembles the most common groupage contract because there is a standard bilateral contract between the carrier and the created company. The main difference concerns the shippers' shareholdings in the latter. For example, since the shippers hold shares in the company, they eventually contribute indirectly to loses that it cannot recover through recourse actions (see Chapter 8). A variation on this motif occurs when it is an LSP (such as a TO or an online platform) rather than a company that concludes the contracts of carriage. As mentioned earlier,

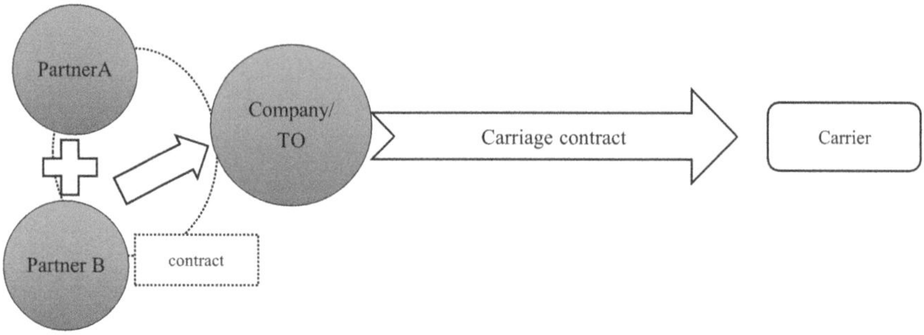

Figure 1.9 The execution model of cargo bundling co-operation that involves a single contract with a carrier, and this is based on institutional co-operation

the responsibilities of the TO or platform vis-à-vis the co-operation scheme may be both internal and external in character. The internal character of those responsibilities entails matching co-operating partners, planning co-operation, and preparing loading plans. At the same time, the TO or platform influences the external relations of the partners by choosing carriers. The positions of the company, the TO, and the platform cause taxonomical difficulties that can exert a significant influence on the liabilities of intermediaries and shippers (see Chapter 8).

6 Cargo bundling co-operation and problems related with uniform transport law

The main characteristics of co-operation in cargo bundling is the combination of horizontal and vertical arrangements in supply chains with a view to the joint transportation of goods. The horizontal elements are reflected in the matching of similar shipper capabilities (flows of goods) to achieve efficiencies. The vertical elements are reflected in the practice of outsourcing transportation to specialised LSPs, such as carriers. As with other business networks, the schemes of co-operation in cargo bundling may take various organisational forms (see Section 5), which are liable to clash with established legal concepts.

Firstly, it is unclear whether each of the co-operating partners has individual rights and obligations towards the carrier under the transport conventions, whether each bears sole liability, or whether each partner is considered jointly with its partners. This proposition holds true in respect of both the effect of the shippers' multilateral contracts on the liability scheme of the transport conventions and in respect of merchant clauses. International transport laws do not address the consequences of multiparty contracts explicitly. It is also not entirely certain how merchant clauses that impose joint liability on cargo interests operate under these frameworks. Thus, national courts retain a broad margin of discretion. Court must assess whether the international regimes govern the consequences of multiparty contracts and merchant clauses. That assessment is marred by two difficulties. Firstly, national judges tend not to interpret international conventions autonomously but instead rely on their national legal background.[114] Secondly, the consequences of multiparty contracts differ across national regimes of contract law. For example, German law favors solidarity, but Polish law attaches more importance to the individual position of the parties (see further Chapter 6). Similarly, the rules that govern the rights and liabilities of third parties differ across jurisdictions, which makes the outcomes of disputes unpredictable, especially since most carriage conventions preclude the use of exclusive jurisdiction clauses, making it impossible to predict which court would be competent. Partners to co-operation in cargo bundling would doubtless benefit from a clear statement of the extent to which the conventions recognise the joint liability of shippers or senders and an enumeration of the matters that are left to national law.

Secondly, the uncertainty of the application of mandatory and non-mandatory regimes extends beyond the issues discussed in the preceding section. The legal classification of internal co-operation between the shippers and the role of new actors in transport chains, such as TOs and online platforms, are also uncertain.

As far as internal co-operation is concerned, it is unclear which rules govern liability for errors in the organisation of co-operation. Internal co-operation should address the adverse effects of the ambiguity of the regime that governs the joint or individual liability of a shipper under the transport conventions. The co-operating shippers could self-regulate their co-operative arrangement by, for example, creating recourse mechanisms that govern instances in which a claim under the carriage contract is affected by the acts or omissions of a partner. However, mandatory carriage law can also impact such agreements. For example, if the partners decide on a company-based solution, judges may, at their discretion, classify the contracts between the individual partners and the company as contracts of carriage. Because the co-operation models may take many forms, the appropriate strategies are likely to be context specific. The design of a co-operation agreement inevitably entails substantial transaction costs,[115] which can also be an obstacle to co-operative logistics.

As far as new intermediaries are concerned, if a TO or platform is classified as a carrier, mandatory law applies. When transport law is mandatorily applicable, shippers cannot modify their liability vis-à-vis the carrier contractually.

---

114 E.g.: Wouter Verheyen (ed), *CMR 60 Years. Time for Retirement or Future Proof?* (Paris Legal Publishers 2017) 9–106.

115 E.g.: Oliver E. Williamson, 'The Economics of Organization: The Transaction Cost Approach' (1981) 87(3) *American Journal of Sociology* 548.

Instead, if the TO or platform is not deemed a carrier, national law is important. The co-operating shippers would then be capable of regulating the liability of the TO or platform. Once more, the need to draft tailored rules generates transaction costs, which could be overcome through the design and adoption of standardised solutions.

The general purpose of this study is to explain the sources of legal uncertainties that can hinder co-operation in logistics and to propose various legal solutions (contractual and regulatory) that can support co-operative models for cargo bundling. Relatedly, since practice already indicates that certain co-operative models prevail on the market and can be executed in several ways (see Section 5), it is interesting to discover which model, if any, would be less vulnerable to legal uncertainties under the legal frameworks that are investigated in this study.

CHAPTER 2

Transport conventions – interpretative framework for mandatory transport law in changing business and technological circumstances

Marta K. Kołacz

1 Introduction

Mandatory transport law occupies a special position in the regulatory framework of cargo bundling co-operation (Figure 2.1). Mandatory transport law creates the overarching legal framework for the issues governed by the conventions. In essence, mandatory law has two effects. It standardises liability schemes in different countries, and it restricts freedom of contract, regardless of the bargaining power that the parties may possess.

The main problem with the application of mandatory law is that national courts tend to refer to national law for issues that are not addressed directly in the conventions. However, they are equipped with tools, particularly the interpretative framework provided by the Vienna Convention on the Law of Treaties (VCLT),[1] that enable them to decide convention issues without immediate recourse to national laws. The VCLT framework ensures that interpretation does not automatically proceed to the meanings and the particular concepts of a specific domestic law, and it requires terms and concepts from conventions to be interpreted in the context of a convention itself.[2] In that interpretative framework, recourse to domestic law should constitute an *ultima ratio*, occurring only if an autonomous principle cannot be derived from the convention or when the convention so requires (e.g. Article 29 of the Convention on the Contract for the International Carriage of Goods by Road of 1956 (CMR)).[3] The VCLT framework also allows for evolutionary and systemic interpretation. Evolutionary and systemic interpretation can overlap, but they are presented separately later for the purposes of the exposition (see Section 3 and Section 4).

1 Vienna Convention on the Law of Treaties (adopted 23 May 1969, entered into force 27 January 1980) 1155 UNTS 331 (Vienna Convention).

2 Martin Gebauer, 'Uniform Law, General Principles and Autonomous Interpretation' (2000) 5(4) *Uniform Law Review* 683, 686.

3 Convention on the Contract for the International Carriage of Goods by Road (CMR) (adopted 19 May 1956, entered into force 2 July 1961) 399 UNTS 189.

DOI: 10.4324/9781003450801-2

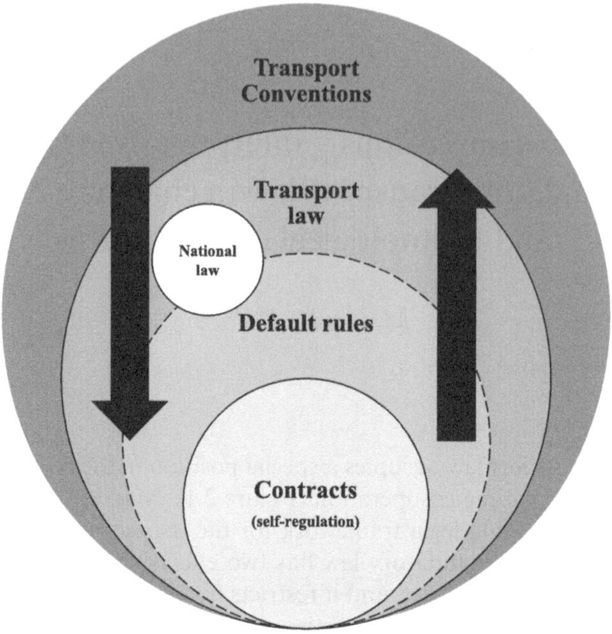

Figure 2.1 Overarching position of transport conventions in the legal framework relevant for cargo bundling co-operation

The framework of Article 31, Article 32, and Article 33 of the VCLT[4] should be the primary instrument for the interpretation of the scope and contents of transport conventions.[5] It is of no import that the transport conventions are forms of uniform private law that mostly regulate the relations

4 Art. 33 VCLT is not given further attention.

5 Oliver Dörr and Kirsten Schmalenbach (eds), *Vienna Convention on the Law of Treaties a Commentary* (Springer 2018) 568. In the literature, it has been noticed that courts struggle with the application of VCLT. Therefore, the possibility of interpreting transport conventions through EU soft law instruments, such as the Draft Common Frame of Reference or the Principles of European Contract Law, has been considered. However, even the proponents of this solution admit that it is incompatible with the principles of public international law, including the hierarchy of norms. See: Cécile Legros, 'Interpreting International Shipping Law with EU Soft Law Instruments' (2015) 1/2 *European Journal of Commercial Contract Law* 32, 34. Furthermore, the VCLT also applies to conventions that entered into force before the VCLT because Arts. 31–33 VCLT are regarded as customary law that conforms to the practice of interpretation and reliance on the good faith and the common intentions of the parties. See: Panos Merkouris, '(Inter)Temporal Considerations in the Interpretative Process of the VCLT: Do Treaties Endure, Perdure or Exdure?' (2014) 45 *Netherlands Yearbook of International Law* 121, 147–148. Olena Bokareva, *Uniformity of Transport Law through International Regimes* (Edward Elgar 2019) 128.

between private parties.[6] The overriding function of these conventions is to secure uniform contractual rights and liabilities for the parties that participate in international trade. Thus, the purpose of the interpretation of these conventions should be the effective operation of the concepts and institutions contained therein.

The construction of a contract that has already been qualified as falling under the transport conventions should proceed in two steps.[7] Firstly, the terms of international mandatory law should be implied into the contract. They should also serve as the primary means of plugging contractual gaps. Gap-filling should accord with the VCLT mechanisms. Secondly, if an issue is not solved in the first step, the judge should refer to mandatory national law (if any), the solutions proposed by the parties, and, failing that, default contractual rules.

2 General interpretation framework

Article 31 of the VCLT lays down the general rule of interpretation:

> The text of a convention shall be interpreted in good faith in accordance with the ordinary meaning to be given to the terms of the treaty in their context and in the light of its object and purpose.

The general rule is non-hierarchical, and thus equal importance should be afforded to the plain meaning, the object, the purpose, and the context of a treaty.[8] In this interpretative framework, the court should balance different means and principles of interpretation, drawing on grammatical, systemic, teleological, and historical arguments.[9]

When interpreting the text of a convention, a court should examine the actual and natural meanings of the words or the special meanings intended by the parties.[10] This grammatical interpretation does not occur in a vacuum.

---

6 Marian Hoeks, *Multimodal Transport Law, the Law Applicable to the Multimodal Contract for the Carriage of Goods* (Erasmus University Rotterdam 2009) 110. Campbell McLachlan, 'The Principle of Systemic Integration and Article 31(3)(C) of the Vienna Convention' (2005) 54(2) *International and Comparative Law Quarterly* 279, 287. Moreover, the constitutional aspects of conventions do not imply that the VCLT rules on treaty interpretation can be ignored. See: Ian Sinclair, *The Vienna Convention on the Law of Treaties* (2nd edn, Manchester University Press 1984) 134.

7 On the process of contract legal qualification see further: Wouter Verheyen, 'National Judges as Gatekeepers to the CMR Convention' (2016) 21 *Uniform Law Review* 441, 441–446; Susan Niessen, *The Legal Position of Terminal Operators in Hinterland Networks. Mixed Contracts and Third Parties* (Paris Legal Publishers 2017) 50.

8 International Law Commission, 'Draft Articles on the Law of Treaties with Commentaries [1966]' 219–220 <https://bit.ly/3ClEP2r> accessed 10 January 2019.

9 Gerald G. Fitzmaurice, 'The Law and Procedure of the International Court of Justice: Treaty Interpretation and Certain Other Points' (1951) 28 *British Yearbook on International Law* 1, 7–25.

10 Fitzmaurice (n 9); Gebauer (n 2) 687; Juha Raitio, *The Principle of Legal Certainty in EC Law* (Kluwer Academic Publishers 2003) 307.

Good faith prevents the sole or exaggerated literal interpretation of a term in a convention.[11] Grammatical interpretation should be further supported by teleological arguments and by viewing the terms as integral components of the convention as a whole.[12] So much is confirmed by the importance of the underlying context of the convention, which includes evolutionary elements, such as modifications, subsequent agreements and practices, and applicable rules of international law (Article 31.2 and Article 31.3 VCLT; see further: Section 3 and Section 4). The terms of a convention should be given the most weight, and their effect should be consistent in all parts of a convention. When the ordinary meaning of a treaty provision has been found to be vague, the object and the purpose of the convention in question should be used to determine its meaning.[13] Mindfulness of the purpose of a convention should prevent the interpretation from rendering parts of its text superfluous.[14]

It is only when interpretation on the basis of the preceding points leads to conflicting results that the courts can refer to interpretative aids such as *travaux preparatoires*. The list of such aides is not exhaustive.[15] The supplementary means of interpretation include, among others, preparatory works, the circumstances of the conclusion of a treaty (which can include the factual situation that the signatories intended to change), and material and substantive matters.[16] In any case, the supplementary means of interpretation should only be used to facilitate establishing the meaning of the convention under consideration.[17] Article 32 VCLT explicitly states that the preparatory work of the treaty has a supplementary character, and the recourse to it should be taken only when application of Article 31 VCLT is unsuccessful.[18] Thus,

11 Mark E. Villiger, *Commentary on the 1969 Vienna Convention on the Law of Treaties* (Martinus Nijhoff Publishers 2009) 426.

12 See: (n 10).

13 Villiger (n 11) 426–427.

14 Dörr and Schmalenbach (n 5) 584.

15 Although it is acknowledged that 'supplementary means of interpretation' is a generic term, such means should be recorded in writing and accessible to all parties. See: Luigi Sbolci, 'Supplementary Means of Interpretation' in Enzo Cannizzaro (ed), *The Law of Treaties Beyond the Vienna Convention* (Oxford University Press 2011) 153–154.

16 Dörr and Schmalenbach (n 5) 620–632; Sbolci (n 15) 151–162.

17 Accordingly, the framework of Arts. 31–33 VCLT confirms the objective approach to interpretation, under which supplementary means of interpretation serve principally to confirm the meaning of a convention. See: Sbolci (n 15) 147–151.

18 Similarly: Malcom Clarke, *International Carriage of Goods by Road: CMR* (5th edn, Informa Law 2009) 9–10; Ulf Linderfalk, 'Is the Hierarchical Structure of Articles 31 and 31 of the Vienna Convention Real or Not? Interpreting the Rules of Interpretation' (2007) 54(1) *Netherlands International Law Review* 133. Contrary e.g.: J.D. Mortenson, 'The Travaux of Travaux: Is the Vienna Convention Hostile to Drafting History' (2013) 107(4) *The American Journal of International Law* 780. For the arguments pro and against the recourse to historical arguments see also: Jan Klabbers, 'International Legal Histories: The Declining Importance of Travaux Préparatoires in Treaty Interpretation?' (2003) 50(3) *Netherlands International Law Review* 267.

travaux preparatoires should give precedence to evolutionary and systemic interpretations allowed under Article 31 VCLT.

3 Evolutionary interpretation

As far as dynamic concepts and practices are concerned, the interpretative framework of the VCLT leaves room for evolutionary interpretation. The Study Group on the Fragmentation of International Law has provided guidance on this matter by explaining when a concept can be considered evolutionary:

> (a). . . is one which implies taking into account subsequent technical, economic or legal developments; (b). . . sets up an obligation for further progressive development for the parties; or (c). . . has a very general nature or is expressed in such general terms that it must take into account changing circumstances.[19]

Evolutionary interpretation is possible as long as there is a link with the intention of the parties.

There are two approaches to evolutionary interpretation in international law. The first reflects subsequent practice, as expressed in Article 31.3(b) VCLT.[20] The second is based on Articles 31.1 and 3(c) of the VCLT, which permit evolutionary interpretation when there is evidence that the original intention of the parties was that the treaty would be evolutionary in character and when the applicable rules of international law have changed.[21] Following Arato, those who engage in interpretation should consider the short- and long-term consequences of both approaches in light of the general framework of interpretation, in which grammatical interpretation is inseparable from the context, object, and purpose of the treaty.[22] If a term is interpreted on the basis of subsequent practice, its new interpretation remains fixed unless practice changes again.[23] However, if there are signs in the text that the meaning of

19 ILC, 'Report of the Study Group of the International Law Commission on the Fragmentation of International Law: Difficulties Arising from The Diversification and Expansion of International Law' (13 April 2006) UN Doc A/CN.4/L.682 par. 23.

20 Julian Arato, 'Subsequent Practice and Evolutive Interpretation: Techniques of Treaty Interpretation Over Time and Their Diverse Consequences' (2010) 9 *The Law and Practice of International Courts & Tribunals* 443, 458–465. The concept of subsequent practice is still developing. Therefore, some inconsistency in its application across various dispute settlement bodies remains. See: Georg Nolte, 'Subsequent Practice as a Means of Interpretation in the Jurisprudence of the WTO Appellate Body' in Enzo Cannizzaro (ed), *The Law of Treaties Beyond the Vienna Convention* (Oxford University 2011) 138–144.

21 Arato (n 20) 465–477; Malgosia Fitzmaurice, 'Dynamic (Evolutive) Interpretation of Treaties, Part I' (2008) 21 *Hague Yearbook of International Law* 101, 102.

22 Arato (n 20) 447, 451, 477–478. More on the problem of choice between the two see: Arato (n 20) 453–455.

23 Arato (n 20) 480–493.

a term is dynamic, it will require reinterpretation whenever a new case comes under consideration.[24]

There is little explicit evidence that the texts of the transport conventions are evolutionary in character *per se*, yet that character can be inferred from the fact that they aim at creating uniform rules for international carriage contracts. Striving for uniformity is a continuous process, which is embedded in a broader context, and thus the terms 'uniform' and 'uniformity' should be, in my opinion, understood as being unvarying and identical in all places and at all times. The conventions should be thus able to adapt business and technological innovations.

The United Nations Convention on Contracts for the International Carriage of Goods Wholly or Partly by Sea of 2008 (Rotterdam Rules)[25] and the Uniform Rules concerning the Contract of International Carriage of Goods by Rail (COTIF-CIM)[26] indicate that uniform application is embedded in a broader context. Article 2 of the Rotterdam Rules states that their interpretation needs to 'promote uniformity in [their] application and the observance of good faith in international trade'. This approach places uniformity within a broader dynamic context, leaving the door open for adaptations to changes in the realities of trade.[27] Here, it is also worth noting that the Rotterdam Rules are considered to regulate subsequent practice in the application of the Hague-Visby Rules (HVR).[28],[29] Article 8 COTIF-CIM also promotes uniformity. It emphasises that the international character of the convention should be taken into account when it is interpreted. That COTIF-CIM belongs to international law, which is constantly changing and developing,[30] implies that interpretation should be sensitive to developments in the area of international law.[31]

24 Arato (n 20).

25 United Nations Convention on Contracts for the International Carriage of Goods Wholly or Partly by Sea (adopted 11 December 2008) C.N.563.2012.

26 Uniform Rules concerning the Contract of International Carriage of Goods by Rail (COTIF-CIM) adopted 9 June 1999, entered into force 1 July 2006) [International Carriage by Rail (COTIF) of 9 May 1980, as amended by the Vilnius Protocol of 3 June 1999] CR 24/NOT/Add.5 21.12.2009]

27 Nevertheless, this should still happen within the boundaries of the general rule of interpretation set out in Article 31 VCLT. See: Dörr and Schmalenbach (n 5) 576.

28 The Brussels Convention for the Unification of Certain Rules of Law relating to Bills of Lading (adopted 25 August 1924, entered into force 2 June 1931) Trb. 1953, 109, 004127 and Protocol to Amend the International Convention for the unification of certain rules of law relating to bills of lading, signed at Brussels on 25 August 1924 (adopted 23 February 1968, entered into force 23 June 1977) No. 23643.

29 Tomotaka Fujita, 'Obligations and Liabilities of the Shipper' in Meltem Deniz Güner-Özbek (ed), *The United Nations Convention on Contracts for the International Carriage of Goods Wholly or Partly by Sea. An Appraisal of the "Rotterdam Rules"* (Springer 2011) 220.

30 Rosalyn Higgins, *Problems and Process: International Law and How We Use It* (Oxford University Press 1994) 1, 8.

31 McLachlan (n 6) 287.

The CMR and the Convention on the Contract for the Carriage of Goods by Inland Waterway (CMNI)[32] favour a stricter form of uniformity. They employ solutions that prevent their further revision and amendment. Article 1.5 of the CMR provides that the contracting parties agree not to vary any of the provisions of the Convention by special agreement. Furthermore, in Article 49 of the CMR, a review conference is permissible only if supported by a fourth of the contracting parties. Article 36 and Article 37 of the CMNI also refer to similar rules for reviewing or amending the convention.[33] The CMR solution has been adopted to avoid the failings of the Convention for the Unification of Certain Rules Relating to International Carriage by Air of 1929 (the Warsaw Convention),[34] in which amendments forced by the evolution of air transport resulted in the emergence of multiple applicable regimes and thus in lack of uniformity.[35] On this line of reasoning, the CMR can be adapted to changes in land transportation without the necessity of further amendments, and the same is true of the CMNI.

The HVR and the Convention for the Unification of Certain Rules Relating to International Carriage by Air of 1999 (Montreal Convention)[36] refer only to the unification of certain rules.[37] Still, such a general approach is sufficient to promote uniformity in the evolutionary understanding of the texts because the value of uniformity attaches to the entire transport law setting. In transport law, uniformity has begun to be analysed in the wider framework of the transport conventions (see further Section 4).[38] This tendency implies that uniform application should be sensitive to developments that aim at uniformity and to changes that are driven by the constant progress of business and technology.[39]

32 Budapest Convention on the Contract for the Carriage of Goods by Inland Waterway (CMNI) (adopted 3 October 2000, entered into force on 1 April 2005) CMNI/CONF(99)2/FINAL.

33 Isabelle Bon-Garcin, 'The 50th Anniversary of the CMR Convention – Future and Perspectives of International Road Transport' (2006) 11 *Uniform Law Review* 698, 703.

34 Convention for the Unification of Certain Rules Relating to International Carriage by Air (adopted 12 October 1929, entered into force 13 February 1933) (Warsaw Convention).

35 The Warsaw Convention was amended by the Hague Protocol of 1955. According to Art. XIX of the Protocol, as between the parties, the convention and the protocol must be read and interpreted together as a single instrument and known as the Warsaw Convention as amended at The Hague, 1955. In fact, a new and separate legal instrument, which is only binding between the parties, was created. If one nation is a party to the Warsaw Convention 1929 and another a party to the amended 1955 version, there is no mutual international ground for litigation.

36 Convention for the Unification of Certain Rules Relating to International Carriage by Air (adopted on 28 May 1999, entered into force 4 November 2003) International Civil Aviation Organization Doc 9740 (Montreal Convention).

37 Preamble HVR, Preamble Montreal Convention.

38 Bokareva (n 5) 70.

39 Bokareva (n 5) 70, 132.

Despite the foregoing considerations, the transport conventions include generic terms that indicate their evolutionary character.[40] For the most part, they are of a very general nature and aver to subsequent developments. Accordingly, understanding them requires alertness to changes in circumstances. The term 'ship' under the HVR supplies an example.[41] The introduction of containers has made it unclear whether they ought to be treated as parts of a ship when supplied by a carrier or a shipper.[42] For example, in a decision of the Dutch Hoge Raad from 1 February 2008, the court decided that a container may be considered a part of a ship if it is provided by a carrier.[43] The court decided to refer to the status and definition of a container as described in Article 1(24) in conjunction with Article 14(c) and Article 17.5(a) and to Article 16(1) Rotterdam Rules. The court therefore acknowledged the technical change that had resulted from the introduction of container ships.

The application of the VCLT framework and its evolutionary concepts has proven difficult, resulting in different national interpretations.[44] Nevertheless, it switches the perspective away from the identification of new regulatory solutions that accommodate the evolution of business and technology at the international level. Those may be unfeasible, for example, because the process of their adoption would be lengthy.[45] Uniform application and interpretation can become feasible if there is active judicial co-operation. Not only should judges consider foreign rulings, but judicial co-operation should also be strengthened by dedicated networks and bodies (see further Chapter 9).

40 The dynamic nature of generic terms is also recognised by some supporters of interpretation of treaty terms in accordance with their meaning at the time when the treaty was concluded. See: Sinclair (n 6) 125.

41 For the evolutionary meaning of the term 'vehicle' under the CMR and loading and stowing operations as far as the groupage service is concerned, see: Marta Katarzyna Kołacz and Gerald Hopster, 'When Technology Takes the Wheel Is the CMR Ready to Meet the Demand for Autonomous Transportation?' (2017) 1/2 *European Journal of Commercial Contract Law* 41, 45–48.

42 See further: W. David Angus, 'Legal Implications of the Container Revolution in International Carriage of Goods' (1968) 14(3) *McGill Law Review* 395, 405–407.

43 Hoge Raad 1.02.2008 C06/082HR.

44 Wouter Verheyen, *CMR 60 Years. Time for Retirement of Future Proof* (Paris Legal Publishers 2017) 11–104.

45 To Bokareva, although uniformity implies progressive understanding and the need for a more flexible approach to the search for tools that aim at uniformity, all solutions (e.g. optional protocols to the Rotterdam Rules, dividing the Rotterdam Rules into two parts, amendments of unimodal conventions) still require international consent, which is difficult to achieve in practice. See further: Bokareva (n 5) 300–317.

4 Systemic interpretation

Finally, Article 31.3(c) of the VCLT lays the foundation for the systemic approach to interpretation in international transport law.[46] The notion of 'systemic interpretation' refers to recourse to other conventions in the same area of the law for the purpose of clarifying the meaning of certain concepts and principles.[47] This allows the judge to use analogical reasoning when the law is unclear or when a novel situation arises, with certain limitations to which I will return shortly. This proposition is supported by the fact that analogical reasoning already features in the codification of international transport law.[48]

Article 31.3(c) of the VCLT refers to the relevant system of international law, which, alongside its context, should be taken into consideration in the application of a treaty.[49] Some already consider the international transport conventions to constitute a distinct field of law, namely international transport law.[50] These conventions can be considered the relevant system of international law for the purpose of Article 31.1(c) of the VCLT because they concern similar subjects.[51] This yields a codification of the corresponding area of uniform commercial law, whose constituent elements rest on similar general principles.[52] At this point, concrete examples of interconnectedness may be

46 Contrast: Jurgen Basedow, 'Uniform Private Law Conventions and the Law of Treaties' (2006) 11(4) *Uniform Law Review* 731, 744–745. Basedow is of the opinion that systemic interpretation is neither allowed nor prohibited, but, in any event, Arts 31–33 VCLT are silent on the matter. See also: Franco Ferrari, 'The Relationship between International Uniform Contract Law Conventions' (2003) 22(2) *Journal of Law and Commerce* 57, 67–68. Ferrari seeks the justification of macro-systemic interpretation in the existence of identical rules of interpretation under each convention. In other words, according to him, macro-systemic interpretation is possible when conventions have identical rules of interpretation.

47 The term 'systemic interpretation' also has a broader meaning under which it permits recourse to international law instruments from other fields. See: McLachlan (n 6).

48 See further on analogy in international law: Fernando Lusa Bordin, *The Analogy between States and International Organizations* (Cambridge University Press 2018) 15–48; Against the use of analogy in international transport law, see: Krzysztof Wesołowski, *Umowa międzynarodowego przewozu drogowego towarów na podstawie CMR* (Wolters Kluwer Polska 2013) 86–87, who argues that international transport conventions do not constitute a separate system of law. The author recognises only the narrow meaning of a 'system', acknowledging it only for conventions and their amendments. Accordingly, he opposes the usage of analogy in the interpretation of international transport conventions but sees the benefits of comparative studies on the topic. Also: Dorota Ambrożuk, 'Legitymacja do dochodzenia roszczeń odszkodowawczych z umowy przewozu towarów w transporcie lądowym' in Dominika Wetoszka (ed), *Prawo transportowe. Morze. Ląd. Powietrze* (Legalis C.H. Beck 2017).

49 Dörr and Schmalenbach (n 5) 603.

50 Basedow (n 46); Eric Van Hooydonk, *Proeve van Belgisch Scheepvaartwetboek (privaatrecht): algemene toelichting* (Maklu 2011) 100–102. Contrary: Wesołowski (n 48).

51 Anselm Brandi-Dohrn, 'Auslegung internationalen Einheitsprivatrechts durch die internationale Rechtsprechung' (1996) *Transport Recht* 45, 49.

52 A proposal has even been made to consolidate international conventions in the area of commercial and transport law into a single instrument. See: Michael Joachim Bonell, 'Modernisation and Harmonisation of Contract Law: Objectives, Methods and Scope an Overview' (2003) 8 *Uniform Law Review* 91, 95.

helpful. Firstly, the transport conventions were designed along the lines of pre-existing conventions. For example, the CMR was modelled after the CIM of 1890[53] and then served as the base for the COTIF-CIM.[54] Secondly, it is possible to observe general principles in international transport law and similarities in the operation of certain legal institutions, such as liability limits.[55]

Recourse to other conventions requires circumspection. Specifically, Article 31.3(c) of the VCLT refers only to the law that is applicable between the parties. The applicable rules are those that were in force at the time of the interpretation of the convention. Thus, at present, the Rotterdam Rules cannot as such be taken into consideration (see nevertheless the observations in Section 3). Furthermore, when there is a conflict between the internal rules of a convention and external concepts, autonomous interpretation and gap-filling require that internal rules be afforded priority.[56] These also concern mode-specific rules that cannot be transposed automatically onto other modes. Accordingly, it might not be possible to draw the same conclusions about an issue across different conventions. Multimodal transport supplies a salient example. Since the international transport conventions that are in force are unimodal and there is no uniform international law on multimodal contracts for the carriage of goods, the application of unimodal conventions to single legs of multimodal carriage has become problematic.[57] For example, in the *Godafoss* case,[58] the Dutch Supreme Court relied on the scope and jurisdiction rules of the CMR to decide that it does not apply to multimodal transport contracts.[59] The court based its finding on Article 1 of the CMR, read in conjunction with Article 2.1. The latter makes the CMR applicable to ro/ro and piggyback transportation and thus refers to carriage by road that is interrupted by carriage by another mode when the goods are not unloaded from the original vehicle. The court also concluded that, for the sake of avoiding problems with unlocated damage, the place of taking over to which Article 31.1(b) of the CMR refers

53 International Convention concerning the Carriage of Goods by Rail, 14 October 1890; See also the preparatory documents to CMR, e.g.: Commission Economique pour L'Europe Comite des Transports Inerieurs, Sous-Comite des transports routiers, Groupe de travail charge des questions juridiques, 'Project de Convention Relative au Contract de Transport International de Merchandises par la Route' TRANS/WP.9/11 10 October 1949, 27 et seq.; Economic Commission for Europe, Inland Transport Committee, Sub-Committee on Road Transport, Working Party on Legal Questions, 'Report of the Small Committee, Preliminary Draft Convention Concerning the Contract for the International Transport of Goods By Road' TRANS/WP9/22 21 December 1953.

54 See further: Hoeks (n 6) 114.

55 Niessen (n 7) 42–44. Similarly: Bokareva (n 5) 70, who places transport conventions within transport law as whole.

56 Gebauer (n 2) 702.

57 See further: Hoeks (n 6); Wouter Verheyen, *Contractuele aansprakelijkheid van vervoersintegratoeren* (die Keure 2014).

58 Hoge Raad, 01.06.2012, 10/05322 S&S 2012/95.

59 The court did not follow the judgement in *Resolution Bay* (see: Rechtbank Rotterdam, 28.10.1999, S&S 2000, 35), a leading Dutch case at that time which was also considered by the Court of Appeal of England and Wales in *Quantum Corp v. Plane Trucking* (see: *Quantum Corp v. Plane Trucking* [2002] 2 Lloyd's Rep 24).

can only be the place where the contract of carriage commenced. The aforementioned CMR-specific arguments may prejudice the application of other transport conventions to individual legs of multimodal carriage. Nevertheless, the CMR-specific arguments raised in the just described *Godafoss* case would require verification in the context of other transport conventions.

As far as the COTIF-CIM is concerned, its scope rule is almost identical to the scope rule of the CMR. This, together with the fact that the COTIF-CIM is modelled after the CMR, could suggest that the question of whether the COTF-CIM rules can apply to legs of multimodal transport can be answered in the same manner as in *Godafoss*. Nevertheless, a court should also consider that the scope of application of the COTIF-CIM has been extended to internal carriage by road and inland waterways which supplement cross-border carriage by rail (Article 1(3) COTIF-CIM). Furthermore, the COTIF-CIM, unlike the CMR, introduces intermodal transport units (Article 3 and Article 7 COTIF-CIM). Therefore, the COTIF-CIM may be applicable to multimodal contracts of carriage.[60] The *Godafoss* arguments against the application of the CMR to the road legs of multimodal carriage contracts cannot be transposed to the HVR and sea legs for which a multimodal B/L has been issued.[61] That is so due to the wording of Article I(b) of the HVR, which is wider than the wording of Article 1 (1) of the CMR. The HVR refer to: 'any similar document of title, in so far as such document relates to the carriage of goods by sea'. There can be little doubt that the Montreal Convention also applies to the air legs of multimodal carriage. This issue is addressed explicitly in Article 38.1 of the Montreal Convention.[62] Because of the similarity between the scope rules of the CMR and the CMNI, the CMNI might also be considered inapplicable to multimodal contracts. However, the exact wording of the scope rule in Article 2.2. of the CMNI, in particular the words 'without transshipment', which indicate that the CMNI only governs unimodal contracts of carriage by inland waterways, should be decisive.

5 Interpretative framework – importance for cargo bundling co-operation

The proper application of mandatory law is relevant to cargo bundling co-operation because it delineates the co-operating partners' freedom of contract. Due to the fact that the conventions do not address the issues of co-operation explicitly, interpretation of the conventions rules is necessary. The proper application of the VCLT rules of interpretation should be inherently linked with an in-depth understanding of the conventions as expressed in Article 31 (see further Chapter 3). These preconditions turn often very

60 Hoeks (n 6) 216.
61 Hoeks (n 6) 319.
62 See further: Ingrid Koning, *Aansprakelijkheid in het luchtvervoer* (Paris Zutphen 2007) 125.

difficult to execute and may be molded differently in the process of interpretation (see e.g. Chapter 4). For example, a court may rashly decide to treat the analysed issue as falling out of the scope of mandatory law and take a recourse to national law (see e.g. Chapter 6). Furthermore, the rules on the interpretation of conventions may play second fiddle when it comes to issues related to contract validity and legal classification. Contract validity is not governed by the transport conventions. The legal classification of contracts is in practice performed based on the rules of national laws and not starting from the interpretation of the conventions' concept of contract of carriage (see e.g. Chapter 7 and Chapter 8). The potential problems with interpretation exacerbate legal uncertainty of co-operating partners.

CHAPTER 3

Risk management under the transport conventions

Marta K. Kołacz

1 Introduction

Transport law regimes can be generally characterised as reactive liability schemes: The carrier's liability can only be triggered by loss, damage, and, in the case of the Convention on the Contract for the International Carriage of Goods by Road of 1956 (CMR),[1] delay. The Hague-Visby Rules (HVR)[2] introduced a presumption of fault-based liability. As far as the CMR is concerned, the presumption of fault-based liability seems to be supported in Poland, whereas a principle of strict liability is applied in Germany and England. However, managing risk by reference to this general distinction could be cumbersome because the system of subjective liability can have objective elements, and vice versa. This can be seen from the examples that follow. Firstly, in some countries, the obligation of a carrier is considered an obligation of result.[3] In its basic form, it is premised on the assumption that the carrier is liable on the basis of risk. To release itself from liability, the carrier needs to prove the actual cause of the non-performance or the improper performance

1 Convention on the Contract for the International Carriage of Goods by Road (CMR) (adopted 19 May 1956, entered into force 2 July 1961) 399 UNTS 189.

2 The Brussels Convention for the Unification of Certain Rules of Law relating to Bills of Lading (adopted 25 August 1924, entered into force 2 June 1931) Trb. 1953, 109, 004127 and Protocol to Amend the International Convention for the unification of certain rules of law relating to bills of lading, signed at Brussels on 25 August 1924 (adopted 23 February 1968, entered into force 23 June 1977) No. 23643.

3 In Poland, where the obligation of the carrier is categorized as an obligation of result, the basic distinction between obligations of result and obligations of means cannot always serve as guidance because all obligations of result are, in fact, obligations to act with due diligence, and failing to maintain due diligence is one of the conditions for the debtor's liability. See: Konrad Osajda (ed), *Prawo zobowiązań – część ogólna System Prawa Prywatnego t. 5* (3rd edn, Ch. Beck 2020) 511–514; Cf. Krzysztof Zagrobelny, '16.2. Umowa o roboty budowlane' in Mirosław Stec (ed), *Prawo umów handlowych System Prawa Handlowego tom 5c* (1st edn, Legalis C.H. Beck 2020) No 16.2.2.3. On the development of objective and subjective liability regimes and the problems related to the dichotomy between obligations of result and means, particularly the subjectivisation of cause that leads to fault-based liability for breach of promise, see: Dario Alessi, 'Distinction between Obligations de Resultat and Obligations de Moyens and the Enforceability of Promises' (2005) 13 *European Review of Private Law* 657.

DOI: 10.4324/9781003450801-3

of the obligation. It is not sufficient to prove lack of fault. This basic rule does not operate in the HVR, where Rule 2 in Article III refers to the carrier's reasonable skill and care in maintaining and carrying the cargo to the port of discharge.[4] This basic rule might also be inaccurate under the strict CMR regime, in which proof that the loss or damage was due to the acts of the cargo interests, in fact, serves as evidence of lack of fault of the carrier and relives it from liability (Article 17.4 (c) CMR). Secondly, under both regimes, the carrier's obligations of care are higher than under the general rules of contractual liability.[5] The distinctions between fault-based liability and strict risk-based liability are blurred, especially when an objective assessment or a subjective test with an objective standard of recklessness is applied under both the HVR and the CMR.[6]

Under both conventions, risk management should be related to the allocation of the burden of proof, whose purpose is to evaluate whether the carrier fulfilled its contractual obligations under a contract of carriage. The CMR and the HVR establish different rules on the burden of proof in cargo claims and attach different importance to the occurrence of risk and the exercise of reasonable care. Since a carriage contract is synallagmatic, that is, the parties assume reciprocal obligations and have certain obligations vis-à-vis the goods, each needs to respond to the risks created by the other. Acquiring knowledge about certain risks is decisive in allocating the burden of proof. The HVR creates a reactive risk management framework for the carrier, and the CMR requires more proactive risk management. Different risk management frameworks are the result of different thresholds for the minimum knowledge that the carrier is expected to possess to avoid liability. The main problem in risk

---

4 *Albacora SRL v Westcott & Laurence Line* [1966] S.C. (H.L.) 19. See also the discussion on challenges to the classification of the obligation to make a ship seaworthy as an obligation of means in: Malcolm Clarke, *Aspects of the Hague Rules. A Comparative Study in English and French Law* (Martinus Nijhoff 1976) 204–205.

5 See: Víctor Hugo Chacón, *The Due Diligence in Maritime Transportation in the Technological Era* (Springer 2017) 117–118, 157–160; Some authors classify the duty of care for cargo under the HVR as an absolute duty. See: Ilian Djadjev, *The Obligations of the Carrier Regarding the Cargo the Hague-Visby Rules* (Springer 2017) 59 and the literature cited there. Contrast: Frank Stevens, 'Liability for Defective Containers: Charting a Course between Seaworthiness, Care for the Cargo and Liabilities of the Shipper' in Baris Soyer and Andrew Tettenborn (eds), *Carriage of Goods by Sea, Land and Air. Unimodal and Multimodal Transport in the 21st Century* (Informa Law 2014) 35.

6 For the discussions on Article IV.5(e) HVR, see e.g.: Marel Katsivela, 'Loss of the Carrier's Limitation of Liability under the Hague-Visby Rules and the Warsaw Convention: Common Law and Civil Law Views' (2012) 26 *Australian and New Zealand Maritime Law Journal* 118. For discussions of Art. 29 CMR, see e.g.: Francisco Sanchez-Gamborino, 'Article 29 of the CMR Convention Concerns Nothing But Wilful Misconduct of the Carrier' (2016) 21 *Uniform Law Review* 561; Wouter Verheyen, *CMR 60 Years. Time for Retirement of Future Proof* (Paris Legal Publishers 2017) 61–104. Dorota Ambrożuk, *Ustalenie odszkodowania w prawie przewozowym w odniesieniu do przewozu przesyłek* (Wolters Kluwer Polska 2018) 63; Otmar J. Tuma, 'The Degree of Default under Article 29 CMR' (2006) 11(3) *Uniform Law Review* 585.

management and cargo bundling co-operation is the position of the shipper or sender in respect of the carrier's defences and shipper's or sender's liability for damage. Relatedly, determining who bears the risks that are connected to the bundled cargo is critical (see further Chapter 4). The determination could also be relevant to the internal relationship between the co-shippers or the co-senders and to their relationship with the Transport Orchestrator (see further Chapter 8). In Section 2.1, I focus on the rules on the burden of proof and risk management under the HVR. In Section 2.2, I extend the analysis to the CMR. Section 2.3. summarizes the findings, taking into account the uncertainties that are related to co-operation in cargo bundling.

2 HVR

2.1 Burden of proof: Scheme

Under the HVR, claims about consolidated cargo can be based on either Rule 1 or Rule 2 of Article III which regulate the carrier's obligations to exercise due diligence and to care for goods properly and carefully, respectively. In the case of carrier-supplied containers, which are regarded as parts of the ship,[7] any damage or loss of cargo that results from a faulty container is considered a breach of either Rule 1 or Rule 2. When the container is provided by the shipper, the carrier may be found liable for breach of Rule 2.[8] Under both rules, the claimant only needs to establish a *prima facie* case against the carrier by showing that the goods were damaged or lost while in the custody of the latter.[9] The carrier, in turn, needs to resort to Article IV, which provides a

7 This view was supposed to be in line with the United Nations Convention on Contracts for the International Carriage of Goods Wholly or Partly by Sea (Rotterdam Rules) (adopted 11 December 2008) C.N.563.2012, which, in Art. 14(c), provide that a container should be cargoworthy. On the legislative history and the wording of the article, see: Stevens (n 5) 32–33; Contrast: Nick J. Margetson, *The System of Liability of Articles III and IV of the Hague (Visby) Rules* (Paris Legal Publishers 2008) 48, who is of the opinion that the scope of Art. III.1 should not be extended to containers.

8 See e.g.: *Kyokuyo Co Ltd v AP Moller-Maersk A/S (t/a Maersk Line)* [2017] Bus. L.R. 1270, where the court stated that 'package or unit' had to have the same meaning in Art. IV, r.5(a) and r.5(c) of the HVR as it had had under Art. IV r.5 of the Hague Rules. The effect of r.5(c) was that the container would be the only 'package or unit' unless there was sufficient specification of the manner in which the cargo contained therein comprised packages or units; *Vinnlustodin HF v Sea Tank Shipping AS (The Aqasia)* [2017] Bus. L.R. 730. Under Art. IV, r.5 of the Hague Rules, the term 'unit' could only refer to a physical item of cargo or to a combination of physical items bundled together for shipment and therefore did not apply to liquid or other bulk cargo. The claimant's argument that the context in which 'unit' had been used indicated that it was intended to refer to a physical item or composite items rather than to a unit of measurement was compelling.

9 Contrast: Aleka Mandaraka-Sheppard, *Modern Maritime Law (Volume 2): Managing Risks and Liabilities* (3rd edn, Informa Law 2013) 106–107. According to the author, the burden of proof shifts to the carrier when the owner of the cargo proves the cause of damage. The author therefore seems to exclude the *prima facie* claim. In practice, however, relying on the *prima facie* claim might not be sufficient for a cargo claim to succeed, and the claimant might, in the notice of damage or loss and without prejudice to its rights, prove the cause of the damage or loss.

catalogue of exceptions.[10] The exceptions in Rule 2 (i) (m) (n) (o) (q) of Article IV are important for the case of containerised goods.[11] The carrier bears the probative burden when it seeks to demonstrate that a case falls within an exception (*prima facie* proof), and when it relies on exception (q) to establish that the damage occurred without its fault. The question here, as far as cargo bundling is concerned, is how the shipper is to be defined for the purpose of those carrier's defences that relate to facts within the sphere of influence of the shippers and to their liability. Thus, it is not immediately obvious whether the defences and the liability rules can be invoked against all shippers or only against the shipper that is associated with the defective cargo. If each shipper retains its individual right to compensation independently of the rights or obligations of the other cargo interests, the liability scheme would operate as in groupage services (see further Chapter 5 and Chapter 6).

In the next phase, the claimant can argue that the fault of the carrier contributed to a peril or prove that the loss or damage had a different cause, but the carrier was negligent in fulfilling its obligations under Rule 1 or Rule 2 of Article III. In that case, the burden of proof shifts to the carrier.[12] The carrier then has to rebut the claims that are related to its negligence or prove, under Rule 1 of Article IV, that it exercised due diligence to make the ship seaworthy. In relation to Rule 2 of Article III and Rule 2 of Article IV, this conventional burden of proof[13] might be subject to change in England. In *Volcafe Ltd and another v Compania Sud Americana de Vapores SA*,[14] the Supreme Court held that the application of the Hague Rules should be considered against the background of the common law of bailment. It was found that the carrier

10 In case the claimant challenges Art. III(2), the carrier can, alternatively, prove compliance with the duties under that article. In practice, however, a successful defence under Art. IV rebuts allegations of breach of Art. III(2). See: Simon Baughen, *Shipping Law* (Routlege 2019) 113. Furthermore, Art. IV.2(q) imposes a higher burden of proof on the carrier. Thus, it might be invoked when the carrier cannot rely on the exceptions in Art. IV.2(a)-(p). It needs to be noted that the Rotterdam Rules follow the Hague-Visby framework on burden of proof in Art. 17. Art. 17 explicitly stipulates that the carrier and the shipper may rebut the allegations of the opposing party. The defendant carrier can invoke either Art. 17.2 to argue that there is no causal connection between loss or damage and its fault or the fault of any person for whom it is liable or Art. 17.3 to make out the presence of excepted perils. The claimant can draw on Art. 17.4(a) to prove that the excepted peril was caused by the carrier or by another person for whom the carrier is liable, on Art. 17.4(b) to establish that an event or circumstance that is not listed as an excepted peril contributed to the loss, damage, or delay, or on Art. 17.5(a) to show that the loss, damage, or delay was caused, partially or fully, by the unseaworthiness of the vessel.

11 The Art. IV.2(q) exception might be particularly relevant when a container includes other bundles of goods, e.g. palletised cargo. This is so because Art. IV.2(n) might be considered to refer to the packing of the particular goods in respect of which or to which loss or damage arises. See: Margetson (n 7) 157 citing *Goodwin, Ferreira & Co. Ltd., and others v. Lamport & Holt, Ltd.* [1929] 34 Ll.L.Rep. 192.

12 In England, Art. III, Rule 1 is considered to have an overriding effect: If the carrier breaches the seaworthiness obligation, it cannot raise Art. IV defences. See: Stephen Girvin, *Carriage of Goods by Sea* (2nd edn, Oxford University Press 2011) 428–429.

13 This seems to have been confirmed in Poland: Sąd Apelacyjny w Gdańsku 16.07.2003 I ACa 1387/02.

14 *Volcafe Ltd and another v Compania Sud Americana de Vapores SA* [2018] UKSC 61 par. 9.

bears the burden of proving that it exercised due care to protect the goods from damage, including damage arising from the inherent characteristics of the cargo, such as its hygroscopic character, for the following reason:

> Apart from certain articles, such as IV.1 and IV.2(q), which deal in terms with the burden of proof for specific purposes, the Rules do not deal with questions of evidence or the mode of proving a breach of the prescribed standard or the application of an exception. These are matters which in accordance with generally recognised principles of private international law are for the law of the forum. Accordingly, in order to be able to rely on the exception for inherent vice, the carrier must show either that he took reasonable care of the cargo but the damage occurred nonetheless; or else that whatever reasonable steps might have been taken to protect the cargo from damage would have failed in the face of its inherent propensities.[15]

The case concerned inherent vice. Nevertheless its reasoning might also be applicable to the exceptions in Article IV, Rule 2 (i), (n), and (o)[16] because it seems difficult to operationalise them without reference to some assumed standard of care in respect of the cargo.[17] Therefore, the carrier would not be able to rely on these exceptions when it has followed instructions from the shipper that were obviously erroneous, when it could and should have taken precautions that would have prevented damage to its packaging or which would result from some inherent characteristic of the cargo, or when it has not minimised the risks of misidentification and erroneous delivery. The judgement has been rightly criticised for incentivising forum shopping by treating the question of the burden of proof as an issue of procedure and private international law.[18] Regardless of who needs to prove care in respect of the goods and when, it is still unclear whether bundled goods make the care obligation of the carrier more stringent. Furthermore, especially when bilateral carriage contracts are concluded based on a multilateral co-operation contract (see further Chapter 5), it is not obvious whether the assessment of reasonable care concerns individual goods under individual contracts or bundled goods. This uncertainty flows from the questions of whether each shipper retains its individual rights and obligations and how it may influence the carrier's liability under Article IV, Rule 5 (see further Chapter 4, Chapter 5, and Chapter 6).

---

15 *Volcafe Ltd and another* (n 14) 15.

16 See also: *Glencore Energy UK Ltd and Glencore Ltd v Freeport Holdings Ltd (The "Lady M")* [2019] EWCA Civ 388, where the court held that *Volcafe Ltd and another v Compania Sud Americana de Vapores SA* did not affect the allocation of the burden of proof in the case of the fire exception (Art. IV.2(b)) and *Alize 1954 and another v Allianz Elementar Versicherungs AG and others (The Libra)* [2019] EWHC 481 (Admlty), where the court held that *Volcafe Ltd and another v Compania Sud Americana de Vapores SA* did not affect the allocation of the burden of proof under Art. III.1 HVR.

17 *Volcafe Ltd and another v Compania Sud Americana de Vapores SA* (n 14) par. 37; Julian Cooke et al. (eds), *Voyage Charters* (4th edn, Informa Law 2014) 1095, 1101–1102, 1103; Girvin (n 12) 485.

18 Justice Stewart, 'The Fluctuating Incidence of the Burden of Proof Under the Hague-Visby Rules: The Implications *of Volcafe v CSAV* [2019] AC 358 for the position in Australia' (2019) Richard Cooper Memorial Lecture <https://bit.ly/3GmVq8k> accessed 2 August 2023.

2.2 Carrier's duty of care

The HVR ties the allocation of the risks of cargo damage to the carrier's exercise of reasonable care and its level on the basis of the knowledge that it possesses or ought to possess. When the goods are not carried with reasonable care and are consequently lost as a result of the perils mentioned in Article IV, Rule 2, then, if the loss is caused by the previous default of the carrier, it is liable for breach of the care obligation. The point in time on which the assessment is based is that of the receipt of the cargo by the carrier. This proposition can be inferred from Rule 1 of Article III, which states that the ship should be seaworthy before and at the beginning of the voyage, where 'the dual reference is to make doubly sure that with respect to cargo then being loaded the vessel must be seaworthy at the time of the receipt of cargo and must continue in that state until the ship sails'.[19] Rule 1 is followed by the provisions of Rule 3, which stipulate that, after receiving the goods into its charge, the carrier or its master or agent shall supply the shipper with a B/L on the latter's request.[20] From that point onwards, the carrier must load, handle, stow, carry, keep, care for, and discharge the goods properly and carefully. The phrase 'properly and carefully' means caring for goods carefully and in accordance with an adequate system that must reflect all of the knowledge that the carrier possesses or ought to possess about the nature of the goods.[21] The level of knowledge must also reflect the kinds of conditions which the vessel is expected to encounter during the journey.[22] Section 2.2.1 specifies the carrier's duty of care as far as the external condition of goods is concerned. Section 2.2.2 treats about the internal condition of goods.

2.2.1 External appearance of goods

After receiving the goods, the carrier should assess their external appearance on the basis of the actual knowledge that a reasonable carrier would possess in the circumstances. In other words, the HVR imposes an obligation on the carrier to use its knowledge of the outward appearance of the goods when issuing a B/L.

In the case of a defect that is apparent or that the carrier ought to discover, the carrier's failure to include reservations in the B/L might compromise its

19 *Mississippi Shipping Co. v. Zander & Co.* (S.S. Del Sud), 270 F.2d 345 (5th Cir. 1959) which is a prevailing doctrine.

20 Art. I (e) and Art. III, r. 2 mean that the obligation to care for cargo is not limited to the period of the carrier's responsibility under the HVR (from the moment of loading until the point of discharge). The carrier must take care of the cargo during the entire process from loading to discharge, that is, for as long as the goods are in its custody.

21 *Albacora v Westcott & Laurence Line* [1966] S.C. (H.L.) 19 27.

22 *Albacora v Westcott* (n 21); *Bunga Seroja* [1999] 1 Lloyd's Rep 512. See further: Djadjev (n 5) 59–62 and the cases mentioned therein.

defences under Article IV, Rule 2 exceptions (n),[23] (o), or (q) for three reasons. Firstly, Article III, Rule 1 can be triggered by damage caused by a defective container supplied by the carrier prior to loading if the container is unseaworthy.[24] Secondly, actual knowledge at the time of the assessment of the cargo might affect the carrier's obligations under Article III, Rule 2, thus precluding reliance on the exceptions against a third-party B/L holder. The carrier can be bound by the outward condition of the goods if it does not negate a statement that would otherwise constitute a representation under Article III, Rule 3, or if it fails to include the phrase 'said to contain as declared by the shipper' in the B/L.[25] Such omissions result in the B/L becoming conclusive evidence in the hands of the third-party B/L holder.[26] Instead, to exonerate itself against the shipper, the carrier would have to challenge the *prima facie* evidence of receipt of cargo in good condition.[27] Furthermore, although the carrier can delegate loading, stowage, and discharge responsibilities contractually,[28] it is still subject to the burden-of-proof rules because it is not exempt from the obligations in Article III, Rule 2.[29] The more risks the carrier accepts, the higher the standard of care. Thus, for example, if a container that has been loaded by the shipper has reasonably noticeable external defects or develops them during the voyage, the carrier may still be held responsible for failing to remedy the defect if it causes the cargo to be damaged or lost.[30] That the defences under Article IV, Rule 2 (o) do not absolve the carrier from liability for shortfall

23 Contrast: Francesco Berlingieri, *International Maritime Conventions: Volume 1 The Carriage of Goods and Passengers by Sea* (Informa 2014) 40, who, regarding the 'n' defence, writes that the carrier does not bear the burden of drawing the shipper's attention to the insufficiency of packing at the time of receipt of the goods because the obligation to prepare the goods for the carriage lies on the shipper, and the carrier is not in a position to inspect their packing. The HVR exception, although it refers only to insufficient packing, also applies to defective packing. See also: Yvonne Baatz et al., *The Rotterdam Rules: A Practical Annotation* (Informa Law 2009) 56.

24 Baughen (n 10) 126–127; Ralph de Wit, *Multimodal Transport* (LLP 1995) 414–416.

25 Under Art. III(3), the carrier must always state the apparent condition of the goods. See: Baughen (n 10) 69. See also: *Noble Chartering Inc v Priminds Shipping Hong Kong Co Ltd (Tai Prize)* [2021] EWCA Civ 87 pars. 47–53, where the court stated that a draft B/L presented by the shippers to the master of a ship which contained the words 'clean on board' and 'shipped . . . in apparent good order and condition' was not a representation or warranty by the shippers as to the apparent condition of the cargo because the veracity of the information in question was not guaranteed by the shipper under the HVR but deduced exclusively from the master's examination.

26 See further: Djadjev (n 5) 309–311.

27 See further: Paul Todd, 'Representations in Bills of Lading' (2003) *Journal of Business Law* 160.

28 *Societe de Distribution de Toutes Merchandises en Cote D'Ivoire (t/a SDTM-CI) v Continental Lines NV and Another* [2015] EWHC 1747 (Comm), where the court held that the transfer of risk for loading is to be equated to the transfer of responsibility.

29 This concerns both FCL and LCL containers: Alexander von Ziegler, *Haftungsgrundlage im internationalen Seefrachtrecht* (Schulthess 2002) 101.

30 Stevens (n 5) 34. In England, this will also be a result of treating the carrier as the bailee of an FCL container that is provided by the shipper. The carrier has a positive obligation to care for the container. See further: Paul M. Bugden and Simone Lamont-Black, *Goods in Transit and Freight Forwarding* (3rd edn, Sweet & Maxwell 2013) 206–207.

in delivery supplies another salient example.[31] Nevertheless, if the carrier is able to rely on Article IV, Rule 2 (o), it also has recourse against the shipper under Article III, Rule 5, which stipulates that the shipper is deemed to have guaranteed the accuracy of the marks, numbers, quantities, and weights that it furnishes at the time of shipment and that the shipper must indemnify the carrier against all loss, damage, and expense that arises or results from inaccuracies in these particulars. Thirdly, when the carrier has loaded the container, it must prove the inherent defect in the goods in order to avoid liability. In such instances, the question is whether the carrier had a reasonable opportunity to examine the quality of the goods.[32] Thus, the higher the level of care in the assessment of the outward condition of cargo, the greater the likelihood that the carrier can avoid liability.

As far as cargo bundling is concerned, the examination of the outward condition of the goods might differ between cargo bundling models. When issuing separate B/Ls, the carrier could be bound to the outward condition of the goods separately, as in the case of LCL shipments where the contracts of carriage are evidenced by the line's B/Ls. Alternatively, the packing operations might be considered FCL shipments, as in the case of container freight stations or shipping lines that operate on classical delivery terms, such as, for example, container yard/container yard (CY/CY).[33]

2.2.2 Internal condition of goods

As far as the internal condition of the goods is concerned, if the carrier has no means of knowing that the cargo requires special treatment, it should still exercise due care in relation to the goods to fulfil the positive duty[34] that Article III, Rule 2 imposes on it in order to successfully use Article IV, Rule 2 (i), (m), or (q). The exonerations in Article IV, Rule 2 (i), (m), or (q) concern acts or omissions by the shipper, inherent defect, and any other cause that arises without the actual fault or privity of the carrier, respectively. As far as shipper-packed units are concerned, the possibility of invoking the insufficient packing exoneration ground that is regulated by Article IV, Rule 2 (n) HVR is also important. That issue is discussed further in Chapter 4.

Due care should be exercised in light of all general knowledge that the carrier has or that it ought to have about the implicit characteristics of the goods in the given circumstances. For example, carriers have been found in breach of Article III, Rule 2 because they did not secure coffee beans, which are known

31 *Sandeman v Tyzack and Branfoot Steamship Co. Ltd* [1913] A.C. 680.

32 Harmke M.B. Brouwer, *Eigen gebrek in het transportverzekeringsrecht* (Paris 2017) 122–123 and the literature cited therein.

33 The 'CY/CY' term means that there is one FCL shipper at the port of loading and one FCL consignee at the port of discharge. For an overview of contractual terms in container freight, see: Djadjev (n 5) 293–295.

34 Stephen Girvin, 'The Carrier's Fundamental Duties to Cargo Under the Hague and Hague-Visby Rules' (2019) 25 *Journal of International Maritime Law* 443, 455.

to be hygroscopic, properly[35] and because they did not ventilate maize according to general practice.[36] Breaches of Article III, Rule 2 can also occur when the carrier assists with the packing of a container and has the opportunity to inspect it before it is sealed. In this case, the use of the phrase 'said to contain' does not prevent the carrier from being held liable for missing cargo.[37] However, a carrier was relieved from liability when the moisture level of cocoa was proven to have been too high at the time of loading, but the cargo had been in good condition.[38] The judge in *The Flowergate* said:

> If in the future and in the light of what is now known, shipowners continue to accept cocoa for shipment merely on the strength of its apparent condition, and heedless of the implications of what its true condition may in fact be by reason of its moisture content, they may find it said against them hereafter that they have engaged themselves to carry that cocoa safely to destination, whatever that moisture content may ultimately prove to be.[39]

The concept of the general knowledge about the goods that the carrier possesses or ought to possess and the meaning of the term 'properly' in Article III, Rule 2 have evolved over time. Their evolution is reflected in the *Volcafe* case (see also Section 2.1), where the court underlined the importance of knowledge of general industry practice as a criterion that is relevant to care for goods and the fulfilment of the obligation under Article III, Rule 2.[40] Still, the carrier does not need to possess the highest degree of knowledge of the cargo. However, the requirement to be familiar with general industry practice might make the standard of care for goods more stringent if the efficacy of industry practice must be proven.[41] It would be more difficult for the carrier to avoid liability because it would need to prove that damage occurred even though it took reasonable care of the cargo or that the damage would have occurred even if it had taken reasonable steps to protect the cargo.

Similarly, if the carrier is informed that the cargo requires special treatment, the aforementioned standard of care becomes more stringent because it comes to encompass specific knowledge about the cargo. By contracting to carry goods of a specified description, the carrier assents to the presence on its ship of goods that possess the attributes of the goods as described. The carrier may avoid liability when it is not informed that the cargo needs to be kept in a refrigerator[42] or shipped via a recommended route that is different from a usual

35 *Volcafe Ltd and another v Compania Sud Americana de Vapores SA* (n 14).
36 *Alianca Navegacao e Logistica Lda v Ameropa SA (The Santa Isabella)* [2020] Bus. L.R. 360.
37 William Tetley, *Marine Cargo Claims* (4th edn, Thomson Carswell 2008) 1563.
38 *The Flowergate* [1967] 1 Lloyd's Rep 1.
39 *The Flowergate* (n 38) 46.
40 *Volcafe Ltd and another v Compania Sud Americana de Vapores SA* (n 14).
41 Contrast: Richard Hedlund, 'Coffee and Water Don't Mix: Clarifying the Burden of Proof Under the Hague Rules' (2019) 3 *Journal of Business Law* 223, 236.
42 *Albacora v Westcott & Laurence Line* [1966] S.C. (H.L.) 19 28.

and reasonable one.[43] However, if it knows that the cargo will be shipped in reefer containers, it needs to secure a technician to monitor the goods during the voyage.[44] Therefore, the more information the shipper provides to the carrier, the higher the level of risk and the standard of care that the latter assumes. Still, if the carrier proves that it has used appropriate means, its claim succeeds without any need to establish the precise character of the goods.[45] The carrier does not need to possess the highest degree of knowledge of the cargo.[46] This also implies that the carrier might seek additional information from the shipper once the goods are in its custody or require the shipper to provide information and documents that are necessary for the carrier to comply with the law.[47]

2.3 Shipper's fault-based and strict liability

While preparing goods for transport, the shipper must remain mindful of the character of the voyage until the carrier receives the goods. The HVR appear to ascribe strict liability to the shipper in circumstances that involve dangerous cargo but require shipper negligence in other circumstances. Article IV, Rule 3 of the HVR sets out a general rule to the effect that the shipper is only liable when it or its servants or agents are at fault. This general principle affords priority to the *lex specialis* in Article III, Rule 5 and Article IV, Rule 6, which establish the shipper's strict liability in case it provides inaccurate or no information, respectively.[48]

The shipper can be expected to have greater access to and familiarity with the shipped goods, and should thus bear the risks of absent or incorrect information about the goods being passed on to the carrier. For example, if the conventional burden of proof applies, it is the shipper that must ultimately prove lack of inherent vice or hidden defects in the goods that it has packed because the Article IV, Rule 2 (m) burden of proof easily switches to the claimant in such cases.[49] This said, the provision of correct information by the shipper to the carrier increases the risk borne by the latter.[50] For example,

---

43 *Alianca Navegacao e Logistica Lda v Ameropa SA (The Santa Isabella)* (n 36).

44 Djadjev (n 5) 305–307.

45 This is also true of dangerous goods. See: *The Athanasia Comninos and the Georges Chr Lemos* [1990] 1 Lloyd's Rep. 277.

46 Tetley (n 37) 654, 1323–1331; also e.g: Art. III.3 *in fine* HVR.

47 Tomotaka Fujita, 'Obligations and Liabilities of the Shipper' in Meltem Deniz Güner-Özbek (ed), *The United Nations Convention on Contracts for the International Carriage of Goods Wholly or Partly by Sea. An Appraisal of the "Rotterdam Rules"* (Springer 2011) 220.

48 See: *'Giannis N.K' Effort Shipping v Linden Management S.A. and Others* [1998] 1 Lloyd's Rep. 337, where the shipper's obligation under Art. IV, r. 6 of the HVR was said to stand free.

49 Tetley (n 37) 1148–1151.

50 Under Art. IV, r. 6, lack of knowledge of dangerous goods entitles the carrier to discharge them without compensation, and the shipper of such goods is liable for all damages and expenses that arise directly or indirectly from the shipment. However, the carrier's acceptance of the dangerous nature of the goods restricts these remedies to situations in which the goods become a danger to the ship or cargo and where the carrier can land, destroy, or render the dangerous goods innocuous without liability on its part, except in general average.

Article IV, Rule 6 implies that if both parties are aware of the dangerous nature of the goods and damage occurs, the case ought to be resolved like any other cargo case. Still, the shipper cannot be exonerated from liability if it is negligent in fulfilling its duties or if it fails to take the necessary precautions, and the carrier needs to care for the goods while assuming more risk.

In the basic scheme, the shipper should exercise the utmost care in furnishing the carrier with information about marks, numbers, quantities, and weights (Article III, Rule 5 HVR) as well as information about the dangerous nature of the goods (Article IV, Rule 6 HVR). Nevertheless, the information about the nature of non-dangerous goods and information about the proper handling, carriage, and delivery of the goods for carriage call for the exercise of reasonable care because the shipper's liability under Article IV, Rule 3 of the HVR is based on fault.[51] Furthermore, the shipper must deliver the goods to the carrier in a condition in which they can withstand the intended carriage. This implies that the standard of care should be based on what the shipper knew or ought to have known about the characteristics of the goods at the time of their delivery for carriage. For example, in the case of shipper-packed containers, a clean B/L is insufficient for the shipper to prove that goods were in a satisfactory condition upon loading if it bears the risk for loading.[52] The information, instructions, and documents that are necessary for the proper handling and carriage of the goods should be provided only to the extent that they are reasonably necessary. The higher the level of care required to deliver the goods to the carrier in a condition in which they can withstand the intended carriage, the higher the probability that the shipper will succeed in discharging the burden of proof.

3 CMR

3.1 Burden of proof: Scheme

Under the CMR, the claimant needs to prove that damage, loss, or delay[53] have occurred within the period set out in Article 17.1 by duly checking the goods upon delivery or through reservations.[54] The claimant has a *prima facie* case for total loss when the goods have not been delivered within 30 days of the expiry of the agreed time limit, or, if there is no agreed time limit, within 60 days of the time when the carrier took over the goods.[55] The carrier, in turn, can rely on defences, which are set out in Article 17.2 for damage, loss, and delay and in Article 17.4 for damage or loss.

51 *The Athanasia Comninos and The Georges Chr Lemos* [1990] 1 Lloyd's Rep. 277; Tetley (n 37) 1111–1116.

52 Brouwer (n 32) 122–123 and the literature cited therein.

53 Simon Baughen is of the opinion that the types of damage set out in the CMR are not exhaustive. See: Baughen (n 10) 183–184. See also: *Shell Chemicals UK Ltd v P&O Roadtanks* Ltd [1993] 1 Lloyd's Rep. 114 on the delivery of wrong goods.

54 Art. 30 CMR.

55 Art. 20.1 CMR, which states: '[. . .] shall be conclusive evidence of the loss of the goods'.

In fact, invoking the exceptions in Article 17.4 favours the carrier. If it establishes that the damage was probably caused by one or more of the enumerated circumstances, it is presumed that those circumstances were, in fact, the cause of the damage, and the carrier may (wholly or in part)[56] free itself of liability (Article 18.2 CMR). The cause should be real and not theoretical, abstract, or based on unsubstantiated claims.[57] It should also be significant.[58] The exceptions that are particularly relevant to consolidated goods concern the defective packing (Article 17.4 (b)), handling, loading, stowage, or unloading of the goods by the sender, the consignee, or an individual who is acting on their behalf (Article 17.4 (c)), goods whose nature exposes them to a particular risk of total or partial loss or damage (Article 17.4 (d)), and the insufficiency or inadequacy of the marks or numbers on the packages (Article 17.4 (e)). As far as Article 17.4 (d) is concerned, Article 18.4 states explicitly that, in respect of the carriage that is performed in vehicles specially equipped to protect the goods from the effects of heat, cold, variations in temperature or the humidity of the air, the carrier cannot benefit from the liability exemption, unless it proves that all steps incumbent on it in the circumstances with respect to the choice, maintenance, and use of such equipment were taken and that it complied with any special instructions issued to it.

The cargo claimant can respond to the invocation of exonerations by proving that the loss or damage was not, in fact, attributable either wholly or partly to one of the risks mentioned earlier or by pointing to another cause of damage or loss.[59] Should the claimant show that the damage can be attributed wholly or partly to a different cause, the carrier bears the burden of showing what proportion of the damage was attributable to a cause for which it was not liable.[60] If the claimant succeeds in claiming that the damage is not wholly attributable to one of the risks, the dispute turns on Article 17.1 once more, and the carrier should try to invoke Article 17.2. Under Article 17.2, the carrier needs to prove the existence of exonerating events. The claimant needs to present evidence that challenges the defence under Article 17.2 or to indicate other grounds for carrier liability.[61]

56 Art. 17.5 CMR.

57 See e.g.:Sąd Okręgowy w Katowicach 09.08.2018 XIX Ga 1025/17; see also: Sąd Okręgowy w Łodzi 13.03.2017 XIII Ga 892/16; LG Düsseldorf 5.12. 2013 31 O 101/12.

58 Malcom Clarke, *International Carriage of Goods by Road: CMR* (5th edn, Informa Law 2009) 218.

59 Art. 18.2 CMR.

60 See: *Exportadora Valle de Colina SA (t/a Exportadora Santa Elena) v AP Moller-Maersk A/S* (t/a Maersk Line) [2010] EWHC 3224 (Comm).

61 See e.g.: Sąd Apelacyjny w Gdańsku 17.04. 2014. V ACa 136/14, where the gross negligence of the driver, which was based on Art. 29 CMR, excluded the applicability of Arts. 17.2 and 18 CMR, and Sąd Apelacyjny w Gdańsku 28.10.2015 I ACa 410/15, where the court held that carrier's liability under Art. 3 of the CMR excludes the benefits of Art. 17.2 CMR. The case concerned theft committed by the carrier's subcontractor. The court found that theft of goods by the carrier's subcontractor is always 'within the scope of employment'. See also: Sąd Najwyższy

3.2 The carrier's standard of care

Like the HVR, the CMR establishes a general scheme of risk allocation between the parties. The CMR, however, does not tie the allocation of the risk of damage to the exercise of reasonable care (the level of which can be determined from the carrier's knowledge about the cargo) but to the occurrence of damage, loss, or delay for which the carrier might be (partially or wholly) liable and to knowledge of hazards. The carrier is the ultimate risk bearer because it is liable for damage[62] regardless of its cause, including damage whose cause is unknown,[63] unless a ground of exoneration applies. Generally, as soon as the carrier takes over the goods, they fall under its sphere of risk, but it is only obliged to prevent general hazards. The carrier is thus expected to control the risks of damage connected to known or presumed[64] facts about the nature and condition of the goods, to possess information about the means of minimising the degree of loss, either before or after the risky event, and to insure against any residual risk that cannot be avoided feasibly. This rule is further explained in Section 3.2.1. Section 3.2.2 presents the standard of care concerning external condition of goods. Section 3.2.3 focuses on the standard of care concerning internal condition of goods.

3.2.1 Article 17.2 CMR in fine

Article 17.2 *in fine* states that the carrier is not liable if it proves that the damage was caused by circumstances which it could not have avoided and the consequences of which it could not have prevented. Conversely, the carrier is the optimal risk bearer for all avoidable hazards and preventive measures. Avoidance and prevention are important.

Understood autonomously, Article 17.2 *in fine* refers to the necessity of risk management processes. Furthermore, in light of the text and purpose of the Convention, these could be specified as risk management processes in the

---

22.11.2007 III CSK 150/07, where the court found that the application of Art. 17.3 of the CMR is excluded if the carrier can make out an exoneration ground under Art. 17.2 *in fine*. The judgement was mentioned in: Sąd Apelacyjny w Białymstoku 4.12.2019 I AGa 68/19, where the court found that a manufacturing defect of a tire can be exempted under 17.2 CMR. On vehicle defects, see also: Karl-Heinz Thume, 'Beweislastfragen bei Fahrzeugmängeln im Bereich der CMR' (2000) *Versicherungsrecht* 821, who writes that relying on Art. 17.2 CMR is difficult because of the onerous burden of proof and thus unlikely to succeed. However, the carrier can still try to make out other special defences.

62 This is also true of the cause for which the carrier fails to discharge the burden of proof, even if the specific failure is unidentified. See: *Ulster-Swift Ltd. and Another v Taunton Meat Haulage Ltd. v Fransen Transport N.V. (Third Party)* [1977] 1 WLR 625.

63 See e.g: OLG Hamburg 13.2.2020 6 U 182/17, where the unknown cause of the damage was the reason for holding the carrier liable under Art. 29 CMR.

64 In that sense, it also does not matter if the carrier accepts unknown or non-conforming goods. The case will still fall under the framework of Art. 17 CMR, and the carrier will have to bring the case within one of the exoneration grounds to avoid liability. See: *Datec Electronics Holdings Ltd and others v United Parcels Service Ltd* [2007] UKHL 23.

carriage of goods. Risk management should be arranged in a manner that is sensitive to context. There are three contextual factors, namely the risk management framework that the organisation has put into place; the organisation and its activities, structure, and human resources; and the environment in which it operates, including its business sector.[65] To avoid hazards or to prevent their consequences, thus avoiding liability under Article 17, the carrier must identify, assess, mitigate, and monitor risks. In other words, it must have knowledge and control over the hazards that it has already faced or the ones that it might face and possess information about minimising loss before or after the risk occurs.[66] It must also monitor dangers and adopt measures to mitigate any residual risk that cannot be avoided feasibly.[67] The standard from Article 17.2 *in fine* should also be considered a general indicator of the level of care as far as the avoidance of damage on the part of the carrier is concerned. This standard is high because the carrier needs to take active steps to avoid the hazards of the road transport sector that it is familiar with in order to prove the exact cause of the damage.[68]

The main advantage of my approach to Article 17.2 CMR *in fine* is that it supports uniformity in the application of the CMR and thus avoids the need to refer to national concepts of *force majeure* or fault-based liability. However, recourse to national law in the interpretation of Article 17.2 CMR *in fine* is currently common, which adds to the uncertainty of the application of the CMR. Germany is on one side of the spectrum. There, Article 17.2 *in fine* is considered to refer to *force majeure* and thus to cover only extraordinary, unforeseeable, and, critically, external events. The carrier must exercise utmost care, which has two components. Firstly, the carrier needs to observe 'ideal' conduct. Secondly, it must identify an 'ideal' response to the hazard.[69] On

65 See further: Paul Hopkin, *Fundamentals of Risk Management Understanding, Evaluating and Implementing Effective Risk Management* (4th edn, Kogan Page 2017) 82–88; see also: the standard ISO 31000:2018: ISO, 'ISO 31000:2018 Risk Management – Guidelines' <https://bit.ly/3GpXL2e> accessed 8 August 2023.

66 See e.g.: Sąd Okręgowy w Łodzi 4.12.2020 XIII Ga 1378/19.

67 For risk identification, risk assessment, risk mitigation and risk monitoring, see further: William Ho et al., 'Supply Chain Risk Management: A Literature Review' (2015) 53(16) *International Journal of Production Research* 5031 and the literature cited therein.

68 Contrast: Clarke (n 58) 255–256, 265 who argues that the carrier should exercise reasonable care in situations that remain in the sender's risk domain (including packing and loading). See also: Krzysztof Wesołowski, *Umowa międzynarodowego przewozu drogowego towarów na podstawie CMR* (Wolters Kluwer Polska 2013) 437–438, who argues that the carrier's obligation to check the loading derives from Art.17.1 CMR or from national law. Cf. Sąd Okręgowy w Krakowie 23.03.2017 XII Ga 575/16, where the carrier was exonerated because it had fulfilled its obligation to secure the load of stone plates in spite of the unstable condition of the stands on which they had been delivered by securing them with extra straps and also informed the sender about its doubts about the loading of the goods.

69 See further: Beate Czerwenka, 'The Concept of "Unavoidable Circumstances" in Article 17, Para 2, of the CMR in Light of German Jurisprudence' (2016) 21 *Uniform Law Review* 533 and the cases mentioned thereon.

the other side of the spectrum, the Polish courts interpret Article 17.2 *in fine* in light of the presumption of fault and reasonable care. In the opinion of the Polish courts, the list of unavoidable circumstances should remain open because these are not specified by the CMR. The carrier is obliged thus to use the due care that is customarily required in relations of a given type and in certain circumstances.[70] An autonomous approach has emerged in England, where Article 17.2 *in fine* implies a standard ('could not avoid even with utmost care').[71] It requires the carrier to take all possible precautions that are not beyond the bounds of common sense. The understanding of Article 17.2 *in fine* that I propose conforms with this view and identifies exact evaluation criteria. The precautions that are taken should be judged by reference to risk identification, assessment, mitigation, and monitoring.

Since the application of Article 17.2 *in fine* is rather strict, the carrier might be considered to bear the risk of the consolidated cargo. The German case law on *Sammeladungsspedition* serves as a useful indication of the risks that are related to caring for cargo, other than packing, for which the carrier needs to take precautions while performing groupage services. The risks could be the same for cargo bundling. They concern cargo regrouping,[72] transport procedures for palletised cargo that contains both easily removable goods[73] and other types of goods,[74] labelling the truck that is transporting the grouped cargo,[75] organising transshipment,[76] loading (and stowing) groupage units,[77] and notifying the sender, in particular through general conditions of carriage and other documents, of the types of goods that are allowed for grouping and the necessary preparations.[78] Although these risks apply to road transport, they could also be present in other modes of transport.[79]

70 See e.g: Sąd Najwyższy 17.11.1998 III CKN 23/98; Sąd Najwyższy 26.11.2019 IV CSK 415/18; Sąd Najwyższy 08.10.2020 II CSK 773/18.

71 *JJ Silber v Islander Trucking Patenta GmbH v Islander Trucking* [1985] 2 Lloyd's Rep 243.

72 The lack of security measures is often used as a basis not only to conclude that the event would have been avoidable but also to find that the carrier acted recklessly. This could also trigger the application of Art. 29 of the CMR. See the judgements at n 71–76.

73 OLG Nürnberg 04.07.2017 12 U 2204/15.

74 BGH 1.12.2005 I ZR 108/04, where the court stated that high-value parcels require greater care during transport.

75 LG Stuttgart 02.10.2017 44 O 27/17 KfH.

76 LG Hamburg 30.08.2012 409 HKO 126/11; OLG Düsseldorf 02.06.2004 18 U 37/04.

77 OLG Hamburg 16.07.2009 6 U 173/08.

78 OLG Düsseldorf 27.09.2006 18 U 61/06, where the sender had not been told to declare special-value packages; *Datec Electronic Holdings Ltd and Others v United Parcels Service Ltd* [2007] UKHL 23 par. 30, where the contractual restrictions were considered relevant to the carrier's attempt to avoid liability under Art. 17(2) CMR. However, see also: BGH 01.12.2005 I ZR 108/04, where the court stated that general terms and conditions cannot be used to waive checks on goods at the points where responsibility passes from one operator to another or where goods are handed over for the next stage of the transportation process.

79 Hans-Joachim Schramm, *Freight Forwarder's Intermediary Role in Multimodal Transport Chains a Social Network Approach* (Physica-Verlag 2012) 30–33, 70.

3.2.2 External condition of goods

The carrier's defences that concern the external condition of goods and refer to the defective condition of packing (Article 17.4 (b) CMR), sender's loading (Article 17.4 (c) CMR), or the insufficiency or inadequacy of marks (Article 17.4 (e) CMR) should not be successful under the Convention when the defects or special requirements of the cargo were apparent or known to the carrier when it took over the goods.

For Article 17.4 (b), this proposition is supported by two considerations. Firstly, when the consignment note contains no specific reservations, the carrier has to rebut the presumption under Article 9.2.[80] Article 9.2 states that if the consignment note contains no specific reservations by the carrier, it shall be presumed, unless the contrary is proved, that the goods and their packaging appeared to be in good condition when the carrier took them over and that the number of packages, their marks and numbers corresponded with the statements in the consignment note. Given the Article 8.1 duty to check the condition of the packing, rebuttal might be difficult.[81] Secondly, the effectiveness of Article 17.4 (b) can be challenged by reference to Article 10. This means that since the carrier loses its right to a recourse claim against the sender when the defect was apparent or known at the time when it took over the goods and made no reservations (Article 10), the carrier should, in my opinion, also fail to establish a presumption under Article 17.4 (b) for the same reasons. Likewise, under Article 17.4 (e), when the consignment note contains no specific reservations, the carrier must rebut the presumption from Article 9.2. The application of Article 17.4 (c) should instead depend on who is in charge of loading or unloading. If the carrier is responsible, Article 17.4 (c) cannot be invoked.[82] If the sender or its agent performs the loading or if the carrier can witness the loading operations, the carrier also has to rebut the presumption from Article 9.2.[83]

---

80 Sąd Okręgowy w Katowicach 09.08.2018 XIX Ga 1025/17.

81 See e.g: Sąd Okręgowy w Białymstoku 15.10.2018 VII Ga 281/18, where the court considered that, in a situation where a carrier is present during loading and knows that packaging is insufficient, it must take additional protective actions. If it considers that packaging is the only effective security measure while remaining aware of its responsibility for the goods from the moment of taking them over, it should ultimately refuse to carry out the carriage.

82 Cf. Sąd Okręgowy w Szczecinie 3.02.2017 VIII Ga 32/16. The case was decided on the basis of national law, but its holding would likely have been the same if it had been decided under the CMR. The carrier received instructions on the means of securing loads of felt, which were supposed to be delivered to three different receivers. The cargo arrived undamaged only at the first destination. The court found that the risks related to the partial unloading and the further securing of the cargo would be borne by the carrier. Similarly, see: Sąd Okręgowy w Szczecinie 26.09.2014 VIII Ga 241/14.

83 See: BGH 22.05. 2014 I ZR 109/13, where the court found that taking over the goods presupposes that the carrier or its agents willingly acquire direct or indirect custody of them. In the case, loading had been performed by the sender, but the drivers witnessed it and, in the opinion of the court, had the opportunity to observe the process or at least to count the number of packed items after loading had been completed. Nevertheless, they blindly elected to sign an acceptance

Similarly to the HVR, the examination of the outward condition of the goods under the CMR might differ depending on the cargo bundling execution model. When issuing separate consignment notes, the carrier could be bound to the external condition of the separate goods. When it receives a container, it must examine the external condition of the unit.

3.2.3 Internal condition of goods

The carrier's defences that pertain to the internal condition of goods, which are based on Article 17.4 (d) of the CMR and Article 17.2 of the CMR (see above) should also fail when, at the time when the carrier took over goods, the defects, and/or the special requirements of the cargo were apparent or known to it. The reader should also pay attention to the fact that in case of shipper-packed units, packing might encompass external and internal condition of goods. Whether and against whom in such case the carrier can invoke insufficient packing exoneration contained in Article 17.4(b) CMR is discussed in Chapter 4.

Inherent vices include packing that does not enable the goods to withstand a journey and failure to store goods inside a container.[84] If the carrier claims that the goods were not secured properly yet the defect was apparent or known to it at the moment of taking over goods (for example, because it participated in their packing),[85] it should not, in any event, benefit from the liability exclusion. Likewise, if the carrier signs an unconditional delivery note in which the need to cool the goods before transport is recorded, it bears the burden of proving that it was prevented from checking their temperature when it received them for loading.[86]

As far as the models for the execution of cargo bundling are concerned, goods are handed differently depending on the model and the corresponding contractual relations. Therefore, special requirements could be provided for

---

note (recognised as evidence) as a receipt for the indicated packages. Similarly: Sąd Okręgowy w Warszawie 05.08.2016 XXIII Ga 632/16, where the carrier did not make reservations in the consignment note at the moment of taking over the goods but also failed to bring the defects in loading and stowage to the sender's attention. Cf: Sąd Okręgowy w Szczecinie 26.09.2014 VIII Ga 239/14, where the carrier was exonerated because loading had been performed by the sender, and the carrier was found not to have influenced it. See also: Ingo Koller, *Transportrecht Kommentar* (C.H. Beck 2013) 1070, who mentions the obligation of the carrier to check loading and stowage.

84 Clarke (n 58) 223.

85 Cf (n 81, 83).

86 BGH 23.11.2017 I ZR 51/16; see also: Ingo Koller, 'Die Beweislast für den ordnungsgemäßen Zustand des Gutes bei dessen Übernahme, insbesondere für die Vorkühlung' (2019) 42(1) *Transportrecht* 1; Pierre Scavio and Rochus Wallau, 'Die transport- und lebensmittelrechtlichen Rechtsfolgen einer Unterbrechung der Tiefkühlkette' (2018) 41(5) *Transportrecht* 177. However, see also: OLG Brandenburg 15.1.2020 7 U 119/18, where the correct cooling temperature of the transported vaccine that was indicated on the consignment note did not create such a presumption because the goods had not been taken from the manufacturer but from a wholesaler. Thus, the burden of proving that the goods had been handed over undamaged laid with the cargo interest.

single goods or composed units. Since bundling is performed on the basis of the shippers' co-operation agreement and different operational models, the question is whether the risk that the carrier bears is higher in the case of cargo bundling than in the case of groupage services.

3.3 Sender's strict liability

The liability of a sender towards a carrier for inaccuracies or inadequacies in the particulars on the consignment note (Article 7 CMR), for defective packing (Article 10 CMR), for absence or inadequacy of documentation that pertains to the consignment note (Article 11 CMR), and for handing over goods of a dangerous nature for carriage (Article 22 CMR) is strict. The CMR, unlike the HVR, does not distinguish between the fault-based and strict liability of the sender, yet the sender, like the shipper under the HVR, can be expected to have greater access to and familiarity with the goods and should thus bear the risk of failure to convey accurate information to the carrier.

Relatedly, Article 17.4 CMR regulates the 'special risks inherent in one more of the following circumstances', which primarily concern the sender. In general, the sender, being the party that prepares the goods before carriage, knows their nature and sometimes loads them. The sender is optimally positioned to prevent the occurrence of the special risks that are connected with the hazards regulated by Article 17.4 CMR. This proposition is also reflected by the fact that the sender assumes the primary obligation to deliver goods intact and undamaged at the agreed time and place,[87] and in light of its responsibility under Article 7 CMR, to inform the carrier about the goods and their nature.[88] If the special hazard eventuates and the carrier can attribute the damage to it, the sender bears the consequences because the carrier can rely on the exoneration grounds.

The concept of knowledge of a hazard is important here. The special character of the risks in Article 17.4 CMR should be understood to be unknown to the carrier. However, in apportioning risk, the CMR attaches importance to special knowledge about a hazard. Under Article 22 of the CMR, the carrier bears the risk of damage to dangerous goods, similarly to the risk of damage to non-dangerous goods, if it receives information about the exact nature

87 Sąd Okręgowy w Białymstoku 15.10.2018 VII Ga 281/18.

88 The sender should also indicate the special prevention measures that the cargo type necessitates. See: OLG München, 26.10.2017 23 U 1699/17, where the court observed that if the driver cannot see which goods they are transporting from the transport documents, they cannot adopt additional preventive measures. The preventive measures should be included in transport documents or the transport order. Alternatively, they may be communicated at the moment when the goods are taken over or discussed in advance. However, a mere mention in the sender's general terms and conditions would not suffice.

of the danger and the precautions that ought to be adopted. Under Article 10 CMR, the risks connected to defective packing are transferred to the carrier if the defect is apparent or known to it at the time when it takes over the goods and if it makes no reservations. Consequently, it loses its recourse claim against the sender. Relatedly, Article 9.2 CMR establishes a presumption that the goods and their packaging are in a good condition if the carrier makes no specific reservations.

4 Cargo bundling: Considerations

The burden-of-proof schemes of the HVR and the CMR exhibit two similarities in their approach to the risk of damage. Firstly, the carrier must possess a minimum of knowledge about the hazards (see point 'm' on the *y*-axis in Figure 3.1). This minimal level of knowledge implies that the carrier faces a minimum level of risk (see point 'm' on the *x*-axis in Figure 3.1 as well as Section 2.2 and Section 3.2.1). The carrier's knowledge can change. The conventions stipulate that the risk that is borne by the carrier can increase whenever it acquires knowledge about the hazard yet fails to clause the transport document, or when the shipper informs about special characteristic of goods, and the carrier does not take it into consideration. In this sense, an informed carrier is less likely to discharge the burden of proof because it cannot invoke the special exoneration grounds. Instead, it remains obliged to provide proper care for the goods (HVR), to prevent the occurrence of a risk (CMR), or to increase its level of care and risk prevention when the shipper or sender provides special information about the cargo.

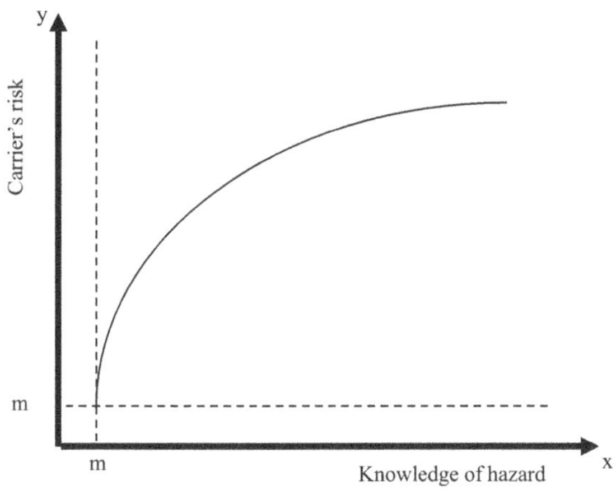

Figure 3.1 Relationship between risk that is born by the carrier and the carrier's knowledge of a hazard

Regardless of the similarities between the two, the HVR creates a reactive risk management framework for the carrier, and the CMR requires more proactive measures. The minimum threshold of knowledge that the carrier is expected to possess differs between the two conventions. It is higher under the CMR, under which the carrier, if it is to be discharged from liability under Article 17.2 CMR, must possess advance knowledge and control over the hazards that it has faced in the past or that it can face in the future as well as information on the means of minimising loss before or after a risk event. It must also undertake measures, for example, by designing procedures, to mitigate residual risks that cannot be avoided feasibly, and it must monitor dangers (see Section 3.2). Under the HVR, the carrier's exercise of reasonable care is based on its knowledge, actual or implied, of the nature of the goods and the journey (see Section 2.2). Therefore, it is important for the carrier to know the consequences of a sender informing it of certain risks and the special requirements that are likely to be apparent or known to it, especially under the CMR.

Producing and distributing companies that are willing to be involved in cargo bundling co-operation should consider three questions that are relevant to anticipate whether and how the risk management under the transport conventions will operate in case of various co-operation models (Figure 3.2). First, are co-operation agreements subject to mandatory law? If one of the partners to co-operation is found to be a carrier, the transport conventions apply, and the partners to co-operation cannot modify the liability scheme vis-à-vis the carrier contractually. If this is not the case, then national law determines the relation between the partners (see further e.g. Chapter 8). Second, can the carrier's defences be invoked against all partners to co-operation or only against the partner whose cargo was defective? Third, are the co-operating partners liable jointly towards the carrier, and relatedly, do they have a joint right to compensation? In the typical case of groupage service which is based on unrelated bilateral shipper- or sender-carrier contracts, where mandatory law applies, the carrier bears limited liability for transport damage in principle.[89] The shipper's or sender's liability is unlimited. If each co-partner retains its individual right to compensation independently of any rights or obligations

89 Except situations where the carrier is not entitled to exclude or limit his liability. See: Art. 29 CMR, Art. 36 COTIF-CIM (Uniform Rules concerning the Contract of International Carriage of Goods by Rail (COTIF-CIM) adopted 9 June 1999, entered into force 1 July 2006) [International Carriage by Rail (COTIF) of 9 May 1980, as amended by the Vilnius Protocol of 3 June 1999] CR 24/NOT/Add.5 21.12.2009]), Art. IV (5) (e) HVR, Art. 61 RR (United Nations Convention on Contracts for the International Carriage of Goods Wholly or Partly by Sea (adopted 11 December 2008) Sea A/RES/63/122), Art. 21 CMNI (Budapest Convention on the Contract for the Carriage of Goods by Inland Waterway (CMNI) (adopted 3 October 2000, entered into force on 1 April 2005) CMNI/CONF(99)2/FINAL), Art. 22.5 Montreal Convention (Convention for the Unification of Certain Rules Relating to International Carriage by Air (adopted on 28 May 1999, entered into force 4 November 2003) International Civil Aviation Organization Doc 9740).

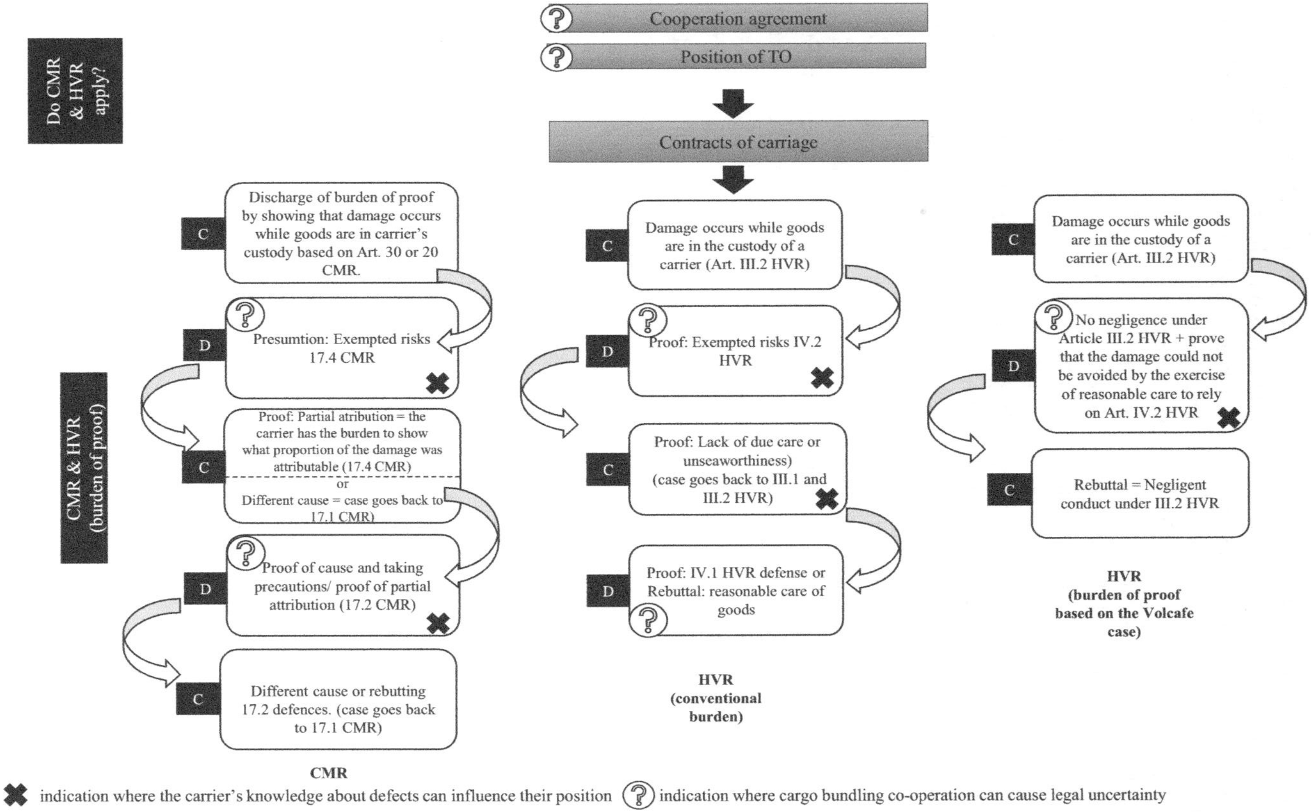

Figure 3.2 Burden of proof under transport conventions and points of legal uncertainty relevant for cargo bundling co-operation. Note 'C' refers to Claimant (cargo interest) and 'D' refers to Defendant (carrier)

of the other cargo interests, the liability scheme in a cargo bundling co-operation will function similarly to that in a groupage service. There might, however, be intricacies. For example, when the cargo bundling company acts as a carrier vis-à-vis the bundling partners but is a shipper or sender vis-à-vis the actual carrier, it faces the risk of being unable to convey accurate information to the latter. Conversely, insofar as the co-operating partners are liable jointly for damage to the carrier, each bears the risk of omissions by the others. Thus, it would seem desirable to draft the co-operation agreement so as to shift the risk to the partner to co-operation to whom the damage is attributable (see further Chapter 7, Chapter 8, and Chapter 9).

Transport Orchestrators that are willing to be involved in cargo bundling co-operation should also anticipate whether and how they will be influenced by the risk management under the transport conventions. The legal classification of a Transport Orchestrator requires here special attention. The classification is relevant because the Transport Orchestrator will in general only be presumed liable in case of classification as a carrier. In case of another classification, the risk for cargo damage lies with the performing carrier. Furthermore, depending on the legal classification the liability for the defective organisation can differ. For example, as far as freight forwarding agents are concerned, the burden of proof is on the cargo interest, who must establish negligence of a freight forwarder and that it caused the loss or contributed to it. Instead a carrier under transport conventions is presumably liable, yet it can invoke exoneration grounds and its liability is limited (see further Chapter 8).

CHAPTER 4

Operation of exoneration grounds and their effect on carrier liability

Marta K. Kołacz

1 Introduction

The discussion in this chapter concerns issues that are typical in the bundled-goods context, that is, instances in which defectively packed goods damage other, adequately packed goods. A question arises as to whether the carrier could then rely on an exoneration ground against the cargo interest whose goods were damaged. The arguments that follow account for the exoneration grounds that refer to packing (Article 17.4 (b) CMR, Article IV Rule 2 (n) HVR).

The literature presents many approaches to the application of the exoneration grounds that refer to packing. As far as the Convention on the Contract for the International Carriage of Goods by Road of 1956 (CMR)[1] is concerned, there are two views in the literature. Under the first, it is argued that the exoneration ground attach only to the specific cargo for which the condition of wrongful or insufficient packing is fulfilled. The second approach allows the exoneration ground to apply to wrongfully packed cargo and to other cargoes that are affected by it. However, all of the cargoes should belong to a single consignment. Under the Hague-Visby Rules (HVR),[2] there are three approaches. Under the first, exoneration applies only to goods that require packing. Under the second, exoneration applies to the consignment as a whole. The third approach extends the operation of the exoneration ground to goods outside of a specific consignment. Thus, the application of the exoneration grounds that refer to packing may range from single parcels to full consignments and beyond (Figure 4.1). As a result, based on existing

1 Convention on the Contract for the International Carriage of Goods by Road (CMR) (adopted 19 May 1956, entered into force 2 July 1961) 399 UNTS 189.

2 The Brussels Convention for the Unification of Certain Rules of Law relating to Bills of Lading (adopted 25 August 1924, entered into force 2 June 1931) Trb. 1953, 109, 004127 and Protocol to Amend the International Convention for the unification of certain rules of law relating to bills of lading, signed at Brussels on 25 August 1924 (adopted 23 February 1968, entered into force 23 June 1977) No. 23643.

DOI: 10.4324/9781003450801-4

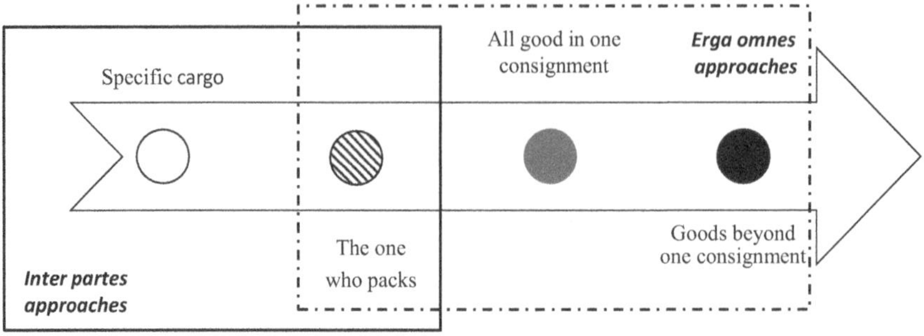

Figure 4.1 Approaches for implementing exoneration grounds related to insufficient packing

approaches the carrier can try to invoke the exoneration grounds *erga omnes* (Section 2). If this proves unsuccessful, the carrier can try to invoke the exoneration grounds against each shipper or sender involved in the bundling of the cargo (Section 3).

However, I argue that risk management in packing operations should be similar to risk management during loading operations: The application of the exoneration grounds depends on the identity of the actor who performs the packing operations (Figure 4.1, Section 4). To support my argument, I rely on the practical aspect of cargo bundling co-operation and the risk management frameworks of the conventions (see Chapter 3): Co-operation can be executed in milk runs or through shipper-packed units that may contain different goods, yet the risk management provisions of the transport conventions should operate similarly, regardless of the execution method. For a reminder, co-operation in cargo bundling is the practice of having manufacturing and distributing companies perform cargo consolidation before a carrier is engaged (see further Chapter 1). These companies can agree on a form of long-term co-operation and identify matching cargo opportunities prior to shipment. A milk run refers to the execution of cargo bundling where one vehicle visits the producing or distributing companies on the established route to pick up the loads. Shipper-packed or sender-packed units refer to cargo units prepared earlier by the co-operating shippers or senders and contain bundled goods. The prepared unit with bundled cargo is further handed over to the carrier at one point of time.

In Section 5, I conclude by presenting the broader consequences of various approaches for cargo consolidation. The reader should be aware of some terminology used in this chapter. The chapter mentions 'shippers' and 'senders' and 'shipper-packed' and 'sender-packed' units to better align the text to the terminology of the CMR and the HVR.

2 *Erga omnes* application – existing approaches

The *erga omnes* approaches vary in their scope and might attach importance to goods in a single consignment (Section 2.1), or all goods carried by a carrier (Section 2.2). Since neither of these approaches predominates, the legal position is uncertain. The uncertainty is compounded by the possibility that a judge denies the *erga omnes* application of the special exoneration grounds (see further Section 3).

2.1 Approach 1: CMR and HVR exoneration can be invoked erga omnes *only as far as the goods belong to a single consignment*

The main problems with this approach are that the concept of a consignment has been interpreted differently and that it has so far not been considered in instances when the loading units are prepared by the shippers or senders and comprise several consignments. As far as the CMR is concerned, Malcolm A. Clarke has argued that if the damage that is caused by Parcel A to Parcel B occurs within the same consignment, the matter is within the sphere of risk of the sender, and the carrier is not liable.[3] If Parcel A and Parcel B are not in the same consignment, the carrier bears the risk because it owes a duty of care to the other consignments, which extends to preventing apparent defects in the packing of the goods of third parties from affecting other goods.[4] This view is also supported by Krzysztof Wesołowski.[5] Under the HVR, William Tetley supports a similar approach to Article IV, Rule 2(n) HVR (in respect of shipper-packed containers)[6] as do Raul Colinvaux,[7] Hakan Karam,[8] and Julian Cook.[9] Conversely, Guenter Treitel and Francis M.B. Reynolds, despite agreeing that the insufficiency-of-packing exception could also apply to damage to other cargo, are of the opinion that such situations are more likely be covered by Article IV, Rule 2(q) of the HVR which consequences I discuss further in Section 3.1.[10]

3 Malcom Clarke, *International Carriage of Goods by Road: CMR* (5th edn, Informa Law 2009) 262.

4 Clarke (n 3); Malcolm Clarke and David Yates, *Contracts of Carriage of Goods by Land and Air* (2nd edn, Informa Law 2008) 45.

5 Krzysztof Wesołowski et al. (eds), *Konwencja o umowie międzynarodowego przewozu drogowego towarów (CMR)* (Lex Wolters Kluwer 2015) 252.

6 William Tetley, *Marine Cargo Claims* (4th edn, Thomson Carswell 2008) 1190–1191. Otherwise, according to Tetley, the issue is subject to Art. III (2) HVR. See: William Tetley, *Marine Cargo Claims* (4th edn, Thomson Carswell 2008) 1201.

7 Raul Colinvaux, *Carver's Carriage by Sea* (13th edn, Stevens and Son 1982) No 539.

8 Hakan Karam, *The Carrier's Liability under International Maritime Conventions – The Hague, Hague Visby, and Hamburg Rules* (The Edwin Mellen Press 2004) 307.

9 Julian Cooke et al. (eds), *Voyage Charters* (4th edn, Informa Law 2014) No 85–340–85–341.

10 Guenter Treitel and Francis M.B. Reynolds, *Carver on Bills of Lading* (4th edn, Sweet and Maxwell 2017) 9–233.

The concept of a consignment is an important aspect of the application of this approach. In Clarke's view, that concept subsumes all cargoes that are shipped by the same sender.[11] This general explanation could be misleading under the conventions, especially when one shipper or sender sends goods to multiple recipients.[12] Generally, the term 'consignment' should refer to one or more pieces of goods received by the carrier from one shipper or sender at one place and at one time to be transported, with a B/L or a consignment note, to a single recipient.[13] Nothing prevents a single consignment from being sent by several shippers or senders. Such situation would trigger *erga omnes* application by default because multiple shippers or senders would likely be considered parties to one contract of carriage with a carrier. To decide which goods comprise a consignment, it is thus important to determine the specific subject of carriage, which should be covered by a single transport document. Wesołowski argues that if several consignment notes must be issued after the conclusion of a contract, that contract should not be divided. Nevertheless, he also argues that the treatment of the goods under each consignment note should reflect the assumption that the carriage contract was concluded exclusively for them. Only in this way is it possible to exercise the right of disposal, to declare the value of the goods, or to allow successive carriage.[14] The same observations would be true, in my opinion, in respect of consignments covered by B/Ls. At the same time, under the CMR, the issue of whether the goods are transported by one means of transport or by several is irrelevant to the identification of a consignment unless one of the parties avails itself of the right under Article 5 (2). Likewise, it does not matter whether goods are carried by one or several carriers.[15] Under the HVR, it is not important

11 Clarke (n 3) 262; similarly, e.g. in Art. 1 of the RHAL Conditions of Carriage 2020: 'Consignment means goods, whether a single item or in bulk or contained in one parcel, package or container, as the case may be, or any number of separate items, parcels, packages or containers sent at one time in one load by or for the Customer from one address to one address'. Road Haulage Association, 'RHA Conditions of Carriage 2020' <https://bit.ly/2XEgYvP>, accessed 8 August 2023.

12 See e.g.: *Ministry of Food v Lamport & Holt Line Ltd* [1952] 2 Lloyd's Rep 371, where the claimants were the owners of a consignment of maize shipped in the lower hold of the defendants' vessel and a cargo of tallow shipped in the 'tween deck, over the maize in the same vessel. On arrival, it was found that the maize had been contaminated by a tallow leakage. It was held that the carrier, knowing the nature of the tallow, had not taken adequate steps to protect the maize and that the exemption clause in the B/L of the maize did not protect the carrier from liability for damage caused by the tallow leak.

13 In this line of cases, see e.g.: Art. 1(g) Ogólne Warunki Przewozu ZMPD – 2016 'przesyłka – ładunek (towar) przyjęty do przewozu, za jednym listem przewozowym CMR' *('consignment – cargo (goods) accepted for carriage under one consignment note')* <https://bit.ly/3jtqucK> accessed 8 August 2023.

14 Krzysztof Wesołowski et al. (eds), *Konwencja o umowie międzynarodowego przewozu drogowego towarów (CMR)* (Lex Wolters Kluwer 2015) 173–175.

15 Tomasz Szanciło, *Odpowiedzialność kontraktowa przewoźnika przy przewozie drogowym przesyłek towarowych* (Legalis C.H. Beck 2013) Chapter 2 Point IV.B.

whether the cargo is divided between different decks on the ship unless the consignments are separate. It has been argued that the HVR would apply to the whole cargo in such a situation.[16]

Under the analysed approach, the division of risk between carrier and shippers or senders for shipper- or sender-packed units differs as a result of variations in the definition of a consignment. As far as the *erga omnes* application of the special exoneration ground, that can be invoked towards all cargoes shipped by the same shipper or sender, is concerned, if the loading unit only contains the goods of one shipper or sender, that shipper or sender bears the risk of damage when some of its insufficiently packed goods cause damage to the rest of its goods. Likewise, if a consignment refers to pieces of goods received by the carrier to be transported with a B/L or consignment note for one recipient and those goods are packed in a loading unit, the risk of damage when some of the insufficiently packed goods damage others lies with the shipper(s) or sender(s). If there is a mix of goods in the loading unit, the exoneration ground does not operate vis-à-vis the goods of the other shippers or senders or vis-à-vis the different consignments. Thus, the risk of damage shifts to the carrier, despite the preparation of the goods being within the discretion of the shipper or sender. This scenario could be seen as derogating from the provisions of the CMR because the burden of proof is, in fact, shifted to the carrier (Article 41.2 CMR).

Under this approach, the division of risk can also be imbalanced when the goods are packed and loaded separately as it happens in milk runs. The possibility of invoking the exoneration ground against all goods of the same shipper or sender can, in fact. disincentivise the carrier to care after them, especially because the carrier must care for the goods that were loaded in the past. Likewise, if the carrier accepts a consignment that it eventually divides inside the vehicle, its ability to invoke the exoneration ground against all goods belonging to one consignment could minimise its efforts to care for the goods.

For the models of execution of cargo bundling, it is important thus to establish whether a co-shipment should be qualified as a single consignment. If this is the case, the carrier could invoke the exoneration ground *erga omnes*. This approach assumes that the shipper or sender is better equipped to avoid the risks that inhere in the preparation of the goods. However, there might be disagreements regarding what a consignment is which hinders legal certainty concerning the application of insufficient-packing exoneration ground to all goods. Furthermore, the presented approach does not account for various methods of cargo bundling execution. Consequently, the risk of damage to goods could be distributed between the parties in a manner contrary to the risk management framework discussed in Chapter 3.

16 Treitel and Reynolds (n 10) No 9–116.

2.2 Approach 2: HVR exoneration generally applies erga omnes

Richard Aikens has argued that the carrier can rely on the Article IV, Rule 2(n) HVR exception not only in relation to damage to the insufficiently packed cargo but also when the insufficiency causes damage to other cargoes.[17] The consequence of this approach for the models of execution of cargo bundling is that, irrespective of the model that is applied, the carrier would be able to invoke the exoneration ground in respect of the insufficient packing of the goods that are damaged and in respect of the damage to other cargoes. This approach has been rejected under the CMR.[18] Furthermore, according to William Tetley, in these situations, the carrier's attempt to avoid liability should be based on Article III, Rule 2 of the HVR that says that the carrier shall properly and carefully load, handle, stow, carry, keep, care for, and discharge the goods carried.[19]

The second approach is certain, in that, in comparison to Approach 1, the application of the exemptions does not depend on the choice of the model of execution of cargo bundling. However, in my opinion, it should be rejected for two reasons. Firstly, it affords additional benefits to the carrier by allowing it to escape, or at least apportion, liability under the conventions, especially when the goods that are damaged by the insufficiently packed cargo have been loaded before the insufficiently packed cargo and the carrier was under an obligation to care for them. Under the CMR, the carrier could, in fact, avoid discharging the burden of proof under Article 17.2. This approach could thus be deemed inconsistent with Article 41 CMR and Article III, Rule 8 of the HVR, as could a clause excluding the carrier's liability for defective packing insofar as it pertains to damage caused by Cargo A to Cargo B. Secondly, the approach neglects Article 10 of the CMR and Article IV, Rule 3 of the HVR, and it imbalances the risk management exercise that carrier and shipper or sender must engage in to the disadvantage of the latter. Article 10 of the CMR and Article IV, Rule 3 of the HVR establish that the shipper or sender is liable to the carrier in instances of inadequate packing or act, fault, or neglect of the shipper respectively. Thus, they give the carrier a cause of action when defectively packed goods cause damage to other goods. Under the conventions, therefore, the carrier is already better placed to bear the risk of defects in the packing of other goods. The application of the second approach could marginalise the importance of Article 10 of the CMR and Article IV, Rule 3 of the HVR, whose application allows the carrier to be compensated for damage that is, in fact, attributable to other cargo interests.

17 Richard Aikens et al., *Bills of Lading* (2nd edn, Informa Law 2016) No 10.276.
18 Clarke (n 3) 262.
19 Tetley (n 6) 1201.

3 *Inter partes* application – existing approaches

The *erga omnes* application of the exoneration grounds causes legal uncertainty. Not only can *erga omnes* application be questioned but also, even when it is recognised, it may be interpreted in several ways. In consequence, the carrier might try to invoke special exoneration grounds against each bundling shipper or sender. In a situation in which Cargo A is damaged because of its insufficient packing and it damages Cargo B, the carrier might try to invoke the exoneration ground against Cargo A and (separately) against Cargo B. For a bundled-goods example, suppose that a cargo of liquids is damaged because of insufficient packing, and it further damages electronics whose packing is not waterproof. Alternatively, during transport, it is possible that one cargo may damage the others. That damaging cargo may appear to be of a totally different (and more dangerous) nature than the one declared. The probability of such occurrences is especially high when shippers or senders avoid sharing information about goods dedicated for cargo bundling for competition law reasons.[20] The question thus arises whether, in the case of cargo bundling co-operation the shipper's or sender's degree of care concerning packing and the general preparation of goods for carriage is limited to its own goods or whether it should also consider the goods of co-shippers or co-senders. Section 3.1 focuses on the approach under which the exoneration ground attaches only to the specific cargo that is packed wrongfully or insufficiently. Section 3.2 inquires whether the shipper's or sender's duty of care could be extended to other goods in the shipment and whether the exoneration ground could be invoked against the other cargo.

3.1 HVR and CMR exoneration apply only to damage to the specific cargo for which the condition of wrongful or insufficient packing is fulfilled

Under the first approach, the exoneration applies only to the specific cargo for which the condition of wrongful or insufficient packing is fulfilled. In the context of the CMR, this approach is supported by Helga Jesser-Huß and Katharina V. Boesche. Jesser-Huß claims that Article 17.4 (b) of the CMR applies only to damage to goods that require packaging but not to damage to individuals or other goods.[21] Boesche is of a similar opinion, supporting it

20 See further: Marta K. Kołacz, 'Co-Operation between Manufacturers and Distributors for Sustainable Freight – Select Legal Obstacles Posed by Laws Oriented to Individual Parties' in Ellen Eftestøl et al. (eds), *Towards a Zero-Emissions and Digitalized Transport Sector: Law, Regulation, and Logistics* (Edward Elgar 2024).

21 Helga Jesser-Huß, 'CMR Art. 17 [Haftungsgrundsatz und Haftungsausnahmen]' in Rolf Herber and Christine Schmidt (eds), *Münchener Kommentar zum HGB bd.7* (4th edn, C.H. Beck 2020) No 60: 'Abs. 4 lit. b betrifft nur Schäden an verpackungsbedürftigen Transportgütern, nicht hingegen Schäden, die Personen oder andere Güter erleiden'. This approach seems to have also been adopted in: Sąd Rejonowy w Bydgoszczy 19.05.2017 VIII GC 2113/15.

by drawing a comparison to Article 10 of the CMR. She argued that, unlike Article 10 of the CMR, Article 17.4(b) does not protect other parties and goods.[22] Thomas Scruton L.J was in favour of this approach in *Silver and Layton v. Ocean Steam Ship Company*,[23] where he took the view that a rectangular metal package that was likely to cause damage to other goods due to lack of covering was not 'insufficiently packed' for reason of that fact.

That the special exoneration ground can only be invoked in respect of the specific cargo for which the condition of wrongful or insufficient packing is fulfilled (Cargo A) does not mean that the carrier cannot defend itself in respect of damage caused to other cargo (Cargo B). In the HVR context, it has been said that Article IV, Rule 2(q)[24] or Article III, Rule 2 might offer that possibility.[25] However, the burden of proof in the case of the (q) exemption is heavier. Firstly, the word 'or' in exception (q) has been said to mean 'and'. Therefore, the exception does exclude alternatives.[26] Furthermore, under Article III, Rule 2 of the HVR, the carrier is required to rebut claims related to its negligence.[27] William Tetley points out that the carrier will be responsible for damage to Cargo B if the packing of Cargo A is apparently defective.[28] The carrier cannot limit its liability contractually because a clause that excuses the carrier from liability for defective packing is void by virtue of Article III, Rule 8 of the HVR. If the insufficiency of the packing is not apparent, the carrier is not liable to the other cargo interests unless stowing the two cargoes closely together was improper.[29] Under the CMR, damage to Cargo B as a result of the wrongful packing of Cargo A could still be covered by Article 17.2 *in fine* discussed in Chapter 3. Since the application of Article 17.2 *in fine* is rather strict, the carrier might be considered to bear the risk in respect of the consolidated cargo. The risk might be lower when the Polish approach to Article 17.2 CMR *in fine*, under which primary importance is attached to the carrier's due diligence, is adopted.

To the carrier, a successful defence would open the possibility of actions under Article 10 of the CMR unless the defect was apparent or known to it,

22 Katharina Boesche, 'CMR Art. 17 [Haftung des Frachtführers. Haftungsausschlüsse]' in Carsten T. Ebenroth et al. (eds), *Handelsgesetzbuch bd.2* (2nd edn, C.H. Beck 2009) No 48: 'Auf den Schutz von Personen oder anderer, zB mitbeförderter Güter kommt es dabei, anders l sim Rahmen des Art. 10 [. . .], nicht an'.; Katharina Boesche, 'CMR Art. 10 [Haftung für mangelhafte Verpackung]' in Carsten T. Ebenroth et al. (eds), *Handelsgesetzbuch bd.2* (2nd edn, C.H. Beck 2009) No 2; confirmed in: Katharina Boesche, 'CMR Art. 10 [Haftung für mangelhafte Verpackung]' in Carsten T. Ebenroth et al. (eds), *Handelsgesetzbuch bd.2* (4th edn, C.H. Beck 2020) No 2.

23 *Silver and Layton v. Ocean Steam Ship Company* [1929] 35 Ll.L.Rep. 49.

24 *Goodwin, Ferreira & Co. v. Lamport & Holt Line Ltd* [1929] 34 Lloyd's Rep. 19.

25 Tetley (n 6) 1201.

26 E.g.: Treitel and Reynolds (n 10) No 9–229.

27 See: *Ministry of Food v Lamport & Holt Line Ltd* [1952] 2 Lloyd's Rep. 371 in fn. 11.

28 Tetley (n 6) 1201.

29 Tetley (n 6).

as well as under Article IV, Rule 3 HVR. In this case, this possibility would, however, also place an additional risk on the carrier. Article 10 of the CMR would operate as a set-off provision when other damaged goods belong to the sender whose first goods were insufficiently packed and this sender is the claimant in the proceedings. However, if the claimant is the consignee, the carrier bears the risk of the sender's insolvency in the recourse action. Instead, Article IV, Rule 3 of the HVR concerns the shipper's negligence. As a result, the carrier bears the risk of damage when shipper negligence cannot be proven.

For the models of execution of cargo bundling, this means that, whatever the model that is applied, the carrier can only invoke the exemption ground in respect of the packing of the goods that are damaged and not in respect of the other affected cargoes. Under this approach, the exoneration applies only to damage to the specific cargo for which the condition of wrongful or insufficient packing is fulfilled, and damage to other cargoes can be excused under the general exoneration grounds. The adoption of this approach has two consequences. Firstly, it only addresses risk management in respect of single-good consignments. Secondly, it increases the risk that the carrier bears for consignments that comprise shipper-packed or sender-packed loading units. The possibility of invoking insufficient packing only in respect of single items in the loading unit might, in fact, shift the risks that inhere in stuffing and securing cargo in shipper-packed or sender-packed loading units onto the carrier: Under the HVR, the carrier must rebut the shipper's arguments about the carrier's lack of due care for the cargo. Under the CMR, it must prove that the conditions for the application of Article 17.2 are met.

The application of Article 17.2 of the CMR might mean for the carrier that it is required to check the content of sender-packed loading units. However, the conventions do not impose a duty on the carrier to inspect cargo in loading units unless its packing is apparently inadequate or the shipper or sender instructs it to do so (see Chapter 3). In this case, it is possible to claim voidness under Article 41 CMR in respect of the interpretation of the special exoneration grounds under which importance is attached only to damage to the specific cargo for which the condition of wrongful or insufficient packing is fulfilled. That is so because this interpretation deviates implicitly from the CMR, under which the risk that inheres in the preparation of the goods for carriage is borne by the sender. Under the HVR, such a solution could nonetheless be valid: Under Article V of the HVR, a carrier is at liberty to surrender, in whole or in part, all or any of its rights and immunities and to increase any of its responsibilities and obligations. In fact, the carrier could surrender the Article IV, Rule 2(n) exoneration concerning insufficient packing. In any case, such a decision would need to be embodied in the B/L that is issued to the shipper.

3.2 Possibility of invoking the exoneration ground separately against all bundled goods

The carrier might try to invoke the exoneration ground separately against all bundled goods, arguing that packing operations must account for the possibility of damage from the goods of co-shippers or co-senders. The carrier could add that the co-operation agreement implies that packing be conducted with a view to the possible mixes of goods that can be shipped. Based on the example presented at the beginning of this section, the carrier would claim that electronics should be packed in waterproof material or loaded in a consolidation unit so as to avoid water damage. Whether this argument can be successful depends on the standard of packing and the degree of care required from the shipper or sender.

Packing entails the assembly of items into a loading unit and an intermediate or an exterior pack with blocking, bracing, cushioning, weatherproofing, and marking. Article 17.4 (b) of the CMR mentions 'improper packing'. Article IV.2 (n) of the HVR refers to 'insufficient packing'. Both proper and sufficient packing refer to a standard that is tied to the ability of the goods to withstand the dangers of the normal carriage that has been contracted for.[30] The degree of packing that is required and the care that ought to be taken are related to the specific cargo. Some cargoes require a higher degree of care and certain types of packing, as in the case of dangerous goods in packaged form.[31] Where the cargo is damaged in its customary packing, it can be concluded that the packing was sufficient.[32] Furthermore, if certain packing has proven sufficient for a certain type of carriage in the past, it will likely meet the standard of propriety or sufficiency.[33] As a result, if goods are packed in accordance with general practice, it is difficult for the carrier to rely on the exception.

The duty of the shipper or sender to pack sufficiently or properly is a natural part of its duties, and the specific packing requirements form part of the statutory or contractual obligations of the shipper or sender. The CMR seems to restrict the necessity of packing to goods that require it by their nature

30 Clarke (n 3) 259; Tetley (n 6) 1178.

31 E.g.: Art. 4.1.1.5 ADR: 'Inner packing shall be packed in an outer packing in such a way that, under normal conditions of carriage, they cannot break, be punctured or leak their contents into the outer packaging. Inner packagings that are liable to break or be punctured easily (glass porcelain) shall be secured in outer packagings with suitable cushioning material'.; Art 4.1.1.6 ADR: 'Dangerous goods shall not be packed together in the same outer packing or in large packaging with dangerous or other goods if they react dangerously with each other . . .'; Article 7.3.3.5 IMDG Code: 'Containers be loaded in a way that incompatible dangerous or other goods are separated'; Article 7.3.3.6 IMDG Code: 'When dangerous goods are transported with other goods (e.g. heavy machinery or crates), all goods shall be securely fixed or packed in the cargo transport units so as to prevent the release of dangerous goods'.

32 Tetley (n 6) 1179.

33 Clarke (n 3) 260.

and for which there may be a causal link between absent or defective packing and loss or damage.[34] Conversely, the wording of the HVR exoneration ground seems to concern a general provision, which states that proof of loss of or damage to the cargo that results from defective packing exonerates the carrier from liability. The carrier has no defence if it issues a clean transport document when the defects are visible to it, yet the estoppel only attaches to packing that is apparently insufficient, that is, when the carrier could have detected it. Even if the carrier cannot rely on the exoneration ground because it knew that the outer packing was visibly insufficient, the insufficiency of the customary packing could also be invoked in respect of the inside packaging, which is not reasonably observable at the moment of loading.[35]

The general rule is applied directly when single-good consignments are handed over to the carrier. As far as cargo bunding is concerned, consignments that comprise single goods can be handed over during the milk run collection of goods. What is important is the moment at which the risk passes to the carrier. Goods are handed over to carriers at different points, and risk passes accordingly. This means that the sufficiency of the packing should be estimated by the carrier whenever the goods are handed to it. The carrier is responsible for determining whether the apparent packing of the goods that are handed over at these different points is sufficient. Once the single goods are handed over, the carrier is under an obligation to care for the goods (the HVR) or to secure them against the hazards of road transport proactively (the CMR). The carrier's duty of care in respect of the goods is not waived even when loading is performed by the shipper or sender. The carrier would still need to secure the goods or even to check their loading and stowage, especially when they are loaded and unloaded on successive occasions (see Chapter 3). If the carrier is performing the loading, including the packing of a loading unit, the stuffing operation forms part of that loading. In such situation, the carrier cannot rely on the exoneration ground when it knew that the outer packing of single goods was insufficient, but it could invoke insufficiency in respect of the inside packaging.

For shipper-packed or sender-packed units, packing includes the condition of the loading unit and the condition of the individual objects inside of it.[36] The exoneration ground could apply to the condition of the inside packaging of a loading unit in two ways. Firstly, under the narrow approach, the

34 Art 17.4(b) CMR. Similarly: Art. 23.3(b) COTIF-CIM (uniform rules concerning the Contract of International Carriage of Goods by Rail (COTIF-CIM) adopted 9 June 1999, entered into force 1 July 2006) [International Carriage by Rail (COTIF) of 9 May 1980, as amended by the Vilnius Protocol of 3 June 1999] CR 24/NOT/Add.5 21.12.2009]), Art. 18.1 (e) CMNI (Budapest Convention on the Contract for the Carriage of Goods by Inland Waterway (CMNI) (adopted 3 October 2000, entered into force on 1 April 2005) CMNI/CONF(99)2/FINAL).

35 Tetley (n 6) 1181; Colinvaux (n 7) No 17, 423.

36 Tetley (n 6) 1190–1191; A pallet has also been held to be a package: Colinvaux (n 7) No 552.

exoneration ground applies only to the inside packaging of single goods, even if bundled. Secondly, under the broader approach, the exoneration ground applies to single goods, but packing also includes the proper stuffing and securing of the cargo within the loading unit and consideration of the surrounding goods.[37]

As far as the narrower meaning is concerned, the exoneration ground operates in the way that it does when single goods are handed over to a carrier. The consequence is that sufficiency of packing is assessed only for the actual packing of goods in the loading unit and excludes risks that emanate from the related operations of stuffing and securing cargo in shipper-packed or sender-packed units. Returning to the example from the beginning of this section, the carrier would not be able to claim that electronics should be packed in waterproof material or loaded onto a consolidation unit to avoid water damage if they have been packed in the customary manner. The carrier would thus be left with the defences under Article IV, Rule 2(q) of the HVR, Article III, Rule 2 of the HVR, or Article 17.2 of the CMR and could, in fact, bear the risks that are related to shipper-packed or sender-packed loading units, especially under the CMR, which stipulates that it must make out the exonerating conditions. In my opinion, this approach should be discarded because it does not account for the fact that goods in shipper-packed or sender-packed units are within the shippers' or senders' domain of risk until handed over to the carrier. The shipper or sender would thus be disincentivised to prepare the goods properly for shipment. Meanwhile, the carrier would need to open shipper-packed or sender-packed loading units to avoid the risk, even though it is not obliged to do so, and this could increase the cost of its operations.

As far as the broader approach is concerned, the sufficiency of the packing of goods in loading units would need to be estimated in light of the possibility that the goods would need to withstand the dangers of normal carriage in a consolidated unit. Packing would thus also include the proper stuffing and securing of the cargo. This understanding of packing, which reflects current market practice, is reflected in Article 27.3 of the United Nations Convention on Contracts for the International Carriage of Goods Wholly or Partly by Sea of 2008 (Rotterdam Rules),[38] which provides that when the shipper packs a container or loads a vehicle, it must stow, lash, and secure the contents properly and in such a way that they do not cause harm to persons or property. Returning once more to the example used in this section, the carrier would be able to claim that the electronics should be packed in waterproof material or loaded in a consolidation unit so as to avoid water damage if there is a presumption or *prima facie* proof to the effect that the electronics were

37 Similarly: Tetley (n 6).

38 United Nations Convention on Contracts for the International Carriage of Goods Wholly or Partly by Sea (adopted 11 December 2008) C.N.563.2012.

packed in a manner that was inconsistent with them being bundled with other goods in a loading unit. At the same time, if the shippers or senders deliver a shipper-packed or sender-packed unit knowing that customary handling and stowage may damage it because of the manner in which the goods are packed and secured, the shippers or senders cannot insist that the carrier did not care for that unit properly.

The possibility of invoking the exoneration ground separately against each shipper or sender involved in cargo bundling nevertheless has certain disadvantages for the carrier. The presumption or *prima facie* proof of insufficient packing would need to be invoked against single goods in a consolidation unit. This could be especially problematic if the goods that damage the other goods transpire to be of a totally different nature than the one declared. This situation could trigger another layer of uncertainty because the judge would need to decide whether the insufficiency of the packing should be assessed on the basis of the shipper's or sender's original knowledge of the types of goods subject to bundling or on the basis of their actual nature. In the former case, the risk would lie with the carrier, who would then need to defend itself under Article IV, Rule 2(q) of the HVR, under Article III, Rule 2 of the HVR, or under Article 17.2 of the CMR. In the latter case, the risk would lie with the shippers or senders.

4 Exoneration can be invoked *erga omnes* when the operation was conducted jointly – suggested approach

I propose an approach, which assumes that the exoneration ground attaches to the performance of an operation. For this reason, it is important to establish whether the obligation of the shippers or senders was shared, discharged by a single shipper or sender, or performed by a carrier. In that sense, this approach is similar to that which is employed in respect of loading operations, whereby the party who loads the goods bears the responsibility for damage resulting from loading.[39] This approach follows the risk management

39 As far as loading is concerned, the CMR does not specify who is responsible for loading. The issue has generated divergent opinions in the literature. On the one hand, it has been argued that, since the issue is not governed by the CMR, national law is applicable (see e.g. Clarke (n 3) 73). Autonomous interpretation has also been proposed. Art. 17 (4)(c), in light of the absence of any provision that imposes obligations on the carrier in this respect, may be taken to mean that unless the parties agree otherwise, the loading activities trigger the liability of the sender (see: Krzysztof Wesołowski, 'Who Is Responsible for Loading Operations, Stowage and Securing with Respect to the Carriage of Consignments?' (2018) 28(1) *European Journal of Service Management* 343, 344–346). Under the HVR, although Art. III.2 states that loading falls within the carrier's obligations, the practice of the courts indicates that it can be the shipper's responsibility (see: *Jindal Iron & Steel Co Ltd v Islamic Solidarity Shipping Co Jordan Inc TCI Trans Commodities AG v Islamic Solidarity Shipping Co Jordan Inc* (The Jordan II) [2004] UKHL 49). Under both conventions, the carrier might still be liable if the sender or shipper performs the packing or loading and there is an apparent or known defect.

scheme established by the conventions, and its *erga omnes* or *inter partes* application depends on spheres of risk.[40] It would be possible to apply the insufficient packing exoneration ground *erga omnes* against those who pack goods together, and packing would include stowing and stuffing. If the packing operation (including the packing of a loading unit) is performed by one shipper or sender *qua* principal, only that shipper or sender bears responsibility for it. This approach equalises the carrier's exposure to risk in respect of shipper-packed or sender-packed goods across instances in which it takes a single package, a consignment composed of a few packages, or a container with different consignments.

This approach seems to be adopted in the Rotterdam Rules. However, it can also be derived from other conventions (see below). Article 17.3(k) of the Rotterdam Rules provides explicitly that the packing exoneration exempts the carrier unless it is packing the goods. Furthermore, Article 27.3 provides that when the shipper packs a container or loads a vehicle, it must stow, lash, and secure the contents in or on the container or vehicle carefully and properly and in such a way that they do not cause harm to persons or property. These articles specify, firstly, the allocation of risk in the performance of certain operations, and they underline that the risk rests with the shipper when it conducts the operation. Secondly, the articles in question make it clear that if the shipper packs a container or loads a vehicle, the relevant operations also include securing the goods. Accordingly, packing and loading should be understood broadly to include ancillary operations, such as, for example, lashing and securing.

Similar conclusions can be derived from the CMR and the HVR. The opponents of this line of reasoning could aver to the literal meaning of Article 17.4 (b) of the CMR, which seems to reflect an approach under which an exoneration ground can be invoked only in respect of goods damaged because of improper packing (see further Section 3). However, the Vienna Convention on the Law of Treaties rule of interpretation[41] cast doubts over this counterargument (see further Chapter 2). The text of a convention must be interpreted in good faith and in accordance with the ordinary meaning of the terms of the

40 Cf. Richard Williams, 'How Much Flexibility Is There in a Voyage Charter? – An Eclectic Conrnucopia!' in Baris Soyer and Andrew Tettenborn (eds), *Charterparties Law, Practice and Emerging Legal Issues* (Informa Law 2018) 161–162, who observes the same scheme in the allocation of the risk of commingling and blending: 'If two different products are loaded contemporaneously by two separate pipes into the same hold, it is possible to argue that the consequent comingling or blending is part of the loading or handling process and the responsibility and risk for such activity can legitimately be passed from the carrier to the cargo owner. But when one cargo is loaded first, and then another cargo is subsequently loaded, then commingling or blending process must logically take place after the loading of that cargo has been completed and cannot be considered to be part of the loading or handling of the first cargo'.

41 Art. 31 Vienna Convention on the Law of Treaties (adopted 23 May 1969, entered into force 27 January 1980) 1155 UNTS 331.

treaty in their context and in the light of its object and purpose. For example, the preamble to the CMR provides that its purpose is the standardisation of the conditions that govern contracts for the international carriage of goods by road with respect to, among others, carrier liability. Furthermore, the conventions reflect the proposition that the shipper or sender is better equipped to acquire information about the goods. The carrier is able to acquire it only at the moment of handing the goods over, and only to a limited extent. While this knowledge can be acquired with relative ease when the defects are apparent, information about the nature of the goods and their inherent condition can only be supplied by the shipper or sender (see further Chapter 3). Only the approach under which the exoneration can be invoked against the one(s) performing packing fulfil the standardization purpose (see Table 4.1). Accordingly, the shipper's or sender's ability to control the preparation of the goods and the carrier's inability to acquire information about that preparation means that it is the shipper or sender who should bear the risk. It should be noted that the carrier has no defence if it issues a clean transport document when the defects are visible, but the insufficiency of the customary packing could still be invoked in relation to inside packaging, which is not reasonably observable at the moment of loading (see further Section 3.2). Moreover, the importance of the performance of the whole operation is also apparent from

Table 4.1 Approaches to insufficient packing and distribution of risk. C-carrier, S-shipper

Operation of exoneration grounds *Example – insufficient packing* *Case: Insufficiently packed Cargo A damages Cargo B*			*Risk of sufficient packing of single goods*	*Risk of damage to other goods in shipper-packed unit*	*Risk of damage to other goods transported by the carrier*
Inter partes	'Sufficient packing' refers only to the packing of single goods		S	C	C
	'Sufficient packing' refers to the packing of single goods in light of the fact that they are bundled		S	S or C	C
Erga omnes	General		S	S	S
	Only as far as the goods belong to one consignment	All cargoes shipped by the same shipper	S	S or C	S or C
		Goods transported with a bill of lading or consignment note for one recipient		S or C	C
	Against those who performed packing		S	S	C

Articles 34–40 of the CMR, which concern successive carriers. Successive carriers become responsible for the whole operation (carriage) under one contract by reason of their acceptance of the goods and a consignment note.

Packing under the CMR and the HVR can be considered an evolutionary concept because its definition is of a very general nature or because it is expressed in such general terms that changing circumstances must be taken into account. Since the evolutionary character of the transport conventions is expressed by their aim to create uniform liability rules (see Chapter 2) novel business practices should be adapted to the convention framework. The allocation of risk under the conventions should therefore not be disturbed when new business models influence practices, such as packing operations. Therefore, containers that are packed by several shippers or senders should be within the sphere of risk of the shippers or senders and not that of the carrier. 'Packing' under the conventions should include inside and outside packing, stowage, and securing operations.

The application of this approach would differ depending on the method through which a cargo bundling model is actuated. If the goods are handed over to the carrier separately, it will be able to invoke the exoneration ground only *inter partes* because the goods are handed over at different points and the risk of damage passes accordingly. However, the carrier will still be safe if insufficiently packed goods damage others because it may avail itself of recourse actions by virtue of Article 10 of the CMR and Article IV, Rule 3 of the HVR. For goods bundled in consolidation units, the exoneration ground could be invoked *erga omnes*: Co-operating shippers or senders share the performance of the packing operations. As a result, invoking Article 10 of the CMR would not be necessary in cases of damage to the other goods in that consolidation unit because the carrier could be exempted under Article 17.4 CMR. Article 10 CMR and the recourse action will nevertheless be useful in respect of goods outside that unit or when the carrier suffers damage. A similar reasoning is possible with regard to Article IV, Rule 3 of the HVR.

However, the presented *erga omnes* application can be hindered by national concepts related to common and divisible obligations (see further Chapter 6). If a judge analyses the joint obligation of the shippers or senders through the concepts of national law, which I consider wrong, depending on jurisdiction it may, for example, arrive at the conclusion that the joint packing obligation is divisible. In consequence, shippers or senders might be considered as having individual position against the carrier when it comes to their liability. Relatedly, the effect of such interpretation may not always lead to joint and several or solidary liability.

An exoneration ground concerning a defect in the goods supplies arguments supporting the approach presented earlier that assumes that the exoneration ground attaches to the performance of an operation. A defect in the goods inside of a package can be classified as an inherent vice.[42] A carrier can invoke the inherent vice of the shipper-packed or sender-packed goods despite there being a clean transport document.[43] However, if the carrier packs the goods, the burden of proving inherent vice rests with the carrier. Likewise, if the goods are handed over to the carrier separately by each shipper or sender, the inherent vice argument can operate only *inter partes*. When, however, the goods of different shippers or senders are in a shipper-packed or sender-packed unit, the carrier would be able to invoke inherent vice *erga omnes*. There is, however, a difference between the burden of proving inherent vice under the CMR and the HVR. Under the HVR, the carrier needs to establish a *prima facie* case for the application of the exoneration ground (Article IV rule 2 HVR). Under the CMR, the burden of proof is more difficult to discharge because the carrier needs to prove that the loss, damage, or delay were due to inherent vice (Articles 17.2 and 18.1 CMR).

5 Summary

Two observations could be made on the basis of the foregoing analysis. Firstly, the variety of the existing approaches to the special exoneration grounds can already affect traditional consignments that comprise single goods which are handed over to the carrier. The second approach concerning *erga omnes* application (Section 2.2), which generally allows the carrier to use the exoneration ground against defectively packed goods and any other goods that are damaged because of defectively packed goods, provides the most vivid example of the impact that the interpretation of the convention can have on a single shipper or sender. Secondly, the variety of approaches can also have a large impact on the shipper-packed or sender-packed units that are subject to common groupage operations or cargo bundling co-operation. Since the conventions do not (directly) address shipper-packed or sender-packed units, it is uncertain which approach the judge decides to adopt.

The optimal solution that ensures legal certainty would be for the risks of packing to be managed similarly, irrespective of the number of those who pack or the number of consignments in a consolidation unit. Since managing the risk that attends to the preparation of the goods for carriage is generally for the shipper or sender, and carriage risks are for the carrier, the preparation of single goods as well as that of shipper-packed or sender-packed units should be the responsibility of the shipper(s) or sender(s). The *erga omnes* approach and invoking the exoneration ground against all who pack a unit ensure the fair distribution of the risk that inheres in the preparation of the goods for carriage (see Table 4.1 and Section 4). This proposal would further

42 Tetley (n 6) 333–336, 1560, 1563.
43 Tetley (n 6).

correspond to the possibility of suing shippers or senders jointly for damage caused to the carrier by their joint operations. I argue, especially in Chapter 6, that this possibility can be derived from the interpretation of the conventions without the need for recourse to national law.

Due to the uncertain status of the *erga omnes* application of exoneration grounds for shipper-packed or sender-packed units, the carrier can alternatively invoke the exoneration ground separately against all bundled goods. In this regard, a strategy better for a carrier would be to argue that 'sufficiency of packing' includes the proper stuffing and securing of the cargo within the loading unit and consideration of the surrounding goods with a focus on their actual nature and not on the knowledge that the shipper or sender had about these goods at the moment of bundling (Section 3.2). However, if this *inter partes* approach is also applied to the carrier's claims for damages, the carrier might bear the risk of the shipper's or the sender's insolvency and the resultant lack of compensation, which, in fact, also imbalances risk management under the conventions that I discuss in Chapter 3.

CHAPTER 5

Separate carriage contracts resulting from the co-operation agreement – first execution model of cargo bundling co-operation

Marta K. Kołacz

1 Introduction

This chapter focuses on the execution model of cargo bundling in which the carrier enters into contracts of carriage with individual shippers or senders that are members of the co-operation for cargo bundling. Together with Chapter 6, this chapter investigates various approaches to defining 'shipper' or 'sender' for the purpose of determining their rights and liabilities. Its focus is mainly on the possibility of joint liability of co-operating partners *vis-à-vis* the carrier and, relatedly, joint compensation. The analysis, although it focuses on the contractual execution of cargo bundling co-operation, reflects also on the operational execution of co-operation that could influence parties contractual obligations. For a reminder, milk runs refer to a situation when the goods are packed and loaded separately along the way and consolidation points refer to situations when consolidation units are prepared by the partners to co-operation in cargo bundling (Figure 5.1).

Although the conventions do not address the problems of several co-operating principals expressly, they do recognise situations in which a traditional bilateral relation can have a multiparty character. Firstly, the conventions deal explicitly with the other type of a multiparty contract that involves a consignee or the bill of lading (B/L) holder. Secondly, the conventions also deal with other types of cargo interests, including apparent and documentary shippers that affect a standard bilateral relation. Therefore, I investigate the existing solutions concerning multiparty contractual relations against the background of the execution model of cargo bundling in which the carrier enters into contracts of carriage with individual shippers or senders that are members of the co-operation for cargo bundling. I specifically inquire whether the carrier could hold all shippers or senders liable despite the existence of separate contracts or to at least have a claim against one shipper or sender for the acts of its co-shippers or co-senders

DOI: 10.4324/9781003450801-5

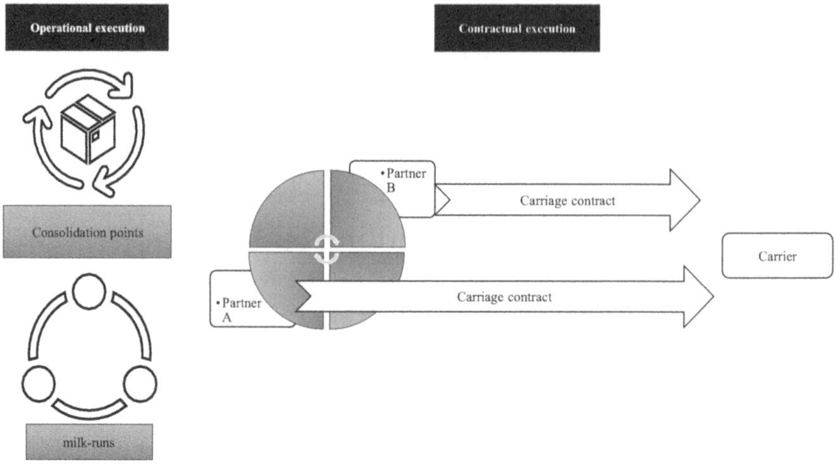

Figure 5.1 The first model of cargo bundling co-operation involves separate carriage contracts that are a result of the co-operation agreement. The operational execution of cargo consolidation can occur either in milk runs or at designated consolidation points

(Sections 3–4). However, because of the importance of the concept of 'principal shipper' or 'principal sender' for the cargo bundling models, this chapter opens by expounding on it (Section 2). The reader should be aware that partners to co-operation agreement for cargo bundling are mainly referred to as co-operating shippers or senders to align the terminology with the legal frameworks that receive special attention in this work. These legal frameworks are the Convention on the Contract for the International Carriage of Goods by Road of 1956 (CMR)[1] and the Hague-Visby Rules (HVR).[2]

1 Convention on the Contract for the International Carriage of Goods by Road (CMR) (adopted 19 May 1956, entered into force 2 July 1961) 399 UNTS 189.

2 The Brussels Convention for the Unification of Certain Rules of Law relating to Bills of Lading (adopted 25 August 1924, entered into force 2 June 1931) Trb. 1953, 109, 004127 and Protocol to Amend the International Convention for the unification of certain rules of law relating to bills of lading, signed at Brussels on 25 August 1924 (adopted 23 February 1968, entered into force 23 June 1977) No. 23643.

2 Principal = contractual

Tying the meaning of 'principal' to contractual relations could be considered the prevalent view in the doctrine.[3] The principal shipper, sender, or consignor does not thus need to be the owner of the goods[4] or the party mentioned in the transport document.[5] Nevertheless, whereas some conventions explicitly define the party that contracts with the carrier, others include no such definition.

The Convention on the Contract for the International Carriage of Goods by Road of 1956 (CMR), the Uniform Rules concerning the Contract of

3 Ingo Koller, *Transportrecht Kommentar* (C.H. Beck 2013) 965, Krzysztof Wesołowski, *Umowa międzynarodowego przewozu drogowego towarów na podstawie CMR* (Wolters Kluwer Polska 2013) 109–110; Simon Baughen, 'The Legal Status of Non-Contracting Shipper' (2000) *The International Journal of Shipping Law* 21, 24; In addition, despite the fact that, under German law, the FOB seller (de *Ablader*) is given certain rights and obligations (e.g. § 513 HGB), it is neither party to the contract of carriage nor bound to the bill of lading conditions. See: Rolf Herber, *Seehandelsrecht Systematische Darstellung* (2nd edn, De Gruyter 2016) 241–243; Marian Paschke, 'HGB § 513 Anspruch auf Ausstellung eines Konnossements' in Hartmut Oetker (ed), *Handelsgesetzbuch* (7th edn, C.H. Beck 2021) No 4–5; Marek Czernis, 'Pojęcie "załadowca" – analiza prawno-porównawcza' in Urszula Jackowiak et al. (eds), *Współczesne Problemy Prawa Księga Pamiątkowa dedykowana Profesorowi Jerzemu Młynarczykowi* (Wyższa Szkoła Administracji i Biznesu im. Eugeniusza Kwiatkowskiego w Gdyni 2011) 199, 204–205, where the author also presents the historical evolution of the understanding of the term 'shipper' under the Polish Maritime Code and the problems that result from accommodation of German and English approaches; See also: Sąd Najwyższy 26.11.2019 IV CSK 415/18, where it was stated that under the CMR the sender is the party that instructs the carrier to transport the goods and undertakes a mutual obligation to pay for the service. Pursuant to Art. 3 of the Convention, the carrier may use a third party (subcontractor). The rule, however, is that the engagement of a third party by the carrier does not lead to the creation of a legal relationship between itself and the sender, and the contract of carriage thus concluded binds only the carrier and the sender. Therefore, the entitled person (consignee) may only claim from the carrier with which the sender concluded the contract.

4 Richard Aikens et al., *Bills of Lading* (2nd edn, Informa 2016) No 3.115; Sąd Rejonowy Szczecin-Centrum w Szczecinie, 07.04. 2016XI GC 1338/15, where the court held that although the CMR does not define the concept of 'sender', there is no doubt that the contractor of the carrier is a sender. The sender does not have to be an owner or to remain in autonomous possession of the goods. Any title to the goods suffices; see also: Sąd Apelacyjny w Krakowie 5.11.2014 I ACa 1097/14. See also: Malcolm Clarke, *International Carriage of Goods by Road: CMR* (5th edn, Informa 2009) 123 where the author underlines that the owner of the goods can sue the carrier subject to assumption that the owner, because of its ownership, concluded a contract of carriage.

5 Sąd Apelacyjny w Szczecinie 5.11.2014 I ACa 19/14 I ACz 23/14; Sąd Najwyższy 03.09.2003 II CKN 415/01; Sąd Apelacyjny w Białymstoku 21.05.2020 I AGa 149/19; see also: *Kala Ltd v. International Freight Services (UK) Ltd* [1998] QBD and *Inco Europe Ltd v. First Choice Distribution* [1999] 1 WLR 270. See also: Sąd Okręgowy w Szczecinie 27.11.2015 VIII Ga 354/15, where the court, drawing on findings from evidentiary proceedings, also denied that the party mentioned on invoices was a party to a contract of carriage. Contrast: Mirosław Stec, *Umowa przewozu w transporcie towarowym* (Kantor Wydawniczy Zakamycze 2005) 119, to whom the fact of appearing on transport documents does automatically trigger the assumption of rights and obligations towards the carrier.

International Carriage of Goods by Rail (COTIF-CIM),[6] the Convention for the Unification of Certain Rules Relating to International Carriage by Air (Montreal Convention),[7] and the Hague-Visby Rules (HVR) are silent on the definition of the party to a carriage contract with a carrier. Nevertheless, it can be inferred from their provisions that the contract is made between carrier and sender[8] in the road carriage, between carrier and consignor[9] in rail and air carriage, and between carrier and shipper[10] in sea carriage. The conventions seem to presuppose that the party that contracts with the carrier also performs other actions, such as those that are related to transport documents or the delivery of the goods to the carrier.

However, in light of the changing market practices, multi-layered cargo interests are a reality. The conventions foresee that the parties to a carriage contract can also use other parties (see Section 4.1.2) to conclude contracts with carriers. This notion is expressed directly in the Budapest Convention on the Contract for the Carriage of Goods by Inland Waterway (CMNI)[11] (Article 1.4 CMNI),[12] but it is also recognised in other conventions.[13] The consequence of attaching the meaning of 'principal' to the contractual position of a shipper or a sender truncates the set of parties that could possibly be considered shippers or senders under the conventions. These can include the seller of the goods but also a freight forwarder or, in the case of sub-carriage, the main carrier. They can also include the recipient if it has instructed the carrier to collect the goods from a specific supplier. For example, in light of the fact that a carriage contract is ancillary to a

6 Uniform Rules concerning the Contract of International Carriage of Goods by Rail (COTIF-CIM) adopted 9 June 1999, entered into force 1 July 2006) [International Carriage by Rail (COTIF) of 9 May 1980, as amended by the Vilnius Protocol of 3 June 1999] CR 24/NOT/Add.5 21.12.2009]

7 Convention for the Unification of Certain Rules Relating to International Carriage by Air (adopted on 28 May 1999, entered into force 4 November 2003) International Civil Aviation Organization Doc 9740.

8 E.g.: Art. 2 and Art. 4 in conjunction with Art. 5 CMR; Similarly: Wesołowski (n 3) 109; Clarke (n 4) 120–121; Marian Hoeks, *Multimodal Transport Law, the Law Applicable to the Multimodal Contract for the Carriage of Goods* (Erasmus University Rotterdam 2009) 36. See also: Sąd Najwyższy 29.10.2008 IV CSK 237/08.

9 E.g. Arts 3.a, 6.3 COTIF-CIM; Arts 6, 39, 18.4 Montreal Convention. Similarly: Hoeks (n 8) 36; Malcolm Clarke, *Contracts of Carriage by Air* (2nd edn, Informa Law 2010) 70.

10 Art. I(a) HVR; Similarly: Aikens et al. (n 4) No 3.108.

11 Budapest Convention on the Contract for the Carriage of Goods by Inland Waterway (CMNI) (adopted 3 October 2000, entered into force on 1 April 2005) CMNI/CONF(99)2/FINAL.

12 Also Art. 1.3 of The United Nations Convention on the Carriage of Goods by Sea (adopted 31 March 1978, entered into force 1 November 1992) 1695 UNTS 4 (Hamburg Rules) and Art. 1.8 of the United Nations Convention on Contracts for the International Carriage of Goods Wholly or Partly by Sea (adopted 11 December 2008) C.N.563.2012 (Rotterdam Rules).

13 For older discussions see e.g.: Christopher M.C. Cashmore, 'Who Are Consignors and Consignees for the Purposes of a Contract of Carriage?' (1990) *Journal of Business Law* 377.

sales contract, a party who hands goods over to a carrier may be deemed to have only been authorised by the principal shipper, sender, or consignor. Such situations may occur in practice in relation to Free on Board (FOB)[14] or Ex Works (EXW)[15] contracts.[16] Thus, the cargo deliverer should not be considered a party to the contract with the carrier by default. This said, these principles would not hold in the case of, among others, Carriage and Insurance Paid (CIP) contracts, under which the seller has to conclude a carriage contract.[17]

3 Legal situation of co-operating shippers and co-operating senders

Under the first model, in which the carrier enters into contracts of carriage with individual shippers or senders that are members of the co-operation, it would benefit the carrier to be able to hold all shippers or senders liable despite the existence of separate contracts or to at least to have a claim against one shipper or sender for the acts of its co-shippers or co-senders (Section 3.1., and Section 3.2.). Furthermore, the co-operating partners may wish to provide exemptions to each other or to limit each other's liability to the carrier, for example, through a *Himalaya* clause and among each other in respect of recourse claims. The carrier instead might try to indemnify itself for all and any claims, losses, damages, fines, or expenses arising or resulting from breach of the shipper's or sender's obligations (Section 3.3.). The analysis touches upon whether the legal position that the carrier wants to have against multiple co-operating shippers or senders as well as shippers' or senders' liability exclusions can be derived from a convention or be decided under national law. The chapter concludes with the observations concerning the operation of the first execution model of cargo bundling as far as shipper or sender right to compensation for damage, shipper or sender liability, and recourse action against the shipper or sender who caused the damage are concerned (Section 4).

14 E.g. *Pyrene v. Scindia Navigation* [1954] 2 QB 402.

15 E.g. Sądu Okręgowego w Łodzi 24.11.2017 X GC 321/14; LG Saarbrücken 27.06.2018 17 HK O 9/16, where it was stated that under the CMR, the term 'sender' covers only those who conclude a contract of carriage with the carrier. When using the Incoterm *ex works*, the seller is not a sender in this sense.

16 For further discussion on the shipper or sender acting on behalf of the consignee, see: Clarke *[on the CMR]* (n 4) 121; Paul M. Bugden and Simone Lamont-Black, *Goods in Transit and Freight Forwarding* (3rd edn, Sweet & Maxwell 2013) 358–359; Frank Stevens, *The Bill of Lading Holder Right and Liabilities* (Routledge 2018) 39–48. For the relation between sender (seller) and receiver (buyer) under Incoterms, see further: Lauri Railas, 'The Identity of a Shipper and Incoterms 2010' (2016) 51(3) *European Transport Law* 239.

17 See e.g.: Sąd Apelacyjny w Szczecinie 23.12.2014 I ACa 461/14.

3.1 Assumption of the liabilities of others

The bilateral carriage contracts concluded by each shipper or sender could include a liability clause that provides that the shipper or sender is responsible for all previous works related to preparation of the goods for carriage, including their packing, loading, and stowing in transport units (see further Chapter 4 on the definition of packing), regardless of the method applied and the identities of the parties that the shippers or senders retain to those ends.[18] This solution is especially important in situations in which a carrier receives a bundled unit of goods that is being sent by different shippers or senders. On that basis, the carrier could try to hold a shipper or sender responsible for omissions that occurred before the goods were passed to the carrier, including the omissions of other co-shippers or co-senders.

3.1.1 Position under the conventions

A liability clause that provides that the shipper or sender is responsible for all previous works related to preparation of the goods for carriage, including their packing, loading, and stowing in transport units, regardless of the method applied and the identities of the parties that the shippers or senders retain to those ends, could be valid under the conventions, which recognise that the shipper or sender may retain other parties to discharge its obligations on different legal bases (apparent shipper or sender), for two reasons. Firstly, the apparent shipper or sender might appear on the transport documents without being a contracting party. Although the name of the sender or shipper is indicated on the transport documents (Article 6.1(b) CMR, Article III, Rule 3 HVR), such indications do not generate rights and obligations towards the carrier automatically.[19] That is so because of the evidentiary nature of transport documents.[20] The evidential effect of transport documents may require a person who appears in documents to be treated as the person who actually

18 See e.g.: Cl. 10 DHL Terms & Conditions: '[. . .] the Shipment was prepared in secure premises by reliable persons and was protected against unauthorized interference during preparation, storage and any transportation [. . .]' DHL, 'Terms & Conditions. DHL Express' <https://bit.ly/30g0n2w>; Cl. 5 Express Service DPD: 'The Customer is exclusively responsible for Parcel packaging, labelling and documentation as it concerns inner and outer packaging [. . .]' DPD, 'GTC Classic/Express Service DPD (Nederland) B.V.' <https://bit.ly/3Ha5dze> all accessed 18 August 2023.

19 Affirming: Sąd Najwyższy, 03.09.2003 II CKN 415/01, where the court held that a person who is not a party to the contract of carriage cannot be considered as the sender of the parcel only because it was described as a sender in the consignment note. Obversely, that the plaintiff had not been included in the consignment note as a sender did not mean that it could not be considered one. According to Arts. 4 and 9 CMR, the consignment note serves as evidence of the contract of carriage. This presumption can, however, be rebutted. This is what happened in this case, where the plaintiff challenged the consignment note by drawing on the written contract of carriage. Contrast: Stec (n 5) 119. See also Section 3.2.1.2 on the Rotterdam Rules and documentary shipper.

20 Clarke (n 4) 121.

consigns the goods and not as the contracting shipper or sender.[21] Secondly, the transport conventions recognise that the principal shipper or sender may retain other parties. I will present now how the retainment of other parties operates under various transport conventions. The HVR mentions agents and representatives as acting on behalf of the shipper (Article IV.2(i) and Article IV.3 HVR). The CMR refers broadly to persons acting on behalf of the sender (Article 17.4(c) CMR). The CMNI avers to persons of whose services the shipper makes use to perform tasks and meet obligations when such persons act within the scope of their employment (Article 8.2 CMNI). The COTIF-CIM mentions agents in the context of customs duties (Article 15.4 COTIF-CIM) and the Montreal Convention mentions servants and agents (Article 18.2(b) Montreal Convention). Therefore, the transport conventions could be read as providing a broad definition of a person whom the shipper or sender can retain.[22] This understanding seems to find support in the United Nations Convention on Contracts for the International Carriage of Goods Wholly or Partly by Sea of 2008 (Rotterdam Rules, RR)[23] which provides that the shipper is liable for the acts or omissions of any person, including an employee, an agent, or a subcontractor, to whom it has entrusted the performance of any of its obligations (Article 34 RR). The impact of these provisions is that the shipper or sender is liable for the acts of the persons who perform any of its obligations or act on its behalf.

3.1.2 Position under national laws

Even if a judge concludes that conventions cannot be read as providing a broad definition of a person whom the shipper or sender can retain,[24] and that the issues that are related to co-operation agreement for cargo bundling are not governed by them,[25] a clause that provides that the shipper or sender is responsible for all previous works related to preparation of the goods for carriage could also be valid as a matter of national laws.

21 Clarke (n 4); Aikens et al. (n 4) No 7.74–7.82.

22 For the same conclusion on the agents and servants of the carrier under the CMR, see: Clarke (n 9) 125; Andrew Messent and David A. Glass, *Hill & Messent CMR: Contracts for the International Carriage of Goods by Road* (3rd edn, LLP 2000) 63–65; See also: Sąd Okręgowy w Poznaniu 12.04.2019 XII C 2611/14, where the court shared the view that the phrase 'persons acting within the scope of their employment' in Art. 3 CMR should be understood broadly and without reference to national concepts.

23 United Nations Convention on Contracts for the International Carriage of Goods Wholly or Partly by Sea A/RES/63/122 3 November 2008.

24 The Note from the Netherlands Government on the liability of the carrier TRANS/WP9/16 22.12.1950 (CMR *travaux préparatoires*) which stresses the relevance of carrier's liability for damage occurring during transport could support the argument that the intention of the convention drafters was to focus mainly on carrier's liability, including its responsibility for the acts and omissions of his agents and servants and of any other persons of whose services he makes use for the performance of the carriage.

25 See further Chapter 7 on the classification of co-operation agreements.

The first possibility supporting the validity of the mentioned clause in the context of co-operating partners is provided under some rules concerning the liability for others' acts (474 KC,[26] § 278 BGB).[27] In such a case a shipper or sender would be liable, as for its own actions or omissions, for the actions and omissions of the co-partners with whose help it fulfils the obligation, as well as the persons to whom he entrusts the performance of the obligation. Hence, although the carrier will only be able to sue each co-operating shipper or sender separately,[28] the risk for insufficient packing and preparation of bundled cargo for transport will switch to the co-operating shippers or senders because each partner that has its goods in a joint loading unit might be considered helping others in the preparation of their goods for transport. This argument could also be invoked in a milk run situation. Although milk runs imply loading and packing of separate goods, the carrier might try to argue that the obligations to prepare the goods for carriage include schedules of picking the goods that are required by the co-operating partners and that failures to provide the goods on time for transport and resulting delays are within the risk of partners.[29]

The second possibility supporting the validity of the mentioned clause in the context of co-operating partners is provided by the agency laws. The arguments that follow focus on the practical implications resulting from the common law and civil law agency doctrines, leaving aside the *per se* comparison of different concepts.[30] The application of agency laws could result in making the analysed model of co-operation similar to the model of co-operation that is discussed in Chapter 6. Several co-partners to co-operation could turn out parties to a contract with a carrier. In consequence, the clause stating that shipper or sender is responsible for all previous works related to preparation of the goods for carriage would be applicable to all co-partners acting as co-principals.

The co-operating partners could be perceived as representing one another if they opt for a legal structure that provides for such representation, such as a

26 Ustawa z dnia 23 kwietnia 1964 r. – Kodeks cywilny Dz.U. 1964 nr 16 poz. 93 (with further changes) (Kodeks Cywilny, KC).

27 Bürgerliches Gesetzbuch in der Fassung der Bekanntmachung vom 2. Januar 2002 (BGBl. I S. 42, 2909; 2003 I S. 738) (with further changes) (BGB).

28 For Germany: § 164 BGB, which provides for a general principle that, in case of doubt, it can be assumed that a party acted for itself. For the UK: there might be a presumption that a party acts as principal unless the contrary is proven, see e.g,: *Magellan Spirit ApS v Vitol SA* (The Magellan Spirit) [2016] EWHC 454 (Comm). For Poland, see e.g.: Sąd Rejonowy Szczecin-Centrum w Szczecinie, 07.04. 2016 XI GC 1338/15, where it was acknowledged that the owner of the transported goods may use the aid of other entities when contracting for the carriage of goods. If it uses the services of a forwarder, which in concluding a contract of carriage acts in its own name vis-à-vis the carrier, the forwarder is the party to the contract of carriage. Accordingly, the forwarder acquires the status of a sender. See also: Sąd Najwyższy 03.09.2003 II CKN 415/01 (OSNC 2004/10/163).

29 This argument will likely fail if the carrier accepts the goods and the CMR applies. See further: Chapter 8 Section 4 on the liability for the wrong organisation of bundling co-operation, and Chapter 3 on risk passing and application of the transport conventions.

30 For comparative analysis of agency laws see e.g. Danny Busch et al. (eds), *Agency Law in Commercial Practice* (Oxford University Press 2016).

Polish or German partnership contract (Article 860 KC, §705 BGB) or English partnership (Partnership Act 1890). The action of one partner effects in consequences for other partners, and relatedly the carrier would be able to sue any co-operating partners regardless of whether the collection of goods happens in milk runs or at the consolidation point. The agent's authority could also be implied[31] into the relationship of co-operating partners based on the fact that a contracting co-partner could be compared to a forwarding agent who organizes transport of goods in the name of its clients (Article 794 KC *et seq.*, § 453 HGB[32] *et seq.*).[33] It could be further argued that each of the bilateral contracts of carriage was concluded by one partner to co-operation in cargo bundling who entered into that contract as principal in respect of its interest and also as agent on the co-partners' accounts, making the latter, in fact, parties to that contract. The legal action that the partner performs as an agent would thus have legal effects directly in the sphere of the co-partners (Article 95§2 KC, § 164.1 BGB).[34] The carrier would accordingly enjoy all rights that derive from the carriage contract vis-à-vis the principal co-senders or co-shippers, and vice versa. A similar observation could also concern the legal situation of a consolidation point and a Transport Orchestrator, which is an intermediary that organizes shipper or sender co-operation.[35] When they conclude the carriage contract in the name of the principal shipper or sender, the latter is considered a party to it.[36]

31 For Germany: When it is clear from the circumstances that the agent concluded the carriage contract on behalf of the principal shipper or sender, the latter is considered a party to it. See: Peter Bydlinski, 'HGB § 453 Speditionsvertrag' in Rolf Herber and Christine Schmidt (eds), *Münchener Kommentar zum HGB bd.7* (4th edn, C.H. Beck 2020) No 124–125. For English law: *A/S Dan Bunkering Ltd v FG Hawkes (Western) Ltd* [2009] EWHC 3141 (Comm); *MVV Environment Devonport Ltd v NTO Shipping GmbH & Co. KG MS 'Nortrader MV Nortrader* [2020] EWHC 1371 (Comm), where a shipping agency did not have express or implied actual or ostensible authority to enter into a contract of carriage on behalf of a shipper. For Polish law: Art. 796 KC in conjunction with art 734 § 2 KC, see further: Paweł Mazur, 'Art. 794 KC' in Konrad Osajda and Witold Borysiak (eds), *Kodeks cywilny. Komentarz* (29th edn, Legalis C.H. Beck 2021) No 27, and Sąd Apelacyjny w Warszawie 12.11.2014 VI ACa 89/14.

32 Handelsgesetzbuch vom 10. Mai 1897 (RGBl. S. 219) BGBl. III/FNA 4100–1 (with further changes) (HGB).

33 In England freight forwarders are subject to general agency law. See further e.g.: David A. Glass, *Freight Forwarding and Multimodal Transport Contracts* (Informa 2012) No 2.124 *et seq.*

34 For English law, see e.g.: Bugden and Lamont-Black (n 16) 43; *J. Y. A. Lamaignere v Selene Shipping Agencies Ltd* [1982] C.L.R. 227.

35 The problem of legal classification of consolidation points and other actors engaged in the cargo bundling co-operation is discussed in Chapter 8.

36 In the English law context, the scope of agent's liability to the exclusion of that of the principal shipper or sender is to be determined by the construction of the contract and the relevant and admissible facts. See e.g.: *Filatona Trading Ltd v Navigator Equities Ltd (Danilina v Chernukhin)* [2020] EWCA Civ 109, where the court held that the disclosed principal of a signatory to an agreement was not excluded from exercising contractual rights under that agreement when there were no clear and unambiguous words or indications of a common intention to exclude him, and *Bell v Ivy Technology Ltd* [2020] EWCA Civ 1563, where the court found that to exclude the liability of a disclosed principal under the contract, the terms of the contract would need to exclude liability arising by virtue of a party being the principal of a party who had entered into the contract as its agent.

3.1.3 Evaluation

The legal uncertainty in holding one shipper or sender liable for the acts of its co-shippers or co-senders operates at two levels. Firstly, although it is possible to argue for the shipper's or the sender's assumption of liability of others under the transport conventions, a national judge, in the exercise of their discretion, might not apply the a broad definition of a person whom the shipper or sender can retain. Secondly, and relatedly, if the judge decides to supplement the convention rules with national law, another uncertainty occurs – the outcome of a case might vary as far as the number of parties that can be sued by the carrier is concerned. However, it might be that the carrier suing all co-shippers or co-senders under a contract of carriage would, in fact, not be unexpected from the co-operation partners. The questionnaire conducted among European producing and distributing companies revealed, for example, that responsibility of all partners for daily management of co-operation could be a preferred form of management (Figure 5.2).

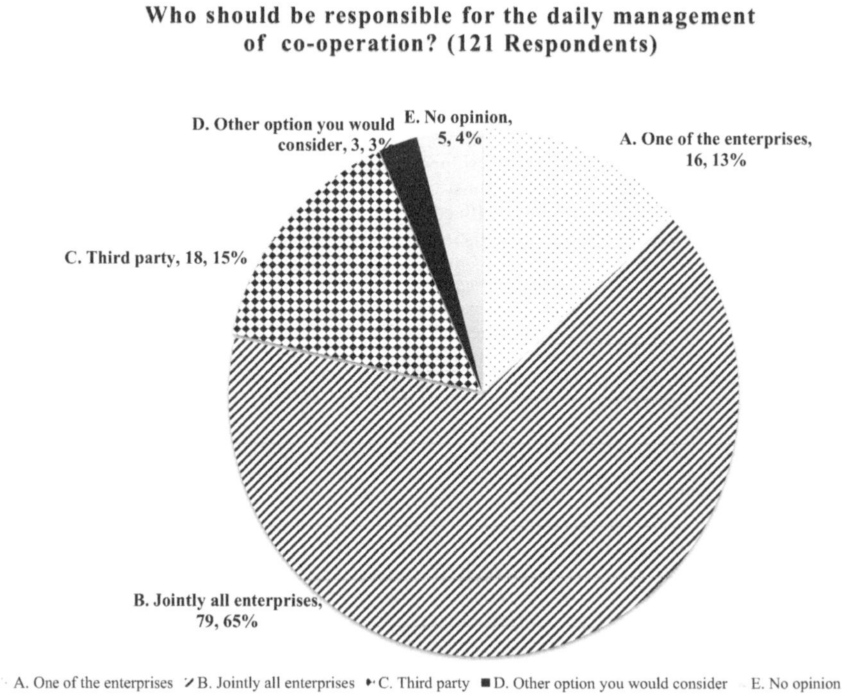

Figure 5.2 Preferences concerning responsibility for the daily management of co-operation for cargo bundling

3.2 Assumption of liability with others

In the context of the HVR, Stephen Girvin has argued that since there is no definition of the term 'shipper', it refers to all persons who may be the shippers of the goods.[37] It seems that Girvin meant that the term 'shipper' refers to the set of actors who can be bound contractually to the carrier, including a voyage or time charterer and the seller or buyer of the goods as per the underlying contract of sale. Nevertheless, this understanding of the term 'shipper' could also imply extending the shipper's obligations and its liability to third parties. Lauri Railas has argued in favour of the joint and several liability of multiple cargo interests on the side of the shipper.[38] Similar considerations could also could also be considered for the CMR. In fact, merchant clauses also attempt to impose joint and several liability on various cargo interests contractually.[39] If these clauses are valid under the conventions, the carrier could claim against any shipper or sender, regardless of the contractual relations between the parties. The multiple shippers or senders, in their capacity as principals and having entered into separate contracts with a carrier, would thus be substitutes for each other and bear concurrent liability. Next, I investigate arguments in favour (Section 3.2.2) and against joint liability (3.2.1.) of co-operating shippers or senders.

3.2.1 Independent position

The arguments against the assumption of liability with others primarily concern contractual privity and its importance under the transport conventions. However, it is noticeable from the Rotterdam Rules that statute can extend some rights and obligations to other parties that represent cargo interests. This possibility, however, does not mean that all rights and obligations are extended through the original contractual relation with a principal shipper or sender.

37 Stephen Girvin, *Carriage of Goods by Sea* (2nd edn, Oxford University Press 2011) 18, 262.

38 Lauri Railas, 'The Identity of a Shipper and Incoterms 2010' (2016) 51(3) *European Transport Law* 255.

39 E.g. Hapag-Lloyd's terms and conditions: 'Clause 1: "Merchant" includes the shipper, holder, consignee, receiver of the goods or of this B/L, and any person owning or entitled to the possession of the goods or this B/L'.; 'Clause 12: All of the persons coming within the definition of Merchant in Clause 1 shall be jointly and severally liable to the Carrier for the fulfilment of all obligations and warranties undertaken by the Merchant either in this Bill of Lading, or required by law and remain so liable throughout the transportation notwithstanding their having transferred this Bill of Lading and/or title to the Goods to another party'. Hapag-Lloyd's, 'Bills of Lading. Terms & Conditions' <https://bit.ly/3EjgtHg>, accessed 10 August 2023.

3.2.1.1 Importance of contract

Three arguments against general joint liability clauses could be made. Firstly, extending liability to shippers or senders outside of a particular contract with a carrier would not be in accordance with the purpose of the conventions, which have the contractual rights and obligation of the parties at their core.[40] The independent co-shippers or senders might, in fact, be neither involved in the handling of the goods of the other shippers or senders (as in the case of milk runs) nor engaged in the handling of transport documents. Therefore, the broad understanding of the term 'shipper' or 'sender' proposed earlier could, in fact, have the anomalous result of imposing liability and granting rights to cargo interests that have no contractual or factual involvement in the shipment of the goods. Secondly, extending liability would also contradict some of the provisions of the conventions. The HVR prohibit shipper liability for damage sustained by the carrier without the fault of the former (Article IV, Rule 3 HVR). Thirdly, since the drafters of the HVR did not foresee extending contractual rights and liabilities to cargo interests that are related to a shipper (apart from a consignee), it is even more difficult to extend them to parties that are not related to the performance of a specific contract or involved in the carriage of particular goods. In addition, during the *travaux preparatoires* of the HVR, it was noticed that a shipper may be difficult to reach. Thus, it was proposed that the particulars of the goods should be guaranteed at the time of shipment by the shipper or the charterer.[41] The proposal implied extending some obligations to persons other than the contractual shipper. Eventually, no obligations were ascribed to the apparent shipper, nor were the obligations of the contractual shipper extended to the other cargo interests on its side.[42] As a result, if the cargo interests conclude carriage contracts *qua* principals, the conventions apply to each contract separately.[43] Likewise, under the CMR, a general merchant clause could be invalid (e.g. in relation to Article 12, Article 14, Article 15, and Article 16 CMR, which refer to the execution of a contract and the right of disposal) when the contractual sender's rights and liabilities are transferred to a third-party cargo interest, that is, outside of a specific sender-carrier contractual relation.[44]

---

40 See also e.g.: Note from the Netherlands Government on the liability of the carrier TRANS/WP9/16 22.12.1950 p. 2, which stresses the relevance of contractual relations.

41 *The Travaux Preparatoires of the Hague Rules and of the Hague Visby Rules* (Comite Maritime International (CMI) 265.

42 Cf. Art. 1.3. The United Nations Convention on the Carriage of Goods by Sea 1978 (Hamburg Rules).

43 Cf. *Cho Yang Shipping Co. Ltd. V Coral (UK) Ltd.* [1997] 2 Lloyd's Rep. 641, where all the intermediaries in the chain of carriage contracts were found to have contracted as principals, and it was thus not possible for the shipowner to claim against the original shipper of the goods, who was not liable for the payment of freight.

44 Similarly: Carsten Vyvers, "Zum Begriff des Absenders" im internationalen Straßengüterverkehr' (2019) 2 *Neue Zeitschrift für Verherrecht* 101, where he further clarifies that, in view of the exclusionary effect of the CMR, the EXW seller cannot rely on national law on a subsidiary basis to establish its active legitimation.

3.2.1.2 Rotterdam Rules: Documentary shipper

Under the Rotterdam Rules, the carrier is free to make some claims against the shipper or the documentary shipper. Whereas a 'shipper' is defined as a person who enters into a contract of carriage with a carrier, a 'documentary shipper' is a person other than the shipper who agrees to be named as 'shipper' in the transport document or electronic transport record.[45] If a co-shipper whose name is on the transport document is also a contractual shipper, it will neither acquire double status nor qualify as a documentary shipper.

The situation of a documentary shipper is governed by a uniform liability regime because it is subject to some obligations and liabilities that are imposed on the shipper and because it is entitled to shipper rights and defences.[46] The limitation of the documentary shipper's obligations means that, for instance, the carrier cannot make a claim for freight payment against the documentary shipper.[47] The obligations and liabilities of the documentary shipper are thus not substitutes for those of the shipper.[48] Some uncertainty could, however, manifest in respect of joint liability. A view was expressed in the *travaux preparatoires* of the Rotterdam Rules to the effect that there was no intention to create joint and several liability as between shipper and documentary shipper.[49] Johan Schelin[50] is of the view that Article 33.2 of the Rotterdam Rules, which concerns assumption of shipper's rights and obligations by the documentary shipper, does not stipulate joint liability as between shipper and documentary shipper and that this state of affairs is a consequence of the separateness of their obligations. Filippo Lorenzon,[51] conversely, seems to treat Article 33.2 of the Rotterdam Rules as an indication of joint liability. The differences in interpretation could result in differences in liability. Suppose that the shipper has instructed the documentary shipper to submit certain instructions to the

---

45 The same is true of Arts. 1.8 and 1.9 of the Rotterdam Rules.

46 Art. 33 Rotterdam Rules. A documentary shipper is only subject to the obligation and liability imposed on the shipper pursuant to Chapter 7 and Article 55, and it is entitled to the shipper's rights and defences provided by Chapters 7 and 13.

47 The shipper's obligation to pay freight is outside the scope of the Rotterdam Rules and is left to the applicable national law. On the issue of regulating the duty to pay freight under the Rotterdam Rules, see: Frank Stevens, 'Duties of Shippers and Dangerous Cargo' in Rhidian Thomas (ed), *The Carriage of Goods By Sea Under the Rotterdam Rules* (Informa 2014) par.11.4–11.12.

48 Tomotaka Fujita, 'Chapter 8 Obligations and Liabilities of the Shipper' in Meltem Deniz Güner-Özbek (ed), *The United Nations Convention on Contracts for the International Carriage of Goods Wholly or Partly by Sea. An Appraisal of the "Rotterdam Rules"* (Springer 2011) 226–227.

49 41st Session of UNCITRAL (A/63/17) UNCITRAL, 'Consolidated Official Reports on the Preparation of the United Nations Convention on Contracts for the International Carriage of Goods Wholly or Partly by Sea ("The Rotterdam Rules")' p. 346 <https://cutt.ly/owcMccnG> accessed 10 August 2023.

50 Johan Schelin, 'Obligations of the Shipper to the Carrier' in Alexander von Ziegler et al. (eds), *The Rotterdam Rules 2008: Commentary to the United Nations Convention on Contracts for the International Carriage of Goods Wholly or Partly by Sea* (Wolters Kluwer 2010) 158–159.

51 Filippo Lorenzon, 'Obligations of the Shipper to the Carrier' in Yvonne Baatz et al. (eds), *The Rotterdam Rules: A Practical Annotation* (Informa Law 2009) 94–96.

carrier, and the documentary shipper fails to do so. In the case of joint liability, its failure would mean that the shipper is also automatically liable for the omission. The different approaches to these provisions suggest that the legal position of multiple cargo interests might be unpredictable.

3.2.2 Joint liability

It is possible to derive certain arguments against the individual position of the cargo interests from the conventions, especially when the individual contracts with the carrier result from a pre-existing co-operation agreement. The literature calls such contractual structures 'independent linked contracts' or 'network contracts'. Under these arrangements, autonomous contracts are linked by a global purpose that is reflected further in their individual objectives.[52] In my opinion, such structures can be captured by treating the references to a contract in the conventions as being of a functional or an evolutionary character. Considering a contract in this way would prevent business partners from creating complicated contractual chains to minimize liability risks.

Treating contract as a functional concept would mean that a contract is understood autonomously, without reference to national formulations. It would be a shift from the current formalistic approach to a flexible functional one, whereby the focus would be on the function of a contract or a group of contracts reflected in how they contribute to the movement of goods from A to B point. Alternatively, a contract could be seen as an evolutionary concept.[53] A concept can be considered evolutionary if it is very general in nature or if it is expressed in terms so general that changing circumstances, including economic realities (see Chapter 2), must be accounted for in its interpretation. Thus, the references to a contract (or, to be precise, the performance of an obligation under the conventions) could be approached not only from the perspective of bilateral contracting but also from that of multilateral contracting (see Chapter 6), long-term contracting (see Chapter 7) and network contracting, whereby the network contract includes a contract of carriage. Contract, as a functional or evolutionary concept, would still need to fit the risk management framework established by the conventions.

Networks such as the one discussed here, under which two parties have a contract and a third party performs an obligation thereunder are, in fact, already recognised by the transport conventions to a certain extent. For example, the carrier's defences and liability limitations operate to the benefit of the parties that it uses for the performance of its obligations, which have

52 E.g.: Rodrigo Momberg Uribe, 'Linked Contracts: Elements for a General Regulation' in Ilse Samoy and Marco B.M. Loos (eds), *Linked Contracts* (Intersentia 2012) 159–160; Hugh Collins, 'Introduction to Networks as Connected Contracts' in Gunther Teubner (ed), *Network as Connected Contracts* (Michelle Everson tr., Hart Publishing 2011).

53 These arguments may not hold for the HVR because of the necessity of the Bill of Lading. See further: Chapter 7.

no contractual link with the shipper or sender (Article IV', Rule 2 HVR, Article 28.2 CMR). In addition, under the CMR, the provisions that pertain to carriage by successive carriers (Articles 34–40 CMR) also regulate liability for the performance of the same (carriage) operation. Recognition of the carrier's liability for organizational errors that result in damage, loss, or late delivery under the CMR could be another example (see Chapter 8). Since the CMR has the sender liable for insufficient packing, organisational errors that result in insufficient packing which causes damage to a carrier could be analysed in a similar manner. The shippers or senders would therefore be responsible individually, under their own contracts of carriage, except for the shared obligation, for which they would bear joint liability to the carrier.

In my opinion, there could be room for shipper or sender network contracts under the transport conventions. The carrier liability scheme of standardised international law is expected to operate in the same manner irrespective of the economic structures that are chosen by the shippers. The HVR forbids only clauses that relieve the carrier from liability for loss of or damage to, or in connection with, the goods (Article III, Rule 8 HVR).[54] Therefore, a merchant clause that involves several cargo interest on the side of the shipper might be found not to shift liability for carrier negligence away from the carrier but only to extend the shipper's liability to other parties contractually.[55] The CMR instead invalidates any stipulation which would directly or indirectly derogate from the provisions of the convention (Article 41 CMR). Thus, an increase in the sender's liability would be invalid.[56] This proposition would apply to typical groupage service, where the carrier contracts with each sender individually, and there are no economic or contractual links between the senders. However, a merchant clause that involves several cargo interests on the side of a shipper or sender who has previously agreed to share some of the obligations (e.g. through a co-operation agreement) or who has actually performed such obligations (e.g. packing) need not derogate from the conventions.

In the absence of any published case law on the matter and the general hesitance to recognise a network contract as a legal concept doctrinally,[57] a judge might find that there is an internal or external gap in respect of the third-party shipper's participation in the performance of an obligation or concerning that

54 Cf. Art. 79 (2) Rotterdam Rules, which explicitly renders terms that extend the obligations of the shippers (and those of other cargo interests) void.

55 This effect of a merchant clause has been also recognised in some judgements on the shipper-consignee relation under the US COGSA. See further: Richard L. Kilpatrick Jr, 'The Joint and Several Liability of Merchants under Maritime Bills of Lading' (2016) 47(4) *Journal of Maritime Law and Commerce* 411.

56 Cf. Art. 23 The United Nations Convention on the Carriage of Goods by Sea 1978 (Hamburg Rules), which also prohibits any clause which directly or indirectly derogates from the convention.

57 Catherine Mitchell, 'Network Commercial Relationships: What Role for Contract Law?' in Roger Brownsword et al. (eds), *Contract and Regulation A Handbook on New Methods of Law Making in Private Law* (Edward Elgar 2017).

a carrier may claim under the shippers or senders' co-operation agreement. The judge may thus have recourse to national law. For example, under English law, to decide on the validity of a clause, the judge considers the facts or circumstances that were known to both parties when the contract was made. The judge is also unlikely to depart from the natural meaning of a term simply because it seems imprudent for a party to have agreed to it.[58] When bilateral contracts are concluded with a carrier on the basis of a framework agreement, it might be difficult for the shipper or sender to deny having assumed joint liability for shared obligations.[59] Such clauses could, however, also be limited by the rules on third-party rights, which in all three jurisdictions consider contracts that impose detriments on third parties ineffective.[60] In addition, in the jurisdictions under observation, judges can investigate the validity of merchant clauses by reference to, among others, agency relations (Germany, Poland, England; see further Section 3.1.2), unfair contract terms (Germany, Poland, England), the possible agreement of other cargo interests to share the debt (Germany, Poland), rules on contracts in favour of third parties and the possibility of establishing a claim in favour of a carrier (Germany, Poland, England), implied contracts (England, Germany), and the indivisibility of obligations (Poland, Germany; see further Chapter 6).[61] Thus, joint liability clauses are not automatically valid.

58 *Arnold v Britton* [2015] UKSC 36.

59 Cf. *Midlothian Council v Bracewell Stirling Architects* [2018] CSIH 21 on the scope of liability under the framework agreement.

60 Małgorzata Bednarek et al., *Umowy odnoszące się do osób trzecich* (Legalis C.H. Beck 2005) §1.I; Martin Fries and Reiner Schulze, 'BGB § 328 Vertrag zugunsten Dritter' in Reiner Schulze (ed), *Bürgerliches Gesetzbuch* (11th edn, C.H. Beck 2021) 5; H.G. Beale (ed), *Chitty on Contracts* (31st eds, Sweet & Maxwell 2012) vol I, No 18–134.

61 For Germany, see further: Dieter Rabe, 'HGB § 521 Ablieferung gegen Rückgabe des Konnossements' in Dieter Rabe and Kay Uwe Bahnsen (eds), *Seehandelsrecht: fünftes Buch des Handelsgesetzbuches mit Nebenvorschriften und Internationalen Übereinkommen* (5th edn, C.H. Beck 2018) No: 14 and the case law mentioned therein; Stefan Grundmann, 'Contractual Networks in German Private Law' in Fabrizio Cafaggi (ed), *Contractual Networks, Inter-Firm Cooperation and Economic Growth* (Edward Elgar 2011) 111 and the special focus on § 328.2 BGB (contract in favour of third parties inferred from the circumstances, in particular from the purpose of the contract) and § 311.3 BGB (debt relation arising from a high level of trust). For England, see further: *Cho Yang Shipping Co. Ltd. V Coral (UK) Ltd.* [1997] 2 Lloyd's Rep. 641 and Simon Baughen's observations on the case in: Baughen (n 3) 26–27, where he implies that the joint liability of the original shipper could be triggered if foreseen in the contract with the carrier or the shipowners, see also: Edwin Peel and Guenter H. Treitel, *Treitel's Law of Contract* (Sweet and Maxwell 2015) No 14–072; Simon Whittaker, 'Contract Networks, Freedom of Contract and the Restructuring of Privity of Contract' in Frabrizio Cafaggi (ed), *Contractual Networks, Inter-Firm Cooperation and Economic Growth* (Edward Elgar 2011) 163. For Poland, see further: Sąd Apelacyjny w Szczecinie 5.11.2014 I ACa 19/14 I ACz 23/14, Mateusz Grochowski, '§11.5. Pośrednictwo sieciowe' in Mirosław Stec (ed), *Prawo umów handlowych System Prawa Handlowego tom 5b* (1st edn, Legalis C.H. Beck 2020); Piotr Machnikowski, 'Rozdział VI. Treść umowy §33. Umowy związane (związki umów)' in Konrad Osajda (ed), *Prawo zobowiązań – część ogólna System Prawa Prywatnego t.5* (3rd edn, Legalis C.H. Beck 2020) 645, who underlines the special function of Art. 56 KC, which is the basis for linking contracts to reflect a trade custom.

3.2.3 Evaluation

In the absence of published case law, co-operating shippers or senders cannot predict which approach a judge would adopt to resolve a dispute. Nevertheless, although there are two approaches to the situation of contractually independent co-shippers or senders, the notion that they enjoy independent status is more likely to prevail, for two reasons. The first is the importance of the privity doctrine in contemporary contract law. The second is that any exception to the rule of privity is considered to be the result of agreement or statute. If these are not present, the contractual chain is highly likely to be treated as a chain of independent bilateral contracts.

3.3 Liability for the same damage

The limitations of contract law, particularly those that result from the privity doctrine and the impossibility of concluding contracts to the detriment of third parties, can force the carrier to have engaged the extracontractual liability of the shippers or senders. Shippers or senders that have independent contracts with a carrier might still be jointly responsible if their conduct contributes to the same damage. Although in principle they act independently of each other or they bear independent responsibility for different sources of danger, they are cumulatively liable where the same damage is attributable to each. Shippers or senders might be held solidarily (§ 840 BGB, 441 KC) or jointly and severally liable (Section 1(1) Civil Liability (Contribution) Act 1978).[62] In the context of the cargo bundling models, liability could also extend to company directors or board members.[63] In addition, in Poland, if the damage is the result of different legal relations that link the carrier with each shipper or sender (e.g. tort and contract or two independent contracts), if there are no grounds for assuming solidarity on the part of the shippers, and if the divisibility of performance prevents the application of the rules on indivisible obligations, the shippers or senders could be liable *in solidum*.[64] Liability *in solidum* will, *per analogia*, trigger the application of the rules on solidarity.[65]

---

62 Beale (n 60) No 17–004, 17–029–17–030.

63 See further: Michael Jones et al., *Clerk & Lindsell on Torts* (23rd edn, Sweet & Maxwell 2017) No 4–04. Solidary liability would also apply to the board members of a limited liability company in the event of execution against the company being ineffective (Article 299 Ustawa z dnia 15 września 2000 r. Kodeks spółek handlowych Dz.U. 2000 nr 94 poz. 1037 with further changes).

64 Cf. Janusz Strzępka, 'Rozdział 13. Umowy w zakresie inwestycji budowlanych' in Mirosław Stec (ed), *Prawo umów handlowych System Prawa Handlowego tom 5* (5th edn, Legalis C.H. Beck 2017) No 802–803, where the author analyses related construction contracts. See further e.g.: Małgorzata Pyziak-Szafnicka, 'Rozdział IV. Wielość dłużników i wierzycieli' in Konrad Osajda (ed), *Prawo zobowiązań – część ogólna. System Prawa Prywatnego t. 5* (Legalis C.H. Beck 2020).

65 Pyziak-Szafnicka (n 64) No 158.

Extracontractual claims require the carrier to prove sufficient causation between the actions of the shipper or sender and a single occurrence of damage.[66] The damage for which one shipper or sender is liable to a carrier must correspond, at least in part, to the damage for which the second shipper or sender is liable. As a result, this mechanism would not operate in every case of damage that a carrier suffers due to insufficient packing. For example, instances in which the insufficient packing of the goods sent by the Shipper A (or Sender A) damages the carrier's vehicle and the insufficient packing of goods sent by Shipper B (or Sender B) results in expenses that the carrier must pay to Shipper C (or Sender C) would not be an instance of a single occurrence of damage. However, if the insufficient packing of the goods sent by Shipper A (or Sender A) and Shipper B (or Sender B) results in expenses that the carrier must pay to Shipper C (or Sender C), Shipper A and Shipper B (or Sender A and Sender B) may be said to have contributed to the same damage. In case of liability *in solidum*, it would be necessary to establish the basis of liability in relation to each shipper or sender, and the conditions might vary depending on whether the individual relation is based on contract or tort. In conclusion, each solidarily or jointly and severally liable shipper or sender would be liable to the carrier for the whole damage. The obvious advantage of this solution for the carrier, however, is limited by the more onerous evidentiary burden.

The form of internal relation between the co-shippers or co-senders can be established in the co-operation agreement. Issues such as legal classification of co-operation agreement, validity, and its relation to executory contracts are discussed in Chapter 7. The importance of a valid co-operation agreement is particularly significant for the regime under which a shipper or sender can be compensated by another shipper or sender for damage to goods. However, internal limitation or exclusion clauses included only in the co-operation agreement do not bind the carrier (cf. Section 3.4.2). Such clauses can be seen as imposing detriment on the carrier and thus be ineffective.[67] If there are no contractual arrangements concerning internal recourse actions, the matter would need to be resolved extra-contractually. Under English and Polish law, the co-shippers or co-senders are liable to the extent of their contribution to the damage in question (s. 2(1) Civil Liability (Contribution) Act 1978, Article 441.2 and Article 441.3 KC). Under German law, the shippers or senders are liable in equal shares unless it is possible to apportion their contributions otherwise (§ 426.1 BGB).

66 Witold Borysiak, 'Art. 441 KC' in Konrad Osajda and Witold Borysiak (eds), *Kodeks cywilny. Komentarz* (29th edn, Legalis C.H. Beck 2021) No 13; Gerhard Wagner, 'BGB § 830 Mittäter und Beteiligte' in Mathias Habersack (ed), *Münchener Kommentar zum BGB bd.7* (8th edn, C.H, Beck 2020) No 6, where an alternative approach, that is, the rule of attribution from § 830 BGB, is presented; Jones et al. (n 63) No 4-03–4-04.

67 See further e.g.: Gerhard Wagner, 'BGB § 840 Haftung mehrerer' in Mathias Habersack (ed), *Münchener Kommentar zum BGB bd.7* (8th edn, C.H. Beck 2020) No 34–35; Michał Chajda, 'Art. 441 KC' in Mariusz Załucki (ed), *Kodeks cywilny. Komentarz* (2nd edn, Legalis C.H. Beck 2020). See also (n 59).

3.4 Exclusion clauses

The liability of the parties that are involved in cargo bundling could be affected by indemnification clauses and clauses that create rights for third parties. Indemnification clauses protect one party to the contract from liability if a third party is harmed.[68] Clauses that create rights for third parties, such as *Himalaya* clauses, allow them to enjoy benefits under the terms of a contract, such as liability limitations. Such clauses could be introduced to the relationship between shippers or senders and to that between carrier and shippers or senders. While for the carrier, it is important to be indemnified for damage to third-party cargo interests, the shippers or senders might prefer to include exclusion clauses that benefit co-shippers or co-senders which have separate contracts of carriage. Although such clauses are largely not governed by the conventions and free contracting is possible, the conventions do limit the parties' freedom of contract, in that the exclusion clauses cannot derogate from the convention regimes.

3.4.1 Carrier's indemnity

The carrier might try to indemnify itself for all and any claims, losses, damages, fines, or expenses arising or resulting from breach of the shipper's obligations. It may even negotiate a clause that excludes all carrier liability, such as liability for defective packing and the resulting damage caused by Cargo A to Cargo B. The latter clause might be void under the transport conventions, a proposition that is discussed further in Chapter 4. As far as indemnification clauses are concerned, both the CMR and the HVR provide some rules on indemnification (Article III, Rule 5 HVR, Article IV, Rule 2(i) HVR, Article IV, Rule 2(o) HVR, Article III, Rule 6 HVR, Article IV, Rule 6 HVR, Article 7 CMR, Article 10 CMR, Article 12.5(a) CMR, Article 17.4(c) CMR, Article 22.2 CMR). These rules do not, however, exclude the liability of the carrier to third-party co-shippers or co-senders. Furthermore, the conventions provide the carrier with the possibility of recourse. General indemnification clauses that build on the recourse possibilities would be valid unless the conventions attach conditions to recourse. An indemnification clause would not be valid, for example, when the defect was apparent or known to the carrier at the time when it took over the goods and it made no reservations (Article 10 CMR). Likewise, under the HVR a clause would not be valid if the carrier excludes the proof of actual fault or neglect on the part of the shipper (Article IV, Rule 3 HVR).[69] In addition, (full) liability shifting is not possible if the carrier has contributed to a certain damage.

---

68 E.g. Clause 12 Hapag-Lloyd: 'The Merchant shall indemnify the Carrier against all and any claims, loss, damage, fines, or expenses arising or resulting from any breach of these obligations and warranties' <https://bit.ly/3nzesQi> accessed 10 August 2023.

69 On other clauses that would or would not be covered, see: Guenter Trietel and F.M.B. Reynolds, *Carver on Bills of Lading* (4th edn, Sweet and Maxwell 2017) No 9–194. See also: *Datec Electronics Holdings Limited and others v United Parcels Services Limited* [2007] UKHL 23 par. 30, where the court held that, insofar as UPS's terms and conditions purported to exclude liability for loss, damage, or delay which UPS would otherwise incur under Art.17 CMR, they were null and void.

3.4.2 Defences of the co-shipper or co-sender

Generally, clauses that benefit third parties have been added to contracts of carriage to protect stevedores, terminal operators, dry dock companies, and the subcontractors of carriers by limiting their liability.[70] Such solutions are expressly provided for in Article IV' of the HVR and in Article 28 CMR. Such clauses could be included effectively for the benefit of cargo bundling companies and TOs acting on behalf of the carrier.

For comparison, under the Rotterdam Rules, protection extends to the shipper's agents and subcontractors. Furthermore, the provisions of the Rotterdam Rules that provide a defence to the shipper or the documentary shipper apply in any judicial or arbitral proceeding that is instituted against the shipper, the documentary shipper, or their subcontractors, agents, or employees, be it based on contract, tort, or some other cause of action (Article 4.2 Rotterdam Rules). The provision, although beneficial for the shipper's agents and subcontractors, does not touch upon co-contractors or other independent third-party shippers under separate contracts of carriage. For this reason, co-shippers or co-senders that conclude independent contracts of carriage would not able to benefit from this provision unless they are mutually authorised to act on one another's behalf. Furthermore, the cargo bundling company and the TO, if acting on behalf of the shippers, would benefit from Article 4.2 Rotterdam Rules.

The CMR and the HVR do not govern the limitation of liability of persons for whom the shipper or sender is responsible and the limitation of liability of co-principal shippers or senders. At the same time, shippers or senders consider limiting the liability of their partners important (Figure 5.3). Thus, each shipper or sender could try to limit own liability and liability of persons for who they are responsible in their own contracts with the carrier. Furthermore, the co-shippers or co-senders could consider clauses that provide the benefit of a limitation of liability to their co-partners. However, in the last two cases, in all three of the jurisdictions under observation, the operation of such clauses is limited by privity rules. In addition, a judge in England is likely to have regard to the rules on unfair contract terms,[71] and a Polish or German judge would consider the issue of good faith (§ 242 BGB, Article 58 KC).

Under English law, clauses that provide the benefit of a limitation of liability, which look alike *Himalaya* clauses, can be effective in three situations. Firstly, they can be based on agency rules particularly when one of

70 See further: Susan Niessen, *The Legal Position of Terminal Operators in Hinterland Networks. Mixed Contracts and Third Parties* (Paris Legal Publishers 2017) Chapters 8–9; Carlo Corcione, 'The Evolution of Third Parties Protection in Carriage of Goods by Sea: From the Himalaya Clause to the Himalaya Protection' (2014) 49(3) *European Transport Law* 271; Carlo Corcione, *Third Party Protection in Shipping* (Informa Law 2020).

71 Unfair Contract Terms Act 1977; See further: Beale (n 60) No 14–059–14–118.

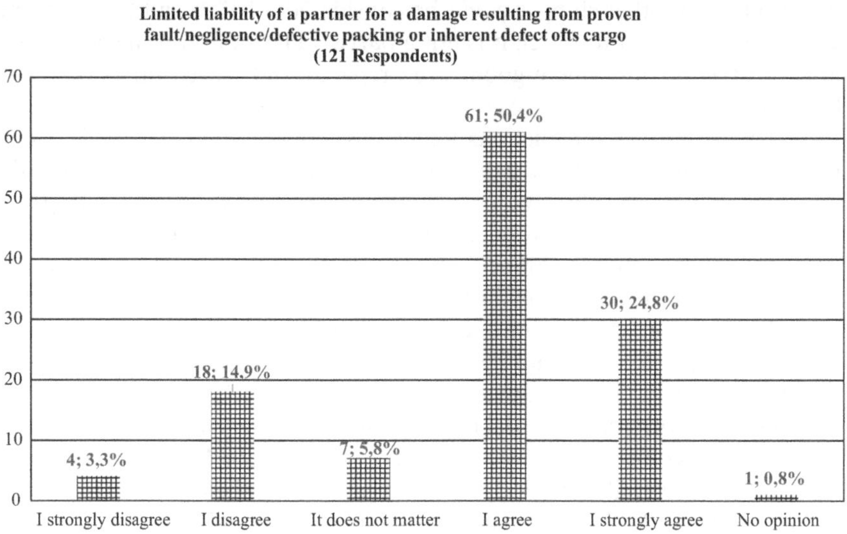

Figure 5.3 Perspectives on the limited liability of partners in co-operation

the contracting parties intended to act as agent for the third party.[72] For the analysed model of cargo bundling it means that the shipper or sender would be treated as having acted as the agent of the co-shipper or co-sender so as to grant it the benefit of the exemption clause. In this case, authorisation to act as an agent of the other shipper can derive from the co-operation agreement between the shippers or senders. However, the co-shipper or co-sender can be protected only while acting in the performance of the contract of carriage in which the clause is contained. While such performance could be easier to prove when the co-shippers or co-sender take part in the preparation of a joint loading unit and there is one contract of carriage, it might be difficult to argue it in a situation of milk runs where goods are prepared and picked up at different locations and several executory contracts of carriage are concluded. Secondly, especially when agency is difficult to prove, a third-party shipper can rely directly on the provisions of the Contracts (Rights of Third Parties) Act 1999 to avail itself of an express exclusion or limitation clause (s. 6(5) Contracts (Rights of Third Parties) Act 1999).[73] The benefit can be provided to more than one party.[74] Thirdly, under bailment law, a co-shipper who handles

72 See further on the *Himalaya* clauses used by carriers and their wording: Treitel and Reynolds (n 69) No 7–046; 7–050-7–057.

73 Beale (n 60) No 14–044, 14–049.

74 E.g. *Nisshin Shipping Co Ltd v Cleaves & Co Ltd* [2004] 1 Lloyd's Rep. 38.

the goods of another shipper could be considered a bailee and benefit from clauses in a contract to which it is not a party.[75] This option seems less likely in case of milk runs where goods are prepared and picked up at different locations.

As far as civil law jurisdictions under investigation are concerned, under Polish law, clauses that provide the benefit of a limitation of liability although possible might be less effective for the beneficiaries (Article 393 KC). In practice, the clause will be directly effective only for the parties to the contract and not for a third party (co-shipper or co-sender), unless it creates a claim for the benefit of a third party against the carrier to conclude a contract to limit the debt to a more convenient one for the third party[76] Thus, the immediate result of the clause would not be the co-shipper's or co-sender's total or partial release from liability. To achieve the immediate benefit for a co-shipper or co-sender in a form of its partial release from debt, a co-shipper or co-sender would need to contract directly with a carrier (Article 508 KC).[77] The German doctrine also generally allows clauses that provide the benefit of a limitation of liability under § 328 BGB. The discussion about the effect of such clauses oscillates between a similar to Polish claim-creation solution that implies an indirect effect of a clause, and anticipated contract by which the creditor releases the debtor from debt, which indicates a direct effect of a clause.[78] The latter approach seems to be preferred.[79]

3.4.3 Evaluation

The liability of the co-shippers or co-senders that are involved in cargo bundling could be affected by clauses that create rights for third parties rather than solutions that operate to their detriment. As a result, although it is possible to speak of limiting the liability of co-shippers or co-senders to the carrier, it is not possible to exclude the carrier's liability unless the conditions prescribed by the conventions are met. Benefits that are created for third parties should also comply with the rules prescribed by different national laws and might thus be impermissible on occasion. For example, general clauses for the benefit of third parties are unlikely to be valid.

75 On the conditions for the bailment relation, see further: Treitel and Reynolds (n 69) No 7–027; 7–041.

76 Andrzej Kubas, 'Rozdział IX. Umowy odnoszące się do osób trzecich' in Konrad Osajda (ed), *Prawo zobowiązań – część ogólna System Prawa Prywatnego tom 5* (Legalis C.H. Beck 2020) 1151–1154.

77 Kubas (n 76).

78 Peter Gottwald, 'BGB § 328 Vertrag zugunsten Dritter' in Wolfgang Krüger (ed), *Münchener Kommentar zum BGB bd. 3* (8th edn, C.H. Beck 2019) No 259.

79 Gottwald (n 78).

4 Operation of the first execution model of cargo bundling model

Under the first co-operation model, in which the carrier enters into contracts of carriage with individual shippers or senders who are members of the co-operation, there are several points of legal uncertainty that pertain to the question of whether the carrier can hold all shippers or senders liable despite the existence of separate contracts or at least claim against one shipper or sender for the acts of the others. Legal uncertainty results from the possible interpretation of the conventions that could, in principle, allow shippers or senders to be held jointly liable or to have one of them held liable for the acts of the others.

These points of legal uncertainty add to the previously discussed problems with the interpretation of the carrier's exoneration grounds that are available under the conventions. These problems were discussed in Chapter 4 which investigated different approaches to the application of the carrier's exoneration ground concerning insufficient packing. Since there is no consensus in the literature on their application *erga omnes* or *inter partes*, cargo interest and a carrier may struggle to anticipate the choice that a judge would make. The carrier should, however, expect most of the approaches to result in a cargo interest receiving compensation despite the damage being attributable to one of the other cargo interests.

This chapter adds to the observations from Chapter 4 and shows that even if a judge considers the exoneration grounds to attach to goods, the rights and liabilities of cargo interests are contractual under the conventions. There could be two approaches to defining the shipper or sender for the purpose of shipper or sender liability for damage. Firstly, despite the existence of independent contracts, shippers or senders can be considered together if a judge recognises the autonomous meaning of the term 'contract for carriage', which can subsume network contracts and the shared obligations that result from them (see Section 3.2.2), and the agency relations (see Section 3.1.). The joint status of shippers or senders can also be upheld in extracontractual claims (see Section 3.3). The convention-level solution regarding joint liability is not yet reflected in the case law. Since there is no guidance, unless a carrier decides to pursue an extracontractual claim, the approach, under which a shipper or sender is considered independent, is likely to be followed. For the first cargo bundling model, this means that each contract between a carrier and a shipper will likely be considered independently, a position that is, in fact, identical to that under groupage contracts. The similarity results mainly from the fact that in groupage it is difficult to hold one shipper or sender contractually liable for the acts of other shippers or senders.

On the pages that follow, I consider the consequences of damage to cargo and damage to a carrier in respect of the following issues: 1) The distribution of compensation between shippers or senders; 2) The liability of individual shippers (the consequences of their joint liability are discussed further in Chapter 6), and 3) Possibilities for recourse against the co-shipper or co-sender who caused the damage.

4.1 Shipper or sender's right to compensation for damage

Under the CMR, in which the limitation of the carrier's liability is 8.33 SDR per kilogram of gross weight (Article 23 CMR), all cargo interests are compensated up to that limit, taking into account the weight of their specific parcels. This means that cargo interests whose cargo has a low per kilogram value are able to recover a higher percentage of their loss than cargo interests whose cargo has a high per kilogram value. Moreover, it might be that the carrier does not have to provide compensation up to the CMR limit even if the average value of the goods exceeds it; for example, when there is a chain of carriers and a recourse gap occurs (see further Chapter 8 Section 5.2).

Similarly, under the HVR, all cargo interests are compensated up to a limit, yet the convention provides two alternatives: 666.67 SDR per package or unit or 2 SDR per kilo of the gross weight of the goods lost or damaged, whichever is higher (Article IV, Rule 5 of the HVR). Suppose that four shippers ship one parcel each. Two of them have cargoes of 5 SDR per kilogram, and the other two have cargoes of 25 SDR per kilogram. The cargo interests whose cargo has a low per kilogram value are able to recover a higher proportion of their loss if the package limitation is applied when the weight of the goods that are lost or damaged is low. When the weight of the goods that are lost or damaged is high, the cargo interests whose cargo has a low per kilogram value are, again, able to recover more, this time by relying on the kilogram limitation. Similarly to the CMR, it might be that the carrier does not have to compensate up to the limit even if the average value of the goods exceeds it because a recourse gap occurs (see Chapter 8 Section 5.2).

4.2 Shipper or sender liability

The carrier can only claim for damages against an individual cargo interest if it can establish that it caused or at least contributed to the damage. Such claims can include compensation paid to other cargo interests. Still, the carrier bears the risk of both default by the shipper or sender that caused the damage and of the existence of contractual clauses that foreclose the possibility of full compensation. Since most carriage conventions do not provide for mandatory rules on the quantum of shipper or sender liability, the carrier, depending on its bargaining position, may be able to secure full compensation or run into a limitation clause (see Section 3.4.2).

4.3 Recourse against the shipper or sender who caused the damage

If damage is caused by the cargo of one shipper or sender to the cargo of co-shipper or co-sender, the latter might be able to launch a claim against the shipper or sender of the cargo that caused the damage. In this respect, the difference between groupage and cargo bundling lies in the nature of the claim. While such a claim would be extracontractual by necessity under groupage, in the case of cargo bundling, the parties to the co-operation agreement can provide for rules on compensation for damage caused by other cargoes contractually. This said, in the latter case an extracontractual claim could also be a possibility.

In the case of groupage, only an extracontractual claim against the shipper or sender of the cargo that caused the damage is possible. Even though this possibility is rarely used in practice, such claims might succeed especially in situations where the cargo has, for example, exploded. Their benefit is that, apart from situations where the other cargo interests are successfully protected by a *Himalaya* clause in the carriage contract (see Section 3.4.2.), the liability of third-party cargo interests is unlimited.

CHAPTER 6

Co-principals under one contract of carriage – second execution model of cargo bundling co-operation

Marta K. Kołacz

1 Introduction

This chapter focuses on the model of cargo bundling in which the carrier enters into one contract of carriage with several senders or shippers as co-principals. Together with Chapter 5, this chapter investigates various approaches to defining 'shipper' or 'sender' for the purpose of determining rights and liabilities. Its focus is specifically on the possibility of joint liability of co-operating partners *vis-à-vis* the carrier and their right to joint compensation from the carrier. The analysis, although it focuses on the contractual execution of cargo bundling co-operation, reflects also on the operational execution of co-operation that could influence parties contractual obligations (Figure 6.1). For a reminder, milk runs refer to situations when the goods are packed and loaded separately along the way, and consolidation points refer to situations when consolidation units are prepared by the partners to co-operation in cargo bundling.

Although the conventions do not address the problems of several co-operating principals expressly, they do recognise situations in which a traditional bilateral relation can have a multiparty character. Firstly, the conventions deal explicitly with the other type of a multiparty contract that involves a consignee or the bill of lading (B/L) holder. Secondly, the conventions also deal with other types of cargo interests, including apparent and documentary shippers. Therefore, I investigate the existing solutions concerning multiparty contractual relations (Section 2) against the background of the execution model of cargo bundling in which the carrier enters into one contract of carriage with shippers or senders that are members of the co-operation in cargo bundling. I specifically inquire whether the carrier could hold all shippers or senders liable based on one contract of carriage or at least have a claim against one shipper or sender for the acts of its co-shippers or co-senders (Section 3). Lastly, based on the collected observations, I present the legal operation of the second execution model of cargo bundling (Section 4). The reader should be aware that partners to co-operation agreement for cargo bundling are mainly referred to as co-operating shippers or senders to align

 DOI: 10.4324/9781003450801-6

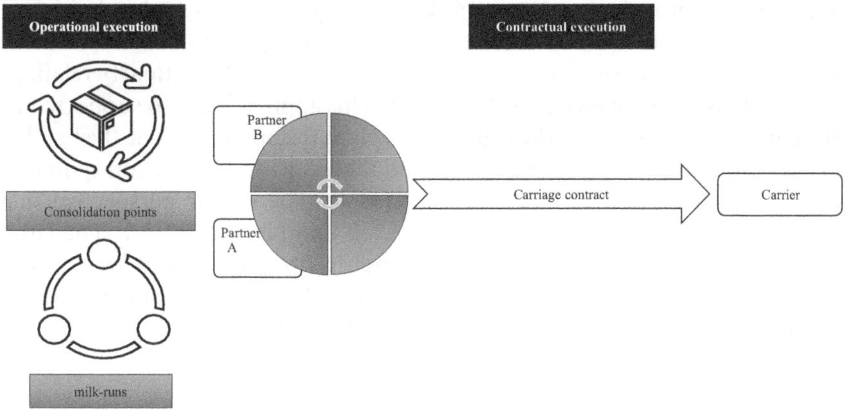

Figure 6.1 The second model of cargo bundling co-operation involves one multiparty carriage contract that is a result of the co-operation agreement. The operational execution of cargo consolidation can occur either in milk runs or at designated consolidation points

the terminology with the legal frameworks that receive special attention in this work. These legal frameworks are the Convention on the Contract for the International Carriage of Goods by Road of 1956 (CMR)[1] and the Hague-Visby Rules (HVR).[2]

2 Rights and liabilities of co-principals – approaches

As far as the shipper or sender is concerned, the HVR and the CMR do not address the consequences of plurality of principal shippers or senders under single contracts of carriage explicitly. It seems, however, that the joint liability of co-shippers and the right to joint compensation can be examined from two perspectives. The discussion on the application of the liability exoneration grounds under the CMR and the HVR showed that the approaches that predominate ascribe importance to the goods (see Chapter 4). Under these approaches, the application of law depends merely on how a judge considers single goods in relation to other goods that are transported by a carrier.

1 Convention on the Contract for the International Carriage of Goods by Road (CMR) (adopted 19 May 1956, entered into force 2 July 1961) 399 UNTS 189.

2 The Brussels Convention for the Unification of Certain Rules of Law relating to Bills of Lading (adopted 25 August 1924, entered into force 2 June 1931) Trb. 1953, 109, 004127 and Protocol to Amend the International Convention for the unification of certain rules of law relating to bills of lading, signed at Brussels on 25 August 1924 (adopted 23 February 1968, entered into force 23 June 1977) No. 23643.

The other approach that can help deciding on the rights and liabilities of co-principals focuses on the nature of the rights, obligations, and liabilities of multiple cargo interests. This approach is at the centre of multiparty relations which involve a consignee or a B/L holder. This approach is also supported by the author of this book as the right approach to the application of the liability exoneration grounds under the CMR and the HVR when joint consignments are transported by a carrier (see Chapter 4). The earlier perspective that ascribes importance to the goods is reflected upon in Section 2.1. The latter that focuses on the on the nature of the rights, obligations, and liabilities of multiple cargo interests is discussed in Section 2.2. Section 2.3. summarizes by giving an indication which approach should be preferable.

2.1 Goods

Tying the rights and liabilities of a plurality of parties to goods could have the following consequences depending on whether the importance is given to single goods, goods in consignments, or all goods being carried.

If a judge finds that shipper's or sender's liability attaches to individual goods, the contractual joint liability of co-shippers or co-senders would be excluded. Similarly, co-shippers or co-senders, particularly those responsible for preparing the loading units containing multiple consignments, would not be entitled to collective compensation for cargo damage under contract of carriage. Their circumstances would closely resemble those under a bilateral carriage contract. In that case, the carrier might be forced to have engaged the extracontractual liability of the shippers or senders. Shippers or senders might still be jointly responsible if their conduct contributes to the same damage (see further Chapter 5).

If the judge instead finds that liability attaches to all goods in a consignment or to all goods being carried, the joint rights and liabilities of co-shippers or co-senders under contract could be engaged. The results of the application of this approach depend on the judge's discretion in deciding how to consider groups of goods (see Chapter 4). For example, if a judge attaches liability to all goods being carried, joint rights and liabilities of co-principals could, in fact, also be triggered in case of the first cargo bundling model in which the carrier enters into contracts of carriage with individual shippers or senders that are members of the co-operation for cargo bundling (see Chapter 5) or in the course of standard groupage transport. This is because the contractual relations between the parties are irrelevant under this approach, and thus the joint liability of cargo interests that have entered into separate contracts with a carrier could also be engaged.

It is difficult to defend either of the presented approaches. The main argument against concerns contractual privity and its importance under the transport conventions, which have the contractual rights and obligations of the parties at their core. The focus on the contractual relations has already been brought while discussing the position of principal shipper and sender (Chapter 5 Section 2). Under both of presented approaches there is a risk of negating the position of principals as these who contract with a carrier and thus undertake various obligations, including proper packing, towards it (see also Chapter 4 Section 2 and Section 3). Another argument against the presented approaches is that these approaches often bypass contractual and extracontractual causes of action. The conventions secure that defences and limits of liability apply in action against the carrier regardless of whether the action is contractual or extracontractual (Article IV bis HVR, Art 28 CMR). Although the provisions securing that defences and limits of liability apply regardless of whether the action is contractual or extracontractual refer to the carrier, they underline the two different causes of action that are possible. The presented approaches that tie the rights and liabilities of co-shippers or co-senders to the goods often go beyond the mentioned causes of action. For example, attaching liability by default to all goods being carried allows the carrier to bypass actual contractual relations with different shippers or senders. Furthermore, attaching liability by default to all goods being carried allows the carrier to avoid proving sufficient causation between the actions of the shipper or sender and a single occurrence of damage while in case of extracontractual liability for the same damage, the damage for which one shipper or sender is liable to a carrier must correspond, at least in part, to the damage for which the second shipper or sender is liable (see Chapter 5 Section 3.3.).

2.2 The nature of an obligation

The conventions do not contain elaborate liability schemes for shipper or sender liability. Likewise, the conventions do not address the internal relations between the shippers or senders. The interpretation guidelines would require these gaps to be bridged on convention grounds and, failing that, by recourse to national law (see further Section 3).

The dichotomy between external and internal gaps is most clearly illustrated through the example of the relationship between a shipper or sender, a carrier, and a consignee or B/L holder, which constitutes a multiparty relation that is governed by the conventions. The situation of a consignee or a B/L holder cannot mirror that of a co-shipper or co-sender because of the special position of the former under the conventions. However, the operation of rights and liabilities in this relationship can be indicative of the problems that a judge would face when called upon to decide on the consequences of certain choices in respect of cargo bundling. The reader should be reminded that the sections that follow present various solutions that a judge can adopt, depending on whether they hold that it is the conventions or national laws that apply.

2.2.1 The Hague-Visby Rules and the Rotterdam Rules

A receiver who is a B/L holder is authorised to dispose of the cargo, in the sense of being able to transfer all rights thereto, including ownership, while the cargo is with the carrier (B/L as a document of title)[3] and is vested with the rights and obligations that result from a B/L contract (B/L as conclusive evidence of a contract of carriage).[4] The latter does not imply, however, that all the rights and obligations of the shipper pass to the B/L holder.[5]

2.2.1.1 HVR: Rights and liabilities regulated in the convention – independent position of the cargo interests

The HVR use the term 'shipper' to describe a particular commercial actor in some of its parts and the term 'B/L holder' to describe a different one in others. Interpreting the convention with a view to the ordinary meaning that ought to be given to its terms in their context and in the light of its object and purpose suggests that the two terms should be treated differently. The HVR provide certain rights to the B/L holder. For example, it can demand that the carrier provides all reasonable facilities for inspecting and tallying the goods (Article III, Rule 6 HVR). At the same time, the HVR impose some duties and liabilities, namely liability for dangerous goods (Article IV, Rule 6 HVR)[6] and acts and omissions (Article IV, Rule 2(i) HVR), solely on the principal shipper, without enabling it to transfer them to the B/L holder.[7] In addition, Article IV,

3 See further e.g: Guenter Treitel and Francis M.B. Reynolds, *Carver on Bills of Lading* (4th edn, Sweet and Maxwell 2017) No 6–001–6-067; Mirosław H. Koziński, 'Zastosowanie instytucji indosu wekslowego w morskim obrocie handlowym' (2006) XXII Prawo Morskie 113; Hans-Joachim Leue, *Die Praxis des Seefrachtgeschäfts* (Springer 2018) 55–56.

4 See further e.g.: Treitel and Reynolds (n 3), No 3–001–3-012; Paul M. Bugden and Simone Lamont-Black, *Goods in Transit and Freight Forwarding* (3rd edn, Sweet & Maxwell 2013) No 7–020; Koziński (n 3); Rolf Herber, 'HGB § 513 Anspruch auf Ausstellung eines Konnossements' in Rolf Herber and Christine Schmidt (eds), *Münchener Kommentar zum HGB bd.7* (4th edn, C.H. Beck 2020) No 5–9.

5 On the position of the B/L holder under various contractual and non-contractual theories, see further: Frank Stevens, *The Bill of Lading Holder Right and Liabilities* (Routlege 2018).

6 Supported, for example, in: Stewart C. Boyd et al. (eds), *Scrutton on Charterparties* (20th edn, Sweet & Maxwell 1996) 453; Julian Cooke et al. (eds), *Voyage Charters* (4th edn, Informa Law 2014) No 18.100. Contrary in: Simon Baughen, 'The Legal Status of Non-Contracting Shipper' (2000) *The International Journal of Shipping Law* 21, footnote 23; Bernard Eder et al. (eds), *Scrutton on Charterparties and Bills of Lading* (23rd edn, Sweet & Maxwell 2015) 373, – where it is stated: 'The previous edition of this work stated that this might be read so as to include a lawful holder satisfying the requirements of COGSA 1992 s. 3 but that it was submitted that it did not do so; and this statement was cited with approval of *the Aegean Sea*. However it is submitted that 1992 Act s. 3 does indeed transfer the shipper's liability for dangerous cargo'. This point was argued by with the reference to D. Mildon QC [1999] I.J.S.L. 99.

7 *Filikos Shipping Corporation of Monrovia v Shipmair B.V. "Filikos"* [1982] 10 WLUK 241, where it was said that 'the shipper or owner of the goods' has to be read as a reference to the charterers. Therefore, the owners were exempted from liability for damage caused by the acts or omissions of the charterers or their agents, the stevedores.

Rule 3 HVR has been found to refer only to the shipper *qua* principal shipper.[8] It has also been argued that the shipper's guarantee of the accuracy, at the time of shipment, of the marks, number, quantity, and weight of the goods (Article III, Rule 5 HVR) can hardly have been intended to apply to third parties.[9] As a result, the validity of merchant clauses that impose joint liability on the B/L holder in respect of the issues mentioned earlier could be questioned. Joint liability is precluded because the shipper's liabilities are exclusive to it and not transferable to the B/L holder.

2.2.1.2 HVR: Rights and liabilities not regulated in the conventions – independent or joint position

As far as issues not governed by the HVR, such as the payment of freight, are concerned, national laws differ on the joint liability of the shipper and the B/L holder. Under English law, in which the transferability of obligations is suggested by Section 3(1) Carriage of Goods by Sea Act 1992, the consignee is liable for the payment of freight along with the original shipper by way of addition. Under § 494.4 HGB,[10] shipper and recipient can be held jointly and severally liable to the carrier.[11] No such provisions exist in Polish law: The consignee is only obliged to pay the amount of freight indicated in the B/L (Article 146.2 Kodeks Morski KM[12]). Thus, the B/L holder does not enter into the obligation to pay freight automatically.[13]

2.2.1.3 Rotterdam Rules – joint position

The United Nations Convention on Contracts for the International Carriage of Goods Wholly or Partly by (Rotterdam Rules)[14] could clarify the position of the shipper and the B/L holder. Article 58.1 contains the general principle that a holder that is not the shipper and does not exercise any right under the contract of carriage does not assume any liability under it solely by reason of being a holder. Article 58.2 states that a holder that exercises any right under the contract of carriage assumes any liabilities imposed on it thereunder to

8 *Aegean Sea Traders Corp v Repsol Petroleo SA & Anor ('The Aegean Sea')* [1998] C.L.C. 1090, where it was said: 'Article IV, r. 3 is dealing with the obligations of the shipper in his capacity as shipper and not with the other liabilities of those who become subject to those other liabilities under the bill of lading by virtue of s. 3 of COGSA 1992'. See also: Stephan Geense, 'De merchant-clausule' (2011) 5 *Nederlands Tijdschrift voor Handelsrecht* 190, 194–195.

9 Eder et al. (n 6) 352.

10 Handelsgesetzbuch vom 10. Mai 1897 (RGBl. S. 219) BGBl. III/FNA 4100–1 (with further changes) (HGB).

11 See further: Marian Paschke, 'HGB § 494 Rechte des Empfängers. Zahlungspflicht' in Hartmut Oetker (ed), *Handelsgesetzbuch* (7th edn, C.H. Beck 2021) No 1–8.

12 Kodeks morski Dz.U. 2001 Nr 138, poz. 1545 (with further changes).

13 See: Sąd Rejonowy w Gdyni 6.11.2019 VI GC 928/18, where the court pointed out that the carrier had waived its rights to secure this claim because of a 'freight prepaid' clause.

14 United Nations Convention on Contracts for the International Carriage of Goods Wholly or Partly by Sea A/RES/63/122 3 November 2008.

the extent that those liabilities are incorporated in or ascertainable from the negotiable transport document. These would include any obligations that are imposed by the terms of the B/L or that originate from the incorporation of the charterparty into it, including the obligation to pay freight. The holder is not, however, subject to any implied obligation that may have been imposed on the original shipper.[15] According to Yvonne Baatz et al., the wording of Article 58.2 of the Rotterdam Rules validates merchant clauses that extend liability to the B/L holder because

> such a clause would make it clear in the bill of lading that all obligations imposed on the shipper were also imposed on the holder: the second requirement for the application of Article 58 would consequently be satisfied because the obligation which the carrier now seeks to impose on the holder would indeed have been imposed by the document "on it".[16]

2.2.2 CMR

A consignee is a person who is entitled to the delivery of the goods and who is mentioned in a carriage contract. The consignee has certain rights and obligations under the contract of carriage, which could be separate from those of the senders or common with them.

2.2.2.1 Article 7, Article 10, and Article 22 CMR – independent position

Under the CMR, certain rules target the sender explicitly, excluding the consignee (Article 7, Article 10, and Article 22 CMR). For this reason, there is no joint liability for inaccurate or inadequate particulars in the consignment note, defective packing, and dangerous goods.

2.2.2.2 Claim against the carrier – independent or joint position

The content of the right to claim against the carrier tend to be derived from national laws,[17] autonomous readings of the convention that link it to the right of disposal,[18] and the nature of the acquisition of rights by both sender

---

15 Simon Baughen, 'Charterparty Bills of Lading – Cargo Interests' Liabilities to the Shipowner' in D. Rhidian Thomas (ed), *The Evolving Law and Practice of Voyage Charterparties* (Informa Law 2009) 248.

16 Yvonne Baatz et al., *The Rotterdam Rules: A Practical Annotation* (Informa Law 2009) No 58–09.

17 E.g.: Sąd Najwyższy 05.10.2011 IV CSK 65/11, where the court found that Art. 13(1) s. 1 CMR does not provide a full answer to the question of who the person who is entitled to claim against the carrier is, and recourse to national law was thus necessary. At the same time, the court found that the recipient's rights were stated explicitly and unambiguously under Art. 13(1)(2) CMR.

18 Krzysztof Wesołowski, *Umowa międzynarodowego przewozu drogowego towarów na podstawie CMR* (Wolters Kluwer Polska 2013) 615–618; also: Sąd Najwyższy 14.04.2016 II CSK 338/15.

and consignee.[19] Thus, the availability of multiple approaches results in different outcomes in respect of joint creditorship.

Krzysztof Wesołowski derives individual position of the sender and the consignee in respect of the right to claim against the carrier from the CMR by taking into consideration the parties' interests.[20] According to him, the sender can withdraw the reservation of performance for a specific recipient until that recipient requires the carrier to deliver the goods. As a result, as between sender and consignee, only one party has the right to instruct the carrier, and only one could sue it. Thus, joint rights are precluded.

However, there is a disagreement on this point, especially because when the goods are lost, the consignee is also entitled to enforce any rights arising from the contract of carriage against the carrier in its own name (Article 13.1 s. 2 CMR). If the right to claim is linked to the right of disposal, as might be expected in Poland,[21] the right to claim is vested in one person at a time, which precludes joint claims for damage to goods. However, in Germany, the recipient and the sender are considered joint creditors because when the goods are lost, the right of the consignee does not dependent on previous transfer. Since the CMR has been found not to govern joint creditors in that country, recourse is made to national laws on joint creditors and double legitimation (§ 428 BGB), under which the sender may, at its discretion, request performance to itself or to the recipient.[22] The status of joint creditors does not imply joint liability on the part of cargo interests.

2.2.2.3 Obligation to pay transport charges – independent or joint position

Turning to the obligation to pay transport charges under Article 13.2 of the CMR,[23] there is a disagreement on whether the sender and consignee can be considered separately or jointly. According to the approach which tends to be favoured by Polish courts and doctrine, the obligation to pay transport chargers rests either with the sender or with the consignee, and there is no need

19 Helga Jesser-Huß, CMR Art. 13 [Rechte und Pflichten des Empfängers] in Rolf Herber and Christine Schmidt (eds), *Münchener Kommentar zum HGB bd.7* (4th edn, C.H. Beck 2020).

20 Wesołowski (n 18) 254.

21 Sąd Najwyższy 14.04.2016 II CSK 338/15; differently: Sąd Okręgowy w Szczecinie 14.12.2012 VIII Ga 385/12, which was in favour of the application of the general principles on the payment of compensation to the sender or recipient, depending on which of the two entities had suffered the damage.

22 Hanno Merkt, 'CMR Art. 13 [Rechte des Empfängers nach Ankunft, Zahlungspflicht]' in Klaus J. Hopt et al. (eds), *Handelsgesetzbuch bd.9* (40th edn, C.H. Beck 2021) No 1.

23 In Poland, these are considered to include freight and other charges; in Germany, only outstanding amounts are included. Wesołowski (n 18) 272; Helga Jesser-Huß, CMR Art. 13 [Rechte und Pflichten des Empfängers] in Rolf Herber and Christine Schmidt (eds), *Münchener Kommentar zum HGB bd.7* (4th edn, C.H. Beck 2020) No 24.

to refer to national law. Therefore, joint debt is precluded. The consignee that accepts the consignment note does not automatically assume all rights and obligations of the sender.[24] Thus, under Article 13.2 CMR, the protection of the interests of the consignee against the carrier's claims is stronger because it only has to pay the carrier for due charges that are mentioned in the consignment note.[25] The existence of the obligation is thus tied to the content of the consignment note. Despite the sender and the consignee not being jointly liable, the carrier is still protected under the CMR because it has the right to security in the event of a dispute about the payment of transport charges (Article 13.2 CMR *in fine*).

In Germany, the consignee's obligation to pay is also considered to depend on the existence of a consignment note with the corresponding entries.[26] However, when there are no consignment note entries that limit the consignee's liability or assign the obligation to pay, then, according to supplementary German law, the sender and the consignee are jointly and severally liable for the costs (§ 421 HGB). The carrier can thus claim against either of them; it has no duty to contact the consignee first.[27] What is noticeable is that the German interpretation of the convention permits recourse to national law, here the rules on joint obligations, more frequently.

24 The same principle exists as a matter of Polish transport law see: Sąd Najwyższy 20.07.2006 V CSK 115/06; Sąd Najwyższy 26.01.2006 V CSK 111/05. The consignee's liability is only additional to the sender's contractual liability. See: Sąd Najwyższy 19.03.1999 II CKN 231/98.

25 Wesołowski (n 18) 272–278, who reflects further on the time of payment; Sąd Najwyższy 19.12.2013 II CSK 70/13; Sąd Apelacyjny w Krakowie 27.05.2014 I ACa 541/14; Cf. Sąd Apelacyjny w Krakowie 27.11.2013 I ACa 1056/13, where the court argued that since the consignment note is not the only evidence of the conclusion of the contract of carriage, contrary evidence can determine the amount of freight and the identity of the persons who are obliged to pay it.

26 Helga Jesser-Huß, CMR Art. 13 [Rechte und Pflichten des Empfängers] in Rolf Herber and Christine Schmidt (eds), *Münchener Kommentar zum HGB bd.7* (4th edn, C.H. Beck 2020) No 22.

27 Jesser-Huß (n 26) No 24–25; Katharina Boesche, 'CMR Art. 13 [Rechte des Empfängers. Zahlungspflicht]' in Carsten T. Ebenroth et al. (eds), *Handelsgesetzbuch bd.2* (4th edn, C.H. Beck 2020) No 11.; This could be the influence of national law: under § 334 BGB, the carrier is entitled to raise all defences that are based on the contract of carriage against the consignee as a third-party beneficiary. Although German law rejects the notion of a contract to the detriment of third parties, it is possible that the carrier and the sender can impose a restriction on the benefit that has been conferred upon a third party. Moreover, the consignee and the shipper can be jointly and severally liable, whereby the latter remains liable for all the amounts payable under contract of carriage (§ 421. 4 HGB). See further e.g.: Basil S. Markesinis, *The German Law of Contract a Comparative Treatise* (Hart Publishing 2006) 197; G. Kirchhof, 'HGB § 421 Rechte des Empfängers. Zahlungspflicht' in Martin Häublein and Roland Hoffmann-Theinert (eds), *BeckOK HGB* (32nd edn, C.H. Beck 2021) No 15–16. Koller does not seem to support any recourse to national law: Ingo Koller, *Transportrecht Kommentar* (C.H. Beck 2013) 1013.

2.3 Observations

In respect of the co-shippers or co-senders, the HVR and the CMR do not explicitly address the consequences of plurality of parties and liability under a carriage contract. The comparison with other multiparty relations that involve a B/L holder, and a consignee reveal the importance of the legal classification of rights and obligations. Therefore, the approach where the rights and the liabilities of the co-principals attach to goods would need to be rejected.

Focusing on the nature of an obligation has several consequences. Firstly, each obligation and the resulting liabilities must be approached individually, and particular attention must be paid to the content of the obligation and its position within the convention. The legal classification of rights and obligations reveals the necessity to decide to what extent the conventions cover the matter and relatedly whether there is an internal or an external gap. Secondly, the consequences of recourse to national laws vary between types of gaps in a convention. In the case of an internal gap, national law solutions must be embedded into the framework of the convention. In the case of an external gap, the solutions are wholly governed by national law. The following section discusses the arguments in favour of internal and external gaps as far as co-operation in cargo bundling is concerned and the extent of application of national laws.

3 Rights and liabilities of co-principals – internal or external gap?

The previous discussion circled on the approaches to rights and liabilities of co-shippers and co-senders. Under the first approach, rights and liabilities of co-shippers and co-senders are tied to the goods. Under the second, right and liabilities are tied to the nature of a contractual obligation. The earlier analysis concluded that the second approach should be preferred. The discussion here continues with such aspects as arguments in favour of internal and external gaps as far as joint rights and liabilities of co-shippers and co-senders are concerned (Section 3.1. and Section 3.2.) and the consequences with following the national law approaches (Section 3.3.) The following sections discuss only the contractual relations between multiple shippers or senders and a carrier. In all cases, extracontractual liability for the same damage could also be invoked (see Chapter 5, Section 3.3). Section 3.4 summarizes by providing a decision-making process concerning joint rights and liability of co-principals under contract of carriage and the impact of the application of national laws.

3.1 Internal gap

Internal gaps in the convention involve matters which are governed by a convention but are not expressly settled by it. The possible existence of internal gaps requires from a judge to engage in an in-depth understanding of the conventions as expressed in Article 31 of the Vienna Convention on the Law of Treaties of 1969 (Vienna Convention, see further Chapter 2).[28] Due to the fact that the conventions do not address the issues of co-operation explicitly, interpretation of the conventions rules is necessary. If a judge finds that an internal gap exists, the issue around it should be first resolved in the context of a convention itself. If that is not possible, national-solutions should be employed. In the case of an internal gap, national law solutions must be embedded into the framework of the convention.

Both the CMR and the HVR provide rules about the liability of shippers and senders (see Chapter 3) but say nothing about the legal effects of shipper or sender co-operation. If this is regarded as an internal gap, the gap arises from the absence of a specification of the consequences related to multiparty contractual undertakings on the side of principal shippers or senders. However, the conventions cannot provide a specification for every business model employed for the purpose of carriage of goods which might be burdened with some inherent ambiguity. Instead, the conventions provide risk management frameworks that secure uniform application of carrier liability regardless of the applied business models including execution models of cargo bundling co-operation. The examination of the nature of obligations in the cargo bundling context requires two characteristics to be considered. In a multilateral contract with a carrier, the contracting co-shippers or co-senders are in an equal position. However, since actual cargo bundling can occur in either milk runs or in consolidation units, the performance of certain obligations that fall on co-shippers or co-senders may vary contextually.

So long as the gap is an internal one, a court should try to find the solution to the investigated issue based on autonomous interpretation applied through the framework of the Vienna Convention. It should only resort to national law solutions if this can be fully justified by the impossibility of finding autonomous solutions (see further Chapter 2). It is argued here that an autonomous solution concerning rights and obligations of co-shippers is possible to be extracted from the framework of the conventions. In my view, the default rule should be that each cargo interest retains its individual rights, including the right to compensation, and performs its obligations independently of the rights or obligations of the other cargo interests. Likely, only joint liability could be triggered as a result of performing operations together. The observations that were introduced while discussing the suggested and proper application of exoneration grounds are useful here (Chapter 4 Section 4): The conventions govern the obligations and liabilities of the shipper or sender. Relatedly, it is important to establish whether the obligation of the shippers

28 Vienna Convention on the Law of Treaties (adopted 23 May 1969, entered into force 27 January 1980) 1155 UNTS 331.

or senders was shared, discharged by a single shipper or sender, or performed by a carrier, and how it affects the risk management scheme established by the conventions. Therefore, containers that are packed by several shippers or senders should be within the sphere of risk of this group of shippers or senders and not that of the carrier. These shippers or senders share their obligation to prepare goods for transport. Instead, if the goods are handed over to the carrier separately, the risk of damage of the goods passes on the carrier accordingly which in turn also implies that each of co-operating shippers or senders should bear the risk for own omissions related to the cargo and its packing.

The abovementioned suggestion for the autonomous approach also implies that there might be no right for joint compensation. The main reason is that conventions govern the liability of the carrier and amount of compensation that it should pay in case of damage to the goods. The co-partners right to joint compensation could be seen as a means of circumventing the limitations on the carrier's liability especially under the CMR (see further Section 4.1). The conventions, however, are unclear on the effects of shipper's or sender's joint rights and obligations, and at this level they could potentially be supported by national laws. The solutions offered by national laws focus on divisible obligations, indivisible and joint obligations, and solidary, joint, and several obligations (see further Section 3.3). These solutions must be embedded into the framework of the conventions and respect the established risk management framework. As a result, it could be that a judge allows the co-operating partners to sue the carrier jointly for damages to the goods; however, if a case is decided under the CMR they might still require the compensation to be calculated per sender.

3.2 External gap

External gaps in the convention involve matters which are not governed by a convention. The possible existence of external gaps also requires from a judge to engage in an in-depth understanding of the conventions as expressed in Article 31 of the Vienna Convention to avoid situations of a premature recourse to national laws. If a judge finds that an external gap exists, the solutions to issues at hand are wholly governed by national laws.

The argument in favour of an external gap as far as rights and liabilities of co-shippers or co-senders are concerned could be that the CMR and the HVR govern mainly those aspects which are central to the performance obligations of the carrier and the existence and use of carriage documents. Relatedly, the plurality of parties under a single contract is regulated explicitly in some transport conventions but, with the exception of the Rotterdam Rules (see

Chapter 5 Section 3.2.1.2), these rules focus on the carrier.[29] Only in these cases the conventions provide explicit mandatory rules, which do not necessarily overlap with national law solutions.[30] Relatedly, the conventions cannot be expected to provide an answer to every possible issue relating to a contract of carriage including the effects of performing obligations jointly by co-shippers or co-carriers, and bearing responsibility for such shared obligations. These must naturally be determined by the national law to which the court is directed through the application of principles of conflicts of law.

The argument in favour of an external gap is risky at least for two reasons. Firstly, the argument in favour of an external gap has a negative effect on achieving uniformity. It facilitates forum shopping as far as the execution of shipper or sender rights and liabilities are concerned (Section 3.3.) and these might also affect the carrier's position under the conventions. Secondly, allowing external gap at this moment would cause an artificial split between the rules on the application of exoneration grounds that were discussed in Chapter 4.

3.3 Solutions provided by national laws

In civil law countries, default rules circle on the nature of the obligation (divisible or indivisible obligation). In England, what matters is the content and the number of the promises (joint and joint and several obligations). Solidarity needs to be agreed by the parties or prescribed by law. In all these schemes, the co-principals might be co-creditors (if the carrier is in breach) or co-debtors (if the co-principals are in breach). The following sections concern issues that are relevant to multiparty contracting, namely 1) the characteristics of obligations under different schemes, 2) liability for the performance of an obligation, 3) liability for damages, 4) recourse claims, 5) the insolvency of one partner and its consequences for the liability of the remaining partners. Their analysis enables an inquiry into the validity of joint liability clauses and the joint enforcement of rights under the conventions depending on whether the judge uses the national law rules to fill internal or external gaps (Section 4).

3.3.1 Divisible obligations (England, Poland, and Germany)

When several shippers or senders bind themselves to a single carrier by way of a common contract or when several shippers or senders under one contract have a single carrier as debtor, their obligations are divisible when the debt or claim is divided into as many independent parts as there are shippers or

29 See further: Simone Lamont-Black, 'Recourse Claims between Carriers: Another Obstacle to Intermodality?' in Rhidian Thomas and Simone Lamont-Black (eds), *Current Issues in Freight Forwarding: Law and Logistics* (Lawtext Publishing Limited 2017).

30 Cf. e.g. Art. 34 and Art. 36 CMR and the rules presented in Section 3.3.

senders. Even then, the fact that the tranches are based on a common contract retains some importance.[31] Polish law clarifies the rules that are relevant to the nature of a divisible obligation further. An obligation is divisible if it can be performed partially without its object or value changing significantly (Article 379.2 KC).[32] This means that the individual parts may differ in quantity, but their quality and value, taken in their totality, do not differ significantly from the quality and value of the whole.[33]

Independence of obligations has at least four consequences. Firstly, the performance of obligations and the payment of remuneration are divisible by default.[34] Thus, the carrier should sue co-shippers or co-senders separately for damages. Relatedly, the carrier cannot claim full performance from one party but must instead divide its claim. As a result, none of the shippers or senders who are party to a divisible obligation are obliged to fulfil it in full. Secondly, when one of the shippers or senders who are parties to a divisible obligation obtains the performance that is due to it, it is not liable to the other partners *qua* creditors for recourse claims.[35] Thirdly, in a divisible obligation, no shipper or sender can claim more that its part, and the insolvency of one does not affect the others. In the case of separate obligations, there is a presumption of equal shares under German (§ 420 BGB) and Polish (Article 379.1 KC) laws, whereas quantum is subject to the construction of the contract at English law. Fourthly, co-shippers or co-senders who are parties to divisible obligations have no right to mutual representation. The actions and omissions of one of the obliged persons do not have any effect on the others (Article 471 KC, § 280 BGB). Relatedly, a debtor can only withdraw from the performance of its part, which does not require the permission of other parties.[36]

The carrier would, in principle, also need to enforce other remedies (i.e. withholding performance or termination) separately towards each shipper or sender in the event of breach. However, there may be some exceptions to the principle of the independence that result from the fact that one contract is a source of obligations. They may depend, for example, on whether performance is due at once or in instalments. Regarding partial performance, in Poland, the carrier would not be able to refuse partial performance if the obligation can be performed in instalments, and acceptance would not infringe

31 § 420 BGB; Art. 379 KC; H.G. Beale (ed), *Chitty on Contracts* (31st eds, Sweet & Maxwell 2012) vol I, No 17–001.

32 Cf. § 752 BGB.

33 Bogusław Lackoroński, 'Art. 379 KC' in Konrad Osajda and Witold Borysiak (eds), *Kodeks cywilny. Komentarz* (29th edn, Legalis C.H. Beck 2021) No 5.

34 Sąd Apelacyjny w Katowicach, 25.10.2017 I ACa 503/17; Susanne Heinemeyer, 'BGB § 420 Teilbare Leistung' in Wolfgang Krüger (ed), *Münchener Kommentar zum BGB bd. 3* (8th edn, C.H. Beck 2019) No 4.

35 Lackoroński, 'Art. 379 KC' (n 33) No 18; Edwin Peel and Guenter H. Treitel, *Treitel's Law of Contract* (Sweet and Maxwell 2015) No 13–033; § 428 BGB.

36 Lackoroński, 'Art. 379 KC' (n 33) No 17.

its legitimate interests (Article 450 KC). In addition, the carrier's right to withhold performance only applies to that part of its performance which corresponds to a part of the other party's performance.[37] Under English law, carrier would in principle also not be able to refuse partial performance unless the failure to perform the other parts is such as to go to the essence of a contract.[38] However, under German law, the carrier would have a general right to withhold all performance in good faith until all shippers or senders have tendered theirs (§ 320 BGB).[39] Furthermore, also termination may be total or partial. Under English law, the right to terminate the whole contract is available when there is a serious breach.[40] However, if the obligation is severable, as opposed to one that should be performed entirely, default justifies refusal to perform the creditor's part only in respect of the outstanding parts.[41] Thus, a party may terminate partially if the default amounts to breach of condition.[42] Under German law, the carrier would be entitled to full termination if it has no interest in partial performance (§ 323.3(5) BGB). Under Polish law, partial performance may be a way of defending the debtor against full termination on the part of the creditor.[43] In case of partial default, the other party's right to terminate is limited, at its discretion, either to the relevant part or to the outstanding performance.[44] Full termination is nevertheless possible when partial performance would infringe on the creditor's legitimate interests (Article 491.2 KC). As a rule, infringement of the creditor's interests is not a reason to terminate the contract in the case of cash payments.[45]

Besides the exceptions mentioned earlier, the effects of divisible obligation rules can be reduced or excluded by the agreement of the parties or statute.

---

37 Fryderyk Zoll, 'Rozdział V[1].Wykonanie i skutki niewykonania lub nienależytego wykonania zobowiązań' in Adam Olejniczak (ed), *Prawo zobowiązań – część ogólna System Prawa Prywatnego – suplement do tomu 6* (Legalis C.H. Beck 2010) No 15.

38 Beale (n 31) No 24–046.

39 Astrid Stadler, 'BGB § 320 Einrede des nicht erfüllten Vertrags' in Rolf Stürner et al. (eds), *Jauernig Bürgerliches Gesetzbuch. Kommentar* (18th edn, C.H. Beck 2021) No 17; Volker Emmerich, 'BGB § 320 Einrede des nichterfüllten Vertrags' in Wolfgang Krüger (ed), *Münchener Kommentar zum BGB bd. 3* (8th edn, C.H. Beck 2019) No 56.

40 Solène Rowan, *Remedies for Breach of Contract: A Comparative Analysis of the Protection of Performance* (Oxford University Press 2012) 72–74.

41 Guenter H. Treitel, *Remedies for Breach of Contract* (Oxford University Press 1988) 307.

42 Treitel (n 41) 376.

43 Rafał Morek, 'Art. 450 KC' in Konrad Osajda and Witold Borysiak (eds), *Kodeks cywilny. Komentarz* (29th edn, Legalis C.H. Beck 2021) No 4.

44 Fryderyk Zoll, 'Rozdział V[1].Wykonanie i skutki niewykonania lub nienależytego wykonania zobowiązań' in Adam Olejniczak (ed), *Prawo zobowiązań – część ogólna System Prawa Prywatnego – suplement do tomu 6* (Legalis C.H. Beck 2010) par. 15.

45 Wojciech Popiołek, 'Art. 450 KC' in Krzysztof Pietrzykowski (ed), *Kodeks cywilny. T II. Komentarz. Art. 450–1088. Przepisy wprowadzające* (10th edn, Legalis C.H. Beck 2021) par. 6; See further also: Kazimierz Zawada, 'Art. 379 KC' in Krzysztof Pietrzykowski (ed), *Kodeks cywilny. T II. Komentarz. Art. 450–1088. Przepisy wprowadzające* (10th edn, Legalis C.H. Beck 2021) No 5, where the author distinguishes between obligations that are divisible because of the plurality of the parties and ones that are divisible due to the divisibility of a single obligation.

Firstly, divisible obligations can be considered solidary or indivisible and imply the applicability of the rules on solidarity as a result of an agreement between the parties.[46] By entering into such an agreement, the parties could, in fact, extend the liability of the debtors to their external relationship with a carrier. Secondly, some laws contain a *lex specialis* whereby, regardless of the type of the obligation, some parties are solidarily liable unless they agree otherwise.[47] For example, under Polish and German laws if several parties have accepted a service contract jointly, their liability towards the other parties is solidary (Article 745 KC, § 427 BGB). Furthermore, some default rules extend the liability of debtors to their external relationship with a creditor. Unless otherwise agreed, debtors who are obliged to perform a divisible obligation bear solidary liability when the creditor's counter-performance is indivisible (Article 380.2 KC; see below).[48] Thirdly, the partners might still be solidarily responsible if their conduct contributes to the same damage, which might occur extra-contractually (see Chapter 5 Section 3.3.).

3.3.2 Common obligations

The common obligations that result from a contract may be construed in three ways, namely 1) as indivisible, 2) as imposing joint liability on the promisors, and 3) as sources of joint and several liability or solidarity. English law favours joint and joint and several liability. Polish law exhibits a preference for indivisible obligations and solidarity. Under German law, there is no special category of rules for indivisible obligations because of a general presumption of solidarity in the case of indivisible obligations (§ 431 BGB). Doctrine, however, recognises the community of debtors and creditors, to which the rules on solidarity might be inapplicable, alongside classical indivisible obligations (the differences are described in the parts on indivisible and solidary obligations).

3.3.2.1 Indivisible obligations (Poland and Germany)

Indivisible obligations are obligations whereby performance is not divisible. The rules on indivisible obligations operate in Poland. Under German law, there is a general presumption of solidarity (e.g. § 431 BGB, see below) in cases when a plurality of debtors must meet an indivisible obligation. In Poland, the

46 Sąd Najwyższy 14.05.1999 I CKN 2/98; Emmerich, 'BGB § 320' (n 39) No 57; Heinemeyer, 'BGB § 420' (n 34) No 17.

47 Rafał Morek, 'Art. 745 KC' in Konrad Osajda (ed), *Kodeks cywilny. Komentarz* (27th edn, Legalis C.H. Beck 2020); Susanne Heinemeyer, 'BGB § 427 Gemeinschaftliche vertragliche Verpflichtung' in Wolfgang Krüger (ed), *Münchener Kommentar zum BGB bd. 3* (8th edn, C.H. Beck 2019) par 4.

48 The courts might also run into difficulties with consequences of the plurality of parties in divisible obligations. For example, Lackoroński reports a judgement of the Polish Supreme Court in which the court did not recognise that fulfilment of a judgement debt to solidary creditors where the obligation was, in fact, divisible was unlawful: Sąd Najwyższy 11.10.2013 I CSK 769/12 mentioned in: Lackoroński, 'Art. 379 KC' (n 33) No 17.1.

obligations assumed by the multimodal transport operator (MTO) have been considered indivisible.[49] The MTO has been found to combine the role of a freight forwarder and a carrier when it offers a door-to-door delivery service to a shipper. When the roles of freight forwarder and carrier are combined, neither of these functions has been found to be decisive.[50] This observation and the construction of an indivisible obligation has an implication on the legal classification of logistics intermediaries. If neither of the assumed legal roles is decisive, the intermediary might be considered a *sui generis* intermediary and thus escape the framework of international uniform transport law that targets only carriers (see further Chapter 8).

Under Polish law, the debtors' indivisible obligation results in the construction of their liability along passive solidarity lines (Article 380.1 in conjunction with Article 366 KC).[51] Solidarity (see below) is nevertheless not a feature of an indivisible obligation but only serves as a model for shaping the obligations of debtors.[52] If the obligation ceases to be indivisible, for example, because it is transformed into cash payments, the debtors are no longer liable under the provisions on solidarity. Instead, the rules on divisible obligations apply.[53] Furthermore, the application of the passive solidarity rules, under which the creditor may demand full or partial performance, is limited in cases of indivisible obligations because the creditor cannot demand partial performance.[54] The creditor may demand the full performance of an indivisible obligation from all debtors jointly, from several of the debtors, or from a single one.[55] All debtors remain liable until the creditor is satisfied fully (Article 366 KC). A debtor who renders indivisible performance (Article 380.3 KC) has recourse against its co-debtors according to the same rules as a joint and several debtor (Article 376 KC; see below). Due to the indivisibility of the

49 Mirosław Stec, 'Rozdział VI. Umowy nienazwane w działalności transportowej, § 19. Umowa przewozu multimodalnego' in Wojciech J. Katner (ed), *Prawo zobowiązań – umowy nienazwane System Prawa Prywatnego t.9* (3rd edn, Legalis C.H. Beck 2018) No 70.

50 Stec (n 49).

51 Cf. Susanne Heinemeyer, 'BGB § 421 Gesamtschuldner' in Wolfgang Krüger (ed), *Münchener Kommentar zum BGB bd. 3* (8th edn, C.H. Beck 2019) No 6–7 on joint obligations in Germany.

52 The rules on indivisible obligations also prevail over the rules on solidarity when the indivisible obligation is solidary.

53 Bogusław Lackoroński, 'Art. 380 KC' in Konrad Osajda and Witold Borysiak (eds), *Kodeks cywilny. Komentarz* (29th edn, Legalis C.H. Beck 2021) No 3.

54 This is a dominant view, expressed, among others, by: Kazimierz Zawada, 'Art. 380 KC' in Krzysztof Pietrzykowski (ed), *Kodeks cywilny. T II. Komentarz. Art. 450–1088. Przepisy wprowadzające* (10th edn, Legalis C.H. Beck 2021) No 1.; Lackoroński (n 53), No 1.1; Wojciech Dubis, 'Art. 380 KC' in Edward Gniewek and Piotr Machnikowski (eds), *Kodeks cywilny. Komentarz* (10th edn, Legalis C.H. Beck 2021) No. 3. Differently: Małgorzata Pyziak-Szafnicka, 'Rozdział IV. Wielość dłużników i wierzycieli' in Konrad Osajda (ed), *Prawo zobowiązań – część ogólna. System Prawa Prywatnego t. 5* (Legalis C.H. Beck 2020).

55 Piotr Horosz, 'Art. 380 KC' in Mariusz Załucki (ed), *Kodeks cywilny. Komentarz* (2nd ed, Legalis C.H. Beck 2020) No 3.

obligation, however, the debtor who fulfilled the obligation can only demand the reimbursement of the value of the relevant part of the obligation in a recourse claim.[56] Lastly, in the case of indivisible obligations, all co-debtors need to terminate the contract through separate declarations of intent. Alternatively, one debtor could terminate if authorised by the others.[57]

In reciprocal contracts, when the debtors' obligation is divisible (e.g. payment for service) but the creditor's counter-performance is indivisible by nature (e.g. the obligation of the MTO mentioned earlier), the co-shippers are solidarily liable unless agreed otherwise (Article 380.2 KC). When the parties to a contract exclude the operation of Article 380.2 KC, Article 379 KC, which concerns divisible obligations (see above), applies.[58] Otherwise, the provisions that govern the solidarity of debtors and creditors are applied directly.[59] Thus, unlike in the case of indivisible obligations, the creditor may demand partial or full performance from all debtors jointly, from several, or from each separately (see further below). All debtors remain liable until the creditor is satisfied in full.[60] Since the partial performance of an indivisible obligation is likely be of no interest to the creditor, it can refuse partial performance (Article 450 KC). The creditor may also terminate the contract for non-performance after a reasonable period has lapsed (Article 491 KC).[61]

The indivisibility model has also been adopted in situations in which one debtor faces a claim from several creditors. In Poland, a single co-creditor can demand full performance (Article 381.1 KC). Alternatively, every creditor can demand full performance in favour of all creditors (Article 381.2 KC). In Germany, only the latter option is available (§ 432 BGB).[62] Turning to claims for damage, under Polish law, the payment of damages could be rendered to one of the co-shippers or co-senders and bind all of them unless the others object. In that case, the sum would need to be provided to all co-shippers or co-senders or deposited in court (Article 380.2, Article 367.2, Article 381.2 KC). Similarly, under German law, claims for damages can be enforced by one co-creditor or by all the co-creditors acting together.[63] As far as the right to termination is concerned, under German law, it can only be exercised by all

56 Aleksander Raczyński, 'Art. 380 KC' in Maciej Gutowski (ed), *Kodeks cywilny. Tom II. Komentarz. Art. 353–626* (2nd edn, Legalis C.H. Beck 2019) par. 6.

57 Bogusław Lackoroński, 'Art. 371 KC' in Konrad Osajda and Witold Borysiak (eds), *Kodeks cywilny. Komentarz* (29th edn, Legalis C.H. Beck 2021) No 5, 12–13.

58 Piotr Horosz, 'Art. 380 KC' in Mariusz Załucki (ed), *Kodeks cywilny. Komentarz* (2nd edn, Legalis C.H. Beck 2020) No 3.

59 Lackoroński, 'Art. 380 KC' (n 53) No 5.

60 Horosz, 'Art. 380 KC' (n 58).

61 A similar solution is provided by § 323.1 BGB.

62 Susanne Heinemeyer, 'BGB § 432 Mehrere Gläubiger einer unteilbaren Leistung' in Wolfgang Krüger (ed), *Münchener Kommentar zum BGB bd. 3* (8th edn, C.H. Beck 2019) No 2.

63 Heinemeyer (n 62) No 5; 7.

co-creditors (§ 351 BGB). Under Polish law, termination by one co-creditor does not affect the others (Article 382 KC).

3.3.3.2 Joint obligations (England)

Under English law, a joint obligation is the consequence of a common promise to do the same thing. As a result, there is a single obligation and a single contract. If several debtors make a single promise, the presumption is that the promise is joint, and each debtor is liable for the performance of the whole promise.[64] An express contractual agreement would be necessary to make liability joint and several (see below).[65] Joint liability is possible in the case of obligations that are due at once or in instalments.

As far as the actions of co-shippers or co-senders are concerned, the consequences of a single joint obligation are as follows: Since the co-shippers or co-senders have identical and indivisible interests in the subject matter of the contract, their individual rights and obligations stand or fall together. Thus, performance by one would suffice to discharge the others. Furthermore, any breach of condition or warranty, wilful misconduct, or a fraudulent claim by one co-shipper or co-sender would affect the rights of the others, allowing the carrier to exercise its remedies against all. Since the debt is joint, if one of joint shippers or senders that are sued jointly[66] makes out a defence that operates to discharge all, the others will escape liability even if they have not pleaded that particular defence. However, if the defence is personal to one co-shipper, the others would not be discharged.[67] In addition, the insolvency of one co-shipper does not discharge the others.[68] The co-shipper that would compensate the carrier under this scheme is entitled to recover contributions from the others. In principle, the amount of the contribution is the amount of the debt divided by the number of co-debtors.[69] This rule can be changed contractually or due to insolvency, in which case the amount of the debt is divided by the number of co-debtors who were solvent when the right to contribution arose.[70] Thus, debtors bear the risk of co-debtor insolvency.

When co-shippers act as creditors, they must all sue the carrier together. Fulfilment of the obligation to one of the joint creditors discharges the carrier from liability to all creditors unless the contract provides otherwise.[71]

---

64 Joint contracts are also used in fields such as insurance and construction law. See further: Raoul P. Colinvaux and Robert M. Merkin (eds), *Colinvaux's Law of Insurance* (11th edn, Sweet and Maxwell 2018) Chapter 15.

65 Beale (n 31) No 17–005.

66 Beale (n 31) No 17–009–17–010.

67 Glanville L. Williams, *Joint Obligations* (Butterworth & Co. 1949) 76–77; Peel and Treitel (n 35) No 13–011; See also: *Pirie v Richardson* [1927] 1 K.B. 448.

68 Beale (n 31) 17–024.

69 Peel and Treitel (n 35) No 13–017.

70 Peel and Treitel (n 35) 13–019.

71 Peel and Treitel (n 35) 13–032.

Likewise, a release granted by one joint creditor discharges the debt.[72] The same could be true of the payment of damages and contract termination.

Turning to the relationship between the carrier *qua* creditor and the co-shippers, the consequence of a joint obligation would be that action on the part of the carrier against one of the shippers also has an effect on the other shippers. This action may, for example, concern the termination of a contract.[73] If the obligation is severable, default would only justify refusal to perform the outstanding parts of the carrier's obligations. In this case, however, all co-shippers would be responsible for each of the severable parts (see further Chapter 7). If the obligation should be performed in whole, default justifies the creditor's refusal to perform the entire contract. If the carrier releases one co-shipper or co-sender, the release is available for the benefit of all the others since it thwarts the cause of action altogether.[74]

3.3.3.3 Solidarity (Poland and Germany) and joint and several obligations (England)

Obligations are solidary when all the debtors are bound to render full performance, and the creditor may require it from any one of them until satisfied in full (§ 421 BGB, Article 366 KC). Solidarity may also be presumed in the case of indivisible obligations (see above). For service contracts, there is a *lex specialis* that establishes a presumption of solidarity in cases of doubt (§ 427 BGB) or unless the parties agree otherwise (Article 745 KC in conjunction with Article 366.1 KC). In the case of joint and several obligations, two or more parties to a contract promise to do the same thing, and each also makes a separate promise to do the same thing severally.[75] Joint and several obligations and solidarity give rise to a single shared obligation.[76] Furthermore, as in the case of the other types of multiparty contract, if the shippers or senders agree to provisions relating, for instance, to the limitation of liability, these provisions apply to all parties.

Joint and several obligations and solidarity have a similar effect on co-debtors in respect of the claim for performance and of the available general defences. The carrier *qua* creditor has the right to choose from which of the debtors it wishes to claim performance, and this debtor might wind up being the defendant in the proceedings.[77] A co-shipper or co-sender *qua* debtor who

72 Peel and Treitel (n 35) 13–030.

73 Williams (n 67) 148–149.

74 Peel and Treitel (n 35) No 13–013.

75 Beale (n 31) No 17–003; Williams (n 65) 34.

76 Beale (n 31) No 17–003; Martin Fries and Reiner Schulze, 'BGB § 421 Gesamtschuldner' in Reiner Schulze (ed), *Bürgerliches Gesetzbuch* (11th edn, C.H. Beck 2021) No 1–6; Pyziak-Szafnicka (n 54) No 30–33, 164–167.

77 Under English law, the creditor can either sue all the promisors together or whichever promisor it thinks fit. In Poland and Germany, the creditor can claim from all debtors together, from the one that it deems fit, or from a group of debtors. For England, see further: Beale (n 31),

has rendered full performance to the creditor or performed more than its internally determined share has a recourse action against the other partners to the amount of its share. The default rule, unless modified contractually, is that the shares of the co-debtors are equal.[78] In case one of the co-shippers or co-senders becomes insolvent, the shortfall must be borne by the other debtors, who are obliged to provide compensation.[79] Regarding general defences, in England, if one of the co-shippers is successful in making out a defence that operates to discharge all, its success would relieve the others from liability even if they have failed to plead it. Similarly in Poland, a judgement rendered in favour of one of the solidary debtors releases the others if defences that are common to all the debtors have been considered (Article 375.2 KC).

However, despite their joint and several obligations and solidarity, the co-shippers or co-senders can often retain their individual positions and avoid the consequences of the actions of their partners. For example, the actions taken by one of the debtors in connection with its relationship with the creditor is effective within that relationship but not in the relationships with the other debtors. If the carrier releases one of the co-shippers from debt or waives solidarity towards it, this decision would have no effect on the joint debtors (Article 373 KC). The personal defences supply another example. Under English law, if a defence is personal to one co-shipper, the others are not discharged.[80] Under Polish law, co-debtors are protected in case one pursues harmful activities (Article 371 KC).

Individual effects are also observed to various extents in claims for damages. Regarding claims for damages, the effect of a carrier's claim for damages might differ between jurisdictions because the default rules might have individual effects. Under English law, it seems that all co-shippers or co-senders could be liable for damages. Since each co-shipper is liable for its separate promise as well as for the joint promise, damages could be claimed from any one of the co-shippers or co-senders, provided that the loss is not a too remote consequence of a breach of contract or unforeseeable at the time of contracting.[81] Remoteness would thus be difficult to claim even when cargo bundling is executed in milk runs because it would be difficult to argue that the co-operating shippers or senders could not have foreseen the various types

No 17–011; Peel and Treitel (n 35) No 13–006; for Poland: Wojciech Dubis, 'Art. 366 KC' in Edward Gniewek and Piotr Machnikowski (eds), *Kodeks cywilny. Komentarz* (9th edn, Legalis C.H. Beck 2019) par. 3; for Germany: Marcus Gehrlein, 'BGB § 421 Gesamtschuldner' in Wolfgang Hau and Roman Poseck (eds), *BeckOK BGB* (59th edn, C.H. Beck 2021) No 11.

78 Heinemeyer, 'BGB § 421' (n 51) No 4; Wojciech Dubis, 'Art. 376 KC' in Edward Gniewek and Piotr Machnikowski (eds), *Kodeks cywilny. Komentarz* (10th edn, Legalis C.H. Beck 2021) No 1; Beale (n 31) 17–027.

79 §426 BGB; Beale (n 31) No 17–027; Dubis, 'Art. 376 KC' (n 78) No 5.

80 Williams (n 67) 76–77; Peel and Treitel (n 35) No 13–011; See also: *Pirie v Richardson* [1927] 1 K.B. 448.

81 Beale (n 31) No 26–108–26–130.

of damage that could have resulted from the shipping of the bundled cargo. Instead, in Poland and Germany, claims for damages, unless otherwise agreed by the parties,[82] only have an individual effect (§425 BGB in conjunction with §280 BGB[83]; Article 471 in conjunction with 371 KC).[84] The rule may not operate in respect of indivisible obligations.[85]

Solidarity under Polish and German law can also be created on the side of the creditors (Article 367 KC, § 428 BGB). A co-creditor can claim full performance independently of other co-creditors, and the debtor is only obliged to effect performance once to the chosen co-creditor, which is effective against all. However, under Polish law, the rules on liability for damages do not provide for the solidarity of the aggrieved creditors. Thus, each co-creditor is individually entitled to compensation, as in the case of divisible obligations.[86] The same seems to be true as a matter of German law.[87]

The discrepancies between the jurisdictions under observation can also be related to the effect of the right to terminate the contract. Under German law, if several parties are involved in a contract on one side or the other, the right to terminate can only be exercised by all and against all (§ 351 BGB).[88] Polish law does not contain a similar provision. As a result, all co-debtors need to terminate the contract by separate declarations of intent. Alternatively, one co-debtor could terminate if authorised by the others.[89] Also, in Poland, the effect of termination by one of the co-creditors has an individual effect.[90] English law also does not contain specific provisions on the issue. However, since each co-shipper would be liable for its separate promise as well as for the joint promise, termination could be exercised by all and against all. In any case, the parties can, however, regulate such situations through their contracts.[91]

82 Kazimierz Zawada, 'Art. 371 KC' in Krzysztof Pietrzykowski (ed), *Kodeks cywilny. T I. Komentarz. Art. 1–449(10)* (10th edn, Legalis C.H. Beck 2020) No 2.; §425 BGB: '[. . .], *soweit sich nicht aus dem Schuldverhältnis ein anderes ergibt* [. . .]'

83 Martin Fries and Reiner Schulze, 'BGB § 425 Wirkung anderer Tatsachen' in Reiner Schulze (ed), *Bürgerliches Gesetzbuch* (11th edn, C.H. Beck 2021) No 4.

84 Pyziak-Szafnicka (n 54) No 40; Wojciech Dubis, 'Art. 371 KC' in Edward Gniewek and Piotr Machnikowski (eds), *Kodeks cywilny. Komentarz* (10th edn, Legalis C.H. Beck 2021) No 2.

85 Susanne Heinemeyer, 'BGB § 425 Wirkung Anderer Tatsachen' in Wolfgang Krüger (ed), *Münchener Kommentar zum BGB bd. 3* (8th edn, C.H. Beck 2019) No. 11–13.

86 Cf. Sąd Apelacyjny w Krakowie 16.09.2015 I ACa 750/15, Sąd Apelacyjnyw Łodzi, 6.11.2014 I ACa 623/14.

87 E.g.: Carsten Herresthal, 'A. Das Giroverhältnis' in Carsten Herresthal (ed), *Münchener Kommentar zum HGB bd.6* (4th edn, C.H. Beck 2019) No 253.

88 Rolf Stürner, 'BGB § 425 Wirkung Anderer Tatsachen' in in Rolf Stürner et al. (eds), *Jauernig Bürgerliches Gesetzbuch. Kommentar* (18th edn, C.H. Beck 2021) No 2.

89 Lackoroński, 'Art. 371 KC' (n 57).

90 Bogusław Lackoroński, 'Art. 377 KC' in Konrad Osajda and Witold Borysiak (eds), *Kodeks cywilny. Komentarz* (29th edn, Legalis C.H. Beck 2021) No 10–14.

91 Astrid Stadler, 'BGB § 351 Unteilbarkeit des Rücktrittsrecht' in Rolf Stürner et al. (eds), *Jauernig Bürgerliches Gesetzbuch. Kommentar* (18th edn, C.H. Beck 2021) No 1–2; Reinhard Gaier, 'BGB § 351 Unteilbarkeit des Rücktrittsrechts' in Wolfgang Krüger (ed), *Münchener Kommentar zum BGB bd. 3* (8th edn, C.H. Beck 2019) No 7; Lackoroński, 'Art. 371 KC' (n 57) No 7.

3.4 Observations

Judges need to answer the following set of questions when deciding upon whether the transport conventions govern the consequences of co-operation contracts as far as the rights and liabilities of the co-principals are concerned (Figure 6.2). This set of questions assume that a judge dealt already with the basic issues concerning the applicability of the conventions such as the existence of a valid contract for the carriage of goods that falls under the scope of the relevant convention.

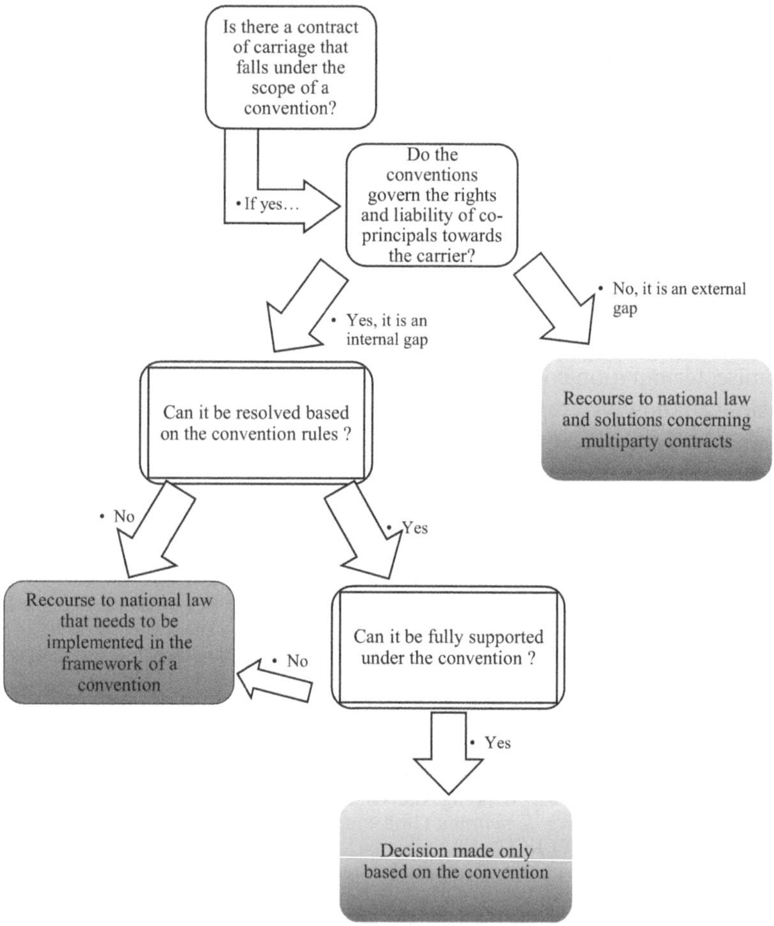

Figure 6.2 A decision-making process concerning joint rights and liability of co-principals under a contract of carriage

The decision-making process can end up with three different results. A judge can make a decision only by interpreting the text of a convention or can recourse to national law when the issue cannot be fully decided under the convention or when it concludes that the issue is not governed by a convention. The number of the possibilities that a judge will recourse to national law is higher comparing to the possibility of deciding a case only based on the text of a convention. The resultant forum shopping would be an argument against uniform carrier liability.

A huge chance that a judge will recourse to the national law has the following implications: As indicated in Section 3.3., the default solutions offered by national laws recognize to a high extent that the effect of multiparty obligations can be shaped by the agreement of the parties. As a result, contractual solutions on the organization of multiparty issues related to co-operation in cargo bundling might matter although views may reasonably differ as to whether the aforementioned freedom of contract and national law concepts operate under the transport conventions especially when a judge recourse to national law based on a decision that there is an internal gap in a convention. One argument in favour of the general operation of joint liability clauses could be that, since joint liability would serve primarily to secure the procedural position of the carrier, who acquires the option to sue all contracting shippers or senders (or one for all) at once, it does not disturb the convention regime. A counterargument could be related to the actual performance of the cargo bundling operations, the number of the consignments that are shipped, and the identity of the party that ships them. It is by virtue of these characteristics that the individual character of certain obligations can still be distinguished regardless on the contractual stipulations as to the effects of multiparty obligations and standard solutions that are set out by national laws (Table 6.1).

Table 6.1 Selected *inter partes* and *erga omnes* effects in divisible, indivisible, joint, and joint and several obligations

	Divisible obligation (PL/DE/EN)	*Indivisible obligation (PL/DE)*	*Joint obligations (EN)*	*Solidarity/Joint and several obligation*
Effect of performance of an obligation by one of the shippers to the carrier	*inter partes*	*Erga omnes*	*Erga omnes* (unless personal defences are effective)	PL – *erga omnes* (unless personal defences are effective) DE – *erga omnes* EN – *erga omnes*

(Continued)

Table 6.1 (Continued)

	Divisible obligation (PL/DE/EN)	*Indivisible obligation (PL/DE)*	*Joint obligations (EN)*	*Solidarity/Joint and several obligation*
Effect of carrier's performance in favour of one of the shippers	*inter partes*	PL – *erga omnes* (unless objected to) DE – no effect (carrier needs to perform in favour of all shippers)	*Erga omnes*	PL – *erga omnes* but might be to the one that sues (if the solidary obligation is also indivisible, in case of an objection, payment must be rendered to all or deposited; Arts. 380.2, 367.2, and 381.2 KC) DE – *erga omnes*
Liability for damage caused by one of the co-shippers	*inter partes*	PL – *inter partes* (Art. 371 & 471 KC) DE – *inter partes* or *erga omnes* when the obligation cannot be fulfilled by one co-shipper	*Erga omnes*	DE – *inter partes* (§ 425.2 & §280 BGB) PL – *inter partes* (Art. 371 & 471) EN – *erga omnes*
Effect of carrier compensating one of the co-shippers	*inter partes*	PL – *inter partes* (damages are of a divisible nature) DE – *erga omnes*	To all co-shippers (*erga omnes* effect of payment)	PL – *inter partes* (471 KC) DE – *inter partes* (§ 280 BGB) EN – *erga omnes*

4 Legal operation of the second execution model of cargo bundling

In Chapter 4, I investigated the carrier's liability for damage to the cargo and, more specifically, the ambit of the exoneration grounds under the CMR and the HVR. The analysis showed that legal certainty could be promoted at the level of the exoneration grounds if judges begin to attach importance to the performance of packing obligations. Based on the analysis in this chapter, attaching the importance to obligations seems also important as far as co-shippers' and co-senders' rights and obligations are concerned under one contract of carriage. However, the conventions are unclear on these aspects. The analysis indicates that a judge might consider the issue as an external or internal gap in the convention. Even if a judge finds that there is an internal gap, they may still recourse to national law.

In the paragraphs that follow, I examine the consequences of damage to the cargo and damage to the carrier by reference to the following issues: 1) The distribution of compensation between shippers and senders, 2) Shipper liability, and 3) Recourse against the shipper who caused the damage. I focus primarily on the consequences of a multiparty contract because the consequences of bilateral contracts were discussed in Chapter 5. Furthermore, I look specifically on the effects resulting from divisible and common obligations, as a result of the fact that there is a huge chance that national laws might come to judges' aid when deciding on the issues of plurality of parties under one contract of carriage (Figure 6.2).

4.1 Shipper or sender's right to compensation for damage

In case the shippers or senders are found to be able to execute their rights jointly, the carrier could discharge its obligation by paying compensation to any of the shippers or senders. The shippers or senders must then divide the compensation between themselves.

The first consequence of this arrangement is that the carrier might, with some exceptions, pay more in collective compensation. This principle might operate differently under the CMR and the HVR. Under the CMR, collective compensation would be higher than individual compensation if it concerns a mix of cargoes with values below and above 8.33 SDR/kg. The carrier pays the same amount for individual compensation and for collective compensation when the individual shipments contain only cargoes of a value not in excess of 8.33 SDR/kg or only in excess of this limit. Under the HVR, collective compensation would be higher than individual compensation when there is a mix of cargoes with values below and above 2 SDR/kg. The carrier pays the same amount in case of individual and collective compensation when the package limitation favours the shippers of both individual and collective shipments, when the package limitation is equal to the value limitation, and when the value limitation is favourable but the individual shipments only contain cargoes with a value that is strictly lower or strictly higher than 2 SDR/kg.

For example, suppose that there are two shippers or senders. One has a cargo with a value of 5 SDR/kg, and the other has a cargo with a value of 25 SDR/kg. Each cargo weighs 1,000 kg and is packed in a separate parcel. When the obligation is considered divisible, the conventions limits apply to each shipper or sender. In the case of collective compensation, one shipper or sender could claim 15 SDR per kilogram on average for a cargo of 2,000 kg in two parcels. Under the CMR, in the case of individual compensation, the carrier would pay a total of 13,330 SDR (5,000 + 8,330), whereas under collective compensation, it would pay 16,660 SDR (8.33 SDR x 2,000). Under the HVR, the carrier faces the same costs for individual compensations and for collective compensation. The individual compensation would be 4,000

SDR (2,000 + 2,000 because the kilogram limitation is more favourable from the perspective of each shipper), and collective compensation would be set at the same amount (because the kilogram limitation is more favourable from the perspective of the cargo interest).

A question arises as to the conditions under which joint creditorship of shippers or senders with *erga omnes* effects arises under a multiparty contract of carriage. The aforementioned operation of joint creditorship is more likely to be accepted under English law than under Polish or German law, where the rules on liability for damages do not provide for the solidarity of the creditors who suffered the damage (see Table 6.1). Thus, each shipper or sender would, as co-creditor, be entitled to compensation individually, as if the obligations were divisible. Accepting the possibility of joint creditorship in multiparty carriage contracts would also supply a means of circumventing the limitations on the carrier's liability. Although such arrangements are possible under the HVR (Article III, Rule 8), they are void under the CMR (Article 41 CMR).

When it comes to the distribution of the collective compensation among shippers or senders, the result depends on contractual stipulations. If such stipulations are lacking, distribution is likely to take into account the value of every shipper's claim. As a result, shippers or senders with lower value cargoes would suffer a detriment. For example, in the previous scenario, the situation would be detrimental to a shipper or sender that has a cargo of 5 SDR/kg, while it would be advantageous for a shipper or sender with a cargo of 25 SDR/kg. Taking into account the average value of 15 SDR/kg and the compensation of 8.33 SDR/kg (CMR), all senders would recover 55% of their claim. This leaves the sender with a cargo of 5 SDR/kg behind, with compensation at 2.77 SDR/kg, while the sender who has a cargo of 25 SDR/kg would recover 13.88 SDR/kg. The shipper or sender suffers a detriment because division is proportional irrespective of whether the carrier faces the same costs for all individual shipments taken together or for collective compensation.

4.2 Shipper or sender's liability

The difference from the first cargo bundling model is that all co-shippers have a contractual link with the carrier under the same contract. Under the first cargo bundling model, it was necessary to examine means of binding parties that were not parties to the contract (see Chapter 5). In the case of a multiparty contract, the focus is on the possible existence of *erga omnes* claims because of which the carrier could claim compensation in full from any of the co-shippers or co-senders as co-debtors. Even though these shippers or senders could then initiate recourse actions against the shipper or sender that caused the damage (see Section 4.3.), the insolvency risk would rests with the other partners to the cargo bundling contract.

A judge must qualify the obligations in a multiparty contract. Unless the convention is read autonomously and the existence of joint liability is decided based on the actual performance of certain operations together, the consequences of qualification will result from national law. Under English law, the obligations are severable unless there is a common promise. A Polish judge would need to decide whether to categorise the obligations as divisible or indivisible. A German one would be able to elect between divisible, indivisible, and solidary obligations. This is so because the concept of solidarity is looser under German law than under Polish law. Unlike in Polish law, under German law there is no rule that states that solidarity results from statute or from a legal act because of which the parties would need to make a contractual reservation in favour of solidarity (cf. Article 369 KC).[92] Instead, solidarity can be derived from the interpretation of the contract.[93] Furthermore, Section 427 BGB contains a rebuttable presumption in favour of joint and several liability, even in the case of a divisible obligation that would spare the carrier from the need to examine the shippers or senders' internal relationship if it is not disclosed in the contract. Uncertainty results because the same obligation can exclude or trigger the joint liability of co-partners in different jurisdictions. A determination in favour of solidarity or joint liability is more likely under German and English law than under Polish law.

If there is a general joint liability clause and the national law is expected to apply, a judge must still determine the extent to which it derogates from the individual effects of the obligations of the parties (see Table 6.1). General joint liability clauses might be more beneficial to the carrier under English law because joint and joint and several obligations have more *erga omnes* effects than civil-law solidarity. In the civil law, the parties need to agree on the solidary payment of damages separately if they are to derogate from the default *inter partes* principles. Otherwise, the carrier will, for example, only be able to invoke Article 10 of the CMR against single senders, and the overall claim for damages would have to be divided by their number.

For the application of national law, legal certainty could, in principle, be achieved at the level of the parties' contract. The option that favours shippers would be to avoid joint or solidary liability and thus to opt for a contract of divisible obligations. If the obligations are of a divisible nature, the shipper's situation would be similar to that which obtains under separate bilateral obligations. The option that favours the carrier is a joint liability clause that is sufficiently detailed to create *erga omnes* effects. The fact that the outcome of the negotiation process depends on the parties' bargaining

92 Bogusław Lackoroński, 'Art. 369 KC' in Konrad Osajda and Witold Borysiak (eds), *Kodeks cywilny. Komentarz* (29th edn, Legalis C.H. Beck 2021) No 7–15.

93 Heinemeyer, 'BGB § 421' (n 51) No 19.

power can result in different contractual arrangements and related different judgements.

4.3 Recourse actions

The discussion that follows concerns the internal distribution of the debt between co-operating shippers or senders that is owed to the carrier. The decision-making process (Figure 6.2) would highly likely end up here with a conclusion that there is an external gap and a judge can fully recourse to national law. The fact that internal arrangements between the co-shippers and co-senders concerning the distribution of the debt that is owed to the carrier once the carrier is already satisfied do not affect the frameworks of the transport conventions supports the argument that this issue can be classified as external gap.

The shippers or senders must be alive to the possibility that a judge might find their obligations to be divisible, indivisible, or solidary. Since there are no recourse actions for divisible obligations, the circumstances of the case, especially the wills of the parties, determine the apportionment of the claims and the debt owed to the carrier. In the absence of any indications, the parts owed to the carrier are equal. This default division might not meet the expectations of the shippers or senders. For example, the respondents to the questionnaire indicated that the costs of transportation should be divided proportionally to the weight or the volume of the goods (see Figure 6.3). Indeed, the lack of a recourse mechanism and the possibility that the carrier may be owed more than shipper's contribution to the co-operation can hinder cargo bundling.

Instead, if obligations are solidary and one shipper or sender compensates the carrier, it may launch recourse actions against its co-partners. It can claim a contribution from each co-debtor to the amount of its share. The default rule is that the shares are equal. Equal division is also the default in the case of the insolvency of a partner. However, the respondents seemed to favour of a proportional division instead (see e.g. Figure 6.4, graph C). The partners may bear additional costs in relation to the equal division, especially when their share is of a very low value.

The shippers or senders may circumvent the aforementioned shortcomings through a multiparty contract. The advantage of a multiparty contract with a carrier over a set of bilateral contracts Section 5.2 is that the parties can introduce certain solutions that are effective for all of them. For example, the liability of the shippers or senders may be unlimited unless otherwise agreed with the carrier. If the shippers or senders have negotiated a limitation of liability, then, under a multiparty contract, the limitation benefits all of them. Such a solution could certainly lower the burden of compensation to the carrier. Relatedly, the shippers or senders can agree on the specifics of recourse actions and derogate from default rules. I expand on these ideas in Chapter 9.

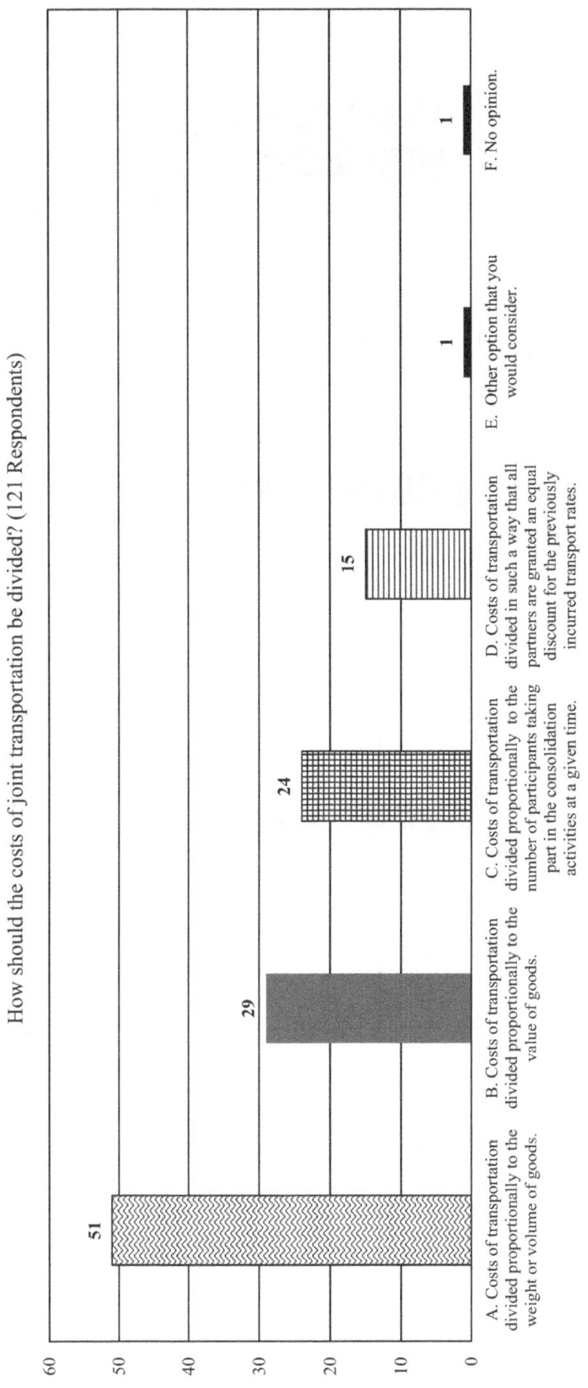

Figure 6.3 Preferences regarding the division of costs for joint transportation

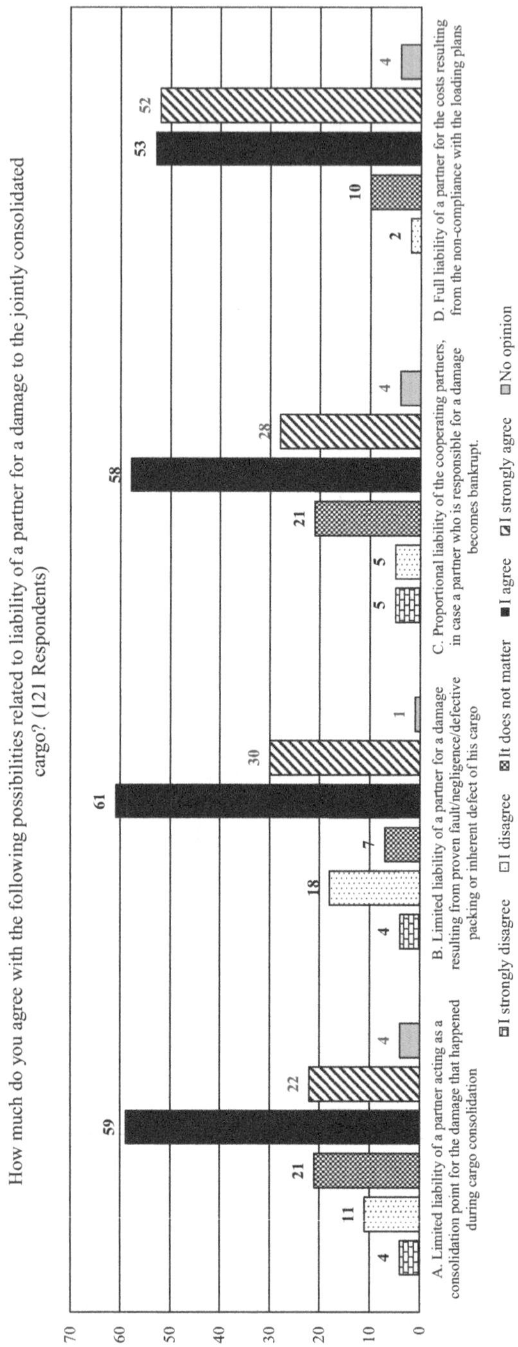

Figure 6.4 Opinions regarding a partner's liability for damage to jointly consolidated cargo

CHAPTER 7

Legal nature of a co-operation agreement for cargo bundling

Marta K. Kołacz

1 Introduction

This chapter discusses the legal nature of a co-operation agreement for cargo bundling. The co-operation agreement possesses the following characteristics: It is a long-term agreement which can govern the parties' rights and obligations and the allocation of responsibilities for agreed commitments concerning cargo bundling to varying degrees. The parties can establish a continuing obligation if they establish multiple contractual obligations for the future in advance (e.g. an obligation to arrange for the shipment of a truckload of canned vegetables once a week from A to B for 12 months). At the same time, the co-operation agreement may be incomplete. In cargo bundling co-operation, incompleteness manifests, for example, when the parties agree that they are willing to participate in joint shipments and that the cargo is to be shipped in various quantities to variable destinations on request. The co-operation agreement can be executed through several underlying bilateral contracts or through one multiparty contract (see Figure 7.1), which can specify the particular features of each delivery, its period, risk, and such like.[1]

Due to these characteristics, I use the term 'co-operation agreement' to refer to concepts such as a framework contract, an incomplete contract, and an umbrella or volume contract. A framework contract organises the process of concluding contracts in the future. The provisions of the executory contracts are included in it in a form that is so unspecific that it is impossible to determine the content of the parties' future performance. An incomplete contract is a contract with missing provisions. An umbrella or volume contract is a contract that provides for carriage on multiple occasions. All of these forms entail a certain degree of generality and only crystalise into individualised performance obligations at a later point in time.

Although the transport conventions attach importance to contracts for the international carriage of goods, they do not define the concept of a carriage contract. Furthermore, although the application of the conventions is tied

1 This chapter does not discuss the model of co-operation that involves a company established by the co-operating companies. For more on this model see Chapter 8.

DOI: 10.4324/9781003450801-7

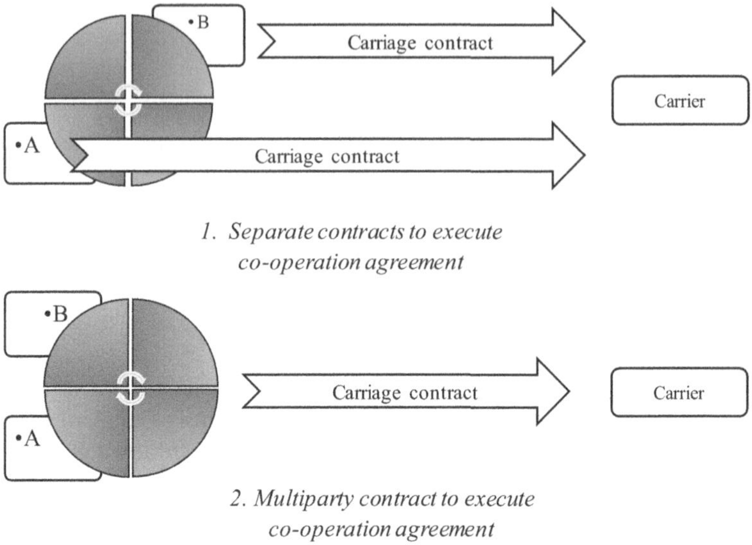

Figure 7.1 Execution of co-operation agreement (A, B – co-operating companies that send goods together)

to contracts, the Hague-Visby Rules (HVR)[2] require additionally documentary evidence of that contract that is mentioned in Article I(b) (documentary scope), and under the Convention on the Contract for the International Carriage of Goods by Road of 1956 (CMR)[3] that the parties need to agree for the scope relevant elements of the convention that are mentioned in Article 1 (contractual scope). Since repeated commitments of varying levels of specificity were not common practice at the time when the conventions were negotiated, the scope rules of mentioned conventions do not elaborate on this issue. Several questions thus arise. Firstly, do the conventions apply to general agreements? Secondly, if the answer to the preceding question is in the negative, when does a general undertaking for the application of the convention become specific? Thirdly, do the conventions apply to series of shipments, and how do multiparty considerations operate in such context? If the co-operation agreement is categorised as a carriage contract to which the conventions apply, the partners to co-operation cannot determine the liability that results from cargo bundling contractually.

2 The Brussels Convention for the Unification of Certain Rules of Law relating to Bills of Lading (adopted 25 August 1924, entered into force 2 June 1931) Trb. 1953, 109, 004127 and Protocol to Amend the International Convention for the unification of certain rules of law relating to bills of lading, signed at Brussels on 25 August 1924 (adopted 23 February 1968, entered into force 23 June 1977) No. 23643.

3 Convention on the Contract for the International Carriage of Goods by Road (CMR) (adopted 19 May 1956, entered into force 2 July 1961) 399 UNTS 189.

The application of the HVR can be determined on the basis of its text, which ascribes considerable importance to a bill of lading (B/L) (Approach 1, Section 2). There are two approaches to the application of the CMR. Under the first, the CMR applies to contracts covered by a consignment note. As will be explained later, this principle is not in line with the CMR scope rule. Since that approach ties the scope of a convention to the existence of a document, it is presented together with the HVR principle. Under the second approach, the CMR applies if the contract of carriage meets the scope requirements of Article 1 CMR (Approach 2, Section 3). Section 4 concludes with an evaluation of the level of legal uncertainty.

2 Approach 1: HVR and (unlikely) CMR – existence of transport documents

The first approach presupposes that a transport document is necessary for the application of the convention. The HVR adopts this approach due to the nature of a B/L. A B/L needs to be issued, or there must be intent to issue one.[4] Some have opined that this approach should also be followed under the CMR. The requirement of a transport document underlines the importance of the actual execution of carriage and excludes the characteristics of long-term contracts (compare Section 3.3), incomplete contracts (compare Section 3.2), and multiparty arrangements other than those under which two shippers are mentioned on a transport document.

The HVR ascribes importance to carriage contracts covered by a B/L or any similar document of title (Article I(b) HVR). Under the CMR, the existence of a consignment note is not decisive (Article 4 CMR). However, the importance of consignment notes for the application of the CMR is evident from some Polish judgements. The necessity of issuing a consignment note results from the argument that the CMR applies only when the goods are ascertained and therefore only to individual executory contracts and not to general co-operation agreements (see Section 3.3.1 and Section 3.3.2).[5] As far as contracts for the carriage of goods by sea are concerned, William Tetley is of the view that classification should proceed on a case-by-case basis. A co-operation contract can have the characteristics of the carriage of goods, yet to be the subject to the HVR, it needs to be covered by a B/L (Article I(b) HVR). Thus, individual shipments on particular ships are treated as falling under the HVR if transported under a B/L that becomes conclusive if in the hands of a third party (Figure 7.2). Once the B/L is transferred, it is a sole contract.[6] Otherwise, the co-operation agreement may form part of the contract of carriage along with the B/L, tariffs, and such like.

4 See further: *AP Moller-Maersk A/S (t/a Maersk Line) v Kyokuyo Ltd* [2018] Bus. L.R. 1481.

5 Sąd Okręgowy w Rzeszowie 16.03.2017 VI Gz 10/17; Sąd Okręgowy we Wrocławiu 23.02.2015 I C 413/14; Sąd Rejonowy w Przemyślu 02.12.2015 V GC 103/15.

6 William Tetley, *Marine Cargo Claims* (4th edn, Thomson Carswell 2008) 33–34.

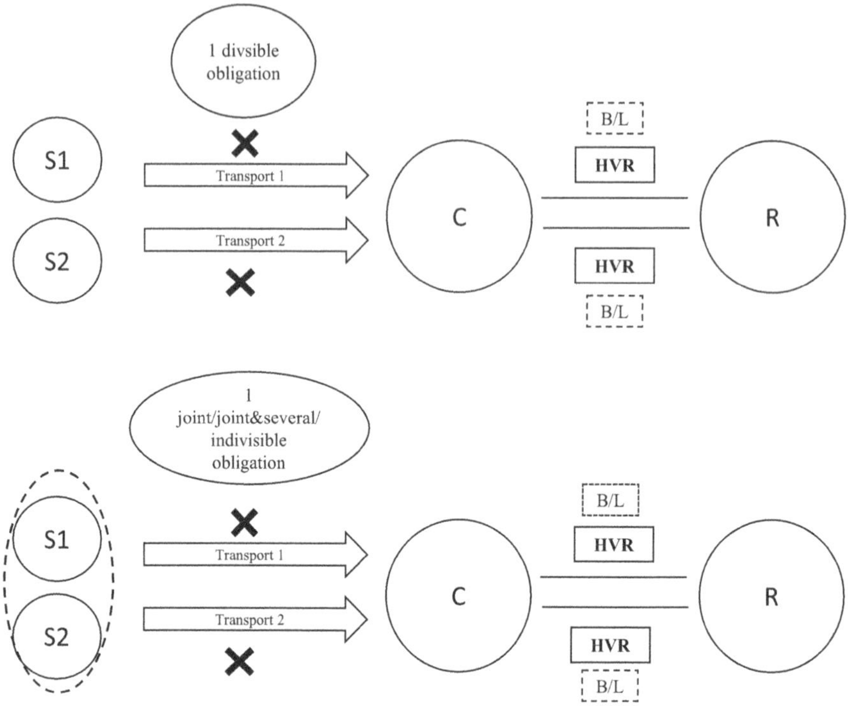

Figure 7.2 Application of the HVR (S= 'shipper/partner to cargo bunding co-operation', C= 'carrier', R= 'receiver', B/L = Bill of Lading, X= HVR not applicable)

As a result, co-operation agreements for series of shipments should be treated similarly to charterparties, which are employed, for example, for consecutive voyages or service contracts concluded by shipowners with regular customers for the carriage of certain volumes of goods and are not protected by mandatory law.[7] Since the HVR do not address co-operation agreements, there is freedom of contract in that respect.

3 Approach 2: CMR – determination of contractual obligations

The application of the CMR depends on whether the contract can be classified as a carriage contract that meets the CMR scope rule (Article 1.1 CMR). Problems may occur if the agreement is general or if only some of its elements are specific. For example, in case of the United Nations Convention on Contracts for the International Sale of Goods (CISG),[8] it has been argued that a frame-

7 Tetley (n 6) 35.

8 United Nations Convention on Contracts for the International Sale of Goods (adopted 11 April 1980, entered into force 1 January 1988) United Nations, Treaty Series, vol. 1489, p. 3.

work contract is a sales contract if it largely determines not only the price but also the quantity of the goods to be delivered so that the individual deliveries are not based on separate sales contracts but only on the goods being demanded.[9] A question arises as to the minimal elements that must be determinable for the CMR to apply to co-operation contracts for cargo bundling. Uncertainty exists at two levels. Firstly, the court must consider the elements that are necessary for the existence of a carriage contract. Given the external gap in the CMR, this assessment necessitates recourse to national laws. Secondly, the court must inquire whether the contract falls under the CMR.

3.1 General framework contracts

The CMR will likely not apply to general framework agreements because they cannot be contracts for the carriage of goods. In Germany, the obligations which the parties assume must be determinable (§ 154 BGB).[10] In England, the parties' agreement and its critical terms need to be sufficiently definite to be enforceable.[11] In Polish law, the object that constitutes the subject matter of the agreement is a necessary element of contracts. In general terms, the object of a contract is the performance of an obligation that is connected with a specifically defined (material or immaterial) interest (Article 353 KC).[12] Therefore, the obligations need to be sufficiently ascertained or ascertainable.[13] Framework contracts could thus be considered ineffective as contracts of carriage if they do not define contractual obligations with sufficient precision.[14] A similar conclusion has been drawn in the context of the CISG, which could serve as a useful point of comparison for a unified international law of contracts. A framework agreement that merely defines the sales relationship conceptually and only identifies delivery and acceptance

---

9 Peter Mankowski, 'CISG Art. 1 [Anwendungsbereich]' in Barbara Gunewald (ed), *Münchener Kommentar zum HGB bd.5* (5th edn, C.H. Beck 2021) No 21–22.

10 Basil S. Markesinis, *The German Law of Contract a Comparative Treatise* (Hart Publishing 2006) 78–79; Konrad Zweigert and Heinz Kötz, *An Introduction to Comparative Law* (3rd edn, Oxford University Press 1998) Chapters 25–31.

11 H.G. Beale (ed), *Chitty on Contracts* (31st eds, Sweet & Maxwell 2012) vol I, No 2-113; Ewan McKendrick, *Contract Law. Text, Cases, and Materials* (8th edn, Oxford University Press 2018) Chapter 4.

12 Witold Borysiak, 'Art. 353 KC' in Konrad Osajda and Witold Borysiak (eds), *Kodeks cywilny. Komentarz* (29th edn, Legalis C.H. Beck 2021) No 67–72; Tomasz Dybowski and Agnieszka Pyrzyńska, 'Rozdział III. Świadczenie, §10.II. Przedmiot świadczenia' in Konrad Osajda (ed), *Prawo zobowiązań – część ogólna System Prawa Prywatnego t.5* (3rd edn, Legalis C.H. Beck 2020) 205.

13 Marek Safjan, 'Art. 353 KC' in Krzysztof Pietrzykowski (ed), *Kodeks cywilny. T. I. Komentarz. Art. 1–449(10)* (10th edn, Legalis C.H. Beck 2020) No 15.

14 Sąd Okręgowy w Rzeszowie 16.03.2017 VI Gz 10/17; Cf. Fabian Reuschle, 'HGB § 407 Frachtvertrag' in in Carsten T. Ebenroth et al. (eds), *Handelsgesetzbuch bd.2* (4th edn, C.H. Beck 2020), where the same conclusion was reached in respect of national law. On the operation of a concept of a framework agreement in Poland, see further: Marcin Krajewski, *Umowa przedwstępna* (2nd edn, Legalis C.H. Beck 2002) Chapter VI.

obligations generally is not a sales contract. Only the individual contracts for the delivery of the goods that are concluded in the course of the execution of such a framework contract are sales contracts under the CISG.[15]

3.2 Incomplete contracts

Different conditions might be deemed necessary for a contract to be classified as one of carriage, which would cause it to fall under the scope of the CMR. The effect of incomplete contracts could differ between Poland on the one side and England and Germany on the other. This is so because, as noted in the preceding section, under Polish law, the contract needs to refer to an object, that is, the performance of an obligation that is connected with a specifically defined interest. Thus, there are some differences in the manner in which the jurisdictions under observation treat the basic obligation of the carrier to deliver goods under the CMR. In Poland, the carrier is under an obligation to deliver conforming goods to the consignee.[16] In England, the carrier assumes a strict contractual duty to deliver goods to the right person.[17] In Germany, the carrier is deemed to have guaranteed the delivery of the goods (*Garantiehaftung, Gewährshaftung*).[18]

The Polish courts underline the importance of a determinable subject of carriage (ascertained goods), a transport route, and due remuneration to the existence of a carriage contract.[19] As a result, a framework contract that lacks these elements will not be classified as a contract of carriage. The final specification of the parties' mutual obligations must occur through executory contracts, which could be qualified as contracts of carriage to which the CMR could apply.[20] As a result, the limitation period for actions runs from the dates indicated on the implementation contracts.[21] In England, conversely, the ascertainability of goods is not necessary for the existence of a contract of carriage and the application of the CMR.[22] In Germany, opinions differ

15 Mankowski, 'CISG Art. 1' (n 9).

16 Krzysztof Wesołowski et al. (eds), *Konwencja o umowie międzynarodowego przewozu drogowego towarów (CMR)* (Lex Wolters Kluwer 2015) 315–320.

17 Malcom Clarke, *International Carriage of Goods by Road: CMR* (5th edn, Informa Law 2009) 184–185.

18 Karsten Otte, 'CMR Art. 17 [Haftung des Frachtführers; Haftungsausschlüsse]' in Franco Ferrari et al. (eds), *Internationales Vertragsrecht* (3rd edn, C.H. Beck 2018) No 1–8.

19 Sąd Apelacyjny w Gdańsku 14.07.2016 I ACa 1106/15; Sąd Okręgowy w Rzeszowie 16.03.2017 VI Gz 10/17; Sąd Rejonowy dla m. st. Warszawy w Warszawie 08.10.2014 XV GC 1377/14; Sąd Okręgowy w Łodzi 30.10. 2018 X GC 270/18.

20 Sąd Okręgowy w Rzeszowie 16.03.2017 VI Gz 10/17; Sąd Okręgowy w Szczecinie 27.11.2015 VIII Ga 354/15; Sąd Rejonowy w Kaliszu 14.09.2016 V GC 1206/15; Sąd Okręgowy w Krakowie 10.04.2017, IX GC 1091/14; Sąd Rejonowy w Przemyślu 02.12.2015 V GC 103/15.

21 See: Sąd Okręgowy w Szczecinie 28.02.2013 VIII Ga 435/12.

22 *Gefco UK Ltd. v Mason* [1998] 2 Lloyd's Rep. 585; *Datec Electronics Holdings Limited and others v. United Parcels Services Limited* [2007] UKHL 23.

as to whether remuneration needs to be ascertained or only ascertainable.[23] The determination of the goods that are shipped has also been said to be important to the volume contracts to which the United Nations Convention on Contracts for the International Carriage of Goods Wholly or Partly by Sea of 2008 (Rotterdam Rules)[24] apply. A volume contract is a contract of carriage that provides for the carriage of a *specified quantity of goods* in a series of shipments during an agreed period of time (Article 1.2 Rotterdam Rules).[25] The Rotterdam Rules thus regulate long-term trade relationships, yet the quantity of goods must still be ascertained. Their ascertainment could occur, for example, if the cargo is shipped in certain minimal or maximal quantities on a weekly basis.

As far as the completeness of agreements on scope components is concerned, special attention has been devoted to leaving the choice of mode of transport to the carrier.[26] According to the strict interpretation of the rules, consent, implicit or explicit, to the use of a particular means of road transport is required at the time of the conclusion of the contract for the CMR to apply. Under the real interpretation, insofar as the contract leaves the choice of means of transportation to the carrier and the carrier performs the contract by road, the contract automatically becomes a contract for the carriage of goods by road, and the CMR can apply. In Germany and England, the carrier can choose to perform carriage by road. In this manner, it may also trigger the application of the Convention.[27] In Poland, no clear approach to this issue has emerged. The case law, as mentioned previously, underlines the importance of agreement, which must be at least implicit, about the transport route, which could also imply agreement as to the choice of transport mode.[28] However, the literature favours the real interpretation of the CMR contractual scope rule.[29]

23 Cf. LG Hamburg 17.7.2015 412 HKO 117/14; BGH 15.01.2009 I ZR 164/06, both decided on grounds of national law.

24 United Nations Convention on Contracts for the International Carriage of Goods Wholly or Partly by Sea (adopted 11 December 2008) C.N.563.2012.

25 On the development of this solution, see further: Prohanto K. Mukherjee and Abhinayan Basu Bal, 'A Legal and Economic Analysis of the Volume Contract Concept under the Rotterdam Rules: Selected Issues in Perspective' (2009) 40 *Journal of Maritime Law and Commerce* 579, 583–590.

26 See further: Wouter Verheyen, 'The Carrier as Designer of Transport' in Rhidian Thomas and Simone Lamont-Black (eds), *Current Issues in Freight Forwarding: Law and Logistics* (Lawtext Publishing Limited 2017) 58–64; Wouter Verheyen, *Contractuele aansprakelijkheid van vervoersintegratoeren* (die Keure 2014) 390–467.

27 Verheyen (n 26); *Datec Electronics Holdings Limited and others v United Parcels Services Limited* [2007] UKHL 23.

28 See (n 19). The Belgian courts follow this approach. See: Verheyen (n 26).

29 Krzysztof Wesołowski, *Umowa międzynarodowego przewozu drogowego towarów na podstawie CMR* (Wolters Kluwer Polska 2013) 63.

3.3 Long-term contracts

The CMR applies to every contract for the carriage of goods by road in vehicles for reward, when the place of taking over of the goods and the place designated for delivery, as specified in the contract, are situated in two different countries, of which at least one is a contracting country, irrespective of the place of residence and the nationality of the parties (Article 1.1 CMR). A question arises as to whether the CMR applies to long-term contracts in general (Section 3.3.1) and contracts for series of shipments (Section 3.3.2 and 3.3.3).

3.3.1 Similar contracts

The CMR does not apply to co-operation contracts that do not have the transport of goods as their purpose.[30] In general, co-operation agreements organise future events, such as the successive performance of specified obligations or future contracts. In the latter case, a more concrete preliminary agreement (Article 389 KC) on the basis of which the parties undertake to conclude a future contract and which specifies the essential provisions of that contract, cannot be qualified as a contract for the carriage of goods because its purpose is only the conclusion of a future contract, not the transport of goods.[31] The same can be said in cases when the parties undertake other obligations or ancillary ones.[32] The executory contracts could, however, incorporate the terms of co-operation agreements in the same way in which they can incorporate the terms of standard contracts.[33] For example, the courts can derive prices, notice periods,[34] payment due dates,[35] and performance

30 See also e.g.: Franco Ferrari, 'CMR Art. 1 [Geltungsbereich. Völkerrechtliche Verbindlichkeit]' in Franco Ferrari et al. (eds), *Internationales Vertragsrecht* (3rd edn, C.H. Beck 2018) No 4, who argues that the following contracts are not included in the terms of the CMR: Contracts for the rental of a vehicle, contracts for the rental of a vehicle with a driver *unless their purpose is the transport of goods from one place to another*, and time charter contracts *unless the entrepreneur undertakes to change the location of the goods* under its own responsibility.

31 Art. 37 Prawo Przewozowe (Polish Transport Law) Dz.U. 1984 Nr 53, poz. 272, which is no longer in force, stipulated that an accepted transport order was evidence of the conclusion of the preliminary contract. The contract of carriage was concluded at the moment when the goods were taken over by the carrier (real contract).

32 See e.g.: Sąd Okręgowy w Rzeszowie 16.03.2017 VI Gz 10/17 and Sąd Rejonowy w Przemyślu 02.12.2015 V GC 103/15, where the courts denied that readiness to perform transport services is tantamount to identifying the subject of transport and its route and thus that it is sufficient to ensure that the contract is classified as one of carriage.

33 Cf. *British American Tobacco Denmark A/S and others (Respondents) v Kazemier Transport BV (Appellant)* [2015] UKSC 65, where the court held that a succeeding carrier becomes a party to the contract of carriage only 'under the terms of the consignment note, by reason of his acceptance of the goods and the consignment note'. It follows that the only terms to which a successive carrier accedes by accepting the goods with the consignment note are those recorded in the note. That indicates the extent to which framework contracts could influence executory contracts; Sąd Okręgowy w Poznaniu 16.12.2016 XII C 101/15, where the court implied that proof that the individual transport contract forms part of another framework forwarding contract could cause the implementing contract to be classified as a forwarding contract. See also § 305.3 BGB.

34 Sąd Apelacyjny w Gdańsku 4.01.2017 I ACa 466/16.

35 Sąd Apelacyjny w Krakowie 26.07.2018 I AGa 176/18.

conditions[36] from the co-operation agreement, provided that they do not violate mandatory law.[37] A similar conclusion could also be drawn in respect of the analysis of related carriage contracts. The CMR does not contain general rules for the transmission of its regulations across two related carriage contracts. The only indication is contained in Article 34 CMR, which concerns subcarriers and furnishes them with additional protection by limiting the content of the contract of carriage to the terms of the consignment note.

The wording of a contract is also important for classification in the Rotterdam Rules, whose application to volume contracts is regulated explicitly. A carrier's public schedule of prices and services, its transport documents, its electronic transport records, and similar documents are not volume contracts. However, a volume contract may incorporate such documents by reference (Article 80.3 RR). Therefore, rate agreements, under which a shipper asks for a quotation for an estimated (but not guaranteed) quantity of goods to be shipped during a certain future period do not fall under the definition of a volume contract. Likewise, a contract that is framed as one for slot charter is not considered a volume contract (Article 6.1 Rotterdam Rules).

3.3.2 Umbrella and volume contracts – types

In practice, contracts for multiple shipments can take many forms. For example, a certain volume of goods may be shipped in a series of shipments during an agreed period of time, the parties may agree on a series of regular shipments for a definite or indefinite period of time, or the carrier may agree to perform carriage when the shipper or sender so requests. Subsequently, I use the terms 'volume contract', which denotes a single obligation to carry a certain volume of goods that can be discharged through multiple shipments over a defined period, and 'umbrella contract', which also concerns contracts for multiple shipments, but the cargo element or the time element is of no relevance.

The Rotterdam Rules and the United Nations Convention on the Carriage of Goods by Sea of 1978 (Hamburg Rules)[38] refer explicitly to series of shipments. The Rotterdam Rules apply to volume contracts (Article 80). According

36 Sąd Okręgowy we Wrocławiu 23.02.2015 I C 413/14. See also: OLG München 13.09.2006 7 U 3872/05, where the breach of the obligation that was contained in a framework contract could justify the presumption of a causal nexus between the wilful misconduct of the carrier and the loss of the goods.

37 See e.g.: Sąd Apelacyjny w Gdańsku 14.07.2016 I ACa 1106/15, where the appellate court agreed with the lower court that the essence of a contract of carriage is the transport of goods for remuneration, not the delivery of original consignment notes, which only has evidential effect. Therefore, a clause that made the payment of remuneration dependent not only on delivery of the intact goods but also on the fulfilment of other conditions (such as delivery of the original consignment notes) was considered contrary to the provisions of the CMR; Sąd Rejonowy w Gorzowie Wielkopolskim 12.09.2012 V GC 693/11, where the court stated that liability for delays in delivery always depends on Art. 41 CMR, no matter how the parties attempt to found it.

38 United Nations Convention on the Carriage of Goods by Sea (adopted 31 March 1978, entered into force 1 November 1992) United Nations, Treaty Series, vol. 1695, p. 3.

to the Rotterdam Rules, the difference between a volume contract and single contract for the carriage of goods are as follows: A single contract only identifies an obligation to carry goods, whereas a volume contract would stipulate that the same obligation to carry the same quantity of goods (which needs to be specified) would need to be discharged through a series of shipments during an agreed period of time. The structural elements which are relevant to volume contracts are the combination of the time factor and the quantity of the cargo. A volume contract thus minimises the importance of the voyage element that typifies voyage charters as well as the use of an individual vessel. A volume contract is more akin to a distributorship agreement.[39] However, Hannu Konka suggests a more nuanced use of volume contracts. Instead of regulating all details in a single volume contract, the contracting parties could cover general issues, such as package deals, series of shipments, and the period of co-operation but agree on each voyage separately depending on whether it needs to be performed by liner services or through the tramp trade.[40] A different approach is employed in the Hamburg Rules. Article 2.4 provides that if a contract is for the 'future carriage of goods in a series of shipments during an agreed period, the provisions of this Convention apply to each shipment'. Therefore, the Hamburg Rules seem to exclude the cargo element that is emphasised in the Rotterdam Rules. Also, the Hamburg Rules do not apply to volume and umbrella contracts but only to the single shipments that result from them.

In my opinion the application of the CMR to both volume and umbrella contracts cannot be precluded. The central issue is the moment at which the scope requirements are fulfilled. The CMR already acknowledges the possibility that a contract can be performed over several transports (Article 34 CMR), which bears semblance to volume contracts, at least as far the possibility of partial performances is concerned. Furthermore, the general wording of Article 5.2 could suggest that multiple shipments can result from any contract of carriage, including ones in which the cargo element and time element are not present.[41] The possibility that several contracts could be considered contracts for multiple shipments would likely engage national law concepts, such as the different types of obligations that can be performed in instalments or successively (*echte Sukzessivlieferungsverträge, świadczenie okresowe, severable obligation, świadczenia częściowe, świadczenia sukcesywne, Dauerschuldverhältnisse*; see Table 7.1; see the following section on the application of the CMR).

39 Lars Gorton, 'Volume Contracts of Affreightment – Some Features and Principles' (2010) *Stockholm Institute for Scandianvian Law* 62 <https://bit.ly/3GrIZbw>, accessed 8 May 2023.

40 Hannu Konka, 'Validity of Contractual Terms' in Alexander von Ziegler et al. (eds), *The Rotterdam Rules 2008: Commentary to the United Nations Convention on Contracts for the International Carriage of Goods Wholly or Partly by Sea* (Wolters Kluwer 2010) 342.

41 Similarly: Wesołowski (n 29) 174–175. The author does not, however, believe that the CMR can apply to such an agreement (see further the next section).

Table 7.1 Comparison of national concepts on the types of obligations (white – concepts that are closer to the definition of a volume contract, black – concepts that are closer to the definition of an umbrella contract)[42]

	Overall obligation determination	Time element
echte Sukzessivliefe-rungsverträge	Yes	No
świadczenia częściowe	Yes	Yes (definite period of time)
Dauerschuld-verhältnisse	No	Yes
świadczenia sukcesywne	Yes	Yes (definite period of time)
świadczenia okresowe	No	Yes
Severable obligation	Yes	No
RR volume contract	Yes	Yes (definite period of time)
HR volume contract	No	Yes (definite period of time)

42 In Germany, two concepts may be relevant. The first is that of the partial delivery contract (*echte Sukzessivlieferungsverträge*), in which the scope of the obligation is specified when the contract is concluded and performance needs to be rendered in instalments, but the time element is of no relevance. The second concept is that of continuous obligations (*Dauerschuldverhältnisse*), which result from uniform contracts concluded for definite or indefinite periods that seek to induce continued behaviour and from which new rights and obligations arise repeatedly for both parties throughout its term. See further: Reinhard Gaier, 'BGB § 314 Kündigung von Dauerschuldverhältnissen aus wichtigem Grund' in Wolfgang Krüger (ed), *Münchener Kommentar zum BGB bd. 3* (8th edn, CH Beck 2019) No 7-12. Several Polish concepts could be taken into consideration. The first is periodical obligation (*świadczenie częściowe*), which exists when the parties stipulate that performance must be rendered in parts within a specified period of time. The second concept concerns successive obligations (*świadczenia sukcesywne*), in which the content of the whole obligation is determined in advance and performance is rendered in the period covered by the contract. There are also periodic one-time successive obligations that make up an entire obligation. The creditor is entitled to full performance and may claim to enforce the successive obligations. The two can be subject to different regulations. The third concept is related to periodical obligations (*świadczenia okresowe*), which, unlike successive obligations, do not constitute the whole obligation. See further: Stanisław Włodyka, '1.7. Umowy długoterminowe' in Mirosław Stec (ed), *Prawo umów handlowych System Prawa Handlowego t. 5a* (1st edn, Legalis C.H. Beck 2020) 50; Tomasz Dybowski and Małgorzata Pyrzyńska, 'Rozdział III. Świadczenie, § 12.II.5. Świadczenia sukcesywne' in Konrad Osajda (ed), *Prawo zobowiązań – część ogólna System Prawa Prywatnego t.5* (3rd edn, Legalis C.H. Beck 2020) 241-242. In England, the relevant concept is a severable obligation, the performance of each of whose parts is independent from the performance of the others. See further: Beale (n 11) No 21-028–21-038.

3.3.3 Application of the CMR to volume or umbrella contracts with a multiparty aspect

Whereas the HVR does not apply to volume contracts due to its documentary scope of application (see Section 2), the issue is not clear in the CMR. Later, I present the consequences of the application of the CMR to umbrella and volume contracts and the operation of their multiparty aspect.

3.3.3.1 Application of the CMR

Three groups of arguments about the classification of a volume or umbrella contract as a contract of carriage to which the CMR can apply can be discerned, namely the contractual, the executory, and arguments that rely on the fact that the application of the CMR does not depend on the existence of a transport document. In Germany, much importance seems to be attached to the construction of the contract and the nature of contracts of carriage. According to Kay Uwe Bahnsen, a contract for the carriage of goods does not necessarily cover a single transport operation and a specific transport route because freight contracts are often concluded in the form of framework or volume contracts for an indefinite number of transport routes.[43] Some cases also indicate that the long-term character of a contract is of no consequence to its classification.[44] In England, it has been held that, due to the fact that a consignment note is not required under the CMR (Article 4 CMR), there is nothing that precludes the application of the convention to a contract for multiple transport operations.[45] The executory argument is influential in Poland. Krzysztof Wesołowski recognises that multiple transport operations can result from one or several contracts of carriage. Nevertheless, what matters is the actual execution of the contract because the performance of each operation can be subject to different rules.[46] In my opinion, all these approaches refer to validity of a contract, the existence of a contract for carriage, and scope of the CMR (in that order) to determine the applicability of the CMR and neither is decisive for the applicability of the CMR in isolation (Figure 7.3).[47]

After the investigation of contract validity (see also Section 3.1), the judge classifies the legal relation as being of a certain contractual type in order to establish what the intentions of the parties were and whether there was a

43 Kay Uwe Bahnsen, 'CMR Art. 1 [Geltungsbereich. Völkerrechtliche Verbindlichkeit]' in Carsten T. Ebenroth et al. (eds), *Handelsgesetzbuch bd.2* (4th edn, 2020) No 27; the same: LG Aachen 21.03.2017 41 O 57/15.

44 Cf. BGH 15.01.2009 I ZR 164/06; Cf. BGH, 02.12.1991 II ZR 274/90 (Hamm); LG Hamburg 17.7.2015 412 HKO 117/14, which reached the same conclusion on the basis of national law.

45 *Gefco UK Ltd. v Mason* [1998] 2 Lloyd's Rep. 585.

46 Wesołowski (n 29) 174.

47 See further: Wouter Verheyen, 'National judges as gatekeepers to the CMR Convention' (2016) 21 *Uniform Law Review* 441.

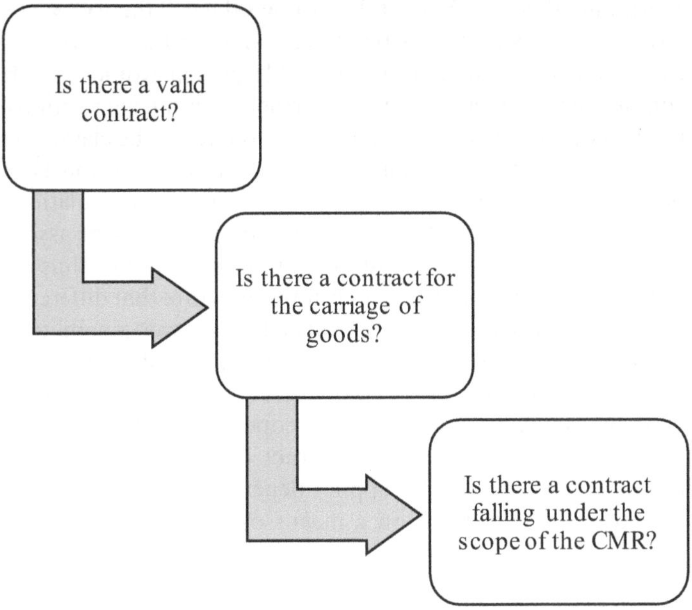

Figure 7.3 Decision matrix for determining the applicability of the CMR to volume or umbrella contracts

contract of carriage (see also Section 3.2).[48] In the scenarios under investigation, classification of contract is relevant not only for umbrella contracts but also for co-operating shippers who only adumbrate the form of their co-operation, including, to varying degrees, issues such as routes, volumes, times, and periods of co-operation, before contracting with a carrier (see Section 3.3.1). Furthermore, classification of contract is relevant to the Transport Orchestrator who may simply match partners and thus establish horizontal co-operation for cargo bundling or go further and administer the co-operation, which can include the preparation of a loading plan and searching for a suitable carrier (see further Chapter 8).

The process of identifying an actual declaration of intent on grounds of national law creates an obstacle to the classification of contracts because of the existence of different theories of contractual obligation. A declaration of intent can be assessed according to the will theory, the declaration theory, or

48 Hugh Collins (ed), *Standard Contract terms in Europe – A Basis for and a Challenge to European Contract Law* (Kluwer Law International 2008) 285.

the plain meaning theory.[49] A court that follows the will theory seeks to establish the true intentions of the parties.[50] According to the declaration theory, the court should focus on what a reasonable person would infer from the conclusion of the agreement at hand.[51] Furthermore, a legal relationship of a mixed nature (composed of many obligations) is likely to be classified through methods of assessment that pertain to mixed contracts. The courts can apply the absorption method, the *sui generis* method, and the cumulation method (see further Chapter 8). The differences in the approaches to the assessment of contractual obligations can result in different classifications, thus increasing legal uncertainty. It is worth mentioning at this juncture that different jurisdictions attach different degrees of importance to the ascertainability of goods in contracts of carriage (see Section 3.2.). Since ascertainability is necessary for a contract to be classified as one of carriage under Polish law, umbrella contracts are presently excluded from the scope of the CMR.

Even if the volume or umbrella contract is qualified as a contract for the carriage of goods, the CMR applies depending on which approach the judge takes towards agreement on a means of transport (Figure 7.4). The severable character of an umbrella or volume contract means that an obligation may be performed in instalments. The performance of an instalment is independent of the performance of the other instalments, which nevertheless constitute the whole obligation. At this point, the application of the CMR may become uncertain. If the parties agree, at the moment at which the contract is made, on all the elements that are necessary to comply with the CMR scope rule, the CMR will apply to each part of the obligation.[52] However, if they make the scope elements optional, as is the case when the carrier selects the mode of transport, the CMR might not apply at all (strict interpretation of the contractual scope rule), or it might apply to some but not all

49 Jacques H. Herbots, 'Interpretation of Contracts' in Jan M. Smits et al. (eds), *Elgar Encyclopedia of Comparative Law* (2nd edn, Edward Elgar 2014) pp. 421–447.

50 E.g. c.f. §133 & §157 BGB and Sąd Najwyższy 29.06.1995 III CZP 66/95 followed e.g. by Sąd Apelacyjny w Krakowie 26.07.2018 I AGa 176/18.

51 See: McKendrick (n 11) 382.

52 OLG München 31.03.1998 25 U 4876/97, where a *Fixkostenspedition* contract, which is subject to application of the CMR, was found to have this effect if concluded in the form of a volume contract for a series of shipments. That was so because the contract was not expressly concluded for every transport operation. Instead, there was one contract between the parties. See also e.g.: Bahnsen, 'CMR Art. 1' (n 43) No 16–17, and Helga Jesser-Huß, 'CMR Art. 1 [Anwendungsbereich, völkerrechtliche Sondervereinbarungen]' in Rolf Herber and Christine Schmidt (eds), *Münchener Kommentar zum HGB bd.7* (4th edn, C.H. Beck 2020) No 21–22, who say that, in case the parties have agreed to transport by air, rail, or sea without any authorisation to use substitutes and the carrier carries out the transport operation across borders by truck in violation of the contract, the CMR does not apply. Conversely, if the parties have agreed on road transport explicitly and the carrier violates the contract and conducts the transport operation by other means, the CMR will still apply; Ferrari, 'CMR Art. 1' (n 30) No 8, who argues that a contract intended by the parties as a contract for national transport does not fall within the scope of the CMR simply because the goods are transported across a border.

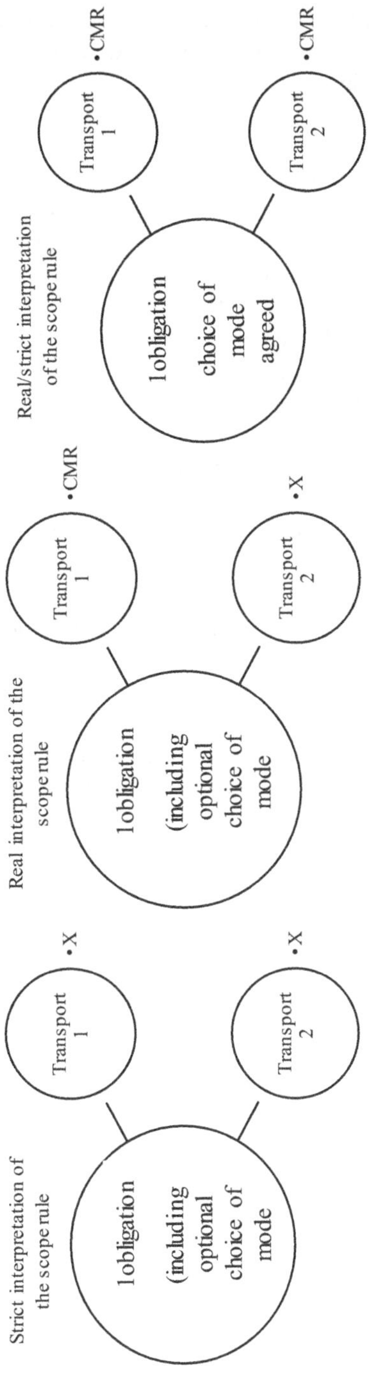

Figure 7.4 Application of the CMR to an obligation to be performed in instalments. (X= CMR not applicable)

instalments (real interpretation of the CMR scope rule). The latter option might be followed in England and Germany, whereas the approach of the Polish courts is uncertain.

3.3.3.2 Multiparty aspect

If several parties owe divisible performance or if divisible performance is due to them, the obligation can be divided into as many parts as there are debtors or creditors (see Chapter 6). The applicability of the CMR to single transport operations would be akin to its application to single obligations that are performed in instalments, with the difference that each sender would be responsible for its part.[53] However, uncertainty can occur because the parts that are attributed to each sender might not overlap with the single transport operation. Unless there is an agreement between the parties, and in case of doubt the obligation is divided into as many independent parts as there are debtors, not transports. Thus, the debtor could bear the risk of being tasked with rendering more extensive performance than what it has agreed with its co-debtors. Nevertheless, in the case of joint or joint and several liability, each debtor is liable for the entire obligation, however, performed. Therefore, all the senders bear responsibility for each transport.

In consequence, the multiparty aspect can create uncertainty, especially in case a real interpretation of the scope provisions is adopted (cf. Figure 7.5 and Figure 7.6). If the carrier exercises its discretion to choose the mode of transport and the obligation is divisible, each sender's position may, in fact, be subject to different transport regimes, especially when the division of the obligation does not correspond to the division of transport operations. In the

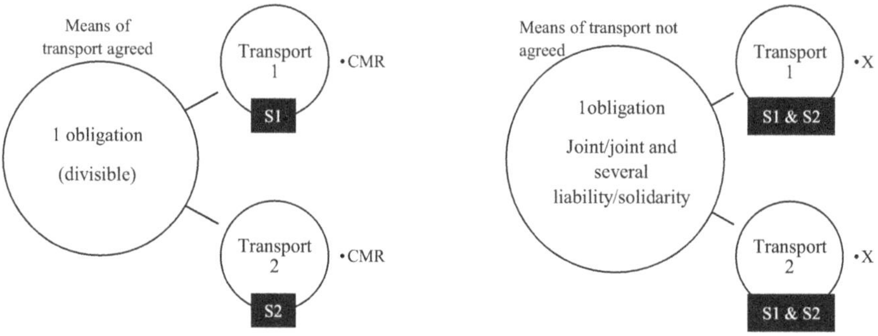

Figure 7.5 Multiparty element under the strict interpretation of the CMR contractual scope rule (S= 'sender liable'; X= 'CMR does not apply')

53 Małgorzata Pyziak-Szafnicka, 'Rozdział IV. Wielość dłużników i wierzycieli §21.II Zobowiązania podzielne' in Konrad Osajda (ed), *Prawo zobowiązań – część ogólna System Prawa Prywatnego t.5* (3rd edn, Legalis C.H. Beck 2020) 459.

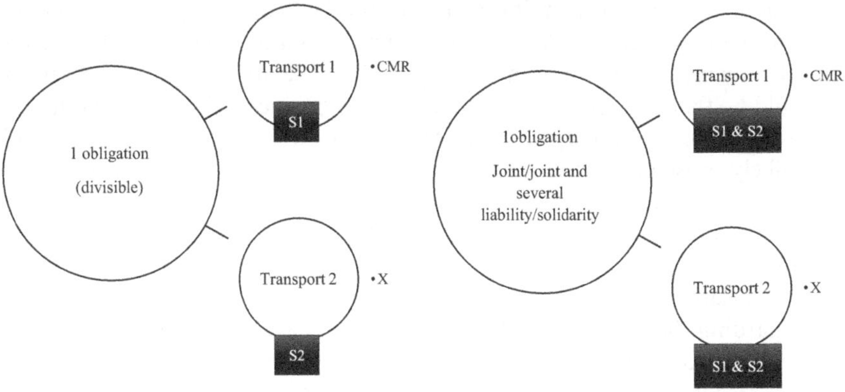

Figure 7.6 Multiparty element under the real interpretation of the CMR contractual scope rule (S= 'sender liable'; X= 'CMR does not apply')

cases of joint liability, joint and several liability, and solidarity, although each transport operation can still be subject to different transport regimes, all the senders are liable for each operation.

4 Conclusions

Three questions were formulated at the beginning of this section. Firstly, do the conventions apply to general agreements? Secondly, if the answer to the previous question is in the negative, when does a general undertaking becomes specific for the purposes of the determining the applicability of the conventions? Thirdly, do the conventions apply to series of shipments, and how does the multiparty aspect operate?

The first question must be answered in the negative. The conventions concern legal obligations that are created by mutual agreements between contractors, not with the expectations of one party that the other will do something that it has not undertaken to do. In the case of the HVR, the reason is its documentary scope. In the case of the CMR, obligations need to be defined if an enforceable carriage contract is to be found to exist. This point concerns not only general framework agreements but also more definite arrangements that lack some elements of a contract of carriage. Whereas a general framework agreement is not considered a contract of carriage in any of the jurisdictions under observation, the position of incomplete contracts is uncertain. The principal points of uncertainty have to do with ascertained goods. In the case of co-operation agreements, a contractual undertaking might often become specific at the point when the goods are marked or when they are dispatched to the port of loading for carriage. In addition, the parties might want to secure their individual needs, and this may prompt them to draft more general contractual terms and conditions. For example, if the shipper or sender is a producer of a homogenous product which is sold in large quantities, it has hardly any interest in obtaining the right to supply other cargo. Alternatively, it could be that the shipper or sender is in the business of supplying different types of cargo, and it may be interested in such a right. The courts of Poland, and likely those of Germany, consider agreement on this point necessary for the existence of a contract of carriage. The opposite is true in England. Furthermore, in Germany and in England, the convention apply if the parties confer a discretion on the carrier in respect of the choice of means of transport. The situation in Poland is rather unclear.

Regarding the second and the third questions, which concern the moment when a general undertaking becomes specific and contracts for series of shipments, respectively, the situation is clear under the HVR (Figure 7.7). Under the CMR, judges are required to classify legal relations. Under the HVR, the issuance of a B/L (or a similar document of title) to the holder triggers the application of the convention. Under the CMR, the existence of a contract of carriage and the conditions of the CMR scope rule must be made out. That several variables determine the applicability of the convention increases legal uncertainty. Relatedly, the HVR scope rule excludes contracts for series of shipments. In the case of the CMR, such contracts are not excluded, but applicability, again, depends on the existence of a contract of carriage and the CMR scope rule. Assuming that a contract for a series of shipments is a contract of carriage, then, depending on the interpretation of the CMR scope rule, the convention could affect the partial performances of a contract in different ways. Certainty would be achieved if the mode of transport is fixed by the parties in the contract because the CMR would then apply to partial performance. The same is not true of arrangements whereby the carrier is free to elect between means of transport. In conclusion, under the HVR, the shippers' co-operation agreement is not subject to mandatory law, whereas it

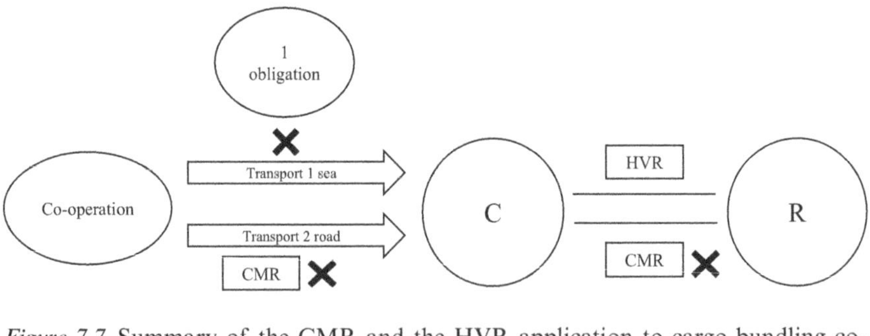

Figure 7.7 Summary of the CMR and the HVR application to cargo bundling co-operation (C= 'carrier', R= 'receiver', X= 'the HVR do not apply'; CMR X= 'uncertain whether the CMR applies')

might be so subject under the CMR. The senders' freedom of contract is thus limited.

The position of long-term contracts and co-operation contracts is also difficult to determine at the level of national laws. Unless the conventions apply, no mandatory law applies, and liability for damage that occurs outside of carriage but as a result of co-operation remains a source of uncertainty. This uncertainty is minimised, to some extent, in respect of the classification of services other than carriage, which trigger fault-based liability in principle, yet this does not solve the problems caused by the interaction of national and international laws. Legal uncertainty can be exacerbated when the conventions do not apply and a co-operation agreement is not considered a contract. For this reason, claims for damage that occurs as a consequence of co-operation must be decided extra-contractually.

Lastly, turning to the multiparty aspect, under national rules the presence of a plurality of parties does not affect the manner of performance but may affect the division of debts or claims. The conventions focus on the carrier's standardized liability regimes for the performance of international transport and to a large extend do not address the consequences related to the existence of plurality of parties to a contract explicitly. When the judge turns to national rules, and finds that the obligation is divisible, absent parties agreement it may cast doubts about its separate parts. In this case, the obligation could be divided into equal parts that might not correspond in number to the transport operations. Furthermore, the division of performance might result in the sender's claim being subjected to different transport regimes when the parties agree to leave the choice of means of transport to the carrier and the judge adopts a real interpretation of the CMR contractual scope rule. The situation that results from the division of the obligation could be avoided in the case of solidarity and that of joint and several obligations.

CHAPTER 8

Legal classification of the bundling company and transport orchestrator – third execution model of cargo bundling co-operation

Marta K. Kołacz

1 Introduction

The chapter addresses the third execution model of cargo bundling where partners establish a joint bundling company, and when a Transport Orchestrator (TO) is involved. A joint bundling company and Transport Orchestrator organize cargo bundling internally between the partners and externally with the carriers (Figure 8.1). The main focus of this chapter is the legal classification of TOs[1] and bundling companies which is analysed also against the background of online logistics platforms. For simplicity, I refer only to the TO in the sections that follow. I distinguish between the two in Section 5.

The online logistic platforms can support co-operation. For this reason, the TO or cargo bundling company can provide identical services on and off the platform. The same platform can provide different types of services that could be subject to different liability rules. While some steps have been taken to attach legal consequences to the use of platforms,[2] the applicability of private law rules is still dependent on the type of obligations that are undertaken by the service provider and not on the (technological) infrastructure through which the services are provided.

Legal classification is important because a TO and bundling company will generally only be presumed to be liable if deemed a carrier. If the TO or a bundling company is classified differently, the risk of cargo damage lies with the carrier who performs the service. Furthermore, liability for defective organisation can differ depending on legal classification. For example, as far as freight forwarding agents are concerned, the burden of proof rests with the cargo interest, who must establish the negligence of the freight forwarder as well as causation or contribution. Under the transport conventions, conversely, a

1 See also Chapter 1 Section 4.3 with the examples of legal self-classification.

2 Regulation (EU) 2019/1150 of the European Parliament and of the Council of 20 June 2019 on promoting fairness and transparency for business users of online intermediation services [2019] OJ L 186/57; Regulation (EU) 2022/2065 of the European Parliament and of the Council of 19 October 2022 on a Single Market For Digital Services and amending Directive 2000/31/EC (Digital Services Act) [2022] OJ L 277

 DOI: 10.4324/9781003450801-8

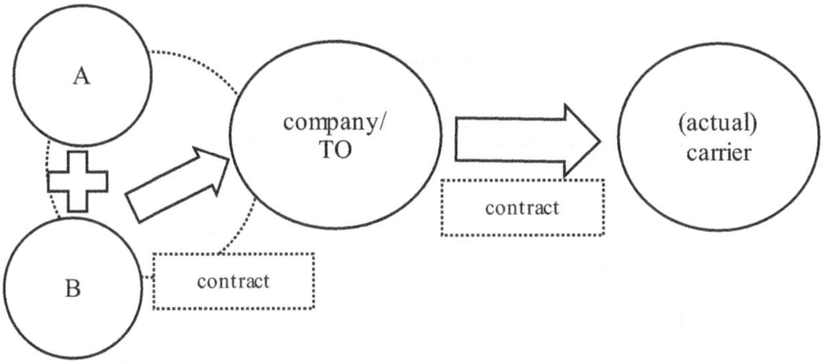

Figure 8.1 The model of cargo bundling co-operation involving a Transport Orchestrator (TO) or cargo bundling company

carrier is presumably liable. However, it can invoke exoneration grounds, and its liability is limited (see further Section 4).

The challenges that are related to legal classification result from existing legislation, with different types of rules applicable to specific service providers, and from online platform self-regulation.[3] Regarding the latter, the platforms predefine the terms and conditions of their intermediation services and often exclude any liability for cargo damage. However, at the same time, platforms could, in fact, fall within the scope of different regimes or at least be subject to general contract law. For example, to the extent that a platform is treated as a carrier, mandatory transport law will override its terms and conditions (e.g. Article 41 Convention on the Contract for the International Carriage of Goods by Road of 1956 (CMR)).[4] Although the judges' role may seem to be limited to applying classification parameters that are referred to in the case law and legislation to logistics service providers, the classification rules are not enumerated in an exclusive way, nor is there any strict hierarchy between them. In addition, there is a vast amount of case law on the classification of logistic service providers, which makes it more difficult to predict future court decisions.

Although this classification issue is far from new in logistics law,[5] TOs and bundling companies that operate through logistic platforms muddle the waters even further (Figure 8.2). One preliminary question that must be answered is whether a TO or bundling company that offers a platform service acts as an information

3 On the top-down and bottom-up approaches to platform regulation, see further: Michèle Finck, 'Digital Regulation: Designing a Supranational Legal Framework for the Platform Economy' (2017) LSE Law, Society and Economy Working Papers 15/2017.

4 Convention on the Contract for the International Carriage of Goods by Road (CMR) (adopted 19 May 1956, entered into force 2 July 1961) 399 UNTS 189.

5 See e.g.: Jes Anker Mikkelsen and Louise Lundsby Wessel, 'From Chameleon to Carrier Freight Forwarders Journey Over 50 Years from a Nordic Perspective' (2015) 50(4) *European Transport Law* 415.

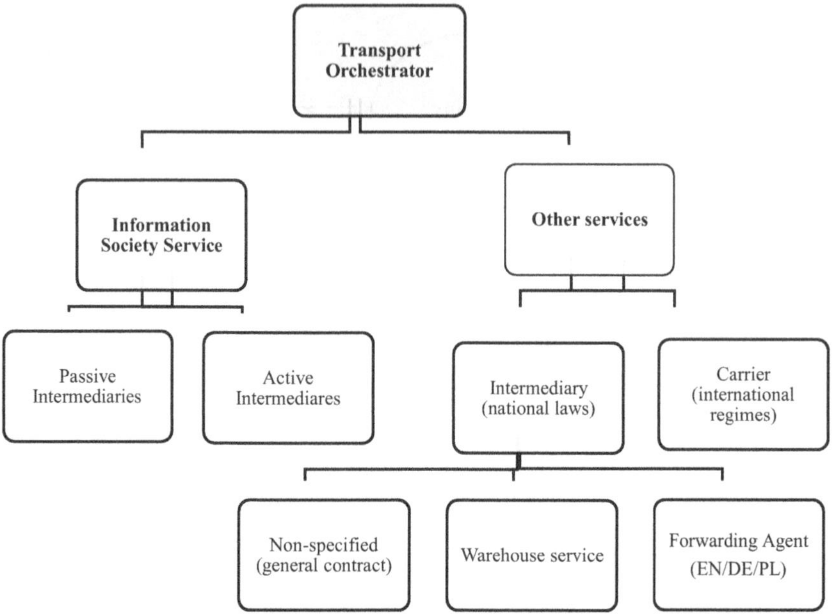

Figure 8.2 Possible legal classifications of a Transport Orchestrator (or a cargo bundling company)

society service or as another service. This distinction is complex for two reasons. Firstly, information society services can assume active roles and influence the presentation of data. While data-transfer platforms in their purest forms are likely be classified as passive information society services, influencing the presentation of data might indicate an active information society service. Secondly, while the key obligation of carriers is to provide the material service of transport, the key obligation of intermediaries is to provide intellectual services that are related to transport, together with accessory functionalities. This might sometimes result in the line between transport intermediaries that are information society services and those that offer other services becoming very thin. In consequence, judges, when classifying a TO or bundling company, must answer four questions:

1 Does the TO meet the criteria for an information society service, or does it provide another service (Section 2)?
2 In case the TO provides another service, is it a carrier or a transport intermediary (Section 3)?
3 If the TO is a transport intermediary, then what is its liability for organisational errors (Section 4)?
4 If the TO is a transport intermediary, what are the liability consequences for contractual chains (Section 5)?

2 TO: Information society service or other service

The starting point in assessing the character of a service offered by a TO is to decide whether it is an intermediary that meets the criteria for classification as an information society service under Article 1 (b) of Directive 2015/1535[6] and Article 2(a) of Directive 2000/31/EC[7] or whether it is likely to be classified as a form of 'other service'. If it is classified as another service, it might be subject to Directive 2006/123/EC[8] or the common transport policy.[9]

2.1 Information society service

An information society service, according to Article 1(b) of Directive 2015/1535,[10] is any service that is normally provided for remuneration,[11] at a distance, by electronic means, and at the individual request of the recipient. Article 1(b) specifies what this definition entails further. 'At a distance' means that the service is provided without the parties being present simultaneously. 'By electronic means' refers to the service being sent and received by means of electronic equipment that processes (including through digital compression) and stores data as well as to it being transmitted, conveyed, and received entirely by wire, by radio, by optical means, or by other electromagnetic means. 'At the individual request of a recipient of services' means that the service is provided through the transmission of data on individual request. Information society services include a wide range of business activities that are conducted online (Rec. 18 Directive 2000/31/EC).[12] It can be inferred that information society services consist of the transfer of data. Thus, these can include, for example, the sale of goods online but also the mere transmission

6 Directive (EU) 2015/1535 of the European Parliament and of the Council of 9 September 2015 laying down a procedure for the provision of information in the field of technical regulations and of rules on Information Society services [2015] OJ L 241/1. Art. 1(b) of the Directive (EU) 2015/1535 referred to for the purpose of ascertaining the meaning of Directive 2000/31/EC of the European Parliament and of the Council of 8 June 2000 on certain legal aspects of information society services, in particular electronic commerce, in the Internal Market (Directive on electronic commerce) [2000] OJ L 178/1.

7 Directive 2000/31/EC (n 6); Directive (EU) 2015/1535 (n 6).

8 Directive 2006/123/EC of the European Parliament and of the Council of 12 December 2006 on services in the internal market OJ L 376, 27.12.2006, p. 36–68.

9 For an overview see: European Parliament, 'Common transport policy: Overview' (2023) <https://rb.gy/zps5n> accessed 8 August 2023.

10 Directive 2015/1535 (n 6).

11 In light of Recital 18 of Directive 2000/31/EC (n 6), the definition also includes online services that are not remunerated but constitute an economic activity, such as online information, commercial communications, search tools, and access to and retrieval of data. Directive 2000/31/EC (n 397); see also: Case C-484/14 *Tobias Mc Fadden v Sony Music Entertainment Germany GmbH* [2016] ECLI:EU:C:2016:689 par 43. See further: Case C-18/18 *Eva Glawischnig-Piesczek v Facebook Ireland Limited* [2019] ECLI:EU:C:2019:821.

12 Directive 2000/31/EC (n 6).

of information or access to communication networks. Activities such as the delivery of goods or the provision of offline services are not covered.

Directive 2000/31/EC identifies information society services that are exempt from liability. Article 12, Article 13, and Article 14 of Directive 2000/31/EC state that the provider of information society services should not be liable for being a mere conduit, for hosting, and for caching. Thus, only services which play a neutral, purely technical, and passive role in respect of the data are covered by the liability exemption. To be precise, a platform that acts neutrally would not initiate transmission across a communication network, select the receiver of the transmission, or select or modify the information contained therein. In the case of caching, 'a neutral, merely technical and passive role' means that the service provider does not modify the data or interfere with the lawful use of technology to obtain it. Still, the platform needs to act expeditiously to remove or disable access to the information that it has stored upon obtaining information that it might, for example, be illegal. In the case of hosting, a platform acts neutrally if it refrains from illegal activities and if it removes illegal content immediately upon becoming aware of a violation. In such cases, the platform needs to observe the average care standard of a diligent economic operator which would realise that the content in question is unlawful.[13]

The judgements of courts in Europe have specified the activities that fall within the scope of an information society service and are thus not exempt. An active platform is one which, instead of confining itself to the neutral provision of services through the technical and automatic processing of data provided by customers, plays an active role so as to acquire knowledge of or control over the data in question. Knowledge and control are of a particular importance. They include processing data that is entered into the platform by users through the use of software and displaying the data under conditions which the platform controls.[14] The 'conditions which the platform controls' include processing frequency, ways of displaying information, and providing suggestions to clients.[15] Information that the platform adopts as its own could also be included.[16] At the same time, the active status of a platform does not depend merely on a referencing service that is subject to payment or on concordance between the selection of a keyword and a search term that is entered by a platform.[17] The platform needs to provide assistance, which entails, in

13 Case C-324/09 *L'Oréal SA and others v eBay International AG and others* [2011] ECR I-06011.

14 Case C-236/08 *Google France and Google* [2010] ECR I-02417; Case C-291/16 *Schweppes SA v Red Paralela SL and Red Paralela BCN SL* [2017] ECLI:EU:C:2017:990.

15 Case C-236/08 (n 14), par. 118.

16 See further: LG Hamburg 3.9.2010 308 O 27/09 (Germany).

17 Case C-236/08 (n 14) paras. 116–117.

particular, optimising the presentation of the data or promoting information.[18] Thus, an active platform can be identified through activities such as filtering, selecting, indexing, organising, classifying, aggregating, evaluating, using, modifying, extracting, or promoting content if it is due to the corporate achievements of the platform as well as the application of techniques to evaluate user behaviour in order to enhance their loyalty to the platform.[19]

The activities of logistic platforms, which include providing search engines to freight marketplaces or services that give rise to online contracting, are likely to extend beyond mere conduit, caching, and hosting, and thus, the TO might not benefit from the liability exemptions in Directive 2000/31/EC.

2.2 Other services

Information society services should be distinguished from other services. Nevertheless, some information society services might be inherently linked to other services and thus create a precondition for their operation. This point is important in two scenarios. The first concerns instances in which a TO offers services in addition to information society services, and the second has to do with the TO linking information society services to other services that are delivered by external providers. Two alternatives seem plausible: The information society service may be a part of the other service such as, for example, organization of co-operation for cargo bundling; or the information society service may be offered alongside the other service such as, for example, carriage of goods.[20]

If an information society service essentially consists of providing a tool for presenting, finding, and matching business partners, thereby facilitating the conclusion of future agreements, it is likely to be separate.[21] However, when information society services form part of subsequent services, the subsequent services become a dominant characteristic of the contract.[22] In that case, the TO might, in fact, be found legally obliged to perform these other services or to have acquired the status of a subcontractor or of a party that performs obligations on behalf of the provider of the subsequent service. Information society services can be considered part of subsequent services in three situations:

---

18 Case C-324/09 (n 13) par. 123.

19 See further: Corte di Cassazione 19.3.2019–9133/2015 (Italy); CA Lyon 15.09.2016 n° 15/06269 (France).

20 Cf. Christiane Wendehorst, 'Platform Intermediary Services and Duties under the E-Commerce Directive and the Consumer Rights Directive' (2016) 5(1) *Journal of European Consumer and Market Law* 30.

21 Case C-390/18 *Airbnb Ireland* [2019] ECLI:EU:C:2019:1112, paras 57–58.

22 Case C-434/15 *Asociación Profesional Élite Taxi v Uber Systems Spain SL* [2017] ECLI:EU:C:2017:981.

Firstly, information society services can be considered part of subsequent services when they are ancillary to the subsequent service to which they relate. Ancillary services are not ends in themselves for the users; instead, they supply a means of benefiting from the principal service.[23] In other words, an information society service would, in that case, aid the performance of the subsequent service, and neither service would be an independent economic activity.[24]

Secondly, information society services can be considered part of subsequent services when they are indispensable to the provision of the subsequent service. The use of the information society services must be a precondition to the use of other services. The availability of the following functionalities might indicate that this condition is *not* met: The online platform operates as an optional tool for estimating prices from market averages taken from that platform,[25] or the platform only constitutes an additional channel for communication between two groups of users. In that regard, the mere fact that the platform competes with other communication channels by providing users with an innovative service that is based on the particular features of commercial activity in the information society does not mean that it is indispensable to the provision of other services.[26] That a platform may be a channel of communication was noticed in the Polish judgement V ACa 163/17,[27] where the platform, despite verifying the credibility of carriers that were active on it, did not acquire the status of another service.

Thirdly, information society services can be considered part of subsequent services in case the service provider has decisive control over the conditions of the subsequent service. Decisive control over the conditions of the subsequent service could mean, for example, being able to determine the maximum fare that the carriers can charge or exercising control over service quality and the conduct of linked service providers, including their exclusion from the online platform environment.[28] The same can be said if the TO controls the maintenance of the key assets that are used by the underlying service provider.

In light of the foregoing, the legal classification of a TO as an information society service or as another service requires a careful analysis of the operational context and the obligations that are undertaken by the TO. If the TO is involved in the electronic processing, organising, and classifying data, it is unlikely to be able to avail itself of the exemptions for information society

23 Case C-432/15 *Odvolací finanční ředitelství v Pavlína Baštová* [2016] ECLI:EU:C:2016:855, par. 71; Case C-71/18 *Skatteministeriet v KPC Herning* [2019] ECLI:EU:C:2019:660, par. 38; Case C-390/18 (n 21) paras 57–58.

24 Case C-425/06 *Ministero dell'Economia e delle Finanze v Part Service Srl* [2008] ECR I-00897, par. 51–52; See also: Case C-434/15 *Asociación Profesional Elite Taxi v Uber Systems Spain SL* [2017] ECLI:EU:C:2017:364, Opinion of AG Szpunar.

25 Case C-390/18 (n 21) par. 54.

26 Case C-390/18 (n 21) par. 55.

27 Sąd Apelacyjny w Katowicach 28.12.2017 V ACa 163/17.

28 Case C-434/15 (n 22).

services. Furthermore, if the information society service seems to inhere in the other service, the TO is liable according to the legal rules that govern that other service, and the exclusion clauses in its terms and conditions are likely invalid. Since the legal classification depends strongly on the judge's understanding of the operational context, legal uncertainty is likely to be high.

3 TO: A carrier or a (*sui generis*) transport intermediary?

The distinction between a carrier and a transport intermediary has the largest impact on the liability of the TO, especially as far as the organisation of co-operation (horizontal relation, Section 3.2) and the performance of transport operations (vertical relation, Section 3.1) is concerned.

3.1 Vertical relation

Demarcation problems concern mostly legal classification as a freight forwarder or carrier (Figure 8.3). Classification as a carrier results in mandatory liability that is often presumed yet limited. This follows from the application of international conventions to contracts for the international carriage of goods. However, the relevant definitions and parameters are not set by the international transport conventions. Furthermore, uniformity in the field of transport intermediaries is lacking. The 1967 draft Convention on Contracts of Agency for Forwarding Agents Relating to International Carriage of Goods never came into force.[29] Legal classification thus depends on domestic concepts of transport intermediaries, which provide more support to judges. The national laws on this point are largely non-mandatory and impose fault-based liability on the intermediary, with the exception of German law (see below), under which the transport intermediary can be subject to mandatory carrier liability. Different classifications can be the result of attaching different weights to the wording of a contract, the actions of the parties, and the different conditions for classification as a carrier or freight forwarder. The topic has already been the subject of many publications.[30] Later, I only outline the

29 On this convention, see: Jan Ramberg, 'Unification of the Law of International Freight Forwarding' (1998) 3(1) *Uniform Law Review* 5; on the Model Law for freight forwarding, see: Simone Lamont-Black, 'Towards Transparency and Predictability in Freight Forwarding the Case for a Model Law' in Jason Chuah (ed), *Research Handbook on Maritime Law and Regulation* (Edward Elgar 2019).

30 For England, see further: Malcom Clarke, *International Carriage of Goods by Road: CMR* (5th edn, Informa Law 2009) 21–26, Paul M. Bugden, 'Freight Forwarder – Agent or Carrier? Categories of Forwarding Contracts' in Rhidian Thomas and Simone Lamont-Black (eds), *Current Issues in Freight Forwarding: Law and Logistics* (Lawtext Publishing Limited 2017); for Germany: Ingo Koller, *Transportrecht Kommentar* (C.H. Beck 2013) 621–718, 941–943: for Poland: Mirosław Stec, 'Rozdział 18. Umowy w działalności transportowo-logistycznej' in Mirosław Stec (ed), *Prawo umów handlowych System Prawa Handlowego tom 5c* (1st edn, Legalis C.H.

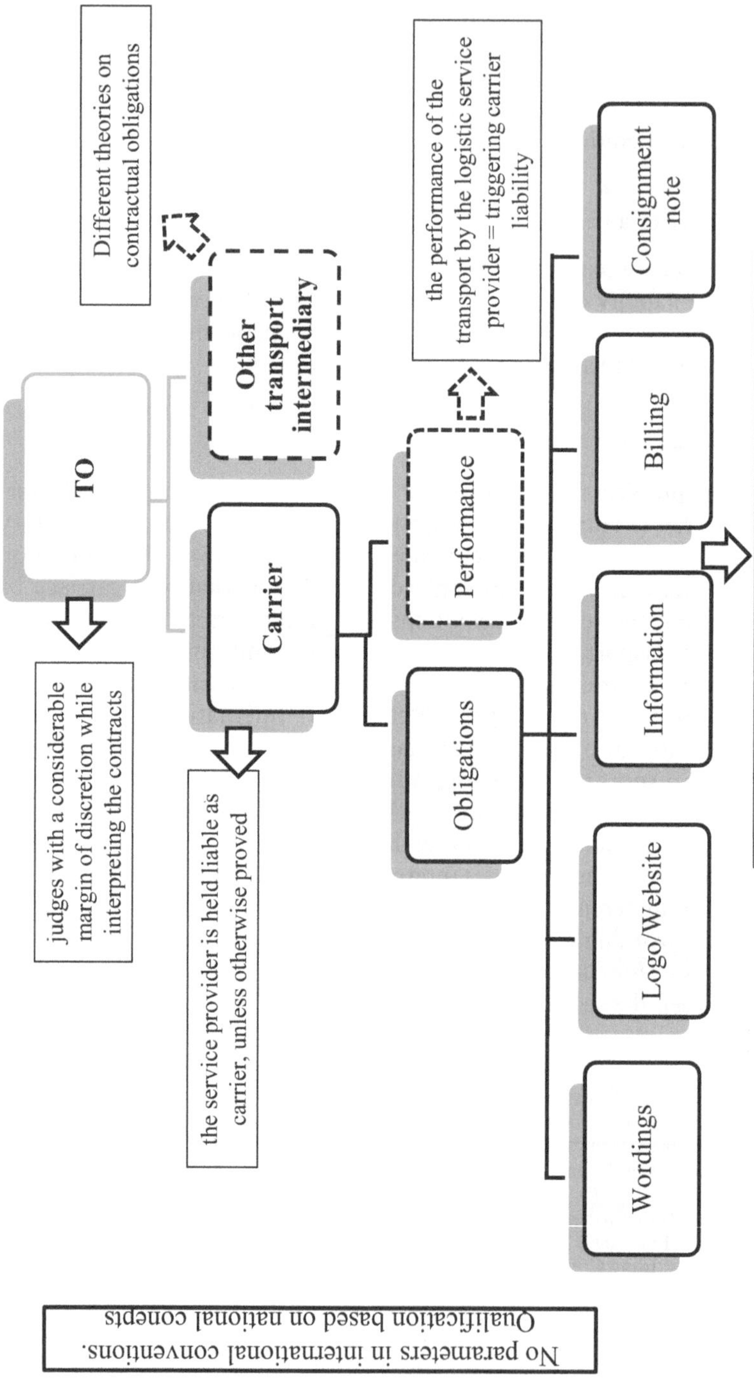

Figure 8.3 Legal classification of a Transport Orchestrator (TO) as a carrier or another transport intermediary

potential points of uncertainty in the three jurisdictions under analysis, which are England, Poland, and Germany.

As far as the wording of the contract and the actions of the parties are concerned, there is a noticeable difference between England and Germany on one side and Poland on the other. In England and Germany, the factual context, including negotiations and the manner in which the contract was performed, are decisive.[31] In Poland, much importance is attached to the scope of the obligations that are undertaken at the moment of contracting. The Polish courts seem to subscribe to the view that the content of the obligation that the service provider accepts, and not its activity, is the basis for distinguishing between a contract of carriage and a freight forwarding contract.[32] If the only obligation that the service provider has offered to assume is to carry goods and the tacit or implicit agreement (*facta concludentia*) do not confirm the existence of additional contractual provisions on services that are related to carriage, then the contract is of carriage, not a forwarding contract.[33] The same was found to be true of a service provider who had subcontracted carriage: The contract did not indicate services other than transport, which would be necessary for classification as a freight forwarder under Article 794.1 KC.[34] As a result, the different approaches to the interpretation of contracts and the broad context in which it occurs in Germany and England make it difficult for parties to predict classification *ex ante*.

The difficulty of predicting the classification of a service provider also results from the different weights that are attached to the relevant factors, which, in any event, lack a clear hierarchical ordering. For example, in England and Germany, lump sum remuneration is indicative of carrier status.[35] The importance of this factor is downplayed in the Polish literature, but since the case law on the matter is sparse, different outcomes are possible.[36] Another factor that could be decisive is the performance of transport

Beck 2020); See also: Frank Smeele, 'Legal Conceptualisation of the Freight Forwarder: Some Comparative Reflections on the Disunified Law of Forwarding' in Rhidian Thomas and Simone Lamont-Black (eds), *Current Issues in Freight Forwarding: Law and Logistics* (Lawtext Publishing Limited 2017); Wouter Verheyen, *Contractuele aansprakelijkheid van vervoersintegratoeren* (die Keure 2014) 115–289.

31 Paul M. Bugden and Simone Lamont-Black, *Goods in Transit and Freight Forwarding* (3rd edn, Sweet & Maxwell 2013) No 15–034; *Tetroc Ltd. v Cross-Con (International)* [1981] 1 Lloyd's Rep. 192; *Investors Compensation Scheme Ltd. v West Bromwich Building Society* [1997] UKHL 28; *Aqualon (UK) Ltd. and Another v. Vallana Shipping Corporation and Others* [1994] 1 Lloyd's Rep. 669; OLG München 12.04.1990 23 U 3161/88.

32 Sąd Najwyższy 20.02.2018 V CSK 205/17; Sąd Apelacyjny w Katowicach 18.04.2005 I ACa 2051/04.

33 Sąd Najwyższy 20.02.2018 V CSK 205/17; Sąd Najwyższy 06.10.2004 I CK 199/04.

34 Sąd Najwyższy 23.05.2018 IV CSK 425/17; Sądu Apelacyjny w Warszawie 7.09.2016 I ACa 1421/15.

35 Clarke (n 30) 25 and case law cited there; OLG München 12.04.1990 23 U 3161/88.

36 Krzysztof Wesołowski, *Umowa międzynarodowego przewozu drogowego towarów na podstawie CMR* (Wolters Kluwer Polska 2013) 130–131.

operations by a logistics service provider, which triggers carrier liability. For a TO that operates on an online platform, classification as a carrier could be triggered if it is found to be the employer of the carrier in charge of the actual transportation.[37]

Considering the wide variety of conditions that are taken into account and the absence of a strict hierarchy, it is unsurprising that these conditions support different classification outcomes. Since classification as a freight forwarder is generally more favorable for the service provider, in some countries, the case law applies the *contra proferentem* rule to instances of ambiguity.[38] Consequently, the logistics service provider qualifies as a carrier. In most cases, the *contra proferentem* rule is applied only to divide the burden of proof: The service provider is held liable as carrier unless it establishes that it contracted only as a freight forwarder.[39]

3.2 Horizontal relation

The characteristic features of the TO's service is the organisation of co-operation between partners that want to ship their goods together and the preparation of transport arrangements. A question arises as to how the courts can treat the first of these characteristics. Since the TO's service is of a mixed nature, mixed contracts doctrines could be important. The rules on mixed contracts are a source of uncertainty, especially because several methods can be employed by the courts to assess contracts. The courts can apply the absorption method, the *sui generis* method, and the cumulation method.[40] The organisation of horizontal co-operation would be subject to the mandatory law of transport conventions if it is considered a part of the obligation to carry and when the freight forwarder acquires carrier liability as under German law (see Figure 8.4).

The absorption method assumes that a contract can be classified according to its dominant element. Therefore, one set of rules applies. The adoption of this method would imply that the organisation of co-operation is ancillary to the main obligation, namely to carry or to organise carriage. For example, when the obligation to carry is incidentally interrupted by storage or transshipment

37 For example, this can happen when the drivers are deemed to be employees of the platform. See: *Uber BV and others (Appellants) v Aslam and others (Respondents)* [2021] UKSC 5.

38 E.g.: *Aqualon (UK) Ltd. and Another v Vallana Shipping Corporation and Others* [1994] 1 Lloyd's Rep. 669.

39 Sąd Najwyższy 27.08.2019 V CSK 191/18; Sąd Apelacyjny w Warszawie 10.03.2016 VI ACa 238/15; Helga Jesser-Huß, CMR Art. 1 [Anwendungsbereich, völkerrechtliche Sondervereinbarungen] in Rolf Herber and Christine Schmidt (eds), *Münchener Kommentar zum HGB bd.7* (4th edn, C.H. Beck 2020) No 5.

40 E.g. Sąd Apelacyjny w Katowicach 27.10.2007 I ACa 400/07; See also: Susan Niessen, *The Legal Position of Terminal Operators in Hinterland Networks. Mixed contracts and Third Parties* (Paris Legal Publishers 2017) 75–104.

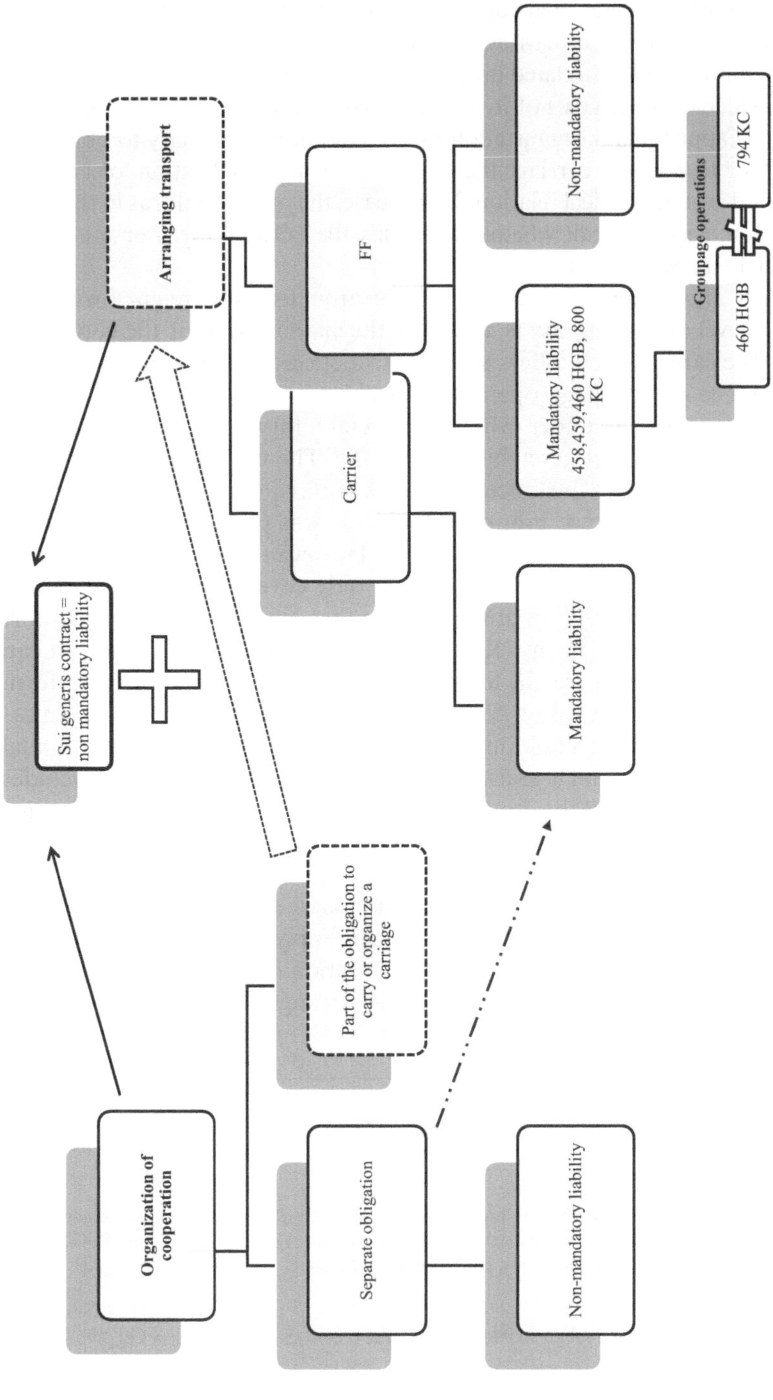

Figure 8.4 Possible legal classifications of the Transport Orchestrator's obligations and liability consequences (HGB – German Commercial Code Handelsgesetzbuch, KC – Polish Civil Code Kodeks Cywilny, FF – Freight Forwarder)

issues, actions of operational convenience have been found not to prevent the existence of a contract of carriage and the applications of the CMR.[41] In that case, an individual load-related order that was related to the transport contract was considered to form part of it, and the CMR applied.[42] In fact, if absorption method is applied, and organization of co-operation is ancillary to obligation to carry or to organise carriage there could be a single obligation for both the horizontal and the vertical relation. In this case, the judge would, as in the vertical relation, need to decide whether to classify the TO as a carrier or as a freight forwarder (see Section 3.1).

Even if the judge classifies the service provider as a freight forwarder, another level of uncertainty is added by the classification of the consolidation of the cargo, which differs across jurisdictions. Under German law, the performance of groupage operations establishes a special type of freight forwarding contract, under which the freight forwarder acquires carrier liability (§ 460 Handelsgesetzbuch (HGB)).[43] The collective shipment can thus be seen as a special instance of the execution of a forwarding contract.[44] A similar construction of groupage transport was provided by the rules of the previous Polish law of obligations.[45] However, in the present version of that law, a freight forwarding contract only covers sending or receiving a consignment or providing other services that are related to its transport (Article 794 Kodeks Cywilny (KC)).[46] However, the collective shipment can still be organised by a freight forwarder, and it will be considered to form part of the freight forwarding contract if it is inseparable from the organisation of transport.[47] Such holdings have been issued in respect of multimodal freight forwarding, which assists multimodal transportation and includes reloading and possibly the storage of goods enroute.[48] The main outcome is that consolidation of cargo can trigger different liability rules in Poland and Germany.

The *sui generis* method is applied in situations when the contract is regarded as being of its own kind. This method would imply that the combination of the TO's tasks that are related to the organisation of co-operation for cargo bundling and the preparation of transport arrangements would result in a

41 Clarke (n 30) 37.
42 OLG Nürnberg 14.04.2015 3 U 1573/14.
43 Handelsgesetzbuch vom 10. Mai 1897 (RGBl. S. 219) BGBl. III/FNA 4100-1 (with further changes).
44 Similarly: Clarke (n 30) 268.
45 See further: Leszek Ogiegło, 'Umowa spedycji' in Jerzy Rajski (ed), *Prawo zobowiązań – część szczegółowa System Prawa Prywatnego tom 7* (4th edn, C.H. Beck 2018) 1146–1147.
46 Ustawa z dnia 23 kwietnia 1964 r. – Kodeks cywilny Dz.U. 1964 nr 16 poz. 93 (with further changes).
47 Stec (n 30) 329–331.
48 Sąd Okręgowy w Szczecinie 20.04.2018 VIII Ga 133/18; Sąd Rejonowy w Gdyni 6.11.2019 VI GC 532/19.

completely new form of contract. For example, since the TO often claims to be a *sui generis* transport intermediary who is thus not subject to standard liability rules, its situation could be compared to that of a multimodal transport operator. In Germany, multimodal contracts are *sui generis* contracts to which the CMR does not apply.[49] In Poland, a multimodal contract could also be considered *sui generis* because it constitutes a specific mix of carriage and freight forwarding, and it is thus impossible to discern a dominant obligation.[50] The likelihood that the Polish courts would qualify the TO's position as *sui generis* is also supported by the fact that even courier services are regarded as *sui generis*. In the recent judgement the Supreme Court said that in typical cases, the scope of courier services goes beyond that of postal or transport services. This means that the parties enter into a *sui generis* contract, and sometimes possibly into a mixed contract.[51] *Sui generis* classification could also be possible when horizontal co-operation is led by one of the shippers or senders if it is not acting in a professional context. Under national laws, freight forwarder and carrier status depend on professional conduct. Peer service providers would thus be subject to general rules of contract law.

The cumulation method implies that different sets of rules can be applied to different types of obligations. Under this method, the organisation of co-operation for cargo bundling is separate from the obligation to carry or to organise carriage, and the two would thus be subject to different rules. If German law is applicable, the argument in favour of the cumulation method could be that § 460 HGB does not apply because the organisation of bundling happens through horizontal co-operation,[52] and the situation of a carrier that receives bundled goods is similar to the situation of a forwarder who prepares the already consolidated cargo for onward carriage, which is not covered by § 460 HGB.[53] If Polish law applies, three arguments could support the use of the cumulation method. Firstly, by analogy with Article 800 of the KC, the different obligations undertaken by the service provider should fall under different sets of rules. Under Article 800 of the KC, a freight forwarder acquires carrier liability only from the moment when it begins performing the carriage.

---

49 BGH 17.07.2008 IZR 181/05.

50 Mirosław Stec, 'Rozdział VI. Umowy nienazwane w działalności transportowej, § 19. Umowa przewozu multimodalnego' in Wojciech J. Katner (ed), *Prawo zobowiązań – umowy nienazwane System Prawa Prywatnego t.9* (3rd edn, Legalis C.H. Beck 2018) 611.

51 Sąd Najwyższy 28.03.2019 I CSK 387/18. See however: Daniel Dąbrowski, *Umowa multimodalnego przewozu towarów w prawie krajowym i międzynarodowym* (C.H. Beck 2024) 207–208, who underlines that the recourse to national law to classify contracts of carriage is wrong when a judge decides about the application of the CMR.

52 Wouter Verheyen, 'The Transport Architect: New Kids on the Block?' (2016) 53(3) *European Transport Law* 263, 267.

53 Hanno Merkt, 'HGB § 460 Sammelladung' in Klaus J. Hopt et al. (eds), *Handelsgesetzbuch bd.9* (40th edn, C.H. Beck 2021) No 1.

The contract does not become a carriage contract at that point, but acquires, by force of law, a mixed character, combining characteristics of carriage and freight forwarding contracts.[54] Secondly, the cumulative method can be used when the parties' will is to conclude a contract of a mixed and cumulative nature.[55] Thirdly, the obligation to organise co-operation for cargo bundling may also be separate if it is not in a real functional relationship with the service of sending or receiving a parcel.[56] On the one hand, the organisation of co-operation might be considered a concept too broad and distant from the actual organisation of carriage. On the other hand, the list of actions that can be in a real functional relationship with the service of sending or receiving a parcel is open and can extend beyond traditional packing, customs assistance, or the supervision of carriage.[57] If English law applies and the contract is found to be multimodal, the different legs of the transport process are governed by different rules.[58] In consequence, while non-mandatory law would govern the organisation of the shippers' co-operation, the judge would still need to qualify the second part of the TO's service, that is, the arrangement of transport. That could result in the TO's obligations being governed by non-mandatory and mandatory rules simultaneously.

4 TO: Transport intermediary – liability for the wrong organisation of bundling co-operation

In the field of transport intermediaries, uniformity is lacking. In addition, national statutes provide dedicated rules for specific transport intermediaries and for the construction of contractual obligations. The proliferation of transport intermediaries and the types of obligations that they undertake makes classification highly untransparent. Furthermore, there are few scenarios in which the rules that apply to such transport intermediaries are mandatory. For this reason, instead of providing an exhaustive overview of the possible classifications of a TO that is deemed a transport intermediary,[59] I focus on liability for organisational errors in the instances in which the actions of the transport intermediary are governed by mandatory law (Section 4.1) and fault-based liability (4.2).

54 See further e.g.: Julian Jezioro, 'Art. 800 KC' in Edward Gniewek and Piotr Machnikowski (eds), *Kodeks cywilny. Komentarz* (10th edn, Legalis C.H. Beck 2021) No 1.

55 Sąd Najwyższy 20.02.2018 V CSK 205/17.

56 Sąd Apelacyjny w Białymstoku 07.04.2017 I ACa 894/16.

57 Sąd Apelacyjny w Białymstoku 07.04.2017 I ACa 894/16.

58 *Quantum Corporation Inc. and others v Plane Trucking Ltd. and Another* [2002] 2 Lloyd's Rep. 25.

59 For an overview of the possible classifications of the TO, see further: Marta K. Kołacz, 'Cargo Bundling Contribution to Sustainable Transportation' (2015) 459 *MarIus* 263, 276–280. For an overview of a similar problem with the classification of terminal operators, see: Niessen (n 40) Chapters 3–6; Freight Integrators see: Wouter Verheyen (n 30) 557–561.

4.1 Mandatory rules

Mandatory rules are important for the organisation of cargo bundling co-operation in three situations. The first occurs when the obligation to organise co-operation falls under the obligation to carry goods, the second concerns instances in which a logistics service provider is liable as a carrier, and the third covers cases in which, regardless of the type of obligations that the carrier has assumed, goods are damaged, lost, or delayed, and the transport conventions apply (Section 3; Figure 8.4).

Mandatory transport rules can apply when the obligation to organise co-operation is absorbed by the obligation to carry goods (Section 3.2). Under German and Polish law, the mandatory transport rules can also apply in one of the scenarios in which the logistics service provider is liable as a carrier. A German freight forwarder *(Spediteur)* may be held liable as a carrier in three situations: If it consolidates cargo (*Sammelladungsspedition* § 460 HGB),[60] if it charges a lump sum (*Fixkostenspedition* § 459 HGB),[61] or if it performs part of the carriage (*Selbsteintritt* § 458 HGB).[62] Under Polish law, the freight forwarder who originally undertakes to send or receive the shipment or to perform other services related to its transport for remuneration and within the scope of its commercial activities (Article 795 KC) acquires carrier liability when it performs carriage (Article 800 KC).[63] The relevance of these concepts might differ between the cargo bundling models, and online and offline provision of services. For example, while *Selbsteintritt* seems largely irrelevant to the context of online platforms, except for the aforementioned scenario in which the platform is categorised as the employer of a delivery worker,[64] the opposite is true of *Sammeladungspedition* and especially of *Fixkostenspedition*. *Sammeladungsspedition* is mainly relevant when the TO provides solutions for Less-than-Container Load (LCL) transport. *Fixkostenspedition* can have an even broader impact, as it could make all one-stop-shop solutions that aim to provide all-inclusive pricing subject to transport law. All the

60 See further e.g.: Peter Bydlinski, 'HGB § 460 Sammelladung' in Rolf Herber and Christine Schmidt (eds), *Münchener Kommentar zum HGB bd.7* (4th edn, C.H. Beck 2020); Helga Jesser-Huß, 'CMR Art. 1 [Anwendungsbereich, völkerrechtliche Sondervereinbarungen]' in Rolf Herber and Christine Schmidt (eds), *Münchener Kommentar zum HGB bd.7* (4th edn, C.H. Beck 2020) No 5–8.

61 See further e.g.: Peter Bydlinski, 'HGB § 459 Spedition zu festen Kosten' in Rolf Herber and Christine Schmidt (eds), *Münchener Kommentar zum HGB bd.7* (4th edn, C.H. Beck 2020); BGH 14.02.2008 I ZR 183/05.

62 See further e.g.: Peter Bydlinski, 'HGB § 458 Selbsteintritt' in Rolf Herber and Christine Schmidt (eds), *Münchener Kommentar zum HGB bd.7* (4th edn, C.H. Beck 2020); Erwin Abele, 'Kapitel 28 Haftung aus Vertragsverletzung, 9.Beförderungsvertrag' in Kurt Haag (ed), *Geigel, Haftpflichtprozess* (28th edn, C.H. Beck 2020).

63 Sąd Najwyższy18.06.2019 II CSK 670/18.

64 See (n 37).

aforementioned concepts could also be relevant to a partner to co-operation that undertakes to lead the co-operation and carries the bundled goods.

The application of the mandatory rules is particularly relevant when, because of other obligations undertaken by the carrier, there is damage, loss, or, in the case of the CMR, also delay. The carriage conventions do not refer to specific causes of damage but to types. As a result, the conventions seem, in this regard, to deploy a technique that is similar to the absorption method (cf Section 3.2). However, liability does not depend on the dominant obligation but on the type of damage. The CMR absorption method operates from the moment when the carrier takes over the goods.[65] Nevertheless, not all organisational errors result in damage, loss, or delayed delivery. For example, take the case of a bundling partner who does not provide goods for transport or does so belatedly. Article 19 of the CMR, in conjunction with Article 17.1, indicates that the delay that it describes should occur in the actual execution of the transport operation.[66] Thus, the carrier who fails to take the goods will not be captured by the CMR. This point was supported, for example, in a decision of the BGH from 14.07.1993, which concerned a delay in transport that had resulted from the provision of incorrect information about the location of a transport vehicle.[67] At the same time, the TO, in matching shippers and cargoes, could be considered to have assumed the obligation to prepare and oversee the loading operations or to co-ordinate it.[68] If damage to cargo occurs, it may be within the scope of the TO's liability as carrier.

If the transport conventions apply, the carrier can avoid liability for organisational errors by invoking special and general exoneration grounds. To be successful, the carrier must prove that it met the standard of care (see further Chapter 3) at two points: When taking the goods over and from that moment until delivery. Under both the CMR and the Hague-Visby Rules (HVR),[69] the moment of taking over the goods imposes certain information duties on the carrier. Under both conventions, if the carrier discovered or should have discovered deficiencies in the state of the cargo at that moment and gave no

65 Wouter Verheyen, 'The Carrier as Transport Architect: Liability for Bad Choices?' (2017) 5 *Transportrecht* 204, 209.

66 Clarke (n 30) 193; Krzysztof Wesołowski et al. (eds), *Konwencja o umowie międzynarodowego przewozu drogowego towarów (CMR)* (Lex Wolters Kluwer 2015) 290–291.

67 BGH 14.07.1993 I ZR 204/91.

68 Co-operation in loading operations can lead to the apportionment of the liability. See further: Tomasz Szanciło, *Odpowiedzialność kontraktowa przewoźnika przy przewozie drogowym przesyłek towarowych* (Legalis C.H. Beck 2013) Chapter IV §4.3.

69 The Brussels Convention for the Unification of Certain Rules of Law relating to Bills of Lading (adopted 25 August 1924, entered into force 2 June 1931) Trb. 1953, 109, 004127 and Protocol to Amend the International Convention for the unification of certain rules of law relating to bills of lading, signed at Brussels on 25 August 1924 (adopted 23 February 1968, entered into force 23 June 1977) No. 23643.

notice to the shipper or sender, it loses the right to invoke such deficiencies by means of exoneration. Proposals have been made in the literature to extend this information duty to situations in which the shipper or sender agrees to the inclusion of a liberty clause concerning mode of transport into the contract.[70] In such cases, the carrier should, taking into account the information that has been provided to it, warn the shipper if its choice of mode may be detrimental to the cargo. It seems that a similar information duty could also be imposed when the goods are subject to bundling. The carrier, drawing on the information that it has acquired or that it should have acquired, should give notice to the sender or shipper if grouping can harm the cargo. In any case, special audit duties could be imposed by the contract effectively.[71]

Under both the HVR and the CMR, the performance of the carriage contract also requires the carrier to exercise a certain degree of care in respect of the goods (see further Chapter 3). Under the CMR, the standard is high because the carrier must have knowledge and control over hazards that it already faced or that it can face as well as information about minimising losses before or after the risky event occurs. The carrier must also undertake measures, for example, by designing procedures, against any residual risk that cannot be avoided feasibly, and it must monitor dangers, and all this while keeping the nature of the goods that it has taken over in mind. Under the HVR, the carrier needs to perform with reasonable care, augmented by its knowledge of general industry practice. Despite these standards, the duty of the carrier is not absolute in nature, and there is thus no need for the highest degree of knowledge of the cargo. The implications are twofold. Firstly, the carrier may seek additional information from the shipper or sender while the goods are in its custody or require the shipper or sender to provide the instructions, information, and documents that are necessary for the carrier to comply with the law. Secondly, the carrier is under no obligation to choose the safest mode of transport.

4.2 Non-mandatory rules

Mandatory carriage law may not be applicable as between the parties to the horizontal relationship. For instance, the contract between a shipper and a shipper acting as a delivery point could be considered a storage contract. The contract between the shipper and the TO could also be a freight forwarding contract.

National regimes apply to intermediary contracts, such as storage or freight forwarding ones, and impose fault-based liability. The standard of care

70 Verheyen (n 65) 211.

71 Cf. Karl-Heinz Thume, 'Rechtsfolgen der Verletzung vertraglich vereinbarter Prüfungspflichten bei Kühltransporten' (2011) *Recht und Schaden* 503, where the author considers the carrier's duty to check the temperature of the goods at the time of loading.

required of a depositary is described as the duty to take reasonable care (§ 475 HGB, Article 855 KC). When the goods are obviously damaged (§ 470 HGB, Article 857 KC),[72] the depositary is not under any obligation to examine them or to conduct checks and controls unless otherwise agreed.[73] The same standard of care applies to freight forwarders. Both the storage point and the freight forwarder can limit or extend their liability.[74] In these cases, the burden of proof lies with the cargo interest, who must establish that negligence by a storage point or a freight forwarder caused the loss or contributed to it.[75] An organisational error can constitute such default. Among these errors are the selection of an inappropriate carrier,[76] acceptance of terms and conditions that are not in the best interests of the cargo interest,[77] failure to secure the claimant's rights in relation to the carrier,[78] and failure to check that the facts that it was warranting to be true were, in fact, true.[79]

Fault-based liability could be more disadvantageous to the shipper or sender than the application of mandatory transport law and the presumed liability of the carrier. Fault-based liability could disturb the incentive of the delivery point to inspect the goods properly. Absent such inspection and notification of damage, the carrier is no longer presumed to be liable towards the shipper (Article 30 CMR, Article III Rule 6 HVR). In this case, the shipper or sender would either have to establish that the damage was caused by the fault or negligence of the delivery point or that it occurred between the moment when the actual carrier took over the goods and delivery. Since proving either might be difficult, the shipper or sender may be left without redress.

Fault-based liability could also be more disadvantageous for the storage point or freight forwarder. If their liability can be established, it is unlimited by default. This unlimited liability can entail risks in cases of high-value parcels, such as consumer electronics. This level of exposure is not only

72 H.G. Beale (ed), *Chitty on Contracts* (31st eds, Sweet & Maxwell 2012) vol I, No 33–049.

73 A storage contract is concluded when one person places goods at a location and leaves them in the care of another for remuneration, whereby the other person has to redeliver goods on demand. Under German and Polish law, services performed by professional enterprises are regulated as contracts of deposit (§467 HGB, Article 853 KC). If the contract is not of a professional nature, the rules on general storage contracts apply (§ 688 BGB, Article 835 KC). Under English law, contracts for storage are classified as contracts for the provision of services under the Supply of Goods and Services Act 1982 and by the rules on bailment.

74 See e.g.: Sąd Apelacyjny w Krakowie 6.10.2015 I ACa 840/15, where the freight forwarder assumed extended liability and agreed to bear full responsibility for its own actions, for the actions of all persons, under whatever title, that it used in the performance of the contract, and for the actions of the carrier and the third-party carriers that would be commissioned to perform the transport operation.

75 Sąd Najwyższy 25.09.2003 V CK 204/02.

76 Bugden and Lamont-Black (n 31) No 15–044; Koller (n 30) 643, Sąd Najwyższy 27.01.2004 II CK 389/02.

77 Bugden and Lamont-Black (n 31), No 15–045.

78 Sąd Apelacyjny w Krakowie 6.10.2015 I ACa 840/15.

79 *Geofizika DD v MMB International Ltd* [2010] 2 Lloyd's Rep. 1.

disadvantageous for the delivery point but may also deter co-shippers from co-operating with shippers or senders that sell high-value goods.

5 Consequences of the legal classification for the cargo bundling models

The analysis presented earlier indicates various problems with the legal classification of the TO and cargo bundling company. I consider the consequences of these observations for the carrier's liability (Section 5.1.), the distribution of compensation to shippers or senders (Section 5.2), the liability of the shipper or sender and the possibilities for recourse against the shipper or sender who caused the damage (Section 5.3).

5.1 Carrier's liability

This part treats about the legal position of a TO or a bundling company in internal relations with co-operating partners and external with the actual carrier. Particularly, the focus is on the consequences of the legal classification of a TO or a bundling company as a carrier or lack of such classification. The reader while looking at the Figure 8.1 should consider that the TO or a bundling company in its relation with the actual carrier might be legally classified a shipper or sender; a carrier; or an intermediary representing bundling companies where these companies have the legal status of a shipper or sender. When the TO or a bundling company is classified as a carrier, the co-operating companies indicated with letters A and B can also have the legal status of shippers or senders.

As far as the consequences of the legal classification of the TO or a bundling company for the internal relations with co-operating partners, the following can be observed. Firstly, the legal classification as a carrier might be problematic and cause legal uncertainties. If the mandatory transport law applies, the TO or a bundling company will have limited yet presumed liability. However, the observations from Chapter 4, Chapter 5, and Chapter 6 on the multiparty issues are salient. The TO or a bundling company will need to deal with the legal uncertainty concerning the application of exoneration grounds under transport conventions, and whether the co-operating shippers or senders have individual or joint legal positions for the purpose of establishing their rights and liability. Furthermore, a cargo bundling company that acts as carrier is special due to the fact that shippers or senders are also shareholders in this company. The situation under which the cargo bundling company operates as a carrier resembles the position of a TO that acts as a carrier if the company can recover the compensation from the shipper or sender whose cargo caused the damage to the other cargoes. However, if this shipper or sender becomes insolvent, the compensation that is paid to the other cargo interests will reduce the assets of the cargo bundling company and therefore the value of the shares that the cargo interests own. In the case of an unlimited liability company, the results could be even more significant. Suppose that there is a hypothetical bundling company with five shareholders. The shareholder whose cargo caused the damage becomes insolvent, and the company lacks sufficient assets to meet the claim. Among the four remaining shareholders, that is, cargo interests, each could claim compensation from any of the other three. The shareholder whose compensation has been claimed could afterwards claim compensation *pro rata* back from all of the other shareholders. If all cargo interests try to enforce their claims in this way, the result would be that the loss would be distributed between the remaining shareholders. It is even possible that one of them will have to contribute more than it recovers. Secondly, if the TO or a bundling company is not considered a carrier, there is a need to secure the position of partners to co-operation in cargo bundling contractually. In case the conventions do not govern to the relationship between the co-shippers or co-senders and the TO or cargo bundling company, the liability limitations do not apply, and the parties can allocate liability for loss, damage, or delay contractually. Contractual arrangements would especially be relevant concerning the liability for organisational errors (see Section 4) and to clarify the parties' legal positions in a multiparty contract.

As far as the consequences of the legal classification of the TO or a bundling company for the external relations with the actual carrier are concerned, the following can be observed. The relationship between the actual carrier and the bundling company or the TO, if it acts as a shipper or sender, is an example of a standard bilateral contract of carriage. The CMR and the HVR can apply and the actual carrier has limited liability in principle. If the TO or a bundling company have the legal status of a (main) carrier, the actual carrier might be subject to liability for successive carriers (Articles 34–40 CMR).[80] Lastly, in case the TO or a bundling company is an intermediary between the shippers or senders and the carrier, the contract of carriage will likely bind shippers or senders and the actual carrier.

5.2 Distribution of compensation

If the transport conventions apply to the relationship between shippers or senders and a TO, the observations on distribution of compensation in the multiparty context from Chapter 5 and Chapter 6 become important. In this section the focus is on recourse gaps in the distribution of compensation across the vertical chain. Firstly, I examine the chain that involves two carriers, one of which is a bundling company or a TO. For simplicity, I will

80 Simone Lamont-Black, 'The Concept of the Successive CMR Carrier on Trial' (2017) 9(1–2) *European Journal of Commercial Contract Law* 8.

refer to the TO or the bundling company *qua* carrier as Carrier 1, while the performing (actual) carrier is called Carrier 2. Carrier 1 is a shipper or sender in its relationship to Carrier 2. Secondly, I focus on a chain that is composed of shippers or senders, a TO or company that is not a carrier, and a carrier.

When the conventions apply between the shippers or senders and Carrier 1 and between Carrier 1 and Carrier 2, Carrier 1 can claim compensation from Carrier 2, while all individual cargo interests can claim compensation from Carrier 1, up to the limits in the conventions. Carrier 1 can only claim compensation for the damage that it has suffered. A recourse gap can occur, especially when the claims between the shippers or senders and Carrier 1 are divisible.

For example, suppose that there are two senders, that one of them has a cargo with a value of 5 SDR/kg and that the other one has a cargo with a value of 25 SDR/kg. Each cargo weighs 1,000 kg and is packed in a separate parcel, and the CMR applies (8.33 SDR/kg limit). Depending on whether the claim is divisible, and triggers individual or collective compensation, Carrier 1 may need to reimburse the cargo interest by paying it 13,330 SDR or 16,660 SDR respectively. The consequence for the individual claims is that even though the average value of the container that was shipped by Carrier 1 is 15 SDR/kg, Carrier 1 cannot claim compensation up to the limit of 8.33 SDR/kg for the container against Carrier 2. Carrier 1 only has to pay 5 SDR/kg to half of the senders. Thus, the actual damage that it incurs is only 6.66 SDR/kg, which is under the limit.

A similar result would obtain under the HVR. Suppose that the average value of 2,000 kg of goods that are placed in a container is 4 SDR/kg. There are four parcels, but half of the shippers have a cargo of 1,000 kg in two packages and with a value of 1 SDR/kg, and the other shippers have a cargo of 1,000 kg in two packages and with a value of 3 SDR/kg. Carrier 1 must pay the shippers a total of 3,333,34 SDR under the divisible claims and 4,000 SDR in joint compensation. Carrier 1 cannot claim from Carrier 2 compensation up to the limit of 2 SDR/kg for the container if the divisible claims have already been met. The actual damage that the Carrier 1 incurs is only 1.67 SDR/kg, which is below the limit.

Turning to the second chain, the carriage conventions are not applicable to the relationship between shippers or senders and the TO or company. Therefore, cargo interests should, absent contractual stipulations on this point, be compensated in full or proportionally if a limited liability bundling company has become insolvent. In the case of a bundling company with unlimited liability, every cargo interest can claim full compensation from any of the other partners. The result would be that all shareholders would have to contribute according to their share in the company, with some paying more than what they receive. A recourse gap can also occur. If there are two shippers or senders, one has a cargo with a value of 5 SDR/kg and the other has a cargo with a value of 25 SDR/kg, with each cargo weighing 1,000 kg, the TO or the company that does not act as carrier must compensate the cargo interest in full (30,000 SDR). However, in its relationship with the carrier, the TO or company that acts as shipper can only be compensated up to the convention limit. In case the CMR applies, compensation would be set at 16,600 SDR, which leaves the TO or company with a 13,340 SDR shortfall.

5.3 Liability of shipper or sender and the possibility of recourse actions

This section concerns the issues of the shipper's or sender's liability and the possibility of a recourse action against the partner whose cargo caused the damage. The particular focus is on how liability operates when the cargo bundling company is employed and whether exoneration clauses that protect other partners to co-operation are possible.

The TO or cargo bundling company will, as shipper or sender, be liable to the actual carrier. It can then reclaim compensation from the shipper or sender whose cargo has caused the damage. In the case of the bundling company, the risk of insolvency lies with the partners to co-operation: If the partner goes bankrupt, the loss remains with the cargo bundling company. As a result, the shares in this company will lose part of their value (also Section 5.1). Accordingly, all partners must make an indirect contribution to the compensation. In case of a recourse against the unlimited liability company, the TO can, on the insolvency of the company, claim compensation in full from all of the partners to co-operation.

A *Himalaya* clause in the carriage contract between the TO or a cargo bundling company and a carrier would not protect a party to a co-operation agreement against claims by its partners. The operation of such clauses is limited by privity rules (see further Chapter 5 Section 3.4.2.). Furthermore, since only one carriage contract governs the carriage of all the cargo, the other parties or the shareholders in a cargo bundling company cannot be considered third parties for the purposes of the *Himalaya* clause. However, the shippers or senders can regulate the distribution of compensation internally (see further Chapter 9).

6 Summary

The analysis presented earlier indicates that the existing conditions for the legal classification of the TO's services do not allow an answer to be given to the four questions posed at the beginning of this section with sufficient certainty *ex ante*. There are several reasons for this conclusion.

Firstly, the classification matters mainly when the court must decide whether an entity is an information society or a carrier. Information society services and contracts for the carriage of goods are subject to mandatory laws, in particular EU law and international transport conventions, respectively. An information society service essentially provides a tool for presenting and finding business partners without participating in the subsequent services. Treating the TO or a cargo bundling company as one might be difficult, especially when it undertakes many other obligations. In addition, the preceding analysis reveals a mismatch between the legal framework that governs logistics service providers and the rise of logistic platforms. The TO, as a platform for transactions, can assume multiple roles. The same problem arises in respect of traditional logistics service providers, but the mismatch between the advertised functionalities and the assumed responsibilities muddles the waters further. While the courts might later dismiss the platform's choice of classification, the problems remain because they still need to classify the contracts, and the outcomes might be different across the jurisdictions under analysis for reasons such as differences in relevant factors that allow to categorize the transport intermediary as a carrier or various rules on mixed contracts.

Secondly, the uncertainty in the classification of the TO and a cargo bundling company has significant influence on the liability issues in the chains of contracts that are the result of co-operation for cargo bundling. The possibility that mandatory and non-mandatory laws can apply leads to the recourse gaps that are detrimental to the TO or a cargo bundling company. Recourse gaps can also be the reason of the uncertainty related to the aspects of multiparty contracts and particularly divisible and joint claims.

CHAPTER 9

Towards a legal framework for co-operation in logistics

Marta K. Kołacz

1 Introduction

This research is based on the idea that merchants are in the best position for market regulation and can manage their activities through contracts. Contracts can offer businesses a reasonable degree of legal certainty in distributing the legal risks that are related to co-operation in logistics. However, since contracts for co-operation in logistics should be drafted with a view to existing legal frameworks, including mandatory legal ones, freedom of contract can be limited. The transport conventions create three types of problem for cargo bundling co-operation: Firstly, there are no explicit rules on some of the matters that are governed by the conventions. Secondly, the existing rules may have different interpretations. Thirdly, the scope of the conventions is narrow, which leaves many issues to national law. The reader should be aware that partners to co-operation agreement for cargo bundling are mainly referred to as co-operating shippers or senders to align the terminology with the legal frameworks that receive special attention in this work. These legal frameworks are the Convention on the Contract for the International Carriage of Goods by Road of 1956 (CMR)[1] and the Hague-Visby Rules (HVR).[2]

The analysis showed that, regardless of whether the shippers or senders use a standard groupage service or cargo bundling, the problems that concern their identities may be present at the level of the exoneration grounds. If a defense to insufficient packing is made out successfully, the carrier can also hold the shipper or sender liable for the damage that it sustained. However, the interpretation of the exoneration grounds, which depends on whether more importance is attached to the goods or the performance of an operation, results in variations in the extent to which a carrier can exonerate itself from

1 Convention on the Contract for the International Carriage of Goods by Road (CMR) (adopted 19 May 1956, entered into force 2 July 1961) 399 UNTS 189.

2 The Brussels Convention for the Unification of Certain Rules of Law relating to Bills of Lading (adopted 25 August 1924, entered into force 2 June 1931) Trb. 1953, 109, 004127 and Protocol to Amend the International Convention for the unification of certain rules of law relating to bills of lading, signed at Brussels on 25 August 1924 (adopted 23 February 1968, entered into force 23 June 1977) No. 23643.

 DOI: 10.4324/9781003450801-9

liability (see Chapter 2 and Chapter 4). The largest mismatch between the operation of the exoneration grounds and the shippers' or sender's rights and liabilities may be observed when the exoneration grounds are tied to goods yet liability attaches to the performance of the contractual obligation (cf Chapter 4, Chapter 5, and Chapter 6). As a result, it may be difficult for the shipper or sender to anticipate whether it is liable for damages jointly.

Furthermore, defining a shipper or sender for the purpose of determining rights and liabilities is problematic for two reasons. Firstly, the conventions do not explicitly regulate the shipper's or sender's position in multiparty and network contracts. This failure causes legal uncertainty, which makes it difficult for the parties to predict the impact of the adoption of various contractual structures. Litigants must be aware that a judge may decide between internal and external gaps in the conventions, which, in turn, means that national laws might matter to varying degrees. The autonomous reading of the conventions (see Chapter 2) suggests that the joint liability of shippers or senders will not always be triggered (which might be the result of separate contracts or the execution of cargo bundling in milk runs or by packing goods in a single unit) and that the possibility of joint creditorship might be foreclosed because the carrier liability limits could be circumvented (see Chapter 5 and Chapter 6). However, if the judge considers that the conventions do not govern pluralities of shippers or senders, the national schemes for multiparty contracts can be engaged. Although these are similar, they differ in various aspects of their joint and individual effects (see Chapter 6). Consequently, the outcome of a dispute may differ across jurisdictions. For example, it can be presumed that more importance would be ascribed to the independence of the shippers or senders in Poland, whereas in Germany, there is a presumption in favour of solidarity.

Regardless of the contractual model that is chosen for the execution of cargo bundling co-operation (see Chapter 1, Chapter 5, Chapter 6, and Chapter 8), the treatment of long-term contracts and co-operation agreements varies because the scope rules of the conventions and the rules on contract classification are interpreted differently (see Chapter 7). These differences create two layers of uncertainty, one at the level of the conventions and another in national laws. Unless the conventions apply, no mandatory law governs a dispute, and liability for damage resulting from co-operation remains uncertain. This uncertainty is minimised to a certain degree in respect of the classification of a service other than carriage because such services trigger fault-based liability in principle.[3] Legal uncertainty can increase when the conventions do not apply and the co-operation agreement is not considered

3 Some jurisdictions apply general rules for service contracts that imply fault-based liability by default (Art. 750 KC; § 611(2) BGB).

a contract. Therefore, claims for damage that results from the co-operation must be decided extra-contractually.

Finally, legal uncertainty is triggered by the applications of laws to issues that are not regulated by the conventions but which could potentially trigger their application. Apart from the aforementioned problem of co-operation agreements, the classification of transport intermediaries is likely to supply many instantiations of this proposition. For example, to the extent that the Transport Orchestrator (TO) or bundling company is classified as a carrier, the CMR is applicable and the parties can no longer influence their liability vis-à-vis the carrier contractually. It is also important to note that the TO or bundling company, because of its engagement in vertical chains with actual carriers, bears the risks of recourse gaps. Those gaps result from the application of different liability regimes to different links in the contractual chains (see particularly Chapter 8 Section 5.2.).

Given the aforementioned uncertainties, it is not possible to answer which co-operation model would remove the legal obstacles to co-operation in cargo bundling. From the carrier's perspective, the model in which the TO or the cargo bundling company acts as a shipper or sender seems the most inviting because the legal relationship between the parties would be regulated by a traditional bilateral contract. In this relationship, the carrier would largely avoid the problem with the interpretation of the exoneration grounds that concern insufficient packing and the uncertainties that are related to the multiparty aspects of contractual arrangements. From the shippers' or senders' perspective, however, the best model for the relationship with the carrier seems to be the first, in which the latter has contracts of carriage with individual shippers or senders who are members of the co-operation. This is so because the current legal framework struggles to recognize the consequences of linked contractual arrangements. This does not, however, mean that the model in question would not involve legal uncertainty for shippers or senders. Regardless of the benefits of particular models for certain parties, the review of the practice of co-operation (Chapter 1) indicates that market realities might require different models of cargo bundling to be adopted. All of these models should result in the same distribution of risks between the carrier and the co-operating shippers (Chapter 3).

This chapter presents several solutions that could be implemented at different regulatory levels in order to overcome the aforementioned limitations and to support co-operation in logistics on the basis of various co-operation models. Section 2 covers the transport conventions, Section 3 is on national laws, and Section 4 analyses contractual clauses that shippers or senders could include in their co-operation contracts. Clauses will be presented for the selected matters. Those clauses are influenced by other regulatory regimes and, in some cases, left to free contracting. The focus on the solutions supporting contractual frameworks is not accidental. Contracts are preferred way to engage in cargo bundling co-operation (Figure 9.1).

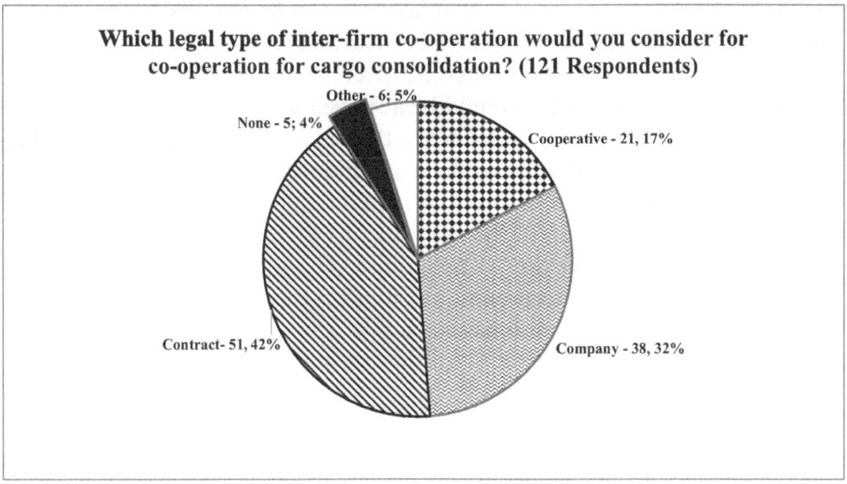

Figure 9.1 Views on the preferred legal form of cargo bundling co-operation

2 The transport conventions

The research indicates that the transport conventions cannot assure legal predictability, not only in respect of the models for cargo bundling but also for standard bilateral contracts pursuant to which the shipper or sender consigns several goods. The conventions are not explicit on the shipper or sender's performance of the packing obligation and the extent to which the carrier can exonerate itself when one of those goods causes damage to the others (see Chapter 4). The cargo bundling models add another layer of uncertainty to the application of the conventions. Firstly, there are no explicit rules on multiparty contracts in the transport conventions. Secondly, it is uncertain how a judge would analyse the common and individual performance of obligations under multiparty contracts, especially when the parties can opt for milk runs or cargo consolidation at the consolidation centre to execute bundling. For a reminder, milk runs refer to situations when the goods are packed and loaded separately along the way, and consolidation points refer to situations when consolidation units are prepared by the partners to co-operation in cargo bundling. Thirdly, since networks of firms were not anticipated by the draftsmen of the conventions, judges need to interpret the substantive rules to decide on liability issues. The research shows that there are several interpretative possibilities concerning shipper liability in cargo bundling models. It seems that the legal position of the carrier is clearer when it contracts with a jointly created company (classified as a shipper or a sender in the relationship with the carrier) that co-ordinates the network of bilateral contracts (Chapter 8). In this way, the carrier avoids the need for a multiparty contract. Uncertainty plagues both multiparty contracts and bilateral contracts of carriage with shippers or senders that are preceded by multiparty co-operation agreements and which involve jointly performed operations.

The unpredictability of the outcome of court cases could be addressed at least partially. Legal certainty could be achieved if the transport conventions are supported with regulatory solutions that address the obligations of shippers that concern delivery for carriage (Section 2.1) and their joint liability (Section 2.2). Whereas direct solutions would reduce the need to interpret the substantive rules (Chapter 2), the most serious challenge to these proposals is related to the general difficulty of updating old conventions and ratifying new ones. Alternatively, the interpretation guidelines can support the autonomous interpretation of the conventions (Section 2.3).

2.1 Shippers' obligations in respect of delivery for carriage

The transport conventions could be supported with a detailed provision on the content of the shipper or sender's obligation to pack a transport unit or load a vehicle. The starting point could be a provision, similar to that of Article 27 of the United Nations Convention on Contracts for the International Carriage of Goods Wholly or Partly by Sea (Rotterdam Rules, RR),[4] which details the shipper's obligations and its liability to the carrier. Whereas in the case of the HVR, such a provision could directly mirror Article 27 RR, in the case of the CMR, it would need to mandate strict liability (cf. Article 10 CMR).

In the context of cargo bundling, a provision like Article 27 RR would secure the carrier's position on four grounds. Firstly, the carrier could specify what 'ready for carriage' means contractually (cf. Article 27.1 RR), and this definition could include an indication that the goods should be capable of withstanding the intended carriage while in a transport unit, taking into consideration the nature and the packing of the other goods that the shipper or sender has placed therein. Furthermore, the model provision stipulates that, in any event, the condition of the goods must not cause harm to persons or property. It thus implies an *a posteriori* assessment of their condition.[5] This assessment imposes a significant burden on the shipper to prepare goods in way to avoid the far-reaching consequences of their unsuitable condition. Since the phrase 'harm to persons or property' is taken to cover situations in which the goods are loaded in such a condition that they cause delays at the port of discharge,[6] it should also cover damage to other goods in the transport unit that is provided by the shipper. Secondly, because containers and

4 United Nations Convention on Contracts for the International Carriage of Goods Wholly or Partly by Sea (adopted 11 December 2008) Sea A/RES/63/122.

5 Yvonne Baatz et al., *The Rotterdam Rules: A Practical Annotation* (Informa Law 2009) Article 27.

6 Baatz et al. (n 5).

other equipment used for the consolidation of cargo would be considered to be goods, the shipper or sender would also need to stipulate that the containers and the other equipment should be in a good condition (Article 1(24) in conjunction with Article 27.1 RR). Thirdly, the carrier could avoid liability if the contents of the shipper-packed container or loaded vehicle are not stowed, lashed, and secured properly and carefully if this results in harm to the goods (Article 27.3 in conjunction with Article 17.3 (i) or (k) RR). The 'properly and carefully' standard, although it may still be high (cf. Chapter IV, Section 2.1.2), would not operate under the CMR, under which the sender is liable to the carrier for any damage to persons, equipment, or other goods due to defective packing. Fourthly, under the two conventions, the rules concerning packing would apply to the loading, handling, stowing, or unloading of the goods if there is an agreement that these will be performed by the shipper, the documentary shipper, or the consignee (cf. Article 27.2 RR).

A provision like Article 27 RR would also clarify the content of the shipper or sender's obligation in respect of the delivery of the goods for carriage, especially in the context of goods that are provided in units. Firstly, it underlines that the risk related to the performance of certain operations is to be borne by the shipper if it performs the operation. Secondly, such a provision would make it clear that if the shipper packs a container or loads a vehicle, these operations must also be taken to include securing the goods. Accordingly, if some of the goods that are wrongly packed, stowed, or loaded by the shipper or sender destroy other goods that are packed by the same shipper or sender in the same unit, the carrier could be able to exonerate itself from the liability in respect of all of the goods. Thirdly, such a provision would also allow the carrier to secure its position in respect of the manner in which the goods should be delivered for carriage. If the contract of carriage imposes on the shipper or sender any further obligations as to the readiness of the cargo for transport, the shipper should also discharge them. In particular, the carrier could specify that if the goods are consolidated by the shipper or sender, their packing should reflect the nature of the goods with which they are packed. Such a provision would be valid under the conventions.

The proposed solution might not solve the issue of several parties performing the same packing operation. Although it would be specified that the activities of packing and loading units trigger risks that rest with the shipper or sender, the judge would still need to be involved in the interpretation of the substantive rules to decide on the consequences of a multiparty contract, and this can result in different outcomes as was indicated in Chapter 6.

2.2 Joint liability for damage resulting from the proximity of performance

The transport conventions could be supported with a provision that grants a right of action to a carrier against an apparent shipper or sender alongside the contractual shipper or sender, who could, in addition, be jointly and severally liable. Furthermore, a similar provision could be used against shippers or senders which perform the same operation of packing or loading jointly, regardless of contractual connections. The transport conventions and German law provide some solutions, which could serve as models for the situation of shippers or senders. These include treating a third party as a party to the contract or drawing on the concept of a quasi-contract with a third party, which is then considered to have undertaken to render characteristic performance.

As far as characteristic performance is concerned, Section 311 (3) of the German Civil Code (BGB)[7] provides that an obligation with duties under section 241 (2) (these are to take account of the rights, legal interests and other interests of the other party) may also come into existence in relation to persons who are not themselves intended to be parties to the contract. In particular, such obligations arise if the third party influences the negotiations or the conclusion of the contract and thus creates a certain level of trust between the parties. This construction could cover a shipper or sender which performs some operations jointly and could therefore be regarded as having provided a personal guarantee for the conclusion and fulfilment of the particular contract of carriage. This solution would be especially relevant to situations in which, acting on the basis of a co-operation agreement, the shippers or senders conclude a separate bilateral contracts of carriage (see Chapter 5). A carrier would thus have a claim against all shippers that are involved in the packing operation, regardless of the existence of separate carriage contracts. Section 311 (3) BGB provides for joint and several liability (see further below on its possible construction).[8]

The liability of co-shippers could also be modelled on the solution for plurality of carriers under which a third-party carrier can be privy to the contract. This solution would also imply joint and several liability. The transport conventions consider the special risk related to jointly performed carriage operations and provide shippers or senders with rights of action against multiple carriers (Article 36 CMR, Article 10.4 Hamburg Rules,[9] Article 4.5 of the Convention on the Contract for the Carriage of Goods by Inland Waterway (CMNI),[10] Article 20.1 RR, Article 27 of the Uniform Rules concerning the

7 Bürgerliches Gesetzbuch in der Fassung der Bekanntmachung vom 2. Januar 2002 (BGBl. I S. 42, 2909; 2003 I S. 738) (with further changes).

8 Volker Emmerich, 'BGB § 311 Rechtsgeschäftliche und rechtsgeschäftsähnliche Schuldverhältnisse' in *Münchener Kommentar zum BGB* (8th edn, C.H, Beck 2020) No 189.

9 The United Nations Convention on the Carriage of Goods by Sea (adopted 31 March 1978, entered into force 1 November 1992) 1695 UNTS 4.

10 Budapest Convention on the Contract for the Carriage of Goods by Inland Waterway (CMNI) (adopted 3 October 2000, entered into force on 1 April 2005) CMNI/CONF(99)2/FINAL.

Contract of International Carriage of Goods by Rail (COTIF-CIM)[11] or at least extend liability for carriage to more carriers (Article 26 COTIF-CIM). Two schemes for liability for the same operation exist. Firstly, the land conventions contain rules on successive carriage (Articles 34–40 CMR, Article 26 COTIF-CIM). Secondly, the sea conventions, CMNI and COTIF-CIM, provide rules on actual carriers (Article 10.4 Hamburg Rules, Article 4.5 CMNI, Article 20.1 RR, Article 27 COTIF-CIM). The applicability of the scheme to successive carriers is dependent on the existence of a single contract of carriage. The system of successive carriers which attaches meaning to the existence of a single contract of carriage has been criticised, among others, due to the ease with which it can be circumvented through the use of independent contracts.[12] It has been suggested that successive carriers should be liable as actual carriers, which can also be sued by cargo interests because the contractual carriers entrust them with the performance of carriage (cf. Article 1.2 Hamburg Rules).[13]

Imposing joint lability on the contractual and the apparent shipper or on the contractual shipper and any other shipper that performs its obligations for delivery for carriage would enable the carrier to join several defendants to its case, thereby enhancing the prospect of recovery. The solvency of the shippers or senders could be a particular risk if their liability is not covered by any insurance schemes. The carrier would be entitled to receive compensation only once and could claim for full compensation from one (or each) of shippers/senders, leaving it up to shippers/senders to seek recourse, recovery, or indemnity, pursuant to their internal arrangements. This solution would also eliminate the discrepancies that result from the application of national default rules on individual or joint liability for damages under multiparty contracts (see Chapter 6).

The system that establishes joint liability for shippers or senders could be based on aggregate liability so that potentially different outcomes can be avoided in cross-border cases, which can be heard by different courts. For example, in cases of damage to a vehicle or equipment, this aggregate liability would not exceed the usual value of the vehicle or equipment on the day and at the place where the damage occurred (cf. Article 30.3 COTIF-CIM). Such a provision would exclude potential claims for vehicle standstill or consequential damage. In the case of damage to a person or other goods, the value of

11 Uniform Rules concerning the Contract of International Carriage of Goods by Rail (COTIF-CIM) adopted 9 June 1999, entered into force 1 July 2006) [International Carriage by Rail (COTIF) of 9 May 1980, as amended by the Vilnius Protocol of 3 June 1999] CR 24/NOT/Add.5 21.12.2009]

12 See further: Michael Spanjaart 'The Successive Carrier: A Relic from the Past' (2016) 21(4) *Uniform Law Review* 522; Simone Lamont-Black, 'The Concept of the Successive CMR Carrier on Trial' (2017) 9(1–2) *European Journal of Commercial Contract Law* 8.

13 Lamont-Black (n 12) 21.

the claim would not exceed the amount that the carrier has already provided as compensation for the damage or loss.

2.3 Interpretative guidelines

The aforementioned solutions would require the revision of the conventions or the creation of new ones. Since that is highly unlikely, the operation of the conventions could be supported with interpretative guidelines that are adapted to the specific problems posed, among others, by co-operation in cargo bundling.

It should be considered whether the existing rules can be applied to co-operation in cargo bundling (or any other innovation that affects mandatory transport regimes). The co-operation in cargo bundling or any other innovation should not automatically be considered as falling outside the scope of the conventions.[14] The interpretative framework of the Vienna Convention on the Law of Treaties (VCLT)[15] provides for the possibility of evolutionary interpretation and contains rules on how evolutionary interpretation should work (see Chapter 2).[16] The transport conventions include generic terms that indicate their evolutionary character. Furthermore, uniformity, when considered as a continuous process, supports the evolutionary character of the transport conventions. This research indicates that the evolutionary character of the conventions could affect the interpretation of Article 17.4 CMR and Article IV, Rule 2 HVR, the concept of a contract, and the HVR concept of 'care of goods'.

The list of the carrier's exoneration grounds includes generic terms which, in my opinion, are more a codification of the context around the performance of a contract of carriage than a list of precise conditions for the applicability of the exclusion grounds. Since the exoneration grounds are expressed in general terms, their interpretation should take into account changing market circumstances, including new business practices but still consider the established allocation of risks between the shippers or senders and the carrier (see Chapter 3). This, in fact, is already happening in the case of standard bilateral contracts, in which the execution of carriage can occur as a result of the collection of goods in milk runs or at consolidation points. In that case, risk passes to the

14 Gregory N. Mandel, 'Legal Evolution in Response to Technological Change' in Roger Brownsword et al. (eds), *The Oxford Handbook of Law, Regulation and Technology* (Oxford University Press 2017) 225.

15 Vienna Convention on the Law of Treaties (adopted 23 May 1969, entered into force 27 January 1980) 1155 UNTS 331 (Vienna Convention).

16 Cf. Wouter Verheyen, 'CMR in Time of Sharing and Platform Logistics a Complex Relationship?' in Andreas Furrer (ed), *Transportation Law on the Move: Challenges in the Modern Logistics World (Schriftenreihe zum Logistik- und Transportrecht Book 11)* (Stämpfli Verlag 2020) 241.

carrier sequentially or at once. Therefore, the shipper-packed containers that are packed by several shippers should be within the sphere of risk of the shippers or senders and should not affect their relationship with the carrier. That would trigger the possibility of the carrier invoking the exoneration grounds *erga omnes* and suing shippers or senders jointly, say for damage caused to a vehicle by a jointly packed container (see also Chapter 4 Section 4).

Secondly, in my opinion, the concept of a contract of carriage could be treated functionally, especially under the CMR. It could accommodate various structures of firm networks and linked contracts. Thus, the references to a contract, or, to be precise, the performance of an obligation under the conventions, could be approached not only from the perspective of a bilateral contract but also from those of a multilateral contract (see Chapter 6) a long-term contract (see Chapter 7, Section 3.3.), and a contract of carriage that is embedded in a network of linked contracts (see Chapter 5, Section 3.2.2). The carrier liability scheme under unified international law is expected to operate in the same way whatever the shippers' choice of a legal structure. A functional approach to the concept of a contract under the conventions and ascribing meaning to performance and the organisation of operations can give effect to the co-operative and behavioral obligations that underpin the relation between the shippers or senders and between them and the carrier.

Lasty, the HVR duty of a carrier to care for goods properly and carefully, particularly the knowledge that the carrier possesses or ought to possess about the goods, can be considered to be evolutionary in nature. The general formulation of this duty permits its extension and the subsumption of general industry practices, of which the carrier should be aware, into the liability regime. This proposition was reflected in the *Volcafe* case,[17] where the court underlined the importance of knowledge of general industry practices as a relevant criterion in the assessment of compliance with the obligation under Article III, Rule 2 HVR (see Chapter 3, Section 2.2). The carrier does not need to possess the highest degree of knowledge about the cargo. However, once the goods are within its sphere of risk, it should be able to evince appropriate knowledge of industry practices. Therefore, it might be more difficult for a carrier to avoid liability: It would need to prove that it took reasonable care of the cargo, but the damage occurred nonetheless or that the damage would have occurred even if it had taken reasonable steps to protect the cargo from it.

Evolutionary interpretation can become a feasible tool for the analysis of the transport conventions in light of changing market practices. It is not, however, perfect. The judges who interpret the substantive rules might arrive at different conclusions, resulting in the differential application of the conventions. This is so mainly because there is no dedicated court that deals with

17 *Volcafe Ltd and another v Compania Sud Americana de Vapores SA* [2018] UKSC 61.

the interpretation of the transport conventions. Uniform application would require active judicial co-operation. That would mean that judges should not only take into consideration judgements from other countries but also strengthen their co-operation through networks and bodies. In this regard, the establishment of an advisory council has been suggested.[18]

The guidelines could also be a cumulative result of individual initiatives conducted by organisations and universities that specialise in international transport law. Such institutions have so far been involved in projects on the national interpretations of the transport conventions[19] and the evaluation of convention provisions.[20] Although certainly important, such projects could be developed further, and networks of experts could examine the adaptative potential of the rules of the conventions. Apart from co-operation in logistics, the adaptive guidelines would be especially important for the technological innovations that influence transport, such as blockchain technology or autonomous cars,[21] and for new models of production, such as the circular economy. The outcomes of these adaptative projects could be aggregated and would operate similarly to soft-law instruments such as the Principles, Definitions, and Model Rules of European Private Law (DCFR).[22]

3 National law

For national law, two main problems are indicated. Firstly, the application of rules related to linked contracts and multiparty contracts can differ between jurisdictions, especially when the judge considers the conventions to be inapplicable. Secondly, the classification of transport intermediaries is problematic.

As far as linked and multiparty contracts and their influence on carriage contracts are concerned, national laws provide, to a certain degree, different rules on the plurality of parties (see Chapter 5 and Chapter 6). This matters, especially when the judge takes the view that there is an external gap in the conventions. For this reason, the outcomes on shipper liability can vary across jurisdictions. The

18 This proposal was made by Wouter Verheyen in: Wouter Verheyen, *Contractuele aansprakelijkheid van vervoersintegratoeren* (die Keure 2014) 598 and is currently being implemented by a group of international scholars who created the CMR Advisory Council. See: <www.cmr-ac.org/> accessed 2 February 2024.

19 See the IDIT database on the interpretation of the CMR in different countries: Institut du Droit International des Transports, 'Base CMR – UNIDROIT – IDIT: Jurisprudence' <https://bit.ly/3IY37mD> accessed 2 February 2024.

20 Wouter Verheyen (ed), *CMR 60 Years. Time for Retirement of Future Proof* (Paris Legal Publishers 2017).

21 For the other project conducted by the author of this book, which concerns the adaptive potential of the CMR, see: Marta Katarzyna Kołacz and Gerald Hopster, 'When Technology Takes the Wheel: Is the CMR Ready to Meet the Demand for Autonomous Transportation?' (2017) 1/2 *European Journal of Commercial Contract Law* 41.

22 Christian von Bar et al. (eds), *Principles, Definitions and Model Rules of European Private Law: EC (DCFR)* (European Law Publishers 2009).

co-operating partners can be solely or jointly liable, which determines whether the carrier will bear the risk of their insolvency. Relatedly, uncertainty surrounds the effects of breach of a contractual obligation in multiparty relations and the carrier's ability to bring a direct claim against all co-operating partners.

The research also indicates the existence of a recurring problem which is related to the classification of transport intermediaries for the purposes of applying mandatory law (see Chapter 8). The analysis touches upon an old classificatory problem: Different legal regimes can apply to the same logistics operation. The research indicates that the difference between Germany and the other analysed jurisdictions is pronounced. This is so because German law mandates carrier liability for a large number of intermediaries. Although several paths to tackling the problem of unification in freight forwarder law have been identified, none have so far found international support,[23] and the issue has been left to national laws and self-regulation (see further Section 4). However, the research also indicates that the classification problem might be more difficult because of the presence of online logistics providers to whom more legal frameworks are potentially applicable.

The aforementioned problems could, to a certain extent, be tackled through the rules on the legal classification of different transport intermediaries (Section 3.1) and the recognition of contractual networks (3.2).

3.1 Transport intermediaries

Online platforms and intermediaries, such as the TOs who operate based on ICT technologies, have changed the logistics landscape. These service

23 Three approaches to the unification of forwarder law at the international level can be distinguished. The first, which has proven unsuccessful, aimed at the promulgation of dedicated forwarder-law convention. Back in 1967, UNIDROIT proposed a draft Convention on Contracts of Agency for Forwarding Agents relating to the International Carriage of Goods. However, this draft Convention was never adopted, and there are no plans for its adoption in the coming future. The second approach, which also failed, was directed at the creation of a multimodal convention. The proposed 1980 United Nations Convention on International Multimodal Transport of Goods has not entered into force. The same is true of the Rotterdam Rules. See further: Jan Ramberg, 'Unification of the Law of International Freight Forwarding' (1998) 3(1) *Uniform Law Review* 5; Jan Ramberg, 'Global Unification of Transport Law: A Hopeless Task' (2009) 27(3) *Penn State International Law Review* 851; Samir Mankabady, 'The Multimodal Transport of Goods Convention: A Challenge to Unimodal Transport Conventions' (1983) 32(1) *International and Comparative Law Quarterly* 120. The third approach, which has been suggested in the literature but not yet attempted, is to create a dedicated Model Law or use solutions from existing Model Laws. See further: Simone Lamont-Black, 'Towards Transparency and Predictability in Freight Forwarding- the Case for a Model Law' in Jason Chuah (ed), *Research Handbook on Maritime Law and Regulation* (Edward Elgar 2019) 99–112; see also Wouter Verheyen, 'Could (Contractual Incorporation of) the DCFR or PECL Be an Answer to the Lack of Harmonisation in the Field of Forwarding Law?' (2015) 7(1–2) *European Journal of Commercial Contract Law* 82, who suggests that the DCFR and the PECL could contribute to harmonization, as far as the division of the burden of proof is concerned, particularly through the incorporation of the *contra proferentem* rule.

providers can escape mandatory liability systems, even though their functionalities exhibit considerable similarities to those of standard logistics service providers. Two solutions are proposed. Firstly, TO or/logistics platform does not offer a *sui generis* service (Section 3.1.1.). Secondly, legal solutions could be designed to channel liability to the TO or platform, which could bear carrier liability (Section 3.1.2).

3.1.1 TO or logistics platform does not offer a sui generis service

It could be sensible to consider limiting the choice between legal classifications, especially for online logistics platforms and TOs that operate through ICT solutions, to information society services and types of transport intermediaries that have already been identified under national law. The benefits of this solution are twofold. Firstly, unless classified as an information society, TOs would not be able to argue for a *sui generis* qualification and thus avoid the specific obligations that have been established for certain transport intermediaries. This consideration follows from the distinction that the case law draws between information society services and other services (see Chapter 8, Section 2). Secondly, offline and online services should be treated equally. This is important because the operational literature and the practice have revealed the existence of new stakeholders in supply chains, which are also considered new intermediaries.[24] Their online operations should not automatically exclude the possibility of classification as a common offline service.

The solution of excluding the *sui generis* classification of TOs, however, is limited and would not have a significant impact on the liability issues that surround classification as a carrier or freight forwarder or the application of mandatory conventions and national laws. The research indicates that only the distinction between an active information society and a carrier matters for liability issues. In other cases, the distinction is mainly theoretical, given the fact that freedom of contract allows the parties to include limitation and exoneration clauses in contracts.

3.1.2 TO or online platform bearing carrier liability

The aforementioned solution can be developed further by channelling the carrier's liability to online logistics platforms and TOs. It would make the classification process easier at the point of choosing between an information society service and other services related to transport because the other service could trigger carrier liability in any event. Furthermore, it could unify the classification of the obligations of TOs or platforms in respect of horizontal and vertical obligations. For a reminder, a vertical obligation refers to the relation

24 E.g.: Riccardo Giusti et al., 'Synchromodal Logistics: An Overview of Critical Success Factors, Enabling Technologies, and Open Research Issues' (2019) 129 *Transportation Research Part E: Logistics and Transportation Review* 92.

between co-operating partners and the intermediary who can potentially be classified as a carrier. A horizontal obligation refers to the TO's service where it organizes co-operation between co-partners.

Channelling carrier liability could be operationalised at two levels. Firstly, that solution could be based on the German model of a freight forwarder, which is held liable as a carrier in case it performs certain operations (§§ 458–460 of the German Commercial Code (HGB),[25] see further Chapter 8, Section 3.1.). Therefore, if the platform or TO offers solutions for less-than-container (LCL) transport or one-stop-shop solutions that are aimed at providing all-inclusive-pricing, it will bear carrier liability. Secondly, that solution could entail use of the absorption method: Orchestration services performed in the course of horizontal co-operation would be considered ancillary to the main obligation in the vertical relation, that is, the carriage of goods or the organisation of LCL transport that can trigger liability as a carrier.

The benefit of the aforementioned solution is twofold. Firstly, it facilitates effective risk externalisation. Legal classification as a carrier triggers limited liability, exoneration grounds, and standard insurance schemes. Secondly, the subsumption of all obligations under a single heading that triggers carrier liability allows risk to be externalised in horizontal and vertical relations.

3.2 Co-operation models with a specific set of rules

The unified liability rules in different co-operation models would improve, to a certain degree, the predictability of judicial outcomes in transport litigation. The most pronounced difference is between contractual and corporate groupings. In the latter case, the jointly created company acquires legal personality. If it is qualified as a shipper or sender, it can be subject to shipper or sender liability. As a result, the contractual agreement for co-operation in the joint transport of goods could result in the creation of a grouping that is subject to principal liability. In case the grouping does not meet its liability, the liability of the individual partners would be engaged. Matters such as legal capacity and the organisation of corporate and quasi-corporate forms are not, however, governed by the conventions, and the unification solutions can only originate from national law. Therefore, the solutions could imply the regulation of contractual forms of co-operation (Section 3.2.1), which should be supported further with the standardisation of liability rules (Section 3.2.2).

3.2.1 Regulation of contractual co-operation models

The co-operation models could be standardised and thus take on a company-like form. Italian law, with its various regulatory options for contractual

25 Handelsgesetzbuch vom 10. Mai 1897 (RGBl. S. 219) BGBl. III/FNA 4100–1 (with further changes).

co-operation (consortium contracts (Article 2602 *et seq* Codice Civile) and network contracts, that is, *rete contratto* and *rete soggetto* (law decree no. 5/2009, converted into law no. 33/2009 and its subsequent amendments))[26] could serve as a model solution.

Italian law offers various legal solutions for contractual co-operation. In a consortium, the contract partners set up a common organisation for the regulation or execution of certain phases of their businesses (Article 2602 Codice Civile). The consortium contract does not involve the absorption of the contracting companies into a unitary body but only the establishment of a common organisation for the performance of certain activities. No common organisation is required for the existence of a network contract. Under an Italian network contract, several entrepreneurs pursue the common aim of increasing, individually and collectively, their innovative capacity and their competitiveness on the market (decree no. 5 of 10 February 2009, converted, with modifications, into Law no. 33 of 9 April 2009 and its subsequent integrations and amendments). The partners establish a common programme for the realisation of aims that they cannot achieve independently because of, say, high costs. As a result, they can, among others, expand their geographical or sectoral reach.[27]

As far as Italian network contracts are concerned, the regulator aimed to enhance the flexibility of the organisational forms that partners can use. The co-operating partners can choose between three main organisational forms. Firstly, the co-operating partners can enter into a contract, based on which they would exchange information. That solution could be particularly useful for companies which bundle goods solely by reference to information on cargo flows and common transport routes. Secondly, the co-operating partners can organise themselves into business clusters. Thirdly, the partners can agree to carry out one or more activities jointly. The last two forms of network contract may therefore entail stronger forms of co-operation between entrepreneurs. Accordingly, they could provide specific support to partners who establish joint consolidation points. Network contracts of the third kind may also provide for the establishment of a common equity fund and the appointment of a common body to take charge of managing, in the name and on behalf of the participants, the execution of the contract or its parts or phases. If there is no equity fund, the partners could include assessment and evaluation criteria for the contributions of each individual partner to the contract.

The consortium is subject to legal responsibility. The same is true of a network contract when the partners choose to register it at the Business Register

26 For an overview, see: RetImpresa, 'Disciplina del contratto di rete' (2019) <https://bit.ly/32NKUHP> accessed 2 February 2024.

27 On the aims of network contracts in the Italian context, see further: Riccardo Leoncini et al., 'Triggering Cooperation Among Firms: An Empirical Assessment of the Italian Network Contract Law' (2020) 37 *Economia Politica* 357, 362–365.

(Art. 3(4-*quarter*), Law no. 33/2009). Registration thus triggers legal subjecthood, in the absence of which participants may be liable *pro quota*. Legal subjecthood further depends on the existence a common equity fund and a managing body. The flexibility of a network contract triggers the application of specific national rules on various organisational forms. A common equity fund and a managing body may engage rules on legal representation, joint liability, or even exclude the direct liability of the partners. Thus, depending on the organisational form of the co-operation, the liability of the co-operating partners might resemble that of a limited or unlimited liability company or that of parties to multilateral or agency contracts (see Table 9.1).

The general rules also support governance structures, including termination. If one of the partners does not fulfil its obligations, the other network partners can seek the termination of the contract in respect of the defaulting partner (see also Section 5.6). However, if the obligation is considered essential for the network contract, then the whole contract must be terminated (Article 1459 Codice Civile). The same rules apply to obligations that have become impossible to discharge. The partners are also free to terminate by establishing a contractual right of withdrawal. For example, it is possible to establish the right of withdrawal *ad nutum*. In such cases, a party may withdraw at will and without justification. The right of withdrawal has effects only for the partner to the co-operation scheme. Nevertheless, a network contract must have at least two parties in order to function. This means that if there are only two parties to the network contract and one of them exercises its right to withdraw, then the network contract ceases to operate.

The advantage of these institutes is that they standardise contractual co-operation in line with known and regulated organisational forms and liability rules. Variety in organisational forms would not, however, facilitate the adoption of unified rules on shipper or sender liability under carriage contracts. Instead, variety of organisational forms would enable the shippers or senders to choose organisational forms that can support their positions, be they weak or strong. As a result, unified rules on contracts of carriage might be impossible to enact not only at the international level but also at the national one (see further Section 3.2.2.1).

3.2.2 Standardisation of the carrier's ability to sue the co-operation scheme and its members

For the carrier, the optimal situation would be for the rules to resemble those that govern bilateral contracts. That would require the elimination of the multiparty aspect that is the cause of legal uncertainty. This could happen when a contractual grouping acquires legal personality and can be sued (Section 3.2.2.1). In that case, there would be a single contract of carriage between the grouping and the carrier. Therefore, the contractual cargo bundling models and the model that involves a jointly established company would

Table 9.1 Liability rules in Italian network contracts

Consortium	*Registered network contract (Subject Network)*	*Unregistered network contract*		
<Article 2602 *et seq.* Codice Civile>	<Combined provisions of Article 3, paragraph 4-ter and Article 3, paragraph 4-quarter decree no. 5 of 10 February 2009 (converted with modifications into Law no. 33 of 9 April 2009) and subsequent consolidations and amendments>	Common equity fund and common managing body <different types of network contract, depending on the existence of common equity fund: Article 3, paragraph 4-ter letter c)	Only the common managing body (the common managing body can act with mandate with or without deputation) <Article 3, paragraph 4-ter letter e) decree no. 5 of 10 February 2009 (converted, with modifications into Law no. 33 of 9 April 2009) and subsequent consolidations and amendments; General rules applicable to the contract of mandate: Articles 1703 *et seq* Codice Civile>	No common equity fund and no common managing body
Members of a consortium have limited liability with respect of obligations (and consequent debts) entered into by the consortium in its own name; only the consortium is liable for those debts, and it meets them with the consortium fund, which is made up of the contributions of the participants.	The network is legally responsible towards third parties	Common managing body acting in the name and behalf *of the whole network*: Third parties can only claim against the common equity fund and not against the network partners. <combined provisions of Article 3, paragraph 4-ter letter c) and Article 2615, paragraph 1 Codice Civile >	*Mandate with deputation*: Obligations to third parties for and on behalf of network partners; obligations produce effects on network partners who are directly responsible => the contract is between third parties and network partners.	In practice, a third party would be able to claim against the assets of the individual network partners which undertook certain obligations.[28]

(*Continued*)

Table 9.1 (Continued)

Consortium	*Registered network contract (Subject Network)*	*Unregistered network contract*	
		Common managing body acting in the name *of individual network partners* in the course of a network programme: Joint liability of the network partners that were involved in the obligations AND the common equity fund. <combined provisions of Article 3, paragraph 4-ter letter c) and Article 2615, paragraph 2 Codice Civile >	Obligations with indivisible performance: All network partners have joint liability => third parties can ask to any individual network partner to fulfil the obligation (or to pay damages resulting from the non-fulfilment of the obligations) {example: An estate that cannot be divided}
		Obligations from the common managing body acting in the *exclusive interest and name of individual network partners* (a power of attorney is required): Third parties can only claim against the specific partners (no solidarity with the common equity fund).	Obligations with divisible performance: It is possible to avoid joint liability if the common managing body indicates which specific network partners will fulfil the given obligations; each network partner is only liable for its own obligations
			Mandate without deputation = obligations to third parties in common managing body's name and on behalf of the network partners; duty to transfer obligations from the managing body to the network partner; prior to the transfer, the common managing body is responsible to third parties, but it can then make claims against the network partners.

operate similarly in respect of liability vis-à-vis the carrier. In addition, since the existence of a quasi-corporate organisation typically implies secondary liability for its members, the unification of the rules would also be necessary to enable members of the co-operation to be sued directly when the grouping cannot meet its principal liability towards the carrier (Section 3.2.2.2). Lastly, I also propose joint liability for damage resulting from the proximity of performance (Section 3.2.2.3).

3.2.2.1 Legal capacity of the contractual groups

The point of departure could be that the carrier should enjoy the same legal certainty irrespective of whether it contracts with a single shipper or with several shippers or senders under a single contract (cf. Chapter 5 and Chapter 6). For this purpose, the contractual grouping cannot be regarded as an assembly of independent legal persons but must be treated as a legal entity.[29] For contractual groupings, the solutions of the European Economic Interest Grouping (EEIG)[30] could serve as a model. For groups of companies linked by jointly established companies, the corporate grouping has not been found to have legal personality in the analysed jurisdictions.[31] However, the carrier's position *vis a vis* corporate grouping would already be more certain when a company that is established by partners co-operating in cargo bundling is classified as a shipper or sender under the transport conventions. Legal personality would allow this company to bear liability towards the carrier for insufficient packing.

The purpose of the EEIG is to facilitate or develop the economic activities of its members that have central administrations in different Member States or when one partner carries on its principal activity in another Member State (Article 3.2 Regulation (EEC) No 2137/85). The activities of a grouping must be related to the economic activities of its members and must not be more than ancillary to them (Preamble, Article 3.1 Regulation (EEC) No 2137/85). The parties which intend to form a grouping must conclude a contract and register it (Article 1 Regulation (EEC) No 2137/85). From the date of its registration, the grouping thus formed has the capacity, in its own name, to assume rights and obligations of all kinds, to make contracts or to execute other legal acts, and to sue and be sued (Article 1.2 Regulation (EEC) No 2137/85). While the grouping bears the principal liability for its debts because it is a legal body that is separate from its members, all the members of the EEIG

29 See also: Gunther Teubner, *Networks as Connected Contracts* (Michelle Everson tr., Hart Publishing 2011) 32–56; Fabrizio Cafaggi, 'Contractual Networks and the Small Business Act – Towards European Principles?' (2008) 4 *European Review of Contract Law* 493, 527–528.

30 Council Regulation (EEC) No 2137/85 of 25 July 1985 on the European Economic Interest Grouping (EEIG) OJ L 199, 31.7.1985, p. 1–9.

31 See also: Karen Vandekerckhove, *Piercing the Corporate Veil* (Wolters Kluwer 2007) 533–534.

have unlimited joint liability for its debts (Article 24.1 Regulation (EEC) No 2137/85). The creditors may not proceed against a member before the liquidation of the grouping concludes unless they have first requested the grouping to pay and payment has not been made within an appropriate period (Article 24.2 Regulation (EEC) No 2137/85). The unlimited liability of a member can be overridden through the insertion of a specific exclusion or limitation into the contract between the grouping and the third party (Preamble).

If a co-operation agreement for the joint transportation of goods can lead to the contractual grouping assuming principal liability, the cargo bundling models that are based on the co-operation agreement and jointly created companies would produce similar outcomes vis-à-vis the carrier when the grouping and the jointly established company are considered as contracting shippers or senders under the conventions. For the carrier, this would mean that it concludes a contract for the carriage of goods as if it is a bilateral contract and that it could claim directly against the company or against the contractual grouping. However, since jointly established companies and contractual groupings are corporate or quasi-corporate forms, at the secondary level, the carrier could try to also claim against the partners to the co-operation agreement (see below).

3.2.2.2 Direct liability of members to co-operation schemes

Assuming that both corporate and contractual groupings could result in the creation of corporate or quasi-corporate forms, at a secondary level, the carrier could also try to claim against the partners to the co-operation scheme. The position of a carrier would be harmonised if all co-operation models provide for an opportunity to claim directly against the members of the co-operation scheme.

However, under the current legal rules, the corporate or quasi-corporate regimes regulate the liability of partners differently. For example, shippers or senders could optimise their liability exposure because jointly established limited liability companies normally grant limited liability to their members and bypassing this limitation occurs infrequently. Polish law implements solutions that imply that only the members of the management board are jointly and severally liable for the obligations of the company when a claim against it has not been met and the directors have failed to file a declaration of insolvency in due course (Article 299 Kodeks Spółek Handlowych (KSH)).[32,33] Under Ger-

32 Ustawa z dnia 15 września 2000 r. Kodeks spółek handlowych Dz.U. 2000 nr 94 poz. 1037 (with further changes).

33 In the comparative setting, see further: Mathias Siems and David Cabrelli, *Comparative Company Law a Case-Based Approach* (2nd edn, Hart Publishing 2018) Chapter 6; Michał Romanowski, 'Wnioski dla prawa polskiego wynikające z uregulowań prawa grup kapitałowych w wybranych systemach prawnych państw UE, Japonii i USA' (2008) 2 *Studia Prawa Prywatnego* 5.

man law, if the declaration of insolvency is not submitted and the company is unable to pay its debts, a carrier would have a direct claim against the directors (BGB, § 823(2) with InsO,[34] § 15a (Germany Insolvency Code)). Piercing the corporate veil and shareholder liability have also been accepted by the German courts, yet they are rarely applied, with successful attempts typically limited to cases of undercapitalisation, the intermingling of the capital of the company and that of a shareholder, withdrawals of funds that result in the destruction of the economic basis of the company, and groups of companies that include joint stock companies.[35] Under English law, shareholders are generally under no liability to creditors unless they are *de facto* or shadow directors (Section 251 Companies Act 2006).[36] Accordingly, if the carrier wants to claim directly from the co-operation partners and it has contracted with a limited liability company, it would enjoy a better position under English law, while its options would be most limited in Poland.

Conversely, if the grouping is based on EEIG rules (see the previous section), the shippers or senders would have fewer possibilities to optimise the partner's liability exposure because of the unlimited liability of the members and the carrier's ability to claim directly against partners when the grouping, despite being requested to cover a liability that has arisen, fails to pay (Article 24.2 Regulation (EEC) No 2137/85). Apart from agreements with carriers, limited liability could also be indirectly implemented in the grouping structure by creating *ad hoc* limited liability companies purely for the purposes of co-operation.[37] This could, however, undermine the flexibility of contractual co-operation. As a result, it seems that establishing a joint limited liability company could protect the co-operating shippers or senders better than a contractual grouping with legal capacity and unlimited member liability.

The foregoing has two implications. Firstly, the unification of liability rules would require similar solutions for corporate groupings in respect of veil piercing and member liability. The English solution for piercing the corporate veil could function as a model. Secondly, and relatedly, restrictions on the limitation of liability would need to be implemented in situations other than post-insolvency veil piercing in order to make it difficult for shippers or senders to hide behind organisational forms.

Three paths, which draw on tort, company, and contract law, have been established to challenge limited liability. Restrictions on limited liability have been developing in torts. For example, in corporate groupings, the parent company can be found liable for its subsidiary's human rights breaches or

34 Insolvenzordnung vom 5. Oktober 1994 (BGBl. I S. 2866), die zuletzt durch Artikel 34 Absatz 13 des Gesetzes vom 22. Dezember 2023 (BGBl. 2023 I Nr. 411) geändert worden ist.

35 (n 33).

36 Companies Act 2006, UK Public General Acts2006 c. 46.

37 Sue Farran et al., *The Diffusion of the Law: The Movement of Laws and Norms around the World* (Routledge 2015) 104–105.

for environmental violations.[38] Enterprise operational liability has also been suggested. It would entail subjecting enterprises to liability regardless of their legal form when avoidable damage results from their combined operational activities.[39] In corporate law, solutions, such as capping the limited liability of small companies, holding shareholders unlimitedly liable,[40] and full unlimited liability for small closely-held corporations,[41] have been proposed, yet they have not been enacted into laws. Solutions could also be established in contract law. This path might require the modification of the general principle of privity in respect of contractual chains and networks.[42] Nevertheless, a direct claim could also be premised on the recognition of an implied contract between a carrier and a member of a co-operation scheme (for example, through the implied agency powers of the members of a co-scheme operation to form a complete multiparty contract)[43] or on quasi-contract (based, for example, on the legally recognised relationship of trust between partners to a network, which would be modelled on § 311.3 BGB).[44] The possibilities offered by the German concept of trustee liability (§ 311.3 BGB) could also allow for the joint liability of a jointly established cargo bundling company and its founders if the carrier claims that the co-operating shippers influenced the negotiations or the conclusion of the individual contracts of carriage or if the carrier claims to have influenced the conclusion of the co-operation agreement. In the context of trust relationships, Aedtner and Teubner discussed a special form of joint and several liability for co-operation scheme members towards third parties on the basis of their actual involvement in the

38 See further e.g: Liesbeth Enneking, 'Paying the Price for Socially Irresponsible Business Practices? Corporate Liability for Violations of Human Rights and the Environment Abroad' (2017) 26(8) *Aktuelle Juristische Praxis/Pratique Juridique Actuelle* 988; Gwynne Skinner, 'Rethinking Limited Liability of Parent Corporations for Foreign Subsidiaries' Violations of International Human Rights Law' (2015) 72 *Washington & Lee Law Review* 1769; Siel Demeyere, 'Liability of a Mother Company for Its Subsidiary in French, Belgian, and English Law' (2015) 3 *European Review of Private Law* 385.

39 E.g.: Gert Brüggemeier and Zhu Yan, *Entwurf für ein chinesisches Haftungsgesetz* (Mohr Siebeck, 2009) 120.

40 Judith Freedman, 'Limited Liability: Large Company Theory and Small Firms' (2000) 63(3) *The Modern Law Review* 317, 344–345.

41 Vandekerckhove (n 31) 535–536.

42 For the ratio of new solutions for the contractual governance, see e.g.: Stefan Grundmann et al. (eds), *Contract Governance: Dimensions in Law and Interdisciplinary Research* (Oxford University Press 2015).

43 Fabrizio Cafaggi, 'Contractual Networks and the Small Business Act – Towards European Principles?' (2008) 4 *European Review of Contract Law* 493 527; See further on implied contracts: Stefan Grundmann, 'Contractual Networks in German Private Law' in Fabrizzio Cafaggi (ed), *Contractual Networks, Inter-Firm Cooperation and Economic Growth* (Edward Elgar Publishing 2011) 111–162, 126–142; David Campbell et al. (eds), *Implicit Dimensions of Contract: Discrete, Relational, and Network Contracts* (Hart Publishing 2003).

44 On the development of § 311.3 BGB for the purpose of multilateral relations, see: Kaya Aedtner and Gunther Teubner, 'Virtual Enterprises: Liability Problems in One- and Multi-Level Networks' in Stefanie Jung et al. (eds), *Business Networks Reloaded* (Nomos 2015) 385–386.

contractual obligations (see further Section 3.2.2.3).[45] Furthermore, the right of a carrier (as a third party) to sue the members of a co-operation scheme could result from the co-operation agreement.[46] Lastly, a network could be recognised as a legal concept in contract law[47] or regulated by a regime similar to that which applies to partnership contracts.[48]

The plausibility of the aforementioned solutions should certainly be scrutinised further in each jurisdiction. However, since the issue of veil piercing is not a problem that is specific to cargo bundling co-operation but instead has to do with the general topic of exceptions to privity for business networks that are based on various organisational forms, it is outside of the scope of this chapter.

3.2.2.3 Joint liability for damage resulting from the proximity of performance

The standardisation of legal rules through the introduction of legal capacity for contractual groupings might not be feasible across the entire contract chain. For example, since national judges retain the discretion to classify contracts, the issues that arise from a contract of carriage might also be important in the internal relation between the shippers or senders when one of them (or the jointly created company) is considered to be a carrier and thus bound to the other shippers by a multiparty contract. The research shows that in the case of multiparty contracts for the international carriage of goods, legal uncertainties manifest at two levels. In the transport conventions, attempts at interpretation may lead to different outcomes as a result of the lack of explicit rules on multiparty contracts. If a judge finds that the issues related to a multiparty contract of carriage fall within the internal or external gap and eventually applies national law, various regimes may govern the classification of obligations and their multiparty or individual effect (see particularly Chapter 6).

The standardisation and unification of the rules on multiparty contracts would need to focus on three considerations. Firstly, the effects of multiparty contracts should be the same across jurisdictions. Secondly, the rules for

45 Aedtner and Teubner (n 44), 392–393.

46 Camila Crea, 'Contractual Business Networks: Interpretation Criteria and Axilogical Perspective' in Stefanie Jung et al. (eds), *Business Networks Reloaded* (Nomos 2015) 359–360; Knut W. Lange, *Virtuelle Unternehmen: Neue Unternehmenskoordinationen in Recht und Praxis* (Fachmedien Recht und Wirtschaft in Deutscher Fachverlag GmbH 2001) 188 et seq. See also: James Gathii and Ibironke T. Odumosu-Ayanu, 'The Turn to Contractual Responsibility in the Global Extractive Industry' (2015) 1 *Business and Human Rights Journal* 69 who consider, among others, contracts that can be construed to allow third parties to sue to address or mitigate the absence of corporate remedy and liability regimes towards those who are adversely affected by business activities.

47 On the recognition of a network as a legal concept, see e.g.: Hugh Collins, 'The Weakest Link: Legal Implications of the Network Architecture of Supply Chains' in Marc Amstutz and Gunther Teubner (eds), *Networks: Legal Issues of Multilateral Co-Operation* (Hart Publishing 2009).

48 Teubner (n 29) 34–39.

multiparty contracts should reflect the nature of carriage contracts, transport operations, or the functioning of contractual networks. Standardisation with a focus on carriage contracts would ensure that a shipper or sender is in the same position across jurisdictions, regardless of whether national judges recognise an internal gap and apply national laws that fit the framework of the conventions or if they position the dispute in the external gap. Thirdly, the rules on multiparty contracts of carriage should imply the same risks for carriers as those that obtain in situations in which there is no multiparty contract yet some co-ordination between shippers or senders occurs (see also Section 3.2). In my opinion, the rules on multiparty contracts and the position of a shipper or sender under such contracts can be derived from the conventions. The rule would be that shippers or senders are individually liable unless the proximity of the performance of the obligations (e.g. joint packing) implies that the obligations have joint effects (Section 2.3). However, since the judge, in their discretion, can arrive at the conclusion that there is a gap in a convention that needs to be supported by national law, national laws could also provide detailed rules on multiparty contracts.

A modified regime for joint and several liability that is based on actual involvement in contractual obligations in multiparty contracts, which was also proposed for the amendment of the conventions and the establishment of direct liability for co-operation partners (see Section 2.2 and Section 3.2.2.2), could also serve as a model. Only those members who have a contractual duty to the carrier that is based on the special network relation and who have breached their obligations should be jointly and severally liable.[49] This solution has two implications. Firstly, it could apply to all cargo bundling models, regardless of contractual or corporate organisation. This is so because, in all the discussed models of cargo bundling execution, the co-operation agreement would create a trust relation that the carrier could rely on to argue that it significantly influenced the conclusion of the contract of carriage and the performance of shippers' or senders' obligations, especially when these involve joint packing. Secondly, the joint and several liability of the partners who are actually in a contractual relation with the carrier would facilitate the internal organisation of co-operation with its often dynamic character. As a result, liability would attach to those partners which are, in fact, engaged in co-operation.

4 Self-regulation

Regulatory uncertainty affects attempts to establish co-operation in cargo bundling. Numerous regulatory changes (Section 2, Section 3) can enhance legal certainty in co-operation, but their enactment would require a significant regulatory effort. Thus, I provide here the solutions that can be implemented

49 C.f. Aedtner and Teubner (n 44) 392–393.

by the partners to cargo bundling. I present the solutions for entrance rules (Section 4.1), division of costs of joint transportation (Section 4.2), liability rules (Section 4.3), and exist rules (Section 4.4). These issues remain sensitive to the manner in which the daily organisation of activities within horizontal co-operation schemes could affect liability. At the same time, due to the limits of this submission, the selected solutions are considered the most important yet not exhaustive.

4.1 Entrance rules

Most of the respondents (62.8%) attached no special importance to the exclusive character of co-operation (Figure 9.2, G). One of the respondents to the questionnaire which was conducted for the purposes of this research made a fair observation on accessible membership: 'Any barriers to membership will make the use of freight forwarding companies more desirable'.[50] However, open membership could trigger free-rider behaviour among shippers, who may wait for the early adopters to make out a business case before joining the scheme. The credibility of a partner is the organisational element that obtains special relevance at the moment of accession to a co-operation scheme and which can later affect liability for damage to cargo. Some partners might be more prone to insolvency and default. Since multiparty contracts can have various (individual or joint) effects across jurisdictions, some partners to cargo bundling co-operation might find themselves in situations in which they bear the risk of the insolvency or default of their partners.

The respondents were asked which conditions they considered important for a new partner to join a co-operation scheme (Figure 9.3). The largest group among the respondents (50.4%) was in favour of purchasing additional insurance coverage that would cover the liability of partners to co-operation schemes. The second largest group of respondents (38.84%) opted for obliging partners to submit their annual financial reports from (at least) the last three years, together with all relevant documents from business activity registers, for review prior to accession. This solution would ensure that only well-established shippers with traceable financial records that have operated on the market for a sufficiently long period join the co-operation scheme. The third largest group of respondents (31.4%) wanted new members to pay entry fees. An entry fee would incentivise a partner to co-operate and minimise the risk of free-rider behaviour. Only 5.78% of respondents were of the view that no entry requirements are necessary. Detailed and more general suggestions were recorded in the open-comment section. Some of those suggestions overlap with the predefined options. The respondents considered matters such as

50 The answer was given in the open-comment section of the question on requirements for becoming a member of a co-operation scheme (Figure 3; author's files).

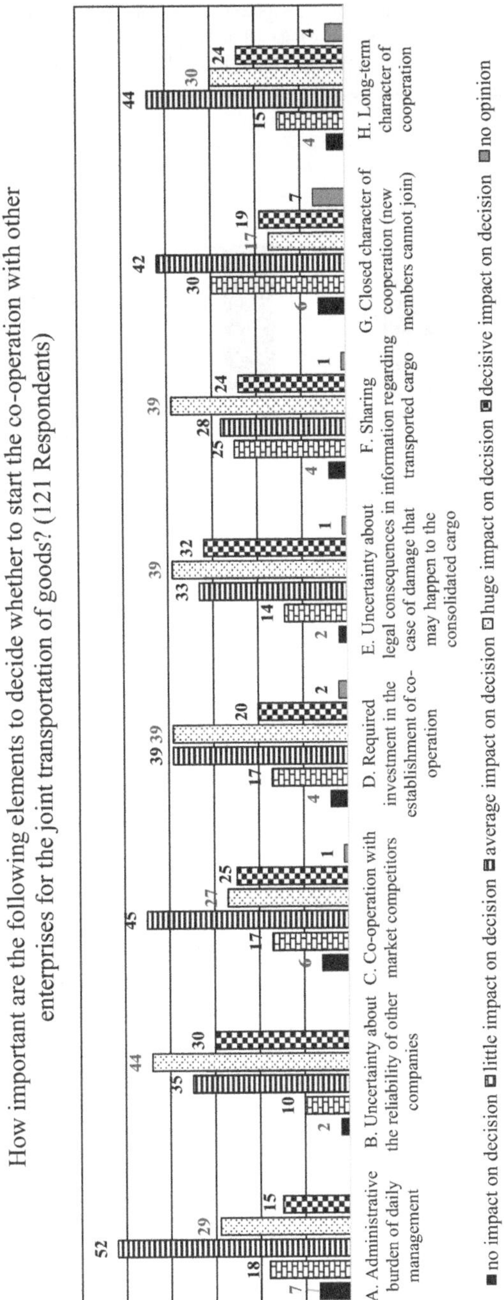

Figure 9.2 Factors relevant to initiating co-operation for cargo bundling

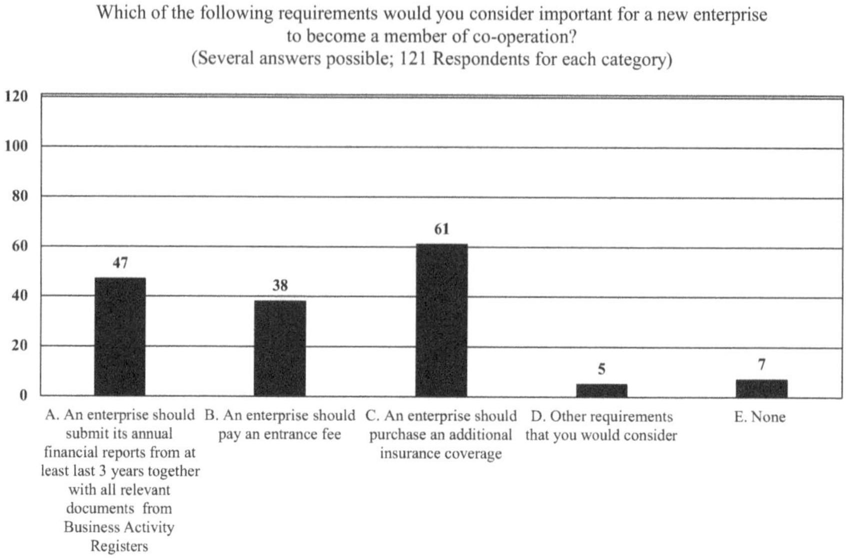

Figure 9.3 The significance of various requirements for a new enterprise to join cargo bundling co-operation

confidentiality clauses, the turnover of a company, its willingness to follow network rules, its reliability, non-competition agreements, the selection of partners according to transport destinations, and the elimination of all barriers, to be relevant.

4.2 Division of costs of joint transportation

The analysis shows that arrangements about the division of costs could be important to carriers' claims for freight payment (see Chapter 6 Section 2.2). This is mainly because there is legal uncertainty about the individual and the joint effects of multiparty contracts. For example, if a judge finds that an obligation to pay freight needs to be examined by reference to national law and is divisible, the default rule is that the debt or claim is divided into as many independent parts as there are debtors or creditors, and there can be a presumption of equal shares (§ 420 BGB, Article 379.1 KC). If an obligation is considered joint, the shipper or sender who pays the carrier has a recourse action against its co-partners. The default rule is that the shares of the co-debtors are equal (see Chapter 6).

The survey of European manufacturing and distributing companies indicates that sector preferences on the methods of costs division (Figure 9.4) could be different from the default rules on multiparty obligations. A total of 42.14%

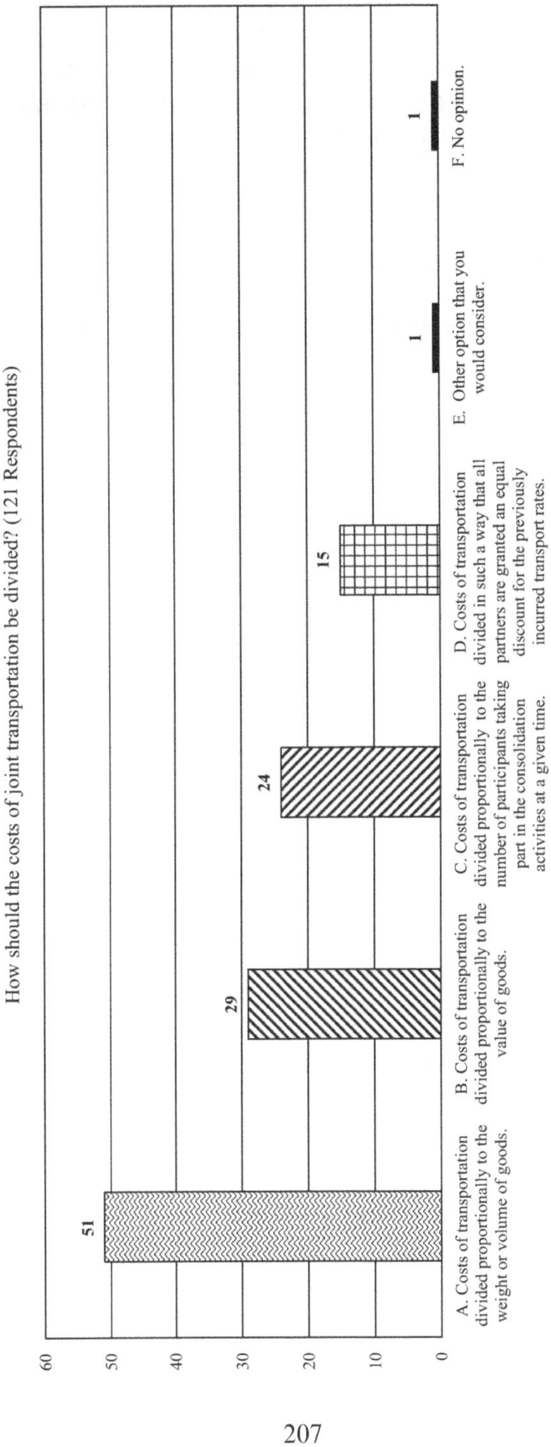

Figure 9.4 Preferences regarding the division of costs for joint transportation

of respondents were in favour of the costs of transportation being divided proportionally to the weight or volume of the goods. Among the respondents, 23.9% opted for the costs of transportation being divided proportionally to the value of goods, and 19.8% were in favour of those costs being divided by the number of participants in the consolidation activities. Furthermore, 12.3% of the respondents opted for an equal discount for transport being applied to previous transport rates. For reasons of feasibility, I could not examine other methods for the division of costs. Nevertheless, I allowed respondents to identify cost division solutions that differed from those that were predefined in the survey. Only one answer was recorded, and it suggests that costs should be divided depending on the distance that each bundle of goods must travel. One respondent had no opinion on cost division. These answers, though inconclusive, indicate that there is a need to regulate the method of cost division contractually to avoid default rules of contract law.

Dividing the costs of transportation in accordance with the weight and volume of the goods, as preferred by the majority of respondents, could be an option, especially for shippers which dispatch similar quantities of cargo. In co-operation schemes in which some companies dispatch more goods than others, those who send large volumes might already enjoy favourable rates and thus benefit less from a proportional division of transportation costs. If proportional cost division is combined with actual participation in the transportation of goods, *ad hoc* contributions to costs increase administrative burdens and make effective cost savings harder to estimate. In addition, the co-operating companies would need to investigate whether this option does not restrict competition. For example, co-operating competitors should avoid commonalities of variable costs in relation to the products in respect of which they compete. That is so because the higher the degree of commonality of costs, the greater the likelihood that price competition will be curtailed.[51] Thus, if competing shippers establish a co-operation scheme whose sole purpose is the joint transportation of goods and compete on transportation costs, a proportional cost division might contribute to a restriction of competition because of the commonality of transport costs that obtains.

A weighted cost distribution, which was not mentioned in the predefined survey answers or by the respondents in the open-comment box, could be an alternative. Weighted cost distribution provides viable benefits to shippers regardless of the amount of cargo that they dispatch.[52] Weighted-cost distribution allows a

51 European Commission, 'Guidelines on the applicability of Article 101 of the Treaty on the Functioning of the European Union to horizontal co-operation agreements' (Communication) C(2023) 3445 final ('New Article 101 Guidelines') paras 164, 342–343.

52 The literature distinguishes between two weighted-cost distribution systems. The first is based on the Shapley value, and it allocates to each shipper the weighted sum of its contributions (see: Marta Anna Krajewska et al., 'Horizontal Cooperation Among Freight Carriers: Request Allocation and Profit Sharing' (2008) 59 *Journal of the Operational Research Society* 1483).

larger company to benefit from a lower per-pallet price than a smaller company. Thus, it may retain its pre-existing competitive advantage. At the same time, the smaller companies can still realise gains. The survey also mentioned an equal discount for cargo transport being granted to all partners in the co-operation scheme in relation to their previous transport rates. The disadvantage of this solution is that it requires honesty about previously obtained rates.

4.3 Liability rules

The research shows that co-operation in cargo bundling is plagued by legal uncertainty, which attaches to external relations with carriers and to internal relations between co-operating companies. As far as external relations are concerned, the uncertainty concerns the joint or individual liability of shippers or senders towards the carrier and its ability to invoke defences *erga omnes* or *inter partes* (see Chapter 4). Since there is a possibility that the co-operating shippers or senders may be liable jointly for damage to the consolidated cargo, it is desirable to draft the co-operation agreement so as to shift the risk to the shipper or sender to whom the damage is attributable (Section 4.3.1). In the internal relation, the uncertainty concerns liability for the management of a co-operation scheme, including the consequences of delays in delivery (Section 4.3.2), the liability of consolidation points (Section 4.3.3), and the position of a TO or a cargo bundling company (Section 4.3.4).

4.3.1 Liability for insufficient packing

The research shows that the issue of shipper's or sender's liability vis-à-vis a carrier in the case of bundled goods is uncertain because, under the conventions, it is unclear whether the shipper and the sender should be treated individually or jointly for the purpose of the carrier's liability exemptions and in the analysis of damages suffered by the latter. My proposal is that the decision on whether shippers or senders should be treated jointly or independently should depend on the performance of their obligations (Chapter 4 and Section 2.3). However, since there are no cases on this issue, a judge, exercising their discretion, can choose a different approach. Since there is a risk that the shippers or senders will be considered jointly, they should regulate the effect of joint liability in their co-operation agreements.

I suggest limiting shipper or sender liability in contracts with carriers and in co-operation agreements. Regardless of the joint or individual consideration of the shipper's or sender's position, it will enjoy the benefit of limited liability

The second is based on the weighted average of a fixed per-pallet price and fixed savings rate (see Wouter Verheyen and Philippe De Bruecker, 'Automated SME Cargo Bundling as a Tool to Reduce Transaction Costs' in Thierry Vanelslander and Christa Sys (eds), *Maritime Supply Chains* (Elsevier 2020)).

in disputes with carriers. Limiting liability could also facilitate the operation of co-operation agreements. If shippers or senders are considered jointly and if one of them cannot recover damages from a carrier who invokes an insufficient packaging exemption towards all of the bundled goods, the shipper or sender may try to claim compensation from its partners. Furthermore, for example, when English law applies, the full compensation is for damage suffered and lost profits. It may therefore be desirable to limit compensation. In the survey, the respondents were asked about different possibilities about the liability of a partner for damage to jointly consolidated cargo. A total of 75.2% of the respondents agreed or agreed strongly that the limited liability of a partner should be engaged by damage resulting from proven fault, negligence, defective packing, or inherent defect (Figure 9.5 B). The model clauses for contracts with carriers and co-operation agreements could be based on the CMR liability limitation model. The clause could read as follows:

> Compensation owed by a shipper, sender, or partner to a co-operation scheme in the event of damage resulting from proven error, negligence, defective packaging, or an inherent defect of its cargo is limited to damages that can be compensated under the CMR, up to the limits applicable under the CMR.

In addition, I also suggest instituting proportional liability for co-operating partners in cases when the partner which is responsible for the damage becomes insolvent (Figure 9.5 (C)). When a judge recognises the joint status of the co-operating partners (see Chapter 6), the risk of one of them becoming insolvent rests with the partners. As a result, co-partners might need to compensate the carrier in lieu of the insolvent partner. At the same time, the research shows that under the default rules, the remaining partners may bear the loss in equal parts. This situation may be undesirable if some shippers have provided fewer goods or goods of lower value for cargo bundling than others. The weighted distribution (see Section 4.2) of damages could be an alternative. The clause could read as follows:

> In the event of the insolvency of a partner which is liable, the damage suffered by the other partners to the co-operation agreement is distributed proportionally (to the volume transported), or on a weighted-cost-distribution basis between the remaining partners.

4.3.2 Liability for delay in the delivery of goods for consolidation

Delays in the delivery of goods that are intended to be bundled may be the result of production problems. Shippers might not have the cargo loads ready at the time of dispatch. Since shippers are often sellers, such occurrences may eventually delay the performance of sales contracts and even result in fundamental breach (see e.g. Art. 73 of the United Nations Convention on Contracts for the International Sale of Goods (CISG)).[53] In any event, delays in the delivery of goods for consolidation can cause additional waiting costs for

53 United Nations Convention on Contracts for the International Sale of Goods (adopted 11 April 1980, entered into force 1 January 1988) United Nations, Treaty Series, vol. 1489, p. 3.

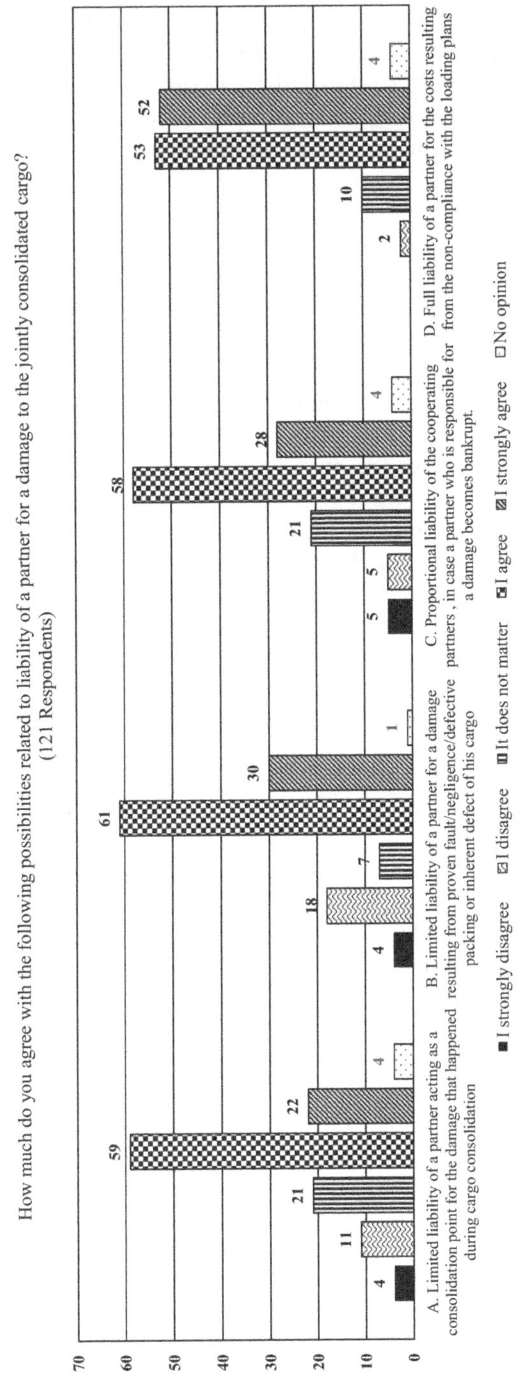

Figure 9.5 Opinions regarding a partner's liability for damage to jointly consolidated cargo

carriers. The survey indicates that a partner of cargo bundling co-operation who does not comply with loading plans should be fully liable for the resulting costs (see Figure 9.5 (D)). Relatedly, the survey shows (Figure 9.6) that partners to co-operation may prefer waiting periods and fines for delay in providing an agreed quantity of goods for bundling (39%). The other options, which account for only 20% of respondents' preferences, include attaching a blocking effect to delay (transport does not leave and no fines), departure without non-complying cargo and without fees, and departure without the cargo of the non-complying partner combined with a contribution to the costs of transport. Three respondents chose more than one option, which rendered their responses invalid. Three respondents expressed no opinion.

The option that was chosen by the respondents is conducive to the flexible and efficient management of co-operation for several reasons. It minimises the possibility that transport would be significantly delayed or no longer performed. The option secures the possibility of excluding a partner in default and departing without its cargo. This possibility can be relevant when the costs of waiting are so high that making the other partners wait would cost more than the organisation of the group shipment. The survey did not solicit further details about the length of an acceptable waiting period and the quantification of fines. Since co-operation arrangements can encompass different market players and operate under different models, the preferred waiting times and fines may vary. For clarity, however, it would be desirable to agree on the details. The following clause can serve as a model:

> If the cargo is not presented in a timely manner, any payments due to the carrier are at the expense of the defaulting partner. In addition, the defaulting partner is obliged to pay €X for each hour of delay to the consolidation point. After X hours, the transport can still depart without the cargo of the defaulting partner, which nevertheless remains bound to share in the cost of transport.

Long waiting periods may disincentivise carriers from collecting goods or even from concluding contracts of carriage in reliance on the co-operation agreement. This is so because of the possible influence of mandatory law. If the transport conventions apply, the carrier can avoid liability for organisational errors only by invoking special and general exoneration grounds for the damage that occurred in the period of responsibility prescribed by the conventions. The application of the conventions does not depend on whether the carrier accepts unknown or non-conforming goods (including also damage as a result of long waiting periods). Furthermore, the carrier, drawing on the information that it has acquired or that it should have acquired, might be expected to give notice to the shipper or sender if bundling can harm the cargo (see further Chapter 8 Section 4, and Chapter 3). Accordingly, the lapse of a long waiting period before the acceptance of the goods imposes on the carrier the additional risk of managing goods that may be susceptible to damage. The

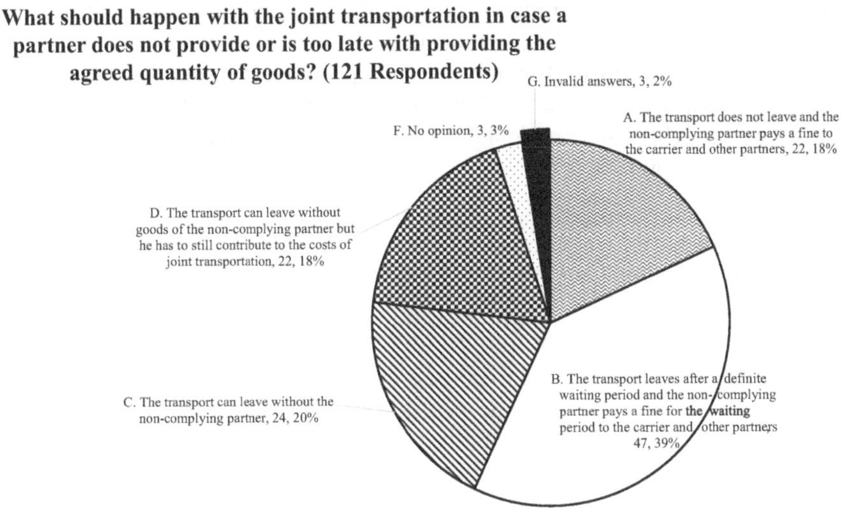

Figure 9.6 Views on delays in providing agreed quantities of goods for joint transport

carrier could try to secure its position by negotiating high fines for waiting periods. However, if a judge finds such terms and conditions to exclude liability for loss or damage (or delay in the case of the CMR), they will be void.[54]

4.3.3 Liability of a consolidation point

Damage to jointly consolidated cargo can occur, among others, when a truck is being loaded by a designated partner. This designated partner might incur liability both towards the carrier (e.g. under Article IV, Rule 3 HVR; see Section 5.5.1) and towards other co-operating partners. Regarding the latter, unlike under mandatory transport law, default liability is unlimited and fault-based.

From the perspective of co-operation in cargo bundling, unlimited and fault-based liability is not a desirable solution. Unlimited liability may disincentivise partners to co-operation from acting as consolidation points unless they can secure excessive fees. Fault-based liability disincentivises delivery points from inspecting goods properly (see also Chapter 8, Section 4.2). Unlimited and fault-based liability also transpired to be undesirable in the eyes of the respondents to the survey. More than half of the respondents (66.94%) agreed that a partner which acts as a consolidation point should enjoy limited liability. Limited liability should, in particular, also attach to

54 *Datec Electronics Holdings Limited and others v United Parcels Services Limited* [2007] UKHL 23 par. 30.

defective packing or an inherent defect of the cargo, according to 75% of respondents (see Figure 9.5 (A) and (B)).

The liability of consolidation points is in principle not mandatory; the parties can thus agree otherwise in their co-operation agreement. Limited liability could be modelled on Article 4.3 of the General Storage Conditions, which provide that liability is

> limited to 8 1/3 special drawing rights (S.D.R.) per kilogramme of lost or damaged goods with an absolute maximum amount to be agreed between parties when concluding the contract. If such an amount has not been agreed, a maximum amount of €453,780.– per event or series of events with one and the same cause of damage will apply.[55]

Alternatively, the partners to co-operation can agree on the CMR liability scheme in the event of damage at the consolidation point. The benefit of such an arrangement is that liability exposure in the event of damage at the consolidation point and during transportation can become uniform. This is particularly important in light of the fact that consolidation points can also be transshipment points. The organisation of horizontal co-operation could be thus subject to the mandatory law of the transport conventions if it is considered a part of the obligation to carry and, sometimes, that to organise carriage (see Chapter 8). One possible wording of the clause runs as follows:

> The partner which acts as a consolidation point is liable for damage that occurs between the delivery of the goods at the point of consolidation and receipt of the goods by the carrier in accordance with (a) the general storage conditions of X or (b) the CMR (choose one option).

4.3.4 Liability of TOs and companies established by shippers for cargo bundling

This research shows that the largest source of uncertainty about the liability of TOs and cargo bundling companies established by partners to co-operation in cargo bundling relates to their legal classification, which can trigger the application of mandatory or non-mandatory regimes. Mandatory regimes are possible in three cases: Classification as an information society (this could be the case when a TO operates through an online platform), classification as a carrier, and when a transport intermediary is deemed to be liable as a carrier (e.g. German *Spediteure*). Sustaining the position of an information society service may be difficult, especially when platforms actively choose intermediaries that provide transport. The research also supplies evidence of the mismatch between the legal framework that governs logistics service providers and the rise of TOs, especially when they operate through logistic platforms.

55 Stichting Vervoeradres, General Storage Conditions (2023) <https://rb.gy/mz479s> accessed 2 February 2024.

Platforms can take on multiple roles, and one platform could assume different capacities in individual contracts. While the same problem arises with traditional logistics service providers and likely with cargo bundling companies, the fragmentation of logistics law is a further example of the maladaptation of the legal framework to the platform economy and makes the classification problem more acute (see Chapter 8). The uncertainty that surrounds the application of mandatory or non-mandatory law also has practical implications. TOs and cargo bundling companies can face a substantial recourse gap if they must bear fault-based liability in their relations with shippers while mandatory law continues to govern their dealings with the actual carrier.

The proposed solutions ensure the application of mandatory law and carrier's liability to TOs, platforms, and bundling companies. Two approaches are possible. The first solution would be to channel legal liability to platforms. This is how transport intermediaries are regulated in Germany (Section 3.1.2). The second solution is directed at the role of a TO or bundling company. For them, legal classification as a carrier would be an optimal quality signal. This solution would be especially important for platforms that attract customers by asserting their trustworthiness. Legal classification as a carrier has several benefits. Firstly, it enables risk to be externalised effectively. Liability is limited, and exoneration grounds are available. Secondly, while a *sui generis* platform would create a specific risk, thus necessitating dedicated insurance coverage, subcontracting or paper carriers are widespread. Consequently, standard insurance policies are available. Thirdly, self-classification as a carrier will likely be upheld by the courts. Thus, the uncertainty related to legal classification by a judge would be avoided. Lastly, this solution would cause the recourse gap to shrink because the liability of TOs and bundling companies would be aligned with that of the performing carrier. The liability of the actual carrier in a dispute with a TO or a bundling company can be limited; the liability of a TO or bundling company in their relations with shippers or senders would also be limited. One possible wording of the clause would run as follows:

> The TO, platform, or bundling company is liable as a carrier for damage that occurs between the delivery of the goods at the point of consolidation and receipt of the goods by the carrier.

4.4 Exit rules

Investigating the exit rules is relevant in light of the numerous challenges to co-operation that Franco Basso and his co-authors described as 'trust in partners', 'actual cost reduction', and 'conflicts of interest'.[56]

---

56 Franco Basso et al., 'A Survey on Obstacles and Difficulties of Practical Implementation of Horizontal Collaboration in Logistics' (2019) 26 *International Transactions in Operational Research* 775.

4.4.1 Unilateral termination

To minimise conflicts of interests, the interests of the partner which wants to leave should be balanced against the interests of the other parties and the co-operation scheme as a whole because the latter may suffer damage as a result of reorganisation.

In the survey, the respondents were asked about the possible means through which co-operation agreements could be terminated unilaterally (Figure 9.7). Among them, 83.47% agreed or agreed strongly that termination should occur after a notice period. Some support was also expressed for termination, conditional upon the payment of a fee (56.19% of the respondents agreed or agreed strongly) and for the proposition that termination should be impossible when partners have already begun to perform obligations that result from the co-operation agreement (52% of the respondents agreed or agreed strongly). The latter solution, however, seems to have encountered some resistance: Whereas large companies seem to be in favour of flexibility and allowing termination even when the partners have already begun to perform their obligations, the smaller companies would prefer to take this option off the menu (cf. Figure 9.8 and Figure 9.9). One explanation could be that large companies have a stronger ability to maintain efficient cargo flows even when co-operation fails. For smaller companies, the exit of a partner might exert downward pressure on returns on investment. Termination only when a new partner is introduced to the scheme seems to have been the least attractive option. Almost 39% of the respondents were in favour, with 36% against and 21.4% expressing no opinion. Interestingly, larger companies seem to be less willing to accept a replacement partner (cf. Figure 9.8 and Figure 9.9). This can be the result of, among others, the need to comply with competition law. The respondents were also given an chance to mention other solutions and indicate how they would be perceived. Some of those answers overlapped with the predefined options in the survey. Four answers were related to termination fees, notice periods, and bans on termination before a minimum period and in cases when the exiting partner owes money to the others. Two respondents suggested a warning system that would prevent partners from breaching their commitments and the subsequent termination of their participation. The other suggestions that could be appreciated by partners to co-operation included insurance coverage (one response), approval of the termination by other partners (one response), and allowing termination only if the partner fulfils their initial obligations (one response). Three respondents focused on the consequences of unilateral termination. One respondent was in favour of maintaining co-operation in such cases, and one responded against this option. One respondent was also in favour of excluding the liability of the partner after it leaves the scheme.

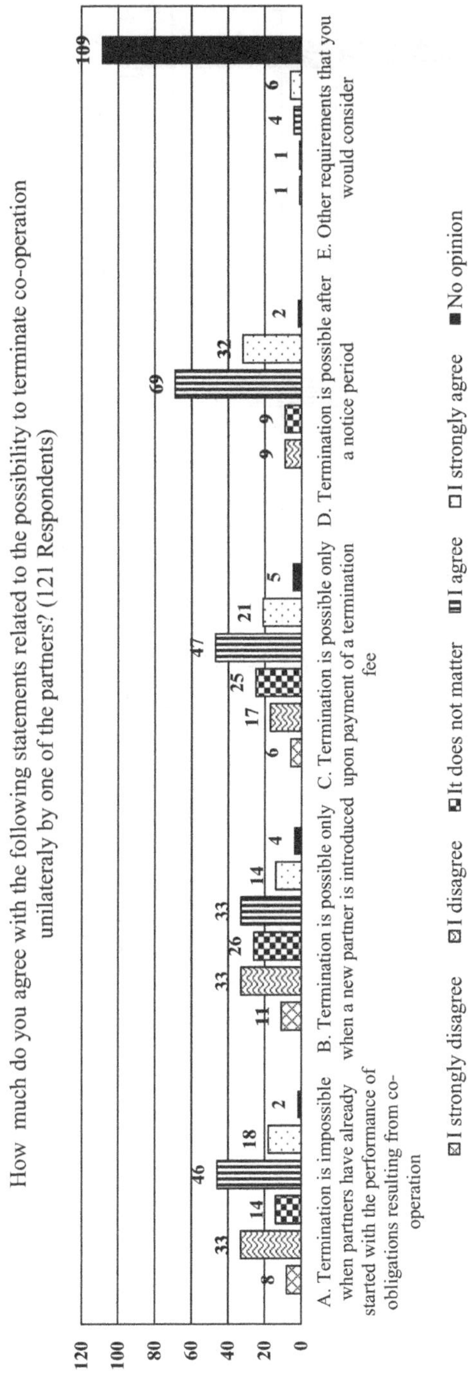

Figure 9.7 Views on unilateral termination (answers for 121 respondents)

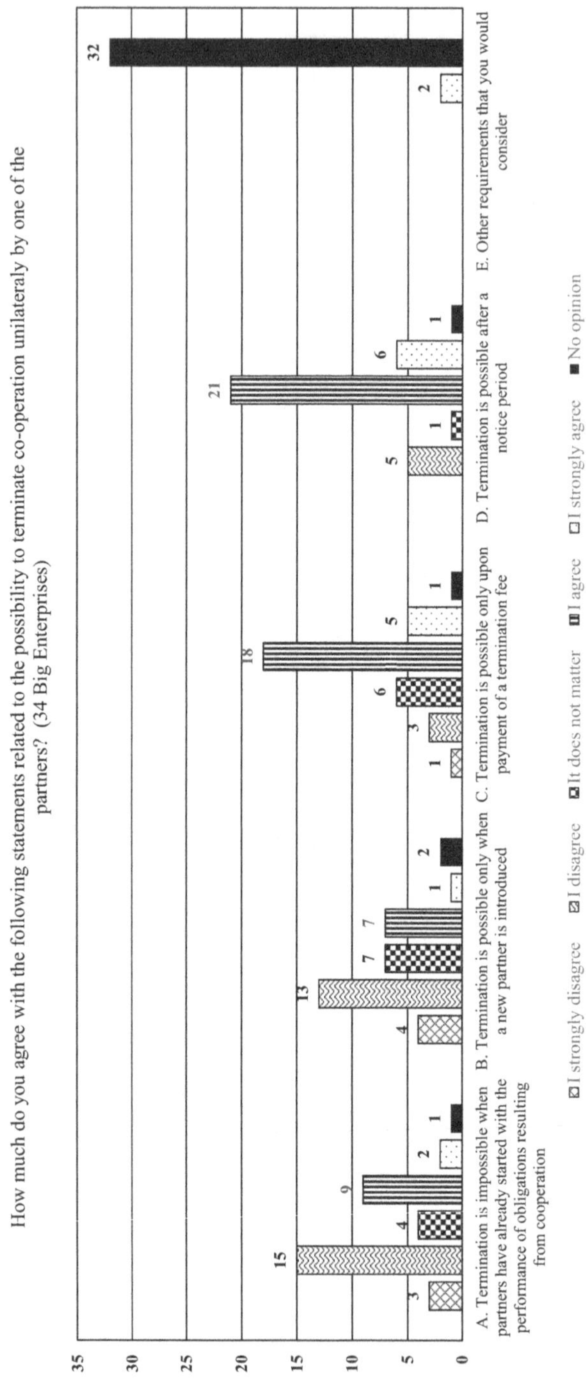

Figure 9.8 Views on unilateral termination (large enterprises)

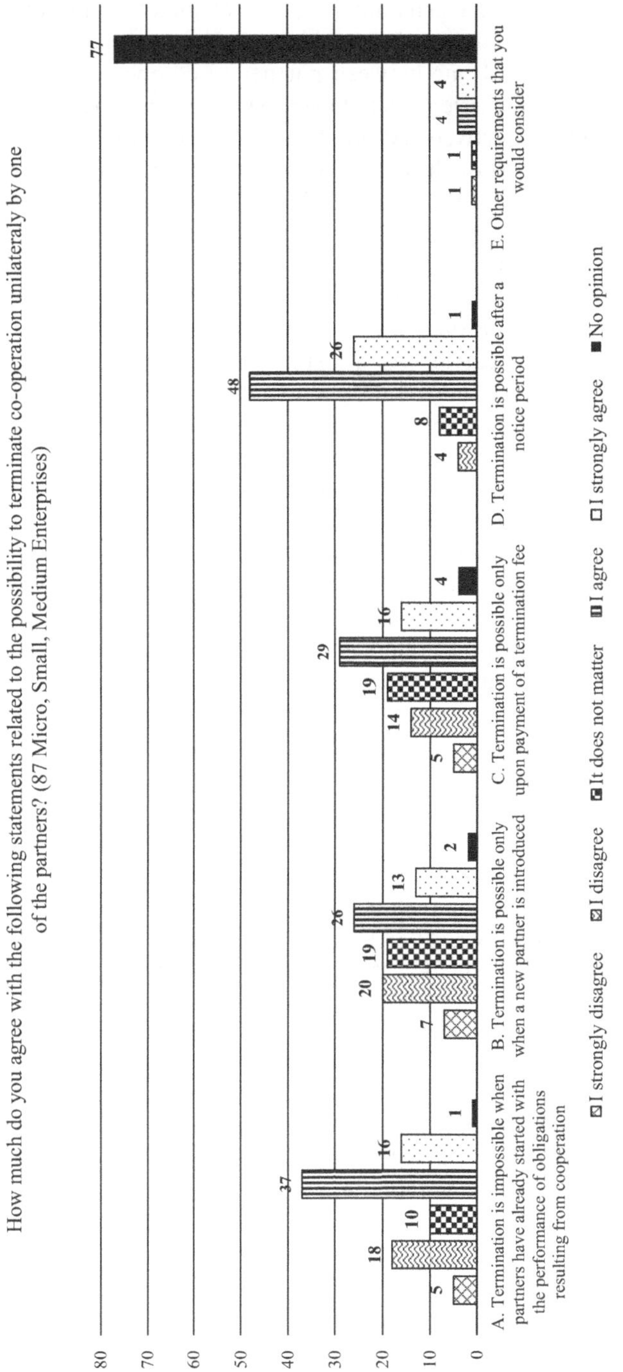

Figure 9.9 Views on unilateral termination (micro, medium, small enterprises)

Although shippers were generally in favour of unilateral termination, unilateral termination might generate problems in the external relation with the carrier and the internal one between partner to co-operation. In the external relation with the carrier, a single shipper might not be able to exercise termination rights effectively. Alternatively, its termination may trigger full termination on the part of the carrier, which can affect the other shippers (see Chapter 6, Section 3.3). In the case of obligations that are due in instalments, the co-operating partners assume the risk that if one of them terminates unilaterally, the carrier might terminate the entire arrangement by reason of a serious infringement of its legitimate interests. At the same time, the effective termination of common obligations often requires all shippers to terminate the contract with the carrier. As a result, unilateral termination may jeopardise the execution of cargo bundling or have no effect at all. In the latter case, the carrier would be able to claim for delays in delivery. Some problems could thus also be encountered at the juncture between the external relation with the carrier and the internal relation between the shippers. For example, when the obligations are joint and several, solidary, or indivisible, the carrier can claim for delayed delivery from any of the co-operating shippers. Consequently, the co-shippers would bear risks related to parties who wish to exit the co-operation scheme.

The preferences of the shippers and the outcomes of the research on the legal rules indicate that the unilateral-termination solution should include several options, which were presented in the survey. One possible solution consists in combining a notice period and a termination fee as well as limiting the possibility of terminating a contract in the external relation with the carrier. The notice period makes it possible to seek new partners. The termination fee allows the costs of reorganisation to be recouped, at least in part. Limiting the possibility of termination during the lifetime of a carriage contract and allocating the risk of damage to the party which wishes to exit the co-operation scheme secures the interests of the other co-shippers. This option should be implemented regardless of the type of carriage contract (spot contract, volume contract, or umbrella contract of carriage; Chapter 7). This is so because, shippers' obligations under these types of contracts may or may not be common or divisible. Although the rules on termination in common obligations are not the same, their practical effect is that all co-shippers would need to terminate contract with a carrier. Therefore, if the partners opt exclusively for solidarity or joint and several obligations, all co-shippers would better be required to terminate at once. A clause may be worded as follows:

> The co-operation agreement can be terminated unilaterally with X months' notice and the payment of a termination fee of €X. Unilateral termination does not exclude the liability of the terminating partners towards the remaining

> partners to the co-operation and towards third parties, including carriers, for obligations undertaken during the period of the co-operation agreement, including the notice period. The unilateral termination of the co-operation agreement has no effect on concluded contracts of carriage, which may only be terminated if all partners terminate the contract with the carrier at once.

4.4.2 Termination for good cause

The rules on the exclusion of partners can prove relevant in cases of conflict within the co-operation scheme or when there are disruptions which make the continuation of the agreement unfeasible. The latter condition may be met when it is no longer efficient to co-operate with a partner. The respondents were asked about this issue in the survey (Figure 9.10). Among them, 67.7% agreed or agreed strongly that it should be possible for a partner to be permanently excluded from the co-operation scheme when all other partners agree. Almost the same percentage of respondents agreed or agreed strongly (63.63%) that a majority of partners should suffice for exclusion. The other options for the exclusion of partners from actual consolidation operations received support from less than 50% of respondents. The survey also recorded other suggestions (29 responses). The majority of these answers overlap with the predefined options. This said, there were suggestions on different mechanisms for exclusion and on other situations in which the exclusion of a partner could be justified. Regarding the latter, the respondents indicated that they would agree to exclude a partner if it is unreliable or if it becomes insolvent. As far as alternative mechanisms of exclusion are concerned, the respondents mentioned the need for a partner to be analysed qualitatively prior to a decision being made, limiting the possibility of using the services through co-operation, or introducing a dispute-settlement mechanism. There was also a suggestion that exclusion (and inclusion) mechanisms should be described in detail in the co-operation contract. Some answers also hinted at the consequences of exclusion. The respondents were sensitive to the need to protect sensitive information about products shipped and customers served.

The support behind the option of allowing all shippers to decide about the exclusion of a partner confirms the willingness of the respondents to manage co-operation jointly (see Figure 9.11). The clause from the preceding section could thus be supplemented with the following wording:

> All partners to the co-operation agreement may terminate the participation of one or more partners thereto with immediate effect for good cause. A good cause shall be deemed to justify termination with immediate effect if mutual trust between the parties has suffered serious disruption or if co-operation has no economic benefits and the continued participation of the partner in question in the co-operation agreement has become unfeasible as a result. The agreement remains valid for the remaining partners.

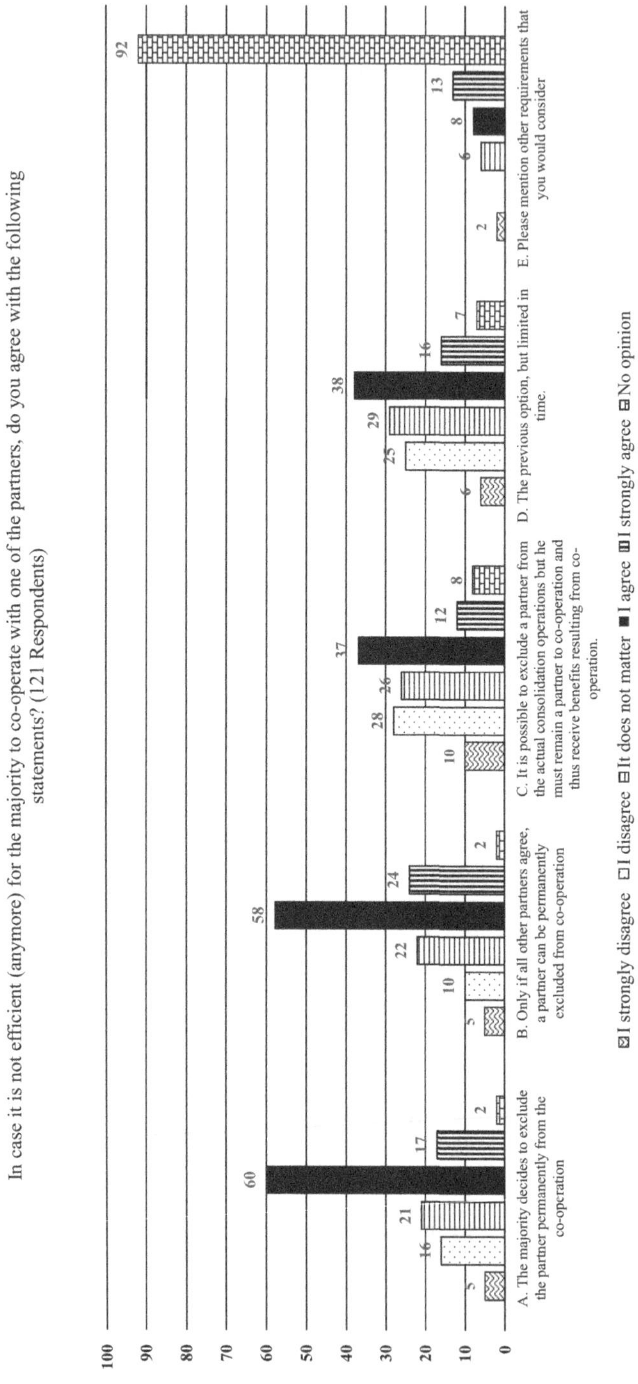

Figure 9.10 Views on the exclusion of a partner to co-operation with whom it is no longer efficient to co-operate

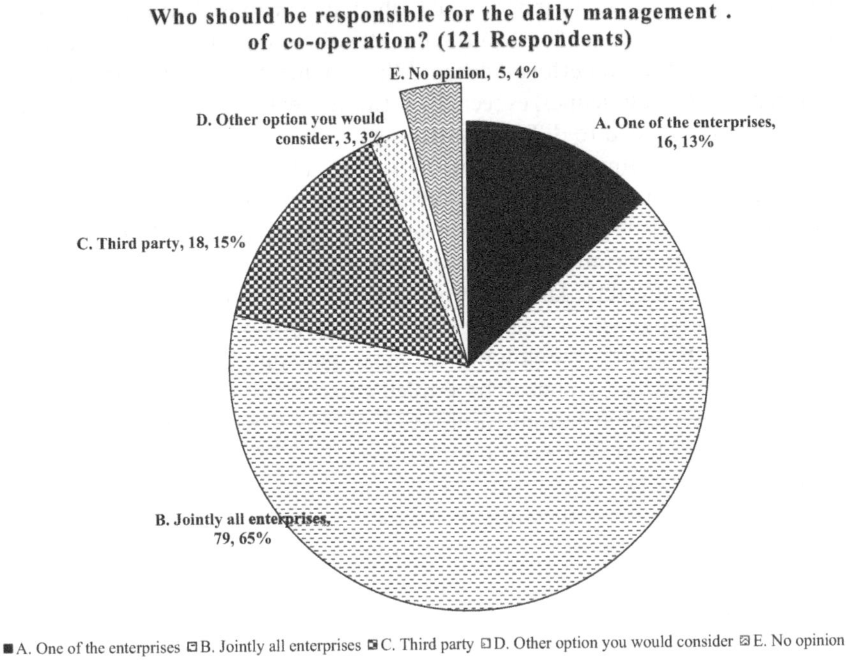

Figure 9.11 Preferences concerning responsibility for the daily management of co-operation for cargo bundling

5 Conclusions

The research shows that all three cargo bundling models are affected by legal uncertainties. The most serious problem is related to the multiparty character of co-operation. I proposed various solutions for improvement, from interpretative guidelines to regulatory changes. I gave indications of the extent to which the proposed solutions would boost co-operation in logistics, I pointed to the regulatory mixes that are likely to prove the most successful. My solutions are designed to facilitate multiparty contractual relations. However, I also acknowledge that turning multiparty arrangements into contractual relations that resemble bilateral contracts could also be fruitful.

Understanding that changes in legal frameworks are difficult to realize, I underlined the necessity and usefulness of interpretative guidelines for the international transport conventions. The international transport conventions contain generic terms and are evolutionary in character. As a result, I proposed that the interpretation of the exoneration grounds that are contained in these conventions take into account changing market circumstances, including new business practices, while retaining the framework of risk allocation between shippers or senders and carriers. Relatedly, I also proposed a functional interpretation of the concept of contract under the conventions, and means of ascribing meaning to performance and the organization of operations.

Interpretative guidelines, especially in the context of the transport conventions, might still lead to different outcomes. Accordingly, I proposed changes to various legal frameworks. I drew on well-established legal solutions for the liability of intermediaries, the plurality of contractors, joint liability, and co-operation models. The introduction of these solutions would, in particular, contribute to uniformity in European private law in the domain of carriage and logistics contracts. The solutions anticipate organizational issues in co-operation and in the interactions between the co-operating partners and third parties. Furthermore, the solutions aim at the standardization of liability issues in contractual chains. The implementation of the solutions that are prescribed by the conventions would result in more transparent liability rules in contractual chains because, among others, mandatory laws would be mirrored in national laws and in contracts.

The foregoing notwithstanding, partners to co-operation can anticipate various legal uncertainties. I proposed improvements in the conduct of co-operation with organizational solutions and model contract clauses. For example, I suggested limiting shipper liability in contracts with carriers and in co-operation agreements as well as limiting the liability of consolidation points. I proposed that partners to co-operation in cargo bundling regulate the effect of joint liability in their co-operation agreements. An appropriate solution would be to introduce proportional liability for co-operating partners in cases in which the partner that is responsible for the damage becomes insolvent. I also proposed means of organizing entry and exit rules, of dividing the costs of transportation to reduce the likelihood of encountering private law problems at the juncture between the partners' external relationship with the carrier and the internal relationship between the partners to co-operation in cargo bundling.

The reader should consider the solutions from various perspectives. Firstly, the mandatory legal frameworks are adaptable. If they are to promote adaptability and remove legal uncertainties, courts across states must work on the uniform application of mandatory transport law. If mandatory law remains uncertain, partners to co-operation can minimize legal risks contractually. However, the complexity and variety of the legal frameworks make such private-ordering solutions difficult and costly. Changes to national laws would be useful. These should minimize the risks that are related to multiparty contracting. For that reason, I proposed a regime of carrier liability for TOs and platforms that offer solutions for LCL transport, regulation of the legal capacity of contractual groups, and joint liability for damage that results from the proximity of performance. These solutions would facilitate the allocation of liability risks, similarly to bilateral contracts.

INDEX

Note: Page numbers in *italics* indicate figures, **bold** indicate tables in the text, and references following "n" refer notes.

For Product Safety Concerns and Information please contact our
EU representative GPSR@taylorandfrancis.com Taylor & Francis
Verlag GmbH, Kaufingerstraße 24, 80331 München, Germany